Power Maths

Year IC

A Guide to Teaching for Mastery

Series Editor: Tony Staneff

Pearson

Contents

Introduction   page 4
What is *Power Maths*?   page 5
Introduction to the author team   page 6
Your *Power Maths* resources   page 7
The *Power Maths* teaching model   page 10
The *Power Maths* lesson sequence   page 12
Using the *Power Maths* Teacher Guide   page 15
Power Maths Year 1, yearly overview   page 16
Mindset: an introduction   page 20
The *Power Maths* characters   page 21
Mathematical language   page 22
The role of talk and discussion   page 23
Assessment strategies   page 24
Power Maths unit assessment grid   page 26
Keeping the class together   page 27
Depth and breadth   page 28
Same-day intervention   page 29
The role of practice   page 30
Structures and representations   page 31
Variation helps visualisation   page 32
Getting started with *Power Maths*   page 33

Unit 12 – Multiplication   **page 34**
Lesson 1 – Counting in 10s, 5s and 2s   page 36
Lesson 2 – Making equal groups   page 40
Lesson 3 – Adding equal groups   page 44
Lesson 4 – Making simple arrays   page 48
Lesson 5 – Making doubles   page 52
Lesson 6 – Solving word problems – multiplication   page 56
End of unit check   page 60

Unit 13 – Division   **page 62**
Lesson 1 – Making equal groups (1)   page 64
Lesson 2 – Making equal groups (2)   page 68
Lesson 3 – Sharing equally (1)   page 72
Lesson 4 – Sharing equally (2)   page 76
Lesson 5 – Solving word problems – division   page 80
End of unit check   page 84

Unit 14 – Halves and quarters   page 86

Lesson 1 – Finding halves (1)   page 88
Lesson 2 – Finding halves (2)   page 92
Lesson 3 – Finding quarters (1)   page 96
Lesson 4 – Finding quarters (2)   page 100
Lesson 5 – Solving word problems – halves and quarters   page 104
End of unit check   page 108

Unit 15 – Position and direction   page 110

Lesson 1 – Describing turns   page 112
Lesson 2 – Describing positions (1)   page 116
Lesson 3 – Describing positions (2)   page 120
End of unit check   page 124

Unit 16 – Numbers to 100   page 126

Lesson 1 – Counting to 100   page 128
Lesson 2 – Exploring number patterns   page 132
Lesson 3 – Partitioning numbers (1)   page 136
Lesson 4 – Partitioning numbers (2)   page 140
Lesson 5 – Comparing numbers (1)   page 144
Lesson 6 – Comparing numbers (2)   page 148
Lesson 7 – Ordering numbers   page 152
Lesson 8 – Bonds to 100 (1)   page 156
Lesson 9 – Bonds to 100 (2)   page 160
End of unit check   page 164

Unit 17 – Time   page 166

Lesson 1 – Using before and after   page 168
Lesson 2 – Using a calendar   page 172
Lesson 3 – Telling time to the hour   page 176
Lesson 4 – Telling time to the half hour   page 180
Lesson 5 – Writing time   page 184
Lesson 6 – Comparing time   page 188
Lesson 7 – Solving word problems – time   page 192
End of unit check   page 196

Unit 18 – Money   page 198

Lesson 1 – Recognising coins   page 200
Lesson 2 – Recognising notes   page 204
Lesson 3 – Counting with coins   page 208
End of unit check   page 212

Introduction

Foreword by the series editor and author, Tony Staneff

For far too long in the UK, maths has been feared by learners – and by many teachers, too. As a result, most learners consistently underachieve. More crucially, negative beliefs about ability, aptitude and the nature of maths are entrenched in children's thinking from an early age.

Yet, as someone who has loved maths all my life, I've always believed that every child has the capacity to succeed in maths. I've also had the great pleasure of leading teams and departments who share that belief and passion. Teaching for mastery, as practised in China and other South-East Asian jurisdictions since the 1980s, has confirmed my conviction that maths really is for everyone and not just those who have a special talent. In recent years my team and I at Trinity Academy, Halifax, have had the privilege of researching with and working with some of the finest mastery practitioners from the UK and beyond, whose impact on learners' confidence, achievement and attitude is an inspiration.

The mastery approach recognises the value of developing the power to think rather than just do. It also recognises the value of making a coherent journey in which whole-class groups tackle concepts in very small steps, one by one. You cannot build securely on loose foundations – and it is just the same with maths: by creating a solid foundation of deep understanding, our children's skills and confidence will be strong and secure. What's more, the mindset of learner and teacher alike is fundamental: everyone can do maths… EVERYONE CAN!

I am proud to have been part of the extensive team responsible for turning the best of the world's practice, research, insights, and shared experiences into *Power Maths*, a unique teaching and learning resource developed especially for UK classrooms. *Power Maths* embodies our vision to help and support primary maths teachers to transform every child's mathematical and personal development. 'Everyone can!' has become our mantra and our passion, and we hope it will be yours, too.

Now, explore and enjoy all the resources you need to teach for mastery, and please get back to us with your *Power Maths* experiences and stories!

What is *Power Maths*?

Created especially for UK primary schools, and aligned with the new National Curriculum, *Power Maths* is a whole-class, textbook-based mastery resource that empowers every child to understand and succeed. *Power Maths* rejects the notion that some people simply 'can't do' maths. Instead, it develops growth mindsets and encourages hard work, practice and a willingness to see mistakes as learning tools.

Best practice consistently shows that mastery of small, cumulative steps builds a solid foundation of deep mathematical understanding. *Power Maths* combines interactive teaching tools, high-quality textbooks and continuing professional development (CPD) to help you equip children with a deep and long lasting understanding. Based on extensive evidence, and developed in partnership with practising teachers, *Power Maths* ensures that it meets the needs of children in the UK.

Power Maths and Mastery

Power Maths makes mastery practical and achievable by providing the structures, pathways, content, tools and support you need to make it happen in your classroom.

To develop mastery in maths children must be enabled to acquire a deep understanding of maths concepts, structures and procedures, step by step. Complex mathematical concepts are built on simpler conceptual components and when children understand every step in the learning sequence, maths becomes transparent and makes logical sense. Interactive lessons establish deep understanding in small steps, as well as effortless fluency in key facts such as tables and number bonds. The whole class works on the same content and no child is left behind.

Power Maths

- ⚡ Builds every concept in small, progressive steps
- ⚡ Is built with interactive, whole-class teaching in mind
- ⚡ Provides the tools you need to develop growth mindsets
- ⚡ Helps you check understanding and ensure that every child is keeping up
- ⚡ Establishes core elements such as intelligent practice and reflection

The *Power Maths* approach

Everyone can!

Founded on the conviction that every child can achieve, *Power Maths* enables children to build number fluency, confidence and understanding, step by step.

Child-centred learning

Children master concepts one step at a time in lessons that embrace a concrete-pictorial-abstract (C-P-A) approach, avoid overload, build on prior learning and help them see patterns and connections. Same-day intervention ensures sustained progress.

Continuing professional development

Embedded teacher support and development offer every teacher the opportunity to continually improve their subject knowledge and manage whole-class teaching for mastery.

Whole-class teaching

An interactive, whole-class teaching model encourages thinking and precise mathematical language and allows children to deepen their understanding as far as they can.

Introduction to the author team

Power Maths arises from the work of maths mastery experts who are committed to proving that, given the right mastery mindset and approach, **everyone can do maths**. Based on robust research and best practice from around the world, *Power Maths* was developed in partnership with a group of UK teachers to make sure that it not only meets our children's wide-ranging needs but also aligns with the National Curriculum in England.

Tony Staneff, Series Editor and author

Vice Principal at Trinity Academy, Halifax, Tony also leads a team of mastery experts who help schools across the UK to develop teaching for mastery via nationally-recognised CPD courses, problem-solving and reasoning resources, schemes of work, assessment materials and other tools.

✚ A team of experienced authors, including:

- ⚡ **Josh Lury** – a specialist maths teacher, author and maths consultant with a passion for innovative and effective maths education

- ⚡ **Jenny Lewis, Stephen Monaghan, Beth Smith and Kelsey Brown** – skilled maths teachers and mastery experts

- ⚡ **Cherri Moseley** – a maths author, former teacher and professional development provider

- ⚡ **Paul Wrangles** – a maths author and former teacher, Paul's goal is to "ignite creative thought in teachers and pupils by providing creative teaching resources."

✚ Professor Liu Jian, Series Consultant and author, and his team of mastery expert authors:

- ⚡ **Hou Huiying, Huang Lihua, Wang Mingming, Yin Lili, Zhang Dan, Zhang Hong and Zhou Da**

Used by over 20 million children, Professor Liu Jian's textbook programme is one of the most popular in China. He and his author team are highly experienced in intelligent practice and in embedding key maths concepts using a C-P-A approach.

✚ A group of 15 teachers and maths co-ordinators

We have consulted our teacher group throughout the development of *Power Maths* to ensure we are meeting their real needs in the classroom.

Your *Power Maths* resources

To help you teach for mastery, *Power Maths* comprises a variety of high-quality resources.

Pupil Textbooks

Discover, Share, and Think together sections promote discussion and introduce mathematical ideas logically, so that children understand more easily.

Using a Concrete-Pictorial-Abstract approach, clear mathematical models help children to make connections and grasp concepts.

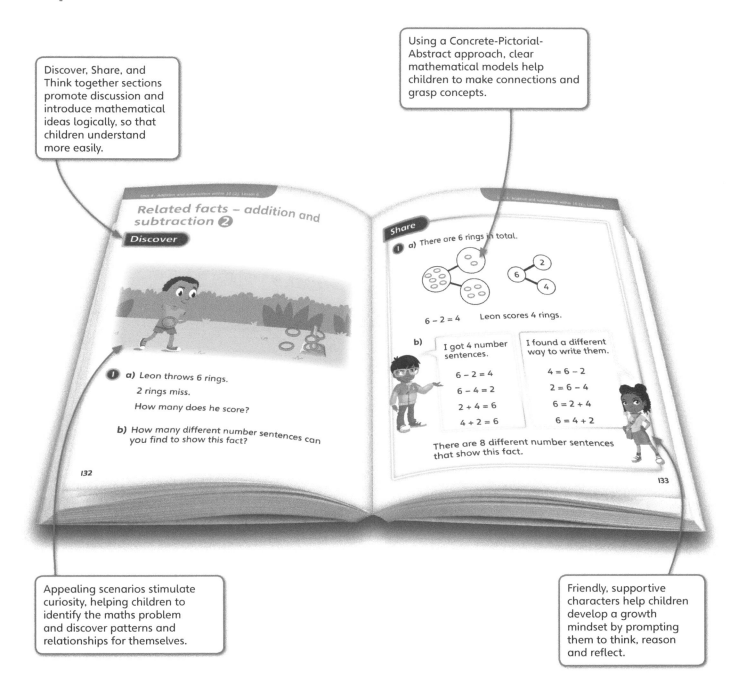

Appealing scenarios stimulate curiosity, helping children to identify the maths problem and discover patterns and relationships for themselves.

Friendly, supportive characters help children develop a growth mindset by prompting them to think, reason and reflect.

The coherent *Power Maths* lesson structure carries through into the vibrant, high-quality textbooks. Setting out the core learning objectives for each class, the lesson structure follows a carefully mapped journey through the curriculum and supports children on their journey to deeper understanding.

Pupil Practice Books

The Practice Books offer just the right amount of intelligent practice for children to complete independently in the final section of each lesson.

The practice questions are for everyone – each question varies one small element to move children on in their thinking. Look at the different parts in question 1!

Calculations are connected so that children think about the underlying concept. In question 3, children have to write out the calculation to find the answer. Concepts are presented differently again in question 4 to challenge children.

Practice questions are finely tuned to move children forward in their thinking and to reveal misconceptions.

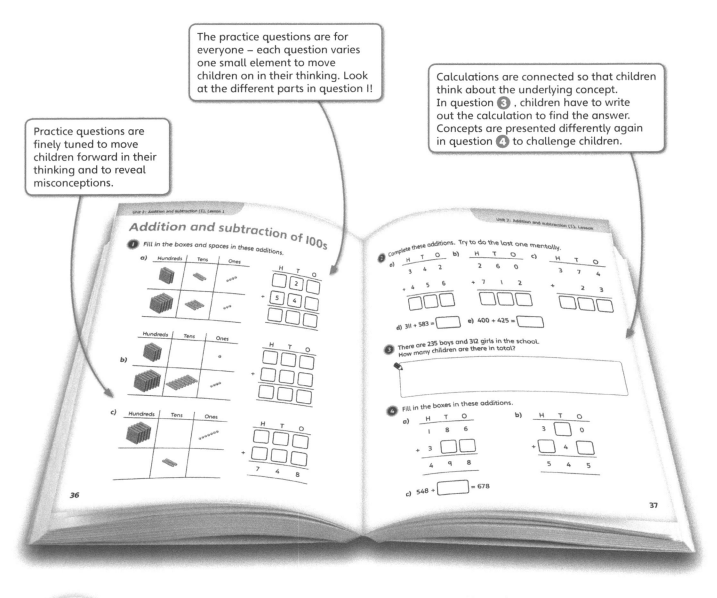

Challenge questions allow children to delve deeper into a concept.

Reflect questions reveal the depth of each child's understanding before they move on.

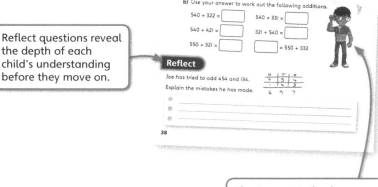

The *Power Maths* characters support and encourage children to think and work in different ways.

Online subscriptions

The online subscription will give you access to additional resources.

eTextbooks

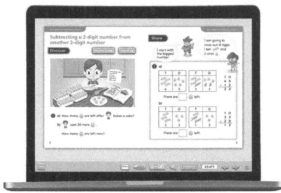

Digital versions of *Power Maths* Textbooks allow class groups to share and discuss questions, solutions and strategies. They allow you to project key structures and representations at the front of the class, to ensure all children are focusing on the same concept.

Teaching tools

Here you will find interactive versions of key *Power Maths* structures and representations.

Power Ups

Use this series of daily activities to promote and check number fluency.

Online versions of Teacher Guide pages

PDF pages give support at both unit and lesson levels. You will also find help with key strategies and templates for tracking progress.

Unit videos

Watch the professional development videos at the start of each unit to help you teach with confidence. The videos explore common misconceptions in the unit, and include intervention suggestions as well as suggestions on what to look out for when assessing mastery in your students.

End of unit Strengthen and Deepen materials

Each Strengthen activity at the end of every unit addresses a key misconception and can be used to support children who need it. The Deepen activities are designed to be low ceiling/high threshold and will challenge those children who can understand more deeply. These resources will help you ensure that every child understands and will help you keep the class moving forward together. These printable activities provide an optional resource bank for use after the assessment stage.

Underpinning all of these resources, *Power Maths* is infused throughout with continual professional development, supporting you at every step.

The *Power Maths* teaching model

At the heart of *Power Maths* is a clearly structured teaching and learning process that helps you make certain that every child masters each maths concept securely and deeply. For each year group, the curriculum is broken down into core concepts, taught in units. A unit divides into smaller learning steps – lessons. Step by step, strong foundations of cumulative knowledge and understanding are built.

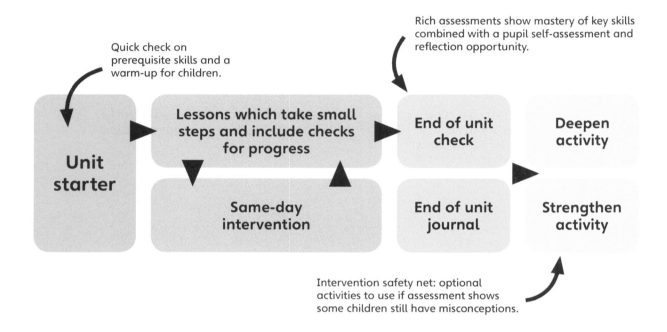

Quick check on prerequisite skills and a warm-up for children.

Rich assessments show mastery of key skills combined with a pupil self-assessment and reflection opportunity.

Intervention safety net: optional activities to use if assessment shows some children still have misconceptions.

Unit starter

Each unit begins with a unit starter, which introduces the learning context along with key mathematical vocabulary and structures and representations.

- The Pupil Textbooks include a check on readiness and a warm-up task for children to complete.

- Your Teacher Guide gives support right from the start on important structures and representations, mathematical language, common misconceptions and intervention strategies.

- Unit-specific videos develop your subject knowledge and insights so you feel confident and fully equipped to teach each new unit. These are available via the online subscription.

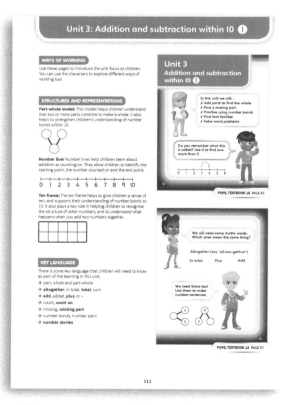

Lesson

Once a unit has been introduced, it is time to start teaching the series of lessons.

- Each lesson is scaffolded with Pupil Textbook and Practice Book activities and always begins with a Power Up activity (available via online subscription).

- *Power Maths* identifies lesson by lesson what concepts are to be taught.

- Your Teacher Guide offers lots of support for you to get the most from every child in every lesson. As well as highlighting key points, tricky areas and how to handle them, you will also find question prompts to check on understanding and clarification on why particular activities and questions are used.

Same-day intervention

Same-day interventions are vital in order to keep the class progressing together. Therefore, *Power Maths* provides plenty of support throughout the journey.

- Intervention is focused on keeping up now, not catching up later, so interventions should happen as soon as they are needed.

- Practice section questions are designed to bring misconceptions to the surface, allowing you to identify these easily as you circulate during independent practice time.

- Child-friendly assessment questions in the Teacher Guide help you identify easily which children need to strengthen their understanding.

End of unit check and journal

At the end of a unit, summative assessment tasks reveal essential information on each child's understanding. An End of unit check in the Pupil Textbook lets you see which children have mastered the key concepts, which children have not and where their misconceptions lie. The Practice Books also include an End of unit journal in which children can reflect on what they have learned. Each unit also offers Strengthen and Deepen activities, available via the online subscription.

> The Teacher Guide offers different ways of managing the End of unit assessments as well as giving support with handling misconceptions.

> The End of unit check presents four multiple-choice questions. Children think about their answer, decide on a solution and explain their choice.

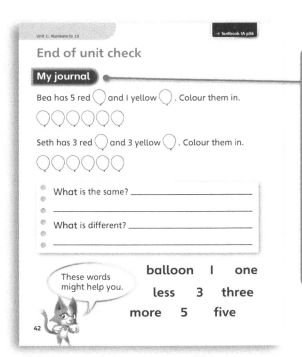

> The End of unit journal is an opportunity for children to test out their learning and reflect on how they feel about it. Tackling the 'journal' problem reveals whether a child understands the concept deeply enough to move on to the next unit.

The *Power Maths* lesson sequence

At the heart of *Power Maths* is a unique lesson sequence designed to empower children to understand core concepts and grow in confidence. Embracing the National Centre for Excellence in the Teaching of Mathematics' (NCETM's) definition of mastery, the sequence guides and shapes every *Power Maths* lesson you teach.

Flexibility is built into the *Power Maths* programme so there is no one-to-one mapping of lessons and concepts meaning you can pace your teaching according to your class. While some children will need to spend longer on a particular concept (through interventions or additional lessons), others will reach deeper levels of understanding. However, it is important that the class moves forward together through the termly schedules.

Power Up ⏱ 5 minutes

Each lesson begins with a Power Up activity (available via the online subscription) which supports fluency in key number facts.

The whole-class approach depends on fluency, so the Power Up is a powerful and essential activity.

TOP TIP
If the class is struggling with the task, revisit it later and check understanding.

Power Ups reinforce the two key things that are essential for success: times-tables and number bonds.

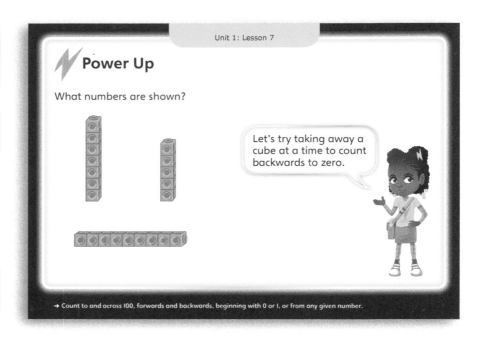

Discover ⏱ 10 minutes

A practical, real-life problem arouses curiosity. Children find the maths through story telling.

TOP TIP
Discover works best when run at tables, in pairs with concrete objects.

Question ❶ a) tackles the key concept and question ❶ b) digs a little deeper. Children have time to explore, play and discuss possible strategies.

Share ⏱ 10 minutes

Teacher-led, this interactive section follows the Discover activity and highlights the variety of methods that can be used to solve a single problem.

TOP TIP
Bring children to the front or onto the carpet to discuss their methods. Pairs sharing a textbook is a great format for this!

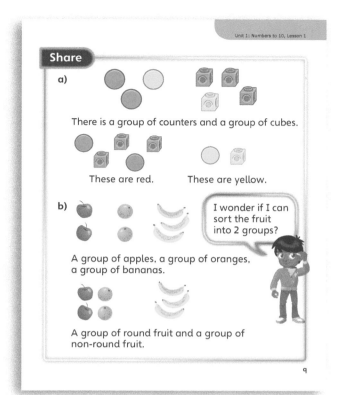

Your Teacher Guide gives target questions for children. The online toolkit provides interactive structures and representations to link concrete and pictorial to abstract concepts.

Bring children to the front to share and celebrate their solutions and strategies.

Think together

⏱ 10 minutes

Children work in groups on the carpet or at tables, using their textbooks or eBooks.

TOP TIP
Make sure children have mini whiteboards or pads to write on if they are not at their tables.

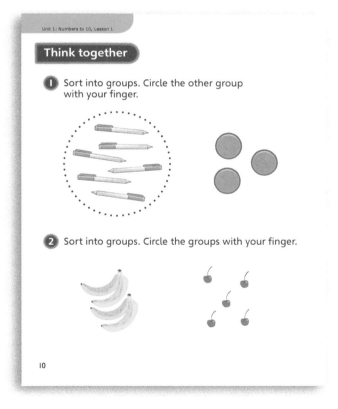

Using the Teacher Guide, model question ① for your class.

Question ② is less structured. Children will need to think together in their groups, then discuss their methods and solutions as a class.

Question ③ – the openness of the Challenge question helps to check depth of understanding.

Practice ⏲ 15 minutes

Using their Practice Books, children work independently while you circulate and check on progress.

Questions follow small steps of progression to deepen learning.

TOP TIP
Some children could work separately with a teacher or assistant.

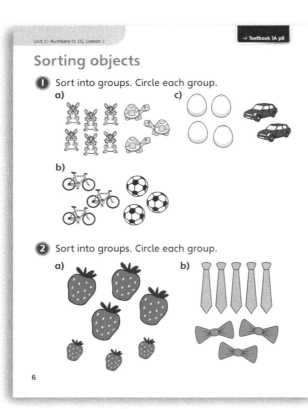

Are some children struggling? If so, work with them as a group, using mathematical structures and representations to support understanding as necessary.

There are no set routines: for real understanding, children need to think about the problem in different ways.

Reflect ⏲ 5 minutes

'Spot the mistake' questions are great for checking misconceptions.

The Reflect section is your opportunity to check how deeply children understand the target concept.

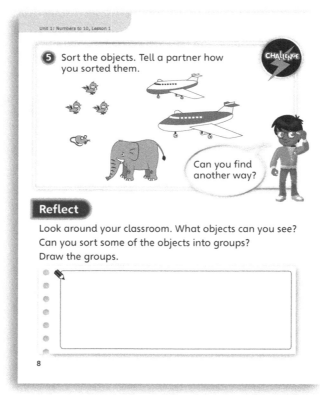

The Practice Books use various approaches to check that children have fully understood each concept.

Looking like they understand is not enough! It is essential that children can show they have grasped the concept.

Using the *Power Maths* Teacher Guide

Think of your Teacher Guides as *Power Maths* handbooks that will guide, support and inspire your day-to-day teaching. Clear and concise, and illustrated with helpful examples, your Teacher Guides will help you make the best possible use of every individual lesson. They also provide wrap-around professional development, enhancing your own subject knowledge and helping you to grow in confidence about moving your children forward together.

There is a Teacher Guide per year group for every term with unit and lesson level guidance and support.

Tips and advice on key elements such as C-P-A approaches, misconceptions, language, modelling growth mindsets and same day intervention.

Annotations for every Pupil Textbook and Practice Book page, providing prompts for key questions to ask to expose understanding and explanations as to why key questions have been chosen.

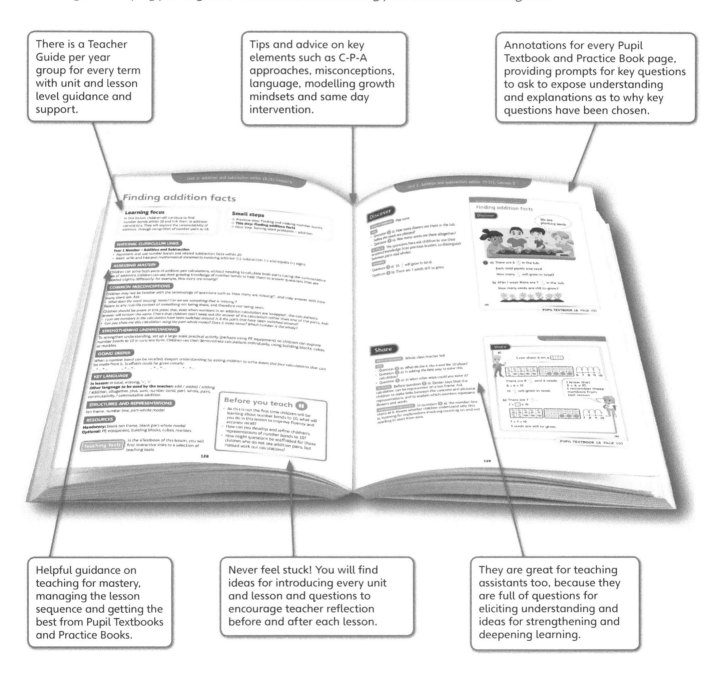

Helpful guidance on teaching for mastery, managing the lesson sequence and getting the best from Pupil Textbooks and Practice Books.

Never feel stuck! You will find ideas for introducing every unit and lesson and questions to encourage teacher reflection before and after each lesson.

They are great for teaching assistants too, because they are full of questions for eliciting understanding and ideas for strengthening and deepening learning.

At the end of each unit, your Teacher Guide helps you identify who has fully grasped the concept, who has not and how to move every child forward. This is covered later in the Assessment strategies section.

Power Maths Year I, yearly overview

Textbook	Strand	Unit	Number of Lessons	
Textbook A / Practice Book A (Term 1)	Number – number and place value	1	Numbers to 10	12
	Number – number and place value	2	Part-whole within 10	5
	Number – addition and subtraction	3	Addition and subtraction within 10 (1)	6
	Number – addition and subtraction	4	Addition and subtraction within 10 (2)	12
	Geometry – properties of shape	5	2D and 3D shapes	5
	Number – number and place value	6	Numbers to 20	7
Textbook B / Practice Book B (Term 2)	Number – addition and subtraction	7	Addition within 20	6
	Number – addition and subtraction	8	Subtraction within 20	8
	Number – number and place value	9	Numbers to 50	11
	Measurement	10	Introducing length and height	5
	Measurement	11	Introducing weight and volume	7
Textbook C / Practice Book C (Term 3)	Number – multiplication and division	12	Multiplication	6
	Number – multiplication and division	13	Division	5
	Number – fractions	14	Halves and quarters	5
	Geometry – position and direction	15	Position and direction	3
	Number – number and place value	16	Numbers to 100	9
	Measurement	17	Time	7
	Measurement	18	Money	3

Power Maths Year I, Textbook IC (Term 3) overview

Strand 1	Strand 2	Unit		Lesson number	Lesson title	NC Objective 1	NC Objective 2	NC Objective 3
Number – number and place value		Unit 12	Multiplication	1	Counting in 10s, 5s and 2s	Count, read and write numbers to 100 in numerals; count in multiples of 2s, 5s and 10s		
Number – multiplication and division		Unit 12	Multiplication	2	Making equal groups	Solve one-step problems involving multiplication and division, by calculating the answer using concrete objects, pictorial representations and arrays with the support of the teacher		
Number – multiplication and division		Unit 12	Multiplication	3	Adding equal groups	Solve one-step problems involving multiplication and division, by calculating the answer using concrete objects, pictorial representations and arrays with the support of the teacher		
Number – multiplication and division		Unit 12	Multiplication	4	Making simple arrays	Solve one-step problems involving multiplication and division, by calculating the answer using concrete objects, pictorial representations and arrays with the support of the teacher		
Number – multiplication and division		Unit 12	Multiplication	5	Making doubles	Solve one-step problems involving multiplication and division, by calculating the answer using concrete objects, pictorial representations and arrays with the support of the teacher	Non-statutory guidance: Through grouping and sharing small quantities, pupils begin to understand: multiplication and division; doubling numbers and quantities; and finding simple fractions of objects, numbers and quantities	
Number – multiplication and division		Unit 12	Multiplication	6	Solving word problems – multiplication	Solve one-step problems involving multiplication and division, by calculating the answer using concrete objects, pictorial representations and arrays with the support of the teacher		
Number – multiplication and division		Unit 13	Division	1	Making equal groups (1)	Solve one-step problems involving multiplication and division, by calculating the answer using concrete objects, pictorial representations and arrays with the support of the teacher		
Number – multiplication and division		Unit 13	Division	2	Making equal groups (2)	Solve one-step problems involving multiplication and division, by calculating the answer using concrete objects, pictorial representations and arrays with the support of the teacher		
Number – multiplication and division		Unit 13	Division	3	Sharing equally (1)	Solve one-step problems involving multiplication and division, by calculating the answer using concrete objects, pictorial representations and arrays with the support of the teacher		
Number – multiplication and division		Unit 13	Division	4	Sharing equally (2)	Solve one-step problems involving multiplication and division, by calculating the answer using concrete objects, pictorial representations and arrays with the support of the teacher		

Strand 1	Strand 2	Unit		Lesson number	Lesson title	NC Objective 1	NC Objective 2	NC Objective 3
Number – multiplication and division		Unit 13	Division	5	Solving word problems – division	Solve one-step problems involving multiplication and division, by calculating the answer using concrete objects, pictorial representations and arrays with the support of the teacher		
Number – fractions		Unit 14	Halves and quarters	1	Finding halves (1)	Recognise, find and name a half as one of two equal parts of an object, shape or quantity		
Number – fractions		Unit 14	Halves and quarters	2	Finding halves (2)	Recognise, find and name a half as one of two equal parts of an object, shape or quantity		
Number – fractions		Unit 14	Halves and quarters	3	Finding quarters (1)	Recognise, find and name a quarter as one of four equal parts of an object, shape or quantity		
Number – fractions		Unit 14	Halves and quarters	4	Finding quarters (2)	Recognise, find and name a quarter as one of four equal parts of an object, shape or quantity		
Number – fractions		Unit 14	Halves and quarters	5	Solving word problems – halves and quarters	Recognise, find and name a half as one of two equal parts of an object, shape or quantity	Recognise, find and name a quarter as one of four equal parts of an object, shape or quantity.	
Geometry – position and direction		Unit 15	Position and direction	1	Describing turns	Describe position, direction and movement, including whole, half, quarter and three-quarter turns.		
Geometry – position and direction		Unit 15	Position and direction	2	Describing positions (1)	Describe position, direction and movement, including whole, half, quarter and three-quarter turns	Non-statutory guidance: Pupils use the language of position, direction and motion, including: left and right, top, middle and bottom, on top of, in front of, above, between, around, near, close and far, up and down, forwards and backwards, inside and outside.	
Geometry – position and direction		Unit 15	Position and direction	3	Describing positions (2)	Describe position, direction and movement, including whole, half, quarter and three-quarter turns	Non-statutory guidance: Pupils use the language of position, direction and motion, including: left and right, top, middle and bottom, on top of, in front of, above, between, around, near, close and far, up and down, forwards and backwards, inside and outside.	
Number – number and place value		Unit 16	Numbers to 100	1	Counting to 100	Count, read and write numbers to 100 in numerals; count in multiples of 2s, 5s and 10s	Identify and represent numbers using objects and pictorial representations including the number line, and use the language of: equal to, more than, less than (fewer), most, least	Count to and across 100, forwards and backwards, beginning with 0 or 1, or from any given number
Number – number and place value		Unit 16	Numbers to 100	2	Exploring number patterns	Count, read and write numbers to 100 in numerals; count in multiples of 2s, 5s and 10s	Given a number, identify one more and one less	
Number – number and place value		Unit 16	Numbers to 100	3	Partitioning numbers (1)	Identify and represent numbers using objects and pictorial representations including the number line, and use the language of: equal to, more than, less than (fewer), most, least	(Year 2) Recognise the place value of each digit in a 2-digit number (tens, ones)	
Number – number and place value		Unit 16	Numbers to 100	4	Partitioning numbers (2)	Identify and represent numbers using objects and pictorial representations including the number line, and use the language of: equal to, more than, less than (fewer), most, least	(Year 2) Recognise the place value of each digit in a 2-digit number (tens, ones)	

Strand 1	Strand 2	Unit		Lesson number	Lesson title	NC Objective 1	NC Objective 2	NC Objective 3
Number – number and place value		Unit 16	Numbers to 100	5	Comparing numbers (1)	Identify and represent numbers using objects and pictorial representations including the number line, and use the language of: equal to, more than, less than (fewer), most, least		
Number – number and place value		Unit 16	Numbers to 100	6	Comparing numbers (2)	Identify and represent numbers using objects and pictorial representations including the number line, and use the language of: equal to, more than, less than (fewer), most, least		
Number – number and place value		Unit 16	Numbers to 100	7	Ordering numbers	Identify and represent numbers using objects and pictorial representations including the number line, and use the language of: equal to, more than, less than (fewer), most, least		
Number – addition and subtraction		Unit 16	Numbers to 100	8	Bonds to 100 (1)	Represent and use number bonds and related subtraction facts within 20	(Year 2) Recall and use addition and subtraction facts to 20 fluently, and derive and use related facts up to 100	
Number – addition and subtraction		Unit 16	Numbers to 100	9	Bonds to 100 (2)	Represent and use number bonds and related subtraction facts within 20	(Year 2) Recall and use addition and subtraction facts to 20 fluently, and derive and use related facts up to 100	
Measurement		Unit 17	Time	1	Using before and after	Sequence events in chronological order using language [for example, before and after, next, first, today, yesterday, tomorrow, morning, afternoon and evening]		
Measurement		Unit 17	Time	2	Using a calendar	Recognise and use language relating to dates, including days of the week, weeks, months and years		
Measurement		Unit 17	Time	3	Telling time to the hour	Tell the time to the hour and half past the hour and draw the hands on a clock face to show these times.		
Measurement		Unit 17	Time	4	Telling time to the half hour	Tell the time to the hour and half past the hour and draw the hands on a clock face to show these times.		
Measurement		Unit 17	Time	5	Writing time	Measure and begin to record the following: time (hours, minutes, seconds)		
Measurement		Unit 17	Time	6	Comparing time	Compare, describe and solve practical problems for time [for example, quicker, slower, earlier, later]		
Number – addition and subtraction	Measurement	Unit 17	Time	7	Solving word problems – time	Solve one-step problems that involve addition and subtraction, using concrete objects and pictorial representations, and missing number problems such as 7 = ? – 9	Compare, describe and solve practical problems for time [for example, quicker, slower, earlier, later]	
Measurement		Unit 18	Money	1	Recognising coins	Recognise and know the value of different denominations of coins and notes		
Measurement		Unit 18	Money	2	Recognising notes	Recognise and know the value of different denominations of coins and notes		
Measurement	Number – number and place value	Unit 18	Money	3	Counting with coins	Recognise and know the value of different denominations of coins and notes	Count, read and write numbers to 100 in numerals; count in multiples of 2s, 5s and 10s	

Mindset: an introduction

Global research and best practice deliver the same message: learning is greatly affected by what learners perceive they can or cannot do. What is more, it is also shaped by what their parents, carers and teachers perceive they can do. Mindset – the thinking that determines our beliefs and behaviours – therefore has a fundamental impact on teaching and learning.

Everyone can!

Power Maths and mastery methods focus on the distinction between 'fixed' and 'growth' mindsets (Dweck, 2007).[1] Those with a fixed mindset believe that their basic qualities (for example, intelligence, talent and ability to learn) are pre-wired or fixed: 'If you have a talent for maths, you will succeed at it. If not, too bad!' By contrast, those with a growth mindset believe that hard work, effort and commitment drive success and that 'smart' is not something you are or are not, but something you become. In short, everyone can do maths!

Key mindset strategies

A growth mindset needs to be actively nurtured and developed. *Power Maths* offers some key strategies for fostering healthy growth mindsets in your classroom.

It is okay to get it wrong

Mistakes are valuable opportunities to re-think and understand more deeply. Learning is richer when children and teachers alike focus on spotting and sharing mistakes as well as solutions.

Praise hard work

Praise is a great motivator, and by focusing on praising effort and learning rather than success, children will be more willing to try harder, take risks and persist for longer.

Mind your language!

The language we use around learners has a profound effect on their mindsets. Make a habit of using growth phrases, such as, 'Everyone can!', 'Mistakes can help you learn' and 'Just try for a little longer'. The king of them all is one little word, 'yet'... I can't solve this...yet!' Encourage parents and carers to use the right language too.

Build in opportunities for success

The step-by-small-step approach enables children to enjoy the experience of success. In addition, avoid ability grouping and encourage every child to answer questions and explain or demonstrate their methods to others.

[1]Dweck, C (2007) The New Psychology of Success, Ballantine Books: New York

The *Power Maths* characters

The *Power Maths* characters model the traits of growth mindset learners and encourage resilience by prompting and questioning children as they work. Appearing frequently in the Textbooks and Practice books, they are your allies in teaching and discussion, helping to model methods, alternatives and misconceptions, and to pose questions. They encourage and support your children, too: they are all hardworking, enthusiastic and unafraid of making and talking about mistakes.

Meet the team!

Creative Flo is open-minded and sometimes indecisive. She likes to think differently and come up with a variety of methods or ideas.

Determined Dexter is resolute, resilient and systematic. He concentrates hard, always tries his best and he'll never give up – even though he doesn't always choose the most efficient methods!

'Let's try again.'

'Mistakes are cool!'

'Have I found all of the solutions?'

'Let's try it this way...'

'Can we do it differently?'

'I've got another way of doing this!'

'I'm going to try this!'

'I know how to do that!'

'Want to share my ideas?'

Curious Ash is eager, interested and inquisitive, and he loves solving puzzles and problems. Ash asks lots of questions but sometimes gets distracted.

'What if we tried this...?'

'I wonder...'

'Is there a pattern here?'

Sparks the Cat

Miaow!

Brave Astrid is confident, willing to take risks and unafraid of failure. She's never scared to jump straight into a problem or question, and although she often makes simple mistakes she's happy to talk them through with others.

Mathematical language

Traditionally, we in the UK have tended to try simplifying mathematical language to make it easier for young children to understand. By contrast, evidence and experience show that by diluting the correct language, we actually mask concepts and meanings for children. We then wonder why they are confused by new and different terminology later down the line! *Power Maths* is not afraid of 'hard' words and avoids placing any barriers between children and their understanding of mathematical concepts. As a result, we need to be planned, precise and thorough in building every child's understanding of the language of maths. Throughout the Teacher Guides you will find support and guidance on how to deliver this, as well as individual explanations throughout the Pupil Textbooks.

Use the following key strategies to build children's mathematical vocabulary, understanding and confidence.

Precise and consistent

Everyone in the classroom should use the correct mathematical terms in full, every time. For example, refer to 'equal parts', not 'parts'. Used consistently, precise maths language will be a familiar and non-threatening part of children's everyday experience.

Full sentences

Teachers and children alike need to use full sentences to explain or respond. When children use complete sentences, it both reveals their understanding and embeds their knowledge.

Stem sentences

These important sentences help children express mathematical concepts accurately, and are used throughout the *Power Maths* books. Encourage children to repeat them frequently, whether working independently or with others. Examples of stem sentences are:

'4 is a part, 5 is a part, 9 is the whole.'

'There are ... groups. There are ... in each group.'

Key vocabulary

The unit starters highlight essential vocabulary for every lesson. In the Pupil books, characters flag new terminology and the Teacher Guide lists important mathematical language for every unit and lesson. New terms are never introduced without a clear explanation.

Symbolic language

Symbols are used early on so that children quickly become familiar with them and their meaning. Often, the *Power Maths* characters will highlight the connection between language and particular symbols.

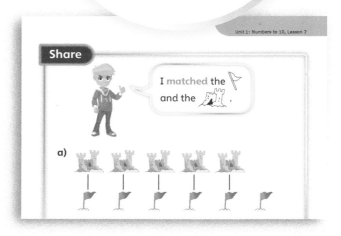

The role of talk and discussion

When children learn to talk purposefully together about maths, barriers of fear and anxiety are broken down and they grow in confidence, skills and understanding. Building a healthy culture of 'maths talk' empowers their learning from day one.

Explanation and discussion are integral to the *Power Maths* structure, so by simply following the books your lessons will stimulate structured talk. The following key 'maths talk' strategies will help you strengthen that culture and ensure that every child is included.

Sentences, not words

Encourage children to use full sentences when reasoning, explaining or discussing maths. This helps both speaker and listeners to clarify their own understanding. It also reveals whether or not the speaker truly understands, enabling you to address misconceptions as they arise.

Working together

Working with others in pairs, groups or as a whole class is a great way to support maths talk and discussion. Use different group structures to add variety and challenge. For example, children could take timed turns for talking, work independently alongside a 'discussion buddy', or perhaps play different *Power Maths* character roles within their group.

Think first – then talk

Provide clear opportunities within each lesson for children to think and reflect, so that their talk is purposeful, relevant and focused.

Give every child a voice

Where the 'hands up' model allows only the more confident child to shine, *Power Maths* involves everyone. Make sure that no child dominates and that even the shyest child is encouraged to contribute – and praised when they do.

Assessment strategies

Teaching for mastery demands that you are confident about what each child knows and where their misconceptions lie: therefore, practical and effective assessment is vitally important.

Formative assessment within lessons

The **Think together** section will often reveal any confusions or insecurities: try ironing these out by doing the first Think together question as a class. For children who continue to struggle, you or your teaching assistant should provide support and enable them to move on.

Performance in **Practice** can be very revealing: check Practice Books and listen out both during and after practice to identify misconceptions.

The **Reflect** section is designed to check on the all-important depth of understanding. Be sure to review how the children performed in this final stage before you teach the next lesson.

End of unit check – Textbook

Each unit concludes with a summative check to help you assess quickly and clearly each child's understanding, fluency, reasoning and problem-solving skills. Your Teacher Guide will suggest ideal ways of organising a given activity and offer advice and commentary on what children's responses mean. For example, 'What misconception does this reveal?'; 'How can you reinforce this particular concept?'

For Year 1 and Year 2 children, assess in small, teacher-led groups, giving each child time to think and respond while also consolidating correct mathematical language. Assessment with young children should always be an enjoyable activity, so avoid one-to-one individual assessments, which they may find threatening or scary. If you prefer, the End of unit check can be carried out as a whole-class group using whiteboards and Practice Books.

End of unit check – Practice Book

The Practice Book contains further opportunities for assessment, and can be completed by children independently whilst you are carrying out diagnostic assessment with small groups. Your Teacher Guide will advise you on what to do if children struggle to articulate an explanation – or perhaps encourage you to write down something they have explained well. It will also offer insights into children's answers and their implications for next learning steps. It is split into three main sections, outlined below.

My journal and Think!

My journal is designed to allow children to show their depth of understanding of the unit. It can also serve as a way of checking that children have grasped key mathematical vocabulary. The question children should answer is first presented in the Textbook in the Think! section. This provides an opportunity for you to discuss the question first as a class to ensure children have understood their task. Children should have some time to think about how they want to answer the question, and you could ask them to talk to a partner about their ideas. Then children should write their answer in their Practice Book, using the word bank provided to help them with vocabulary.

Power check

The Power check allows pupils to self-assess their level of confidence on the topic by colouring in different smiley faces. You may want to introduce the faces as follows:

I am starting to understand. I need more practice

I don't yet know how to do this

I know how to do this, but I will keep practising

Power play or Power puzzle

Each unit ends with either a Power play or a Power puzzle. This is an activity, puzzle or game that allows children to use their new knowledge in a fun, informal way.

How to ask diagnostic questions

The diagnostic questions provided in children's Practice Books are carefully structured to identify both understanding and misconceptions (if children answer in a particular way, you will know why). The simple procedure below may be helpful:

> Ask the question, offering the selection of answers provided.

▼

> Children take time to think about their response.

▼

> Each child selects an answer and shares their reasoning with the group.

▼

> Give minimal and neutral feedback (for example, 'That's interesting', or 'Okay').

▼

> Ask, 'Why did you choose that answer?', then offer an opportunity to change their mind by providing one correct and one incorrect answer.

▼

> Note which children responded and reasoned correctly first time and everyone's final choices.

▼

> Reflect that together, we can get the right answer.

▼

> Record outcomes on the assessment grid (on the next page).

Power Maths unit assessment grid

Year ____   Unit ____ _____

Record only as much information as you judge appropriate for your assessment of each child's mastery of the unit and any steps needed for intervention.

Name	Q1	Q2	Q3	Q4	Q5	My journal	Power check	Power play/puzzle	Mastery	Intervention/ Strengthen

Keeping the class together

Traditionally, children who learn quickly have been accelerated through the curriculum. As a consequence, their learning may be superficial and will lack the many benefits of enabling children to learn with and from each other.

By contrast, *Power Maths'* mastery approach values real understanding and richer, deeper learning above speed. It sees all children learning the same concept in small, cumulative steps, each finding and mastering challenge at their own level. Remember that when you teach for mastery, EVERYONE can do maths! Those who grasp a concept easily have time to explore and understand that concept at a deeper level. The whole class therefore moves through the curriculum at broadly the same pace via individual learning journeys.

For some teachers, the idea that a whole class can move forward together is revolutionary and challenging. However, the evidence of global good practice clearly shows that this approach drives engagement, confidence, motivation and success for all learners, and not just the high flyers. The strategies below will help you keep your class together on their maths journey.

Mix it up

Do not stick to set groups at each table. Every child should be working on the same concept, and mixing up the groupings widens children's opportunities for exploring, discussing and sharing their understanding with others.

Recycling questions

Reuse the Textbook and Practice Book questions with concrete materials to allow children to explore concepts and relationships and deepen their understanding. This strategy is especially useful for reinforcing learning in same-day interventions.

Strengthen at every opportunity

The next lesson in a *Power Maths* sequence always revises and builds on the previous step to help embed learning. These activities provide golden opportunities for individual children to strengthen their learning with the support of teaching assistants.

Prepare to be surprised!

Children may grasp a concept quickly or more slowly. The 'fast graspers' won't always be the same individuals, nor does the speed at which a child understands a concept predict their success in maths. Are they struggling or just working more slowly?

Depth and breadth

Just as prescribed in the National Curriculum, the goal of *Power Maths* is never to accelerate through a topic but rather to gain a clear, deep and broad understanding.

"Pupils who grasp concepts rapidly should be challenged through being offered rich and sophisticated problems before any acceleration through new content. Those who are not sufficiently fluent with earlier material should consolidate their understanding, including through additional practice, before moving on."

National Curriculum: Mathematics programmes of study: KS1 & 2, 2013

The lesson sequence offers many opportunities for you to deepen and broaden children's learning, some of which are suggested below.

Discover

As well as using the questions in the Teacher Guide, check that children are really delving into why something is true. It is not enough to simply recite facts, such as '6 + 3 = 9'. They need to be able to see why, explain it, and to demonstrate the solution in several ways.

Share

Make sure that every child is given chances to offer answers and expand their knowledge and not just those with the greatest confidence.

Think together

Encourage children to think about how they solved the problem and explain it to their partner. Be sure to make concrete materials available on group tables throughout the lesson to support and reinforce learning.

Practice

Avoid any temptation to select questions according to your assessment of ability: practice questions are presented in a logical sequence and it is important that each child works through every question.

Reflect

Open-ended questions allow children to deepen their understanding as far as they can by finding new ways of finding answers. For example, *Give me another way of working out how high the wall is… And another way?*

My friends and I often ask questions that make children think more deeply!

Have I found all of the solutions?

Is that always true?

Online materials

For each unit you will find additional strengthening activities to support those children who need it and to deepen the understanding of those who need the additional challenge.

Same-day intervention

Since maths competence depends on mastering concepts one by one in a logical progression, it is important that no gaps in understanding are ever left unfilled. Same-day interventions – either within or after a lesson – are a crucial safety net for any child who has not fully made the small step covered that day. In other words, intervention is always about keeping up, not catching up, so that every child has the skills and understanding they need to tackle the next lesson. That means presenting the same problems used in the lesson, with a variety of concrete materials to help children model their solutions.

We offer two intervention strategies below, but you should feel free to choose others if they work better for your class.

Within-lesson intervention

The Think together activity will reveal those who are struggling, so when it is time for Practice, bring these children together to work with you on the first practice questions. Observe these children carefully, ask questions, encourage them to use concrete models and check that they reach and can demonstrate their understanding.

After-lesson intervention

You might like to use Think together before an assembly, giving you or teaching assistants time to recap and expand with slow graspers during assembly time. Teaching assistants could also work with strugglers at other convenient points in the school day.

The role of practice

Practice plays a pivotal role in the *Power Maths* approach. It takes place in class groups, smaller groups, pairs, and independently, so that children always have the opportunities for thinking as well as the models and support they need to practise meaningfully and with understanding.

Intelligent practice

In *Power Maths*, practice never equates to the simple repetition of a process. Instead we embrace the concept of intelligent practice, in which all children become fluent in maths through varied, frequent and thoughtful practice that deepens and embeds conceptual understanding in a logical, planned sequence. To see the difference, take a look at the following examples.

Traditional practice

- Repetition can be rote – no need for a child to think hard about what they are doing

- Praise may be misplaced

- Does this prove understanding?

Intelligent practice

- Varied methods – concrete, pictorial and abstract

- Equation expressed in different ways, requiring thought and understanding

- Constructive feedback

All practice questions are designed to move children on and reveal misconceptions.

Simple, logical steps build onto earlier learning.

C-P-A runs throughout – different ways of modelling and understanding the same concept.

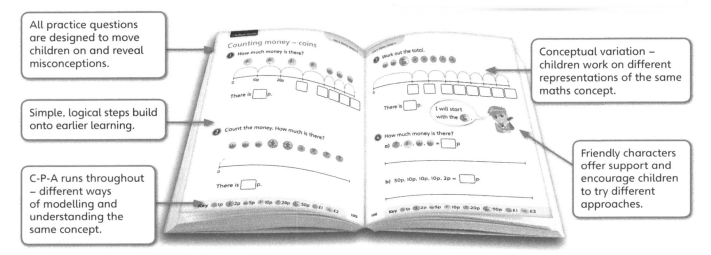

Conceptual variation – children work on different representations of the same maths concept.

Friendly characters offer support and encourage children to try different approaches.

A carefully designed progression

The Pupil Practice Books provide just the right amount of intelligent practice for children to complete independently in the final sections of each lesson. It is really important that all children are exposed to the practice questions, and that children are not directed to complete different sections. That is because each question is different and has been designed to challenge children to think about the maths they are doing. The questions become more challenging so children grasping concepts more quickly will start to slow down as they progress. Meanwhile, you have the chance to circulate and spot any misconceptions before they become barriers to further learning.

Homework and the role of carers

While *Power Maths* does not prescribe any particular homework structure, we acknowledge the potential value of practice at home. For example, practising fluency in key facts, such as number bonds and times tables, is an ideal homework task for Key Stage 1 children, and carers could work through uncompleted Practice Book questions with children at either primary stage.

However, it is important to recognise that many parents and carers may themselves lack confidence in maths, and few, if any, will be familiar with mastery methods. A Parents' and Carers' Evening that helps them understand the basics of mindsets, mastery and mathematical language is a great way to ensure that children benefit from their homework. It could be a fun opportunity for children to teach their families that everyone can do maths!

Structures and representations

Unlike most other subjects, maths comprises a wide array of abstract concepts – and that is why children and adults so often find it difficult. By taking a concrete-pictorial-abstract (C-P-A) approach, *Power Maths* allows children to tackle concepts in a tangible and more comfortable way.

Non-linear stages

Concrete

Replacing the traditional approach of a teacher working through a problem in front of the class, the concrete stage introduces real objects that children can use to 'do' the maths – any familiar object that a child can manipulate and move to help bring the maths to life. It is important to appreciate, however, that children must always understand the link between models and the objects they represent. For example, children need to first understand that three cakes could be represented by three pretend cakes, and then by three counters or bricks. Frequent practice helps consolidate this essential insight. Although they can be used at any time, good concrete models are an essential first step in understanding.

Pictorial

This stage uses pictorial representations of objects to let children 'see' what particular maths problems look like. It helps them make connections between the concrete and pictorial representations and the abstract maths concept. Children can also create or view a pictorial representation together, enabling discussion and comparisons. The *Power Maths* teaching tools are fantastic for this learning stage, and bar modelling is invaluable for problem-solving throughout the primary curriculum.

Abstract

Our ultimate goal is for children to understand abstract mathematical concepts, symbols and notation and, of course, some children will reach this stage far more quickly than others. To work with abstract concepts, a child must be comfortable with the meaning of and relationships between concrete, pictorial and abstract models and representations. The C-P-A approach is not linear, and children may need different types of models at different times. However, when a child demonstrates with concrete models and pictorial representations that they have grasped a concept, we can be confident that they are ready to explore or model it with abstract symbols such as numbers and notation.

Use at any time and with any age to support understanding

Variation helps visualisation

Children find it much easier to visualise and grasp concepts if they see them presented in a number of ways, so be prepared to offer and encourage many different representations.

For example, the number six could be represented in various ways:

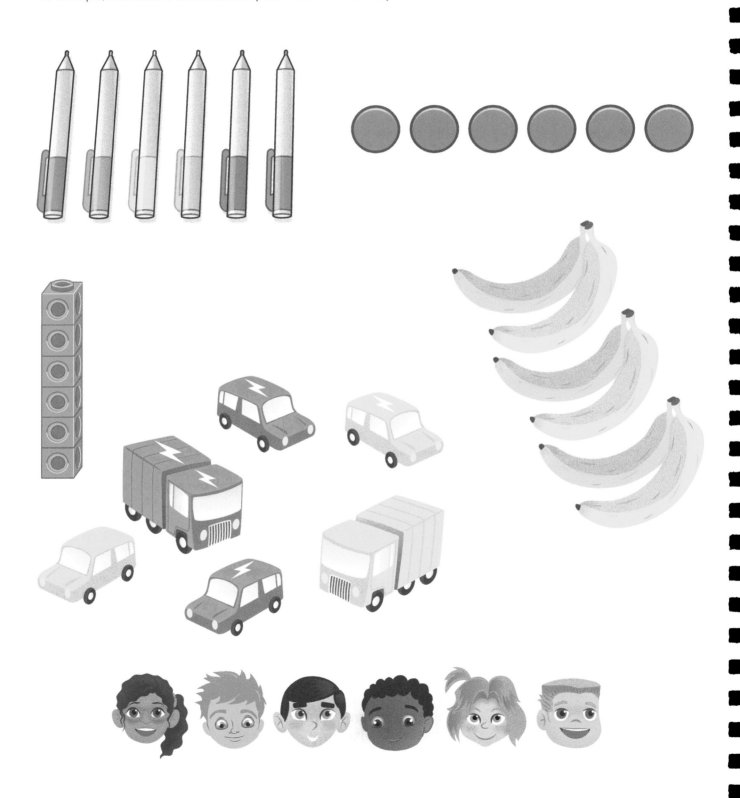

Getting started with *Power Maths*

As you prepare to put *Power Maths* into action, you might find the tips and advice below helpful.

STEP 1: Train up!

A practical, up-front full day professional development course will give you and your team a brilliant head-start as you begin your *Power Maths* journey. You will learn more about the ethos, how it works and why.

STEP 2: Check out the progression

Take a look at the yearly and termly overviews. Next take a look at the unit overview for the unit you are about to teach in your Teacher Guide, remembering that you can match your lessons and pacing to match your class.

STEP 3: Explore the context

Take a little time to look at the context for this unit: what are the implications for the unit ahead? (Think about key language, common misunderstandings and intervention strategies, for example.) If you have the online subscription, don't forget to watch the corresponding unit video.

STEP 4: Prepare for your first lesson

Familiarise yourself with the objectives, essential questions to ask and the resources you will need. The Teacher Guide offers tips, ideas and guidance on individual lessons to help you anticipate children's misconceptions and challenge those who are ready to think more deeply.

STEP 5: Teach and reflect

Deliver your lesson – and enjoy!

Afterwards, reflect on how it went… Did you cover all five stages? Does the lesson need more time? How could you improve it?

Unit 12
Multiplication

Mastery Expert tip! "When I taught this unit my class really enjoyed going on an 'array hunt' around the school. It really engaged them in the learning and had them finding multiplications everywhere around them!"

Don't forget to watch the Unit 12 video!

→ Unit 11: Introducing weight and volume
→ **Unit 12: Multiplication**
→ Unit 13: Division

WHY THIS UNIT IS IMPORTANT

In this unit, children will develop their understanding of multiplication as repeated addition, understanding the difference between equal and not equal groups. They will use their knowledge of skip counting in 2s, 5s and 10s and will use concrete, pictorial and abstract representations to help them to find the total of multiple equal groups and of doubles. These representations will include arrays, a powerful way of developing multiplicative reasoning. This will then feed into their work on division in the following unit.

In the final lesson, children will use their understanding of multiplication as repeated addition to solve simple multiplication word problems. This will give them an opportunity to work with more abstract problems.

WHERE THIS UNIT FITS

→ Unit 11: Introducing weight and volume
→ **Unit 12: Multiplication**
→ Unit 13: Division

Before they start this unit, it is expected that children:
- count reliably in 2s, 5s and 10s
- can sort objects into equal groups
- recognise and use ten frames and number lines.

ASSESSING MASTERY

Children will demonstrate mastery in this unit by counting reliably in steps of 2, 5 and 10. They will be able to use concrete, pictorial and abstract representations to find the total of a given number of equal groups, including repeated addition. They will be able to create arrays based on the numbers given to them and begin to recognise the commutativity that arrays demonstrate. Children will use their conceptual understanding to solve word problems, explaining fluently which representation of multiplication they will use to solve the word problem.

COMMON MISCONCEPTIONS	STRENGTHENING UNDERSTANDING	GOING DEEPER
Children may confuse the number of groups with the number in each group.	Show children two pictures of related groupings, such as 4 groups of 5 stars and 5 groups of 4 stars (not in an array). Ask, for both pictures: • *How many stars are in each group in this picture? How many groups of stars are there?* • *What is the same and what is different about the two pictures?* • *What can you tell me about the number of stars in each row? How many rows are there?* Ask children to arrange both pictures into arrays and ask about each: • *What can you tell me about the number of stars in each row? How many rows are there?* • *Can you write the total number of stars as an addition?*	Children could be given a number with many factors (such as 24). Ask: • *What arrays can you make using this number?* • *Can you write down addition calculations for your arrays?* • *How do you know you have found all the possible arrays?*

Use these pages to introduce the focus to children. You can use the characters to explore different ways of working too.

STRUCTURES AND REPRESENTATIONS

Array: Arrays are a visual representation of multiplication and division. They are an excellent tool for showing what X groups of Y is equivalent to. They also clearly show the commutativity of multiplication (i.e. how 'X groups of Y' has the same total as 'Y groups of X').

Number line: Number lines help children to represent their skip counting. They will help children count on and back from a given starting point and help them identify patterns and groups within the count.

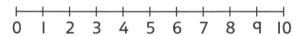

Ten frame: This model will help children visualise 10. In this unit it is used to demonstrate and cement children's understanding of doubles.

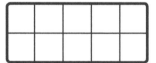

KEY LANGUAGE

There is some key language that children will need to know as part of the learning in this unit:

→ equal groups

→ array

→ row, column

→ double, twice

→ add, addition, adding, altogether, total

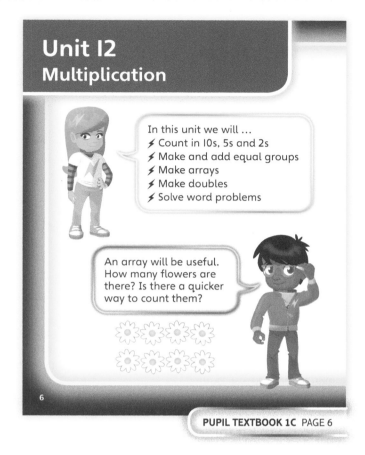

Unit 12
Multiplication

In this unit we will ...
⚡ Count in 10s, 5s and 2s
⚡ Make and add equal groups
⚡ Make arrays
⚡ Make doubles
⚡ Solve word problems

An array will be useful. How many flowers are there? Is there a quicker way to count them?

6

PUPIL TEXTBOOK 1C PAGE 6

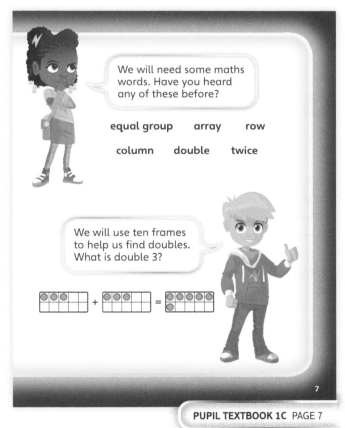

We will need some maths words. Have you heard any of these before?

equal group   array   row

column   double   twice

We will use ten frames to help us find doubles. What is double 3?

7

PUPIL TEXTBOOK 1C PAGE 7

Counting in 10s, 5s and 2s

Learning focus

In this lesson, children will recap counting fluently in steps of 10, 5 and 2. They will investigate the patterns these counts create using different concrete, pictorial and abstract representations.

Small steps

→ Previous step: Solving word problems – weight and capacity

→ **This step: Counting in 10s, 5s and 2s**

→ Next step: Making equal groups

NATIONAL CURRICULUM LINKS

Year 1 Number – Multiplication and Division

Count, read and write numbers to 100 in numerals; count in multiples of 2s, 5s and 10s.

ASSESSING MASTERY

Children can solve 1-step problems involving multiplication and division, by calculating the answer using concrete objects, pictorial representations and arrays with the support of the teacher.

COMMON MISCONCEPTIONS

Children may count inaccurately when counting in one or more of steps of 10, 5 or 2. Ask:
• *Are you sure you are correct? How could you check? Can you show me what you counted using another representation? Does it match what you just counted?*

Children may keep counting beyond where they need to count to. Ask:
• *Can you show me the counting on a number line? How many jumps will you need to make? Can you show me where to stop counting? How is that different from your first count?*

STRENGTHENING UNDERSTANDING

Introduce the concept of this lesson by giving children sorting activities. For example, explain to children that the stationery in the class needs sorting for each table. Each table needs 10 pencils, 5 rulers and 2 glue sticks. Children can then sort this out and give each table the required resources. Once this has been done, ask: *How many glue sticks do we have in total? Is there a quicker way to count than in 1s? How can you check?*

GOING DEEPER

Encourage children to investigate the patterns found in each of these counts, asking them to make generalisations about the patterns. Ask: *What is the same and what is different about the numbers in the count? What do you notice about the ones digit?* Ask children to investigate how these sequences change when you start at a different number.

KEY LANGUAGE

In lesson: count, groups, altogether

Other language to be used by the teacher: total, 2s, 5s, 10s, pattern, sequence, ten frame, number line, 100 square, digit, representation

STRUCTURES AND REPRESENTATIONS

Ten frame, number line, 100 square

RESOURCES

Optional: ten frame, number line, 100 square, countable objects (such as counters or cubes)

 In the eTextbook of this lesson, you will find interactive links to a selection of teaching tools.

Before you teach

• How confident are children with these concepts already?
• Is there a counting pattern that will require more attention than the others?

Discover

Counting in 10s, 5s and 2s

Discover

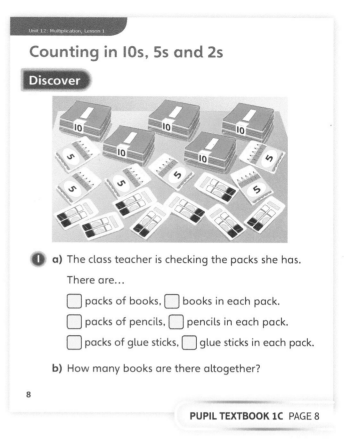

WAYS OF WORKING Pair work

ASK

- *How many books are in each pack?*
- *How can you work out how many books there are in total?*
- *Can you show how many books there are using representations or a picture?*
- *How many pencils are there altogether?*
- *How many objects are there in total?*
- *What representations could you use to make sure you are counting accurately?*

IN FOCUS This part of the lesson provides a good opportunity to recap the methods children can use to ensure they count accurately. Remind children of the representations they have used previously, such as number lines, ten frames and 100 squares, and encourage them to demonstrate how they would use these representations to show their counting.

ANSWERS

Question ❶ a): 5 packs of books, 10 books in each pack.

6 packs of pencils, 5 pencils in each pack.

8 packs of glue sticks, 2 glue sticks in each pack.

Question ❶ b): There are 50 books altogether.

❶ a) The class teacher is checking the packs she has.

There are…

☐ packs of books, ☐ books in each pack.

☐ packs of pencils, ☐ pencils in each pack.

☐ packs of glue sticks, ☐ glue sticks in each pack.

b) How many books are there altogether?

8

PUPIL TEXTBOOK 1C PAGE 8

Share

WAYS OF WORKING Whole class teacher led

ASK

- *What representations are used to show the count in 10s?*
- *How is the number of books shown on the number line?*
- *How has the ten frame helped to show the packs of books?*
- *How has the 100 square been used to show the counting?*
- *What would counting in 2s look like on the 100 square? What about counting in 5s?*
- *Which representation do you think is clearest?*

IN FOCUS Ensure children are clear on how each representation has been used. Provide children with large, printed versions of the three representations of counting which they can record on and manipulate.

Share

For each thing, first count how many groups, then how many in each group.

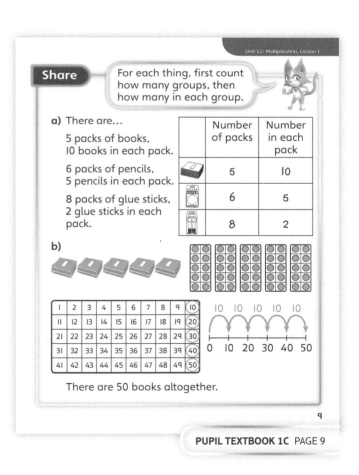

a) There are…

	Number of packs	Number in each pack
5 packs of books, 10 books in each pack.	5	10
6 packs of pencils, 5 pencils in each pack.	6	5
8 packs of glue sticks, 2 glue sticks in each pack.	8	2

b)

There are 50 books altogether.

9

PUPIL TEXTBOOK 1C PAGE 9

Think together

Unit 12: Multiplication, Lesson 1

WAYS OF WORKING Whole class teacher led (I do, We do, You do)

ASK

- *What do you need to know before you can count how many pencils there are?*
- *How many jumps of 5 are you going to need to make?*
- *How do the jumps look similar and different on the number line and 100 square?*
- *Are there any patterns you could use to help you count?*

IN FOCUS For each question, children are given fewer partially completed models of counting. Provide children with copies of these models that they could complete to enable them to count reliably and to recognise patterns. Encourage children to use these to check the accuracy of their counting.

STRENGTHEN If children are struggling to count in steps of 10, 5 or 2, offer objects that they can arrange along a number line in appropriately sized groups. Ask children to show how they would count the objects in groups of 10, 5 or 2. Can children arrange these groups on a 100 square and spot the pattern each creates?

DEEPEN Question ❸ deepens children's ability to count in groups by removing the cardinality of each group (each box shows only 1 pen, while it represents 5). Use Astrid and Ash's comments to elicit children's thinking. Is Astrid's method effective? Will it help Astrid to know how many packs there are? Can Ash count in groups? Challenge children to answer questions such as: *How many pens would there be if there were 10 in each pack?*

ASSESSMENT CHECKPOINT Children should be able to explain how the 100 square, number line and ten frame can help them represent their counting and the patterns within it. They should show greater fluency when counting in 10s, 5s and 2s, realising that counting in this way, rather than in 1s, is more efficient.

ANSWERS

Question ❶ : There are 25 pencils altogether.

Question ❷ : There are 12 glue sticks altogether.

Question ❸ : There are 40 pens altogether.

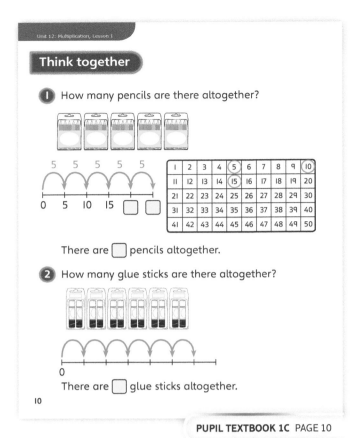

Think together

❶ How many pencils are there altogether?

There are ☐ pencils altogether.

❷ How many glue sticks are there altogether?

There are ☐ glue sticks altogether.

10

PUPIL TEXTBOOK 1C PAGE 10

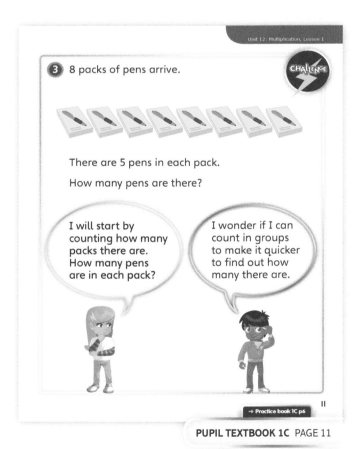

❸ 8 packs of pens arrive.

CHALLENGE

There are 5 pens in each pack.

How many pens are there?

I will start by counting how many packs there are. How many pens are in each pack?

I wonder if I can count in groups to make it quicker to find out how many there are.

→ Practice book 1C p6

11

PUPIL TEXTBOOK 1C PAGE 11

Practice

→ Textbook 1C p6

WAYS OF WORKING Independent thinking

IN FOCUS Questions ❶ and ❷ help children to use a number line to represent their counting efficiently. These questions can be used to help reinforce children's ability to know when to stop counting. It is worth noting that the fingers and sticks could be viewed in groups of 5 or 10. This could be a useful point for discussion while children are solving the problem.

STRENGTHEN If children are struggling with questions ❶ and ❷, have objects ready and available for them to count. Ask children to show how they would count the objects. What size groups will they count in and how will they represent their counting? Does their representation match anything they see in the question?

DEEPEN Question ❹ offers an excellent opportunity for children to begin generalising about the patterns found in different counting sequences. To help children develop this skill, ask them what they notice about the numbers that are coloured in. What is the same? What is different? Ask children to explain any patterns they notice. Can they use this to help them find the next number that has a circle and a colour? What about if they underlined all the numbers that are used when counting in 10s? This could be extended also by offering them the complete 100 square to investigate.

ASSESSMENT CHECKPOINT Children should be able to fluently count in 10s, 5s and 2s using a number line to represent the count. They should be able to recognise and describe patterns in their counting and should be confident when explaining how this will help them to count further. Question ❹ assesses understanding of the patterns in the count of 2s and 5s and gives opportunity for further reasoning about the numbers that will appear in both the 2s and 5s counts, making the connection that these numbers will all be in the 10s count (multiples of 10) because 2 groups of 5 and 5 groups of 2 are both 10.

ANSWERS Answers for the **Practice** part of the lesson appear in the separate **Practice and Reflect answer guide**.

Reflect

WAYS OF WORKING Pair work

IN FOCUS Give children a few minutes to record their method and reasoning then encourage them to share their thinking with a partner. Did they approach the question in the same way? Whose method was more efficient?

ASSESSMENT CHECKPOINT Children should recognise there are 10 bicycle wheels. Look for evidence of efficient counting in children's explanations; they should have recognised they can count 5 groups of 2.

ANSWERS Answers for the **Reflect** part of the lesson appear in the separate **Practice and Reflect answer guide**.

After the lesson ⏸

- Were children equally confident at counting in 10s, 5s and 2s or less confident in one or two areas?
- Were children able to use the specific examples given in the questions to draw out generalisations about the number sequences they were investigating?
- Were children able to apply these generalisations and explain how they could help them count further?

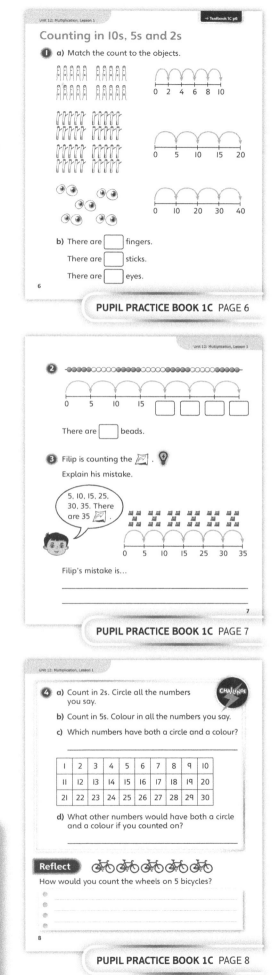

PUPIL PRACTICE BOOK 1C PAGE 6

PUPIL PRACTICE BOOK 1C PAGE 7

PUPIL PRACTICE BOOK 1C PAGE 8

Making equal groups

Learning focus

In this lesson, children will develop their ability to recognise and find equal groups of numbers and say how many groups of a number there are.

Small steps

→ Previous step: Counting in 10s, 5s and 2s
→ **This step: Making equal groups**
→ Next step: Adding equal groups

NATIONAL CURRICULUM LINKS

Year 1 Number – Multiplication and Division

Solve one-step problems involving multiplication and division, by calculating the answer using concrete objects, pictorial representations and arrays with the support of the teacher.

ASSESSING MASTERY

Children can recognise and explain how they know when groups are equal. They can recognise and explain how this can help them count totals more efficiently.

COMMON MISCONCEPTIONS

Children may confuse the number of groups with the number of objects in each group. Ask:
• *How many objects are in each group? How can you check? How many groups of these objects are there? Can you say in a sentence how many groups of objects there are?*

STRENGTHENING UNDERSTANDING

Introduce the topic of this lesson to children through contexts easily recognisable to them: for example, by sharing resources. How do they know when something has been shared equally? Say: *I am going to give each person on this table 2 pencils. How many groups of 2 will that be?*

GOING DEEPER

Children could investigate numbers from 1 to 20. How many ways can each number be shared into equal groups? Ask questions such as: *Can you find out how many ways 10 can be shared into equal groups? Can you tell me how many groups of 2 make 8? Can 9 be shared into equal groups of 2? Which is the smallest number that can be shared into equal groups of 2, 5 and 10? Which numbers cannot be shared into any equal groups of 2, 5 or 10? With a set of 6 objects, can you count 1 group of 6 and 6 groups of 1 as equal groups?*

KEY LANGUAGE

In lesson: equal groups

Other language to be used by the teacher: counting, groups, number, pattern, unequal, amount

STRUCTURES AND REPRESENTATIONS

Cubes, counters

RESOURCES

Mandatory: cubes, counters

Optional: grids showing the group sizes appropriate to the questions in the **Pupil Textbook**, collections of countable objects

 In the eTextbook of this lesson, you will find interactive links to a selection of teaching tools.

Before you teach

• How confident are children in their understanding of 'equal'?
• How could you use children's real-life experiences to broaden and add depth to this lesson?

Discover

Pair work

ASK

- *What is the same and what is different about the boats?*
- *Which colour boats do you think it will be easier to count?*
- *How many people are in the red boats?*
- *How many people are in the yellow boats?*
- *What is different about the groups in the red and yellow boats?*

IN FOCUS Use this picture to focus on why it is easier and more efficient to count the children in the red boats. See whether children can recognise that, as there are unequal numbers of children in the yellow boats, it is not possible to count using a repeating pattern.

ANSWERS

Question **1** a): There are 4 ⛵ .

          There are 2 people in each ⛵ .

Question **1** b): There are 3 yellow ⛵ .

          There are not the same number of people in each ⛵ .

          One ⛵ has 1 person in it.

          One ⛵ has 3 people in it.

          One ⛵ has 5 people in it.

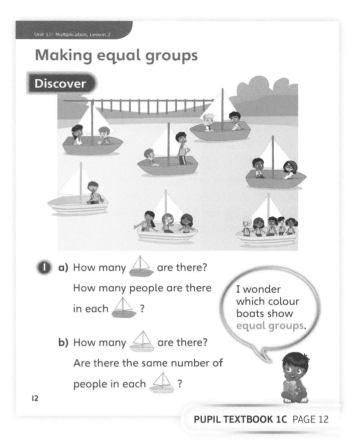

PUPIL TEXTBOOK 1C PAGE 12

Share

Whole class teacher led

ASK

- *How did you count the total amount of people in the red boats?*
- *Which boats are easier to count?*
- *How could you show the groups on a number line? Is a ten frame useful for this count or not?*
- *Could the children in the yellow boats be grouped equally? How do you know?*
- *Is there more than one way to share the children in the yellow boats equally?*

IN FOCUS At this point in the lesson, it would be beneficial to let children explore sharing different numbers of objects into equal groups. Start with the children in the yellow boats. Children should discover that there is only one way to make equal groups: 3 groups of 3. 12 is a useful number to investigate as it can be shared into equal groups of 2, 3, 4 and 6.

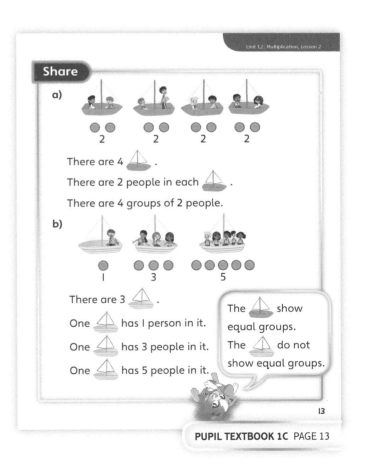

PUPIL TEXTBOOK 1C PAGE 13

Think together

WAYS OF WORKING Whole class teacher led (I do, We do, You do)

ASK
- *How will you know if the objects are shared into equal groups? What two pieces of information will you need?*
- *Does it matter if the objects are arranged differently?*

IN FOCUS All questions in this section will develop children's ability to recognise and describe equal groups. Questions **2** and **3** require children to begin differentiating between equal and unequal groups.

STRENGTHEN If children struggle to recognise equal groups in the pictures, allow them the opportunity to use concrete manipulatives to represent the groups shown. This could be supported further still by giving children grids with a number of boxes matching the group size (for groups of 4 have a grid with 4 boxes). Ask children to place the objects into the grid. Do they have enough to have an equal quantity in each box?

DEEPEN Once children have solved question **3** , challenge them to answer Ash's question. Can they arrange the other shapes into equal groups? Explain that they do not have to be put into 3 equal groups as in the diagrams. Is there only one solution? Are groups of one object in each equal? Discuss the fact that groups of 1 are still equal groups.

ASSESSMENT CHECKPOINT All questions will show whether children understand and recognise equal groups, with questions **2** b) and **3** identifying children who do or do not recognise equal groups when the objects are arranged differently. Question **3** will also identify which children can rearrange objects so that they are in equal groups. Some children may just see that moving one triangle from the first group to the last group will make 3 groups of 4. Other children, having been told that there do not need to be only 3 groups, may explore further to discover more or all solutions.

ANSWERS

Question **1** : There are 5 groups of 2 ice cubes.

Question **2** a): B and C show equal groups because there is a group of 4 cupcakes on each plate.

Question **2** b): There can be two answers, either:

There are 4 equal groups of 4 cupcakes or,

There are 2 equal groups of 8 cupcakes.

Question **3** : A shows equal groups.

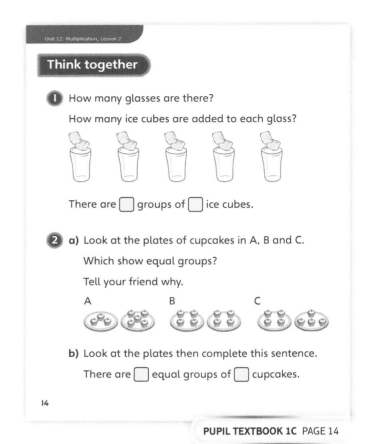

Think together

1 How many glasses are there?

How many ice cubes are added to each glass?

There are ☐ groups of ☐ ice cubes.

2 a) Look at the plates of cupcakes in A, B and C.

Which show equal groups?

Tell your friend why.

A   B   C

b) Look at the plates then complete this sentence.

There are ☐ equal groups of ☐ cupcakes.

14

PUPIL TEXTBOOK 1C PAGE 14

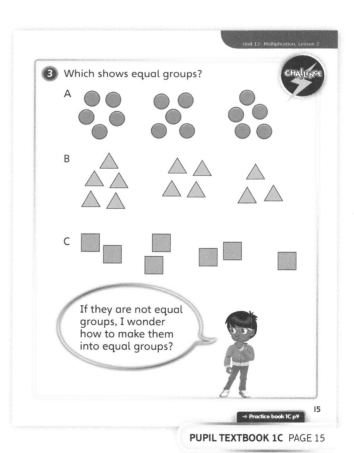

3 Which shows equal groups?

A

B

C

If they are not equal groups, I wonder how to make them into equal groups?

15

→ Practice book 1C p9

PUPIL TEXTBOOK 1C PAGE 15

Practice

WAYS OF WORKING Independent thinking

IN FOCUS Question ❶ scaffolds children's ability to describe equal groups, focusing on how many groups there are and how many are in each group. Question ❷ develops children's understanding of creating equal groups. This question offers a good opportunity to discuss whether groups need to look the same to be equal. Ask children how many dots need to be in each group. Do the groups have to look like the first group? How many ways could they draw the groups?

STRENGTHEN If children are finding it tricky to identify equal groups, ask them to explain what the word 'equal' means. What could be the same about each group? Can they spot where the groups have the same number of objects or pictures?

DEEPEN Use question ❸ to deepen children's understanding of how the arrangement of a group does not impact on the number it represents. Explain that Cora thinks her groups are equal. Why do children think Cora thinks this? What is it about the groups that makes them look equal? What is it about Oliver's groups that makes them look unequal? Challenge children to describe how they could help Cora understand that she is mistaken.

ASSESSMENT CHECKPOINT These questions assess whether children can differentiate between the number of groups and the number in each group, identify equal and unequal groups, and show understanding that equal groups are equal even if the groups are arranged differently. Question ❹ assesses whether children can use the language of equal groups to describe what the picture shows.

ANSWERS Answers for the **Practice** part of the lesson appear in the separate **Practice and Reflect answer guide**.

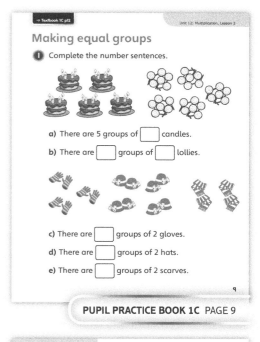

Making equal groups

① Complete the number sentences.

a) There are 5 groups of ☐ candles.

b) There are ☐ groups of ☐ lollies.

c) There are ☐ groups of 2 gloves.

d) There are ☐ groups of 2 hats.

e) There are ☐ groups of 2 scarves.

PUPIL PRACTICE BOOK 1C PAGE 9

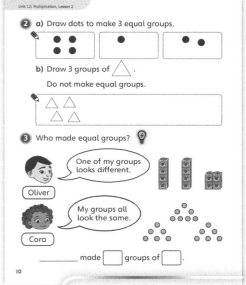

② a) Draw dots to make 3 equal groups.

b) Draw 3 groups of △.
Do not make equal groups.

③ Who made equal groups?

Oliver: One of my groups looks different.

Cora: My groups all look the same.

_____ made ☐ groups of ☐.

PUPIL PRACTICE BOOK 1C PAGE 10

Reflect

WAYS OF WORKING Independent thinking, pair work

IN FOCUS Encourage children to share their ideas with a partner. Have they found the only solution? How do they know? Suggest that children draw the cube as a square (one of its faces) to make the task easier.

ASSESSMENT CHECKPOINT Look for children to have drawn appropriate groups. Children should be able to identify which groups are equal and which are not.

ANSWERS Answers for the **Reflect** part of the lesson appear in the separate **Practice and Reflect answer guide**.

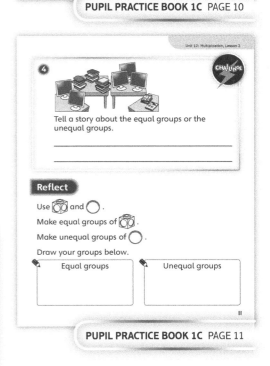

④ CHALLENGE

Tell a story about the equal groups or the unequal groups.

_____

_____

Reflect

Use ☐ and ○.
Make equal groups of ☐.
Make unequal groups of ○.
Draw your groups below.

Equal groups	Unequal groups

PUPIL PRACTICE BOOK 1C PAGE 11

After the lesson

- Were children able to recognise that equal groups can be arranged differently as long as they each contain the same number of objects?
- Did children begin to make the link between equal groups, using this to count a total?

Adding equal groups

Learning focus

In this lesson, children will build on their understanding of equal groups and begin adding equal groups together to find a total.

Small steps

→ Previous step: Making equal groups
→ **This step: Adding equal groups**
→ Next step: Making simple arrays

NATIONAL CURRICULUM LINKS

Year 1 Number – Multiplication and Division

Solve one-step problems involving multiplication and division, by calculating the answer using concrete objects, pictorial representations and arrays with the support of the teacher.

ASSESSING MASTERY

Children can recognise where groups are equal and add these groups together to find a total. They can use a number line to reliably and fluently represent their additions.

COMMON MISCONCEPTIONS

Children may not be able to translate the problem into an addition. Ask:
* *How many counts of (5) do you need to make? How many jumps on the number line are there? How many (5s) should there be in the addition? How can you write this problem as an addition?*

STRENGTHENING UNDERSTANDING

Ask children to arrange counters or cubes into a set number of equal groups, say 4 groups of 2. Children should then practise recording what the counters show in two ways: 4 groups of 2 and as an addition 2 + 2 + 2 + 2. Repeat by asking children to add one counter to each group making 4 groups of 3: 3 + 3 + 3 + 3. Continue to show 4 groups of 4 and 4 groups of 5. Ask: *Which number is changing?* (Number of counters) *Which number stays the same?* (Number of groups) *How many numbers are in each addition?* (4, the same as the number of groups).

GOING DEEPER

Encourage children to investigate a skip count sequence and its related additions. For example, ask children to look into the patterns found if the skip count is in groups of 4. How far can they skip count in 4s? What would the addition look like for each new step of the sequence? Ask children to describe any patterns they notice in the numbers and in the addition calculations. Could they use the patterns to help them count further? Children could also use number lines to draw skip counts, recording each as an addition.

KEY LANGUAGE

In lesson: pair, skip counting, addition, in total, adding

Other language to be used by the teacher: equal groups, counts, add, plus, sum, equals, number line, problem, sequence, pattern, represent

STRUCTURES AND REPRESENTATIONS

Number line, counters

RESOURCES

Optional: collections of countable objects, large printed number line

 In the eTextbook of this lesson, you will find interactive links to a selection of teaching tools.

Before you teach

* How confident are children at recognising when groups are equal and when they are not equal?
* What support will you offer children who count on in 1s rather than using the count number?

Discover

Unit 12: Multiplication, Lesson 3

WAYS OF WORKING Pair work

ASK

- *How many flowers are in a bunch?*
- *Are all the bunches of flowers equal?*
- *What equal groups can you see?*
- *Can you see any unequal groups?*
- *How could you represent the groups you have just counted?*

IN FOCUS This is a good opportunity for children to share the different ways they would represent the addition of the equal groups, before having the more formal model of the number line introduced into the lesson.

ANSWERS

Question ❶ a): Millie bought 15 .

Question ❶ b): Dan bought 10 .

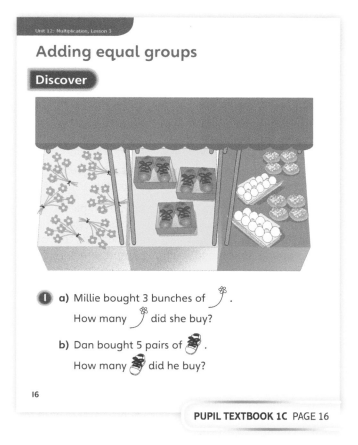

Adding equal groups

Discover

❶ **a)** Millie bought 3 bunches of .
How many did she buy?

b) Dan bought 5 pairs of .
How many did he buy?

16

PUPIL TEXTBOOK 1C PAGE 16

Share

WAYS OF WORKING Whole class teacher led

ASK

- *How did you show the equal groups?*
- *How can this be written as addition?*
- *Can you explain how the number line helps to show the count?*

IN FOCUS Use the opportunities given here to ensure that children are confident and fluent when recognising what number they are skip counting, and how many of that number they need to count. How many groups do they need to count? How many are in each group? How do they know when to stop counting? Ensure children understand that they are being asked to record the number of flowers in 3 bunches, not in all of the bunches shown in the picture, and that the number of pairs of shoes in the question is more than is shown in the picture on page 16.

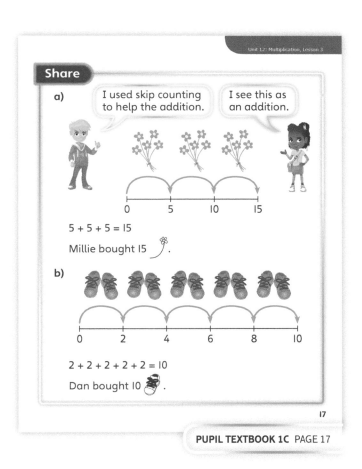

Share

a) I used skip counting to help the addition. I see this as an addition.

$5 + 5 + 5 = 15$

Millie bought 15 .

b)

$2 + 2 + 2 + 2 + 2 = 10$

Dan bought 10 .

17

PUPIL TEXTBOOK 1C PAGE 17

Think together

WAYS OF WORKING Whole class teacher led (I do, We do, You do)

ASK

- *What do you need to know about the bunches of flowers before you can find the total?*
- *What number will you skip count in?*
- *How can you use a number line to represent the count?*
- *How can you show your counting as an addition?*

IN FOCUS Provide children with different examples to skip count using different amounts. Consider using egg cartons in 6s or 10s, empty battery packs or other objects that offer clear groupings. Encourage children to represent each of their skip counts along a number line and link them to an addition calculation.

STRENGTHEN For children who are struggling to relate the pictures of the groups to the number, offer concrete resources that can be used to represent the objects pictured. These could be arranged along a large printed number line to help children link the concrete with the abstract. Ask questions such as: *How many are in each group? How many flowers are in each group? What number do you need to skip count in? How many skip counts do there need to be? What numbers will be recorded along the number line?*

DEEPEN For children who have completed question ❸, deepen their understanding by drawing on the previous lesson. Ask: *Can you share the 12 bread rolls into different equal groups?* Challenge children to record their new equal groups as an addition. How many different ways to do this are there? How will children know when they have found all the possibilities?

ASSESSMENT CHECKPOINT Children should be able to recognise how skip counting is an efficient method of finding the total of a number of equal groups. They should be able to link this to a number line and the written addition calculation. Using these methods children should be increasingly confident when finding the total of a given number of equal groups.

ANSWERS

Question ❶ : 5 + 5 + 5 + 5 + 5 + 5 + 5 = 35

There are 35 flowers in total.

Question ❷ : 10 + 10 + 10 = 30

Dad bought 30 eggs.

Question ❸ : 4 + 4 + 4 = 12

PUPIL TEXTBOOK 1C PAGE 18

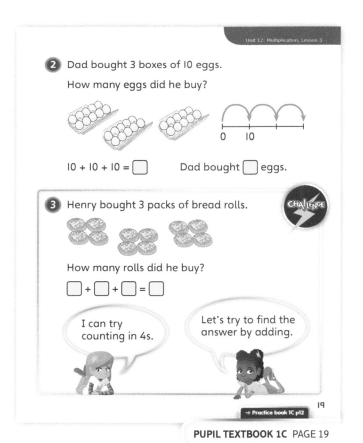

PUPIL TEXTBOOK 1C PAGE 19

Practice

WAYS OF WORKING Independent thinking

IN FOCUS At this point in the lesson, where children are working independently, it will be very important to look out for any child confusing the number of groups with the number in each group. Questions **1** a) and **1** b) help to scaffold children's understanding of this concept, with the elements of the count partially completed for them.

STRENGTHEN To help children working on questions **2** and **3** , ask: *How many are in each group? How many groups do you need to count?* Are there any patterns in children's counting that can help them find the next number? Can they show the count in a different way?

DEEPEN Question **5** offers an excellent opportunity to develop children's reasoning. As the two children actually both have the same number of stickers, the question will also challenge children's assumptions about group size and number of groups, and how these affect the total amounts. Ask children to write down what they think about Oliver and Anna's statements. Is either Oliver or Anna correct? Why? Can children explain how the two collections are similar and how they are different? Do they know what links the two collections?

ASSESSMENT CHECKPOINT At this point in the lesson, children should be able to explain clearly how skip counting is an efficient method for finding the total of a number of equal groups. They will be able to link this to a number line and the written addition calculation. Using these methods, children should be fluent when finding the total of a given number of equal groups.

ANSWERS Answers for the **Practice** part of the lesson appear in the separate **Practice and Reflect answer guide**.

Reflect

WAYS OF WORKING Whole class

IN FOCUS Discuss children's different approaches to the question and encourage children to share their ideas with the class. Ask: *What size groups did you use? Could you have used different-sized groups? How many of these groups were there?*

ASSESSMENT CHECKPOINT Look for children recognising the equal groups within the picture and using these to skip count. Children may have seen different groups (6 groups of 5, 3 groups of 10 or possibly 2 groups of 15). Use this as an opportunity to assess children's fluency and flexibility with the idea of finding and using equal groups to assist counting.

ANSWERS Answers for the **Reflect** part of the lesson appear in the separate **Practice and Reflect answer guide**.

After the lesson ⏸

- Could children confidently explain the link between skip counting and addition?
- Are there any opportunities you could offer, outside of the mathematics lesson, for children to practise skip counting?

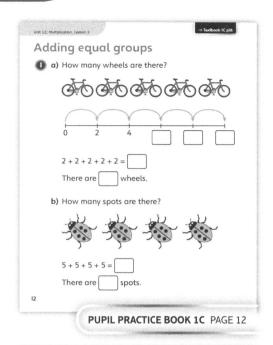

PUPIL PRACTICE BOOK 1C PAGE 12

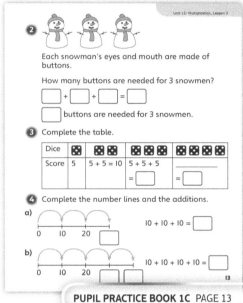

PUPIL PRACTICE BOOK 1C PAGE 13

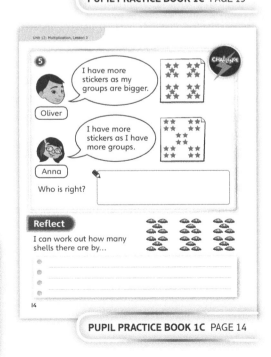

PUPIL PRACTICE BOOK 1C PAGE 14

Making simple arrays

Learning focus

In this lesson, children will learn to recognise, understand and create simple arrays. They will link this representation to their learning about repeated addition.

Small steps

→ Previous step: Adding equal groups
→ **This step: Making simple arrays**
→ Next step: Making doubles

NATIONAL CURRICULUM LINKS

Year 1 Number – Multiplication and Division

Solve one-step problems involving multiplication and division, by calculating the answer using concrete objects, pictorial representations and arrays with the support of the teacher.

ASSESSING MASTERY

Children can recognise an array and explain what it represents fluently using the vocabulary of 'columns' and 'rows'. They can identify and explain how an array can be read in two ways and can show the related repeated additions along a number line.

COMMON MISCONCEPTIONS

When counting or creating an array, children may mistakenly count too many or too few objects in a row or column. Ask:
• *How many should there be in all the rows? How many should there be in all the columns? Can you prove that all the rows are equal and all the columns are equal? Where did you make a mistake?*

STRENGTHENING UNDERSTANDING

Encourage children to look for arrays in the world around them. Examples include egg cartons, window panes, bookshelves, some chocolate box arrangements, cake trays and chess boards. Discuss with children the patterns they can see in the arrays. Ask: *Which equal groups can you see?* Discuss and practise counting using first the rows and then the columns, establishing that the total of all the rows is the same as the total of all the columns.

GOING DEEPER

Encourage children to look for more arrays in the world around them. Ask them to take photos or draw pictures of the arrays that they have found. Challenge children to order their arrays from biggest to smallest and to draw them a different way. Ask them to choose one of the arrays. Ask: *Can you create a different array that represents the same amount? Could you turn or change this array so that the rows become the columns?*

KEY LANGUAGE

In lesson: row, array, column, arrangement, total, count

Other language to be used by the teacher: addition, biggest, smallest, groups

STRUCTURES AND REPRESENTATIONS

Array, number line, counters

RESOURCES

Mandatory: counters

Optional: collections of countable objects, large printed number lines, boards as a base for the arrays

 In the eTextbook of this lesson, you will find interactive links to a selection of teaching tools.

Before you teach

• How could you introduce the lesson's vocabulary of 'rows' and 'columns' using children's real-life experiences?
• How will you make this lesson as hands-on as possible? Could you begin or end with an array hunt around the school environment?

Discover

WAYS OF WORKING Pair work

ASK

- *How have the seeds been arranged?*
- *What equal groups can you see in the picture?*
- *Who planted more seeds, the first group or Anya?*
- *How many ways can you count Anya's seeds?*
- *How many seeds did Anya plant in total?*
- *Can you show Anya's array on a number line? Is there more than one way to do this? Which is easier?*

IN FOCUS To help reinforce the structure of arrays, focus on how both the columns and rows represent equal groups. It is important to discuss how the rows and columns differ in their size and amounts.

ANSWERS

Question ❶ a): There are 10 seeds in each row.

There are 2 rows.

There are 20 seeds in total.

Question ❶ b): There are 20 seeds in total.

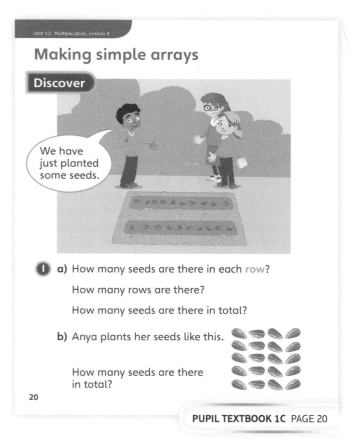

PUPIL TEXTBOOK 1C PAGE 20

Share

WAYS OF WORKING Whole class teacher led

ASK

- *Did you find another way to arrange Anya's seeds into equal groups?*
- *Did your number line look the same as the one shown?*
- *Could you have created another number line that showed the same total but used different groups?*
- *What is the same about all the columns in an array?*
- *What is the same about all the rows in an array?*
- *Compare the number line and the array. What is the same and what is different about them?*

IN FOCUS At this point in the lesson, it is important for children to recognise how the array can show two different sets of equal groups and therefore two separate repeated additions, both amounting to the same total. Encourage children to investigate the different arrays they can make with a given number. Can they find a number where the number of objects in both the array's rows and columns are the same?

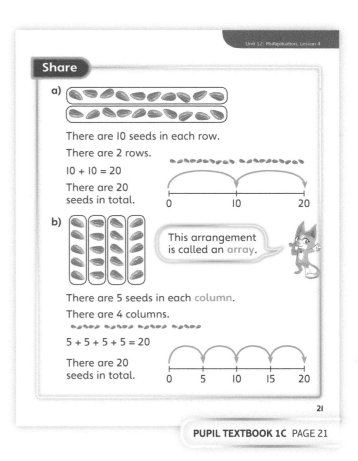

PUPIL TEXTBOOK 1C PAGE 21

Think together

WAYS OF WORKING Whole class teacher led (I do, We do, You do)

ASK

- *How can you find out how many counters are in an array?*
- *Can you show me how to count the rows?*
- *How is counting the rows different from counting the columns?*

IN FOCUS In questions **1** and **2**, continue the patterns that the arrays are showing. Discuss the shapes that can be observed as the arrays grow. Ask children what shape the arrays look like (rectangles). Are there any times when the arrays look different (squares)? What do they notice about the rows and columns at those times?

STRENGTHEN During questions **1** and **2**, encourage children to build the arrays using concrete resources to strengthen their understanding. Ask children to make the arrays they see on the page. How many counters are in each row? How many rows or columns do they need to arrange? Ask children to explain how many counters there are in total. Is there another way of looking at the array?

DEEPEN In question **3**, use Ash's question about the potential totals to deepen children's thinking. Ask children if they think that counting the rows and columns will result in a different total. What is the same about the rows and columns and what is different about them? Can children explain why they total the same amount?

ASSESSMENT CHECKPOINT Children should be able to recognise an array, observing the rows and columns and explaining how many are in each. Children should be able to explain, using question **3**, that the total should be the same whether they count the rows or the columns.

ANSWERS

Question **1** a): 2 rows; 5 counters in each row; 10 counters in the array.

Question **1** b): 3 rows; 5 counters in each row; 15 counters in the array.

Question **1** c): 4 rows; 5 counters in each row; 20 counters in the array.

Question **2** a): 3 columns; 2 counters in each column; 6 counters in the array.

Question **2** b): 4 columns; 2 counters in each column; 8 counters in the array.

Question **2** c): 5 columns; 2 counters in each column; 10 counters in the array.

Question **3** a): 2 chocolates in a row; 3 chocolates in a column; 6 chocolates in the box.

Question **3** b): 5 chocolates in a row; 4 chocolates in a column; 20 chocolates in the box.

Question **3** c): 3 chocolates in a row; 5 chocolates in a column; 15 chocolates in the box.

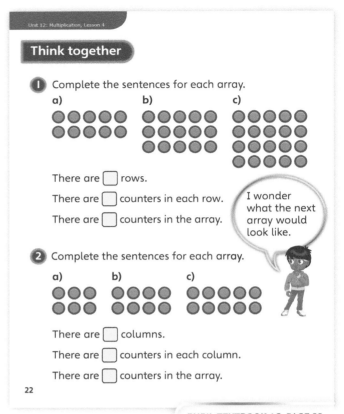

Think together

1 Complete the sentences for each array.

a)   b)   c)

There are ☐ rows.

There are ☐ counters in each row.

There are ☐ counters in the array.

I wonder what the next array would look like.

2 Complete the sentences for each array.

a)   b)   c)

There are ☐ columns.

There are ☐ counters in each column.

There are ☐ counters in the array.

22

PUPIL TEXTBOOK 1C PAGE 22

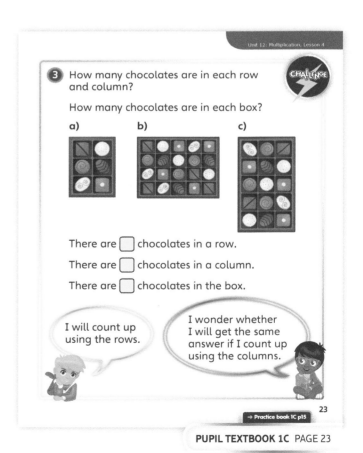

3 How many chocolates are in each row and column?

CHALLENGE

How many chocolates are in each box?

a)   b)   c)

There are ☐ chocolates in a row.

There are ☐ chocolates in a column.

There are ☐ chocolates in the box.

I will count up using the rows.

I wonder whether I will get the same answer if I count up using the columns.

→ Practice book 1C p15

23

PUPIL TEXTBOOK 1C PAGE 23

Practice

WAYS OF WORKING Independent thinking

IN FOCUS While children are working on the questions in this section of the lesson, it is important to reinforce their understanding that arrays can be read in two ways. For example, while solving questions **1** and **2** , ask children to describe the array in another way. Encourage them to describe the array using a full sentence.

STRENGTHEN If children are struggling to link the arrays with a number line and the repeated addition calculation, ask them to find equal groups within the array. Did they look at the rows or columns? Encourage the use of the number line to skip count, linking this to addition. It may be beneficial to allow children to make the array using counters or other resources, then place these along a printed number line, to help reinforce the link between the models.

DEEPEN Question **4** offers an opportunity for children to explain their reasoning about how arrays are arranged. If they have fully explained their thinking about the question given, ask: *Could Tim have made any correct arrays with the number of counters he has?* Challenge children to prove that Tim is able to make at least one correct array. Can they find all possible arrays? Since 19 is a prime number, Tim can only make 2 arrays: 1 row of 19 and 1 column of 19.

ASSESSMENT CHECKPOINT At this point in the lesson, children should be confidently identifying and describing arrays using the correct vocabulary of rows and columns. They should be able to explain which two repeated additions an array shows, and represent these using number lines and addition calculations.

ANSWERS Answers for the **Practice** part of the lesson appear in the separate **Practice and Reflect answer guide**.

Reflect

WAYS OF WORKING Independent thinking

IN FOCUS Once children have completed the **Reflect** section, ask them whether they chose to count the rows or the columns. What did their number line look like? Did it look the same as for someone who chose to count differently? Which number line had more jumps? Which number line was easier to count?

ASSESSMENT CHECKPOINT Children should be able to independently select how they will count the array. They should be able to show this along a number line fluently and confidently explain their thinking using the lesson vocabulary.

ANSWERS Answers for the **Reflect** part of the lesson appear in the separate **Practice and Reflect answer guide**.

After the lesson

- Were children more inclined to count the rows or columns or both?
- If children relied more heavily on one facet of the array, how will you develop their confidence with the other one?
- Were children able to confidently see the link between arrays and repeated addition?

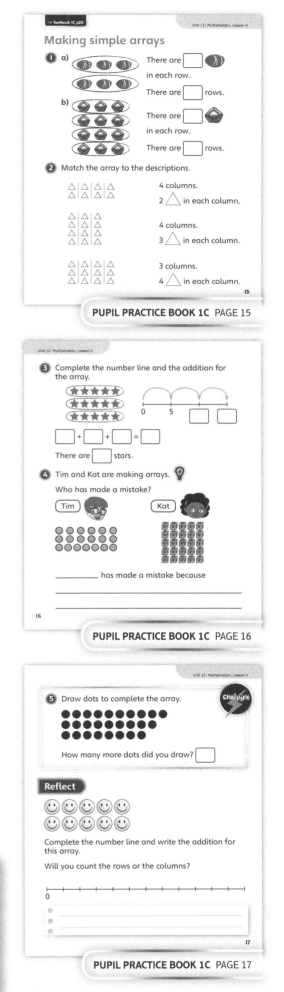

PUPIL PRACTICE BOOK 1C PAGE 15

PUPIL PRACTICE BOOK 1C PAGE 16

PUPIL PRACTICE BOOK 1C PAGE 17

Making doubles

Learning focus

In this lesson, children will learn about the meaning of the word 'double'. Using familiar representations, they will develop their understanding of what a double is and how to find one.

Small steps

→ Previous step: Making simple arrays
→ **This step: Making doubles**
→ Next step: Solving word problems – multiplication

NATIONAL CURRICULUM LINKS

Year 1 Number – Multiplication and Division

Solve one-step problems involving multiplication and division, by calculating the answer using concrete objects, pictorial representations and arrays with the support of the teacher.

Year 1 Non-statutory guidance

Through grouping and sharing small quantities, pupils begin to understand: multiplication and division; doubling numbers and quantities; and finding simple fractions of objects, numbers and quantities.

ASSESSING MASTERY

Children can find the double of a given number and will be able to explain what doubles are, using the appropriate vocabulary. They will be able to use representations they are familiar with to show doubles concretely and pictorially, and use repeated addition calculations to represent doubles in an abstract manner.

COMMON MISCONCEPTIONS

Children may miscount when finding the double of a number. Ask:
• *How can you check your working out? What representation could you use to make sure your double is correct?*

STRENGTHENING UNDERSTANDING

Introduce children to the concept of this lesson by playing a version of the game shown in **Discover**. Working in pairs, children could roll 1 dice each. If the dice land on the same number, the children have rolled a double. The first child to recognise this and shout 'Double!' wins a point. Children could be asked to find the total both dice make.

GOING DEEPER

Ask children to investigate the links between numbers such as double 2 and double 20. For example, ask: *If double 2 is 4 and double 20 is 40, what is double 30?* Ask children to explain how they found the double. Challenge them to find as many doubles of 10s numbers as they can. Can they spot any patterns?

KEY LANGUAGE

In lesson: double, group

Other language to be used by the teacher: add, pair, representation, addition, working out, ten frame

STRUCTURES AND REPRESENTATIONS

Ten frame, counters, array

RESOURCES

Optional: large printed ten frame, 6-sided dice

 In the eTextbook of this lesson, you will find interactive links to a selection of teaching tools.

Before you teach

• Where will children have met this concept before? Could you use their experiences to help introduce the lesson?
• How will you make sure children get sufficient opportunity to observe patterns and explain their generalisations?

Discover

WAYS OF WORKING Pair work

ASK

- *What totals have been made by each pair of dice in the picture?*
- *How will you know if you have thrown a double?*
- *What is double 4?*
- *What other doubles can you make using the two dice?*
- *How else can you make a double? What resources could you use to show a double?*

IN FOCUS Encourage children to play a similar game to begin the lesson. Reinforce the understanding that 'double' is two of a number. Encourage children to model this in different ways, especially the use of an array, making the link with the previous lesson.

ANSWERS

Question ❶ a): Tariq rolled a double.

Double 4 is 8.

Question ❶ b): Double 6 is 12.

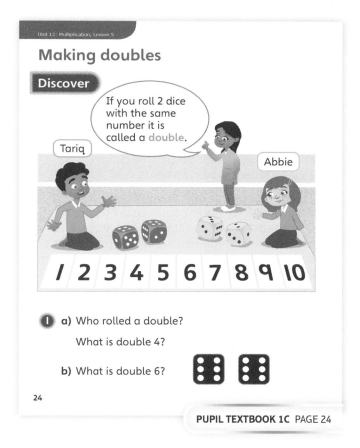

Share

WAYS OF WORKING Whole class teacher led

ASK

- *How did you show a double?*
- *How is your representation similar to that shown in the picture? How is it different?*
- *How does the ten frame help to show the doubles?*
- *What is different about when you double numbers greater than 5?*
- *Can you find the doubles of all the numbers from 1 to 10?*
- *What do you notice about the doubles you have found?*

IN FOCUS Draw children's attention to the similarities and differences between the two representations of doubles. What is the same and different about them? Discuss with children why the picture for double 6 includes two ten frames and not just one, as in the picture for double 4. Children could be encouraged to find other numbers up to 10 that result in numbers bigger than 10.

STRENGTHEN To help practise the skill of finding doubles, give pairs of children a 1–20 number track, a dice and a different coloured counter each so they can play a game. Children roll a dice and find the double of the number shown. Once they have found the double they can move their counter that far along the track. The first child to reach 20 wins. Children can then design their own doubles game.

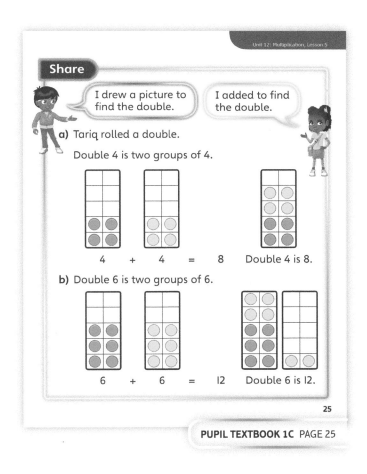

Think together

Unit 12: Multiplication, Lesson 5

Think together

WAYS OF WORKING Whole class teacher led (I do, We do, You do)

ASK

- *How can you show double 4 on a ten frame?*
- *How will you find what double 5 is?*
- *What addition calculation matches the picture?*
- *When will you need two ten frames to show a double?*

IN FOCUS The questions in this part of the lesson help scaffold and reinforce the link between the concrete, pictorial and abstract representations of doubles. Encourage children to make the representations shown on the page to help them understand that doubles are all even numbers and in the 2s count.

STRENGTHEN For children who are not finding doubles accurately, use ten frames to help reinforce the importance of counting carefully. Ask: *If you are finding double 7, how many counters should you place on the ten frames first? How many more should you add to the ten frames to make sure you have found double 7? How can you use what you have made to check the total of your double?*

DEEPEN While completing question ❸, deepen children's understanding by asking them to find a different way of representing each double, perhaps with a number line or an array. Do they see any patterns? Ask: *What is special about all the double numbers? Can you use skip counting to find the next 5 doubles?*

ASSESSMENT CHECKPOINT Children should be able to explain that 'double' means 'two of the same number'. They should be able to show double a number using several representations, in particular through the use of a ten frame. Encourage the link with arrays from the previous lesson.

ANSWERS

Question ❶ : Children should complete all pictures accurately, using two colours to show the double.
1 + 1 = 2
2 + 2 = 4
3 + 3 = 6
4 + 4 = 8
5 + 5 = 10
6 + 6 = 12

Question ❷ : 8 + 8 = 16
Double 8 is 16.

Question ❸ :

Number	1	2	3	4	5	6	7	8	9	10
Double	2	4	6	8	10	12	14	16	18	20

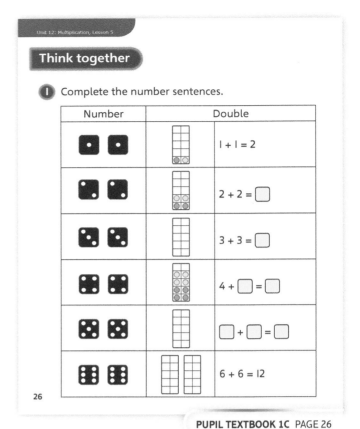

Think together

❶ Complete the number sentences.

Number	Double
	1 + 1 = 2
	2 + 2 = ☐
	3 + 3 = ☐
	4 + ☐ = ☐
	☐ + ☐ = ☐
	6 + 6 = 12

26

PUPIL TEXTBOOK 1C PAGE 26

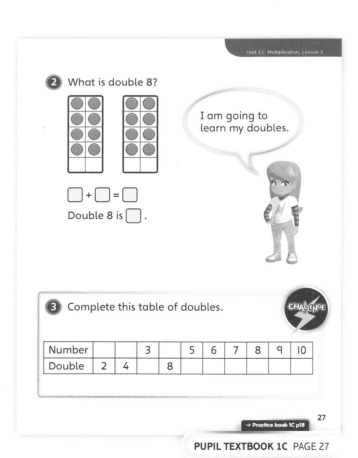

❷ What is double 8?

☐ + ☐ = ☐

Double 8 is ☐ .

I am going to learn my doubles.

❸ Complete this table of doubles.

Number			3		5	6	7	8	9	10
Double	2	4		8						

27

→ Practice book 1C p18

PUPIL TEXTBOOK 1C PAGE 27

Practice

WAYS OF WORKING Independent thinking

IN FOCUS Questions ① to ④ all help children recognise and understand pictorial representations of doubles. It would be beneficial to have concrete resources to match the questions, for children to manipulate. Questions ④ b) and c) informally use the concept that the inverse of a double is a half.

STRENGTHEN For question ③, suggest children count the triangles in each picture in the top row and record the totals. Work systematically left to right and ask: *If there are 3 triangles on the page, how many more do you need to add to have double 3? How many is double 3? Can you find the picture with 6 triangles on it?*

DEEPEN Question ⑤ offers a good opportunity to develop children's pattern recognition and ability to generalise. Ask: *What happens each time you find a new double? Do you think that will happen forever?* Challenge children to predict the next five doubles and to explain their predictions.

ASSESSMENT CHECKPOINT Children should be able to reliably find the double of a given number up to 10, knowing some of them by heart. They should also be able to find the inverse, when given the double as their starting number. Children should be fluent at using concrete and visual representations of doubles to support their reasoning.

ANSWERS Answers for the **Practice** part of the lesson appear in the separate **Practice and Reflect answer guide**.

Reflect

WAYS OF WORKING Independent thinking

IN FOCUS Give children time to self-assess and then feed back their ideas to the class. Ask questions such as: *How did you decide which doubles you knew? Are there any easy ways of remembering your doubles? What could you do to get better at the doubles you still find tricky? How could you practise your doubles later on today?*

ASSESSMENT CHECKPOINT Look for children to explain what doubles they knew and which they found tricky. Check how they respond to the doubles they have identified as knowing: do they count or work them out in some way or do they just know them? Children should be able to give some ideas of the games they could play or resources they could use to practise their doubles, thereby demonstrating their understanding of how these activities link to finding doubles.

ANSWERS Answers for the **Reflect** part of the lesson appear in the separate **Practice and Reflect answer guide**.

After the lesson ⏸

- How capable were children at moving from simple pattern recognition to a generalisation they could apply more widely?
- What games or activities could you play that provide opportunities for further doubling practice?

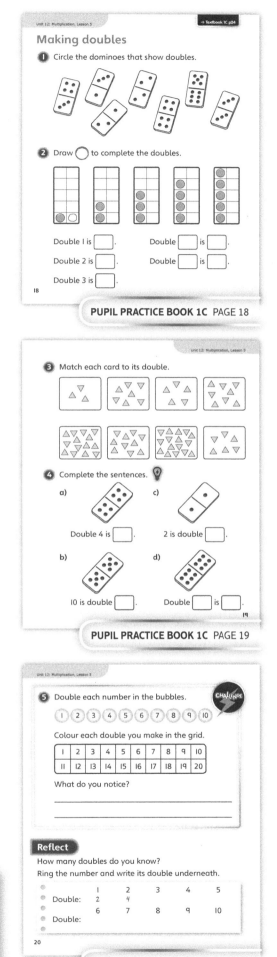

PUPIL PRACTICE BOOK 1C PAGE 18

PUPIL PRACTICE BOOK 1C PAGE 19

PUPIL PRACTICE BOOK 1C PAGE 20

Solving word problems - multiplication

Learning focus

In this lesson, children will use all the strategies they have learned to solve simple word problems based around multiplication. Children will also revisit their understanding of doubling.

Small steps

→ Previous step: Making doubles
→ **This step: Solving word problems – multiplication**
→ Next step: Making equal groups (1)

NATIONAL CURRICULUM LINKS

Year 1 Number – Multiplication and Division

Solve one-step problems involving multiplication and division, by calculating the answer using concrete objects, pictorial representations and arrays with the support of the teacher.

ASSESSING MASTERY

Children can read and understand a word problem. They can explain what the problem is asking them to do and use an appropriate method to represent and solve it.

COMMON MISCONCEPTIONS

Children who struggle with reading or understanding the written vocabulary may misread the problems. Provide word banks or flash cards with matching pictorial representations of the words that children are likely to use in this lesson. Ask:
• *Which word are you finding tricky in this question? Can you find it using the word bank? What does it mean?*

STRENGTHENING UNDERSTANDING

Introduce children to multiplication word problems through role play. For example, ask children to model filling party bags: *10 people are coming to the party. Each party bag needs 2 balloons and 5 stickers. How many balloons and how many stickers do you need altogether?* Encourage children to draw the 10 bags in a row or a column, putting the balloons on top and using skip counting in 2s to work out how many are needed. Repeat for the stickers, counting in 5s. Finally use representations to check these answers.

GOING DEEPER

Encourage children to make up their own word problems for a partner to solve. Challenge them to write a problem that their partner will need to use an array or a number line to solve. They should write their own solution using a number line or an array to check it with their partner's solution. Ask: *Did you both solve it the same way?*

KEY LANGUAGE

In lesson: twice, double, bigger, full, array, organise, row

Other language to be used by the teacher: altogether, addition, group, column, number line

STRUCTURES AND REPRESENTATIONS

Number line, array, counters

RESOURCES

Optional: counting equipment, objects for role play

 In the eTextbook of this lesson, you will find interactive links to a selection of teaching tools.

Before you teach ⏸

• How confident are children at using arrays and number lines?
• Will children be able to use these methods independently?
• What do you need to provide for children who find reading difficult?

Discover

Pair work

ASK

- *What information do you need to solve the question? How is the information presented?*
- *How long does it take for the train to go around the track?*
- *How can you find out how long it would take to go around twice?*
- *How could you represent the problem in a different way?*
- *How long will it take to go around three times? How could you prove it?*

IN FOCUS Discuss what is the same and what is different about the problem that children see in the picture compared with those they have seen before. Discuss how it probably has more words in it than those they have met before.

ANSWERS

Question ❶ a): The train takes 4 minutes to go around the track twice.

Question ❶ b): The train takes 10 minutes to go around the bigger track twice.

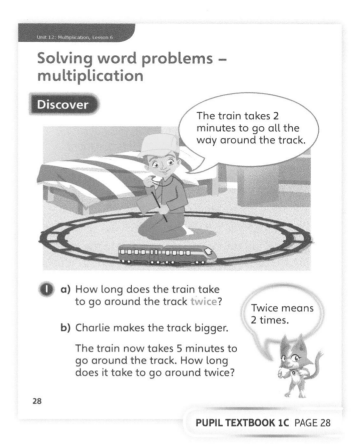

PUPIL TEXTBOOK 1C PAGE 28

Share

Whole class teacher led

ASK

- *What representation has been used to show the problem?*
- *Did you notice the link to the doubles lesson? Can you explain how the work on doubles helps?*
- *How does the number line make the solution clear?*
- *Could you show this using an array? How about an addition calculation?*
- *What if the train took 7 minutes to get around? How long would it take to go twice around?*
- *What if it went around 4 times?*
- *If it took 2 minutes to get around, and it went around for 10 minutes, how many times around is this?*

IN FOCUS To help develop children's familiarity with word problems, write some related questions on paper for them to practise reading: *How long would it take for the train to travel around the track 4 times? A train takes 3 minutes to go around the track. How long will it take to go around 3 times?* Can children suggest other questions?

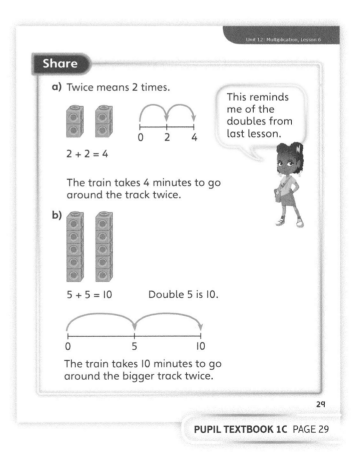

PUPIL TEXTBOOK 1C PAGE 29

Think together

WAYS OF WORKING Whole class teacher led (I do, We do, You do)

ASK
- *What information do you need to solve this question?*
- *Can you show me the equal groups in this question?*
- *How could you represent the equal groups?*
- *Can you arrange the equal groups into an array or along a number line?*
- *Can you show the addition calculations?*
- *How will you know if you can use doubling?*

IN FOCUS It is important to use this point in the lesson to ensure that children are confident when choosing an appropriate representation for their working. For each question, discuss the different ways of approaching their working, encouraging children to try different approaches and discuss their preferences. They could also record each solution as an addition calculation.

STRENGTHEN If children are struggling to draw the array in question ❶ , provide them with a collection of cars to arrange. Ask: *How many groups of 5 cars do you need? How do you know? Can you arrange them into an array?*

DEEPEN When solving question ❸ , use Ash and Flo's comments to deepen understanding and reasoning. Ask: *Is it possible to use doubles for both arrays of counters? Why do you think Flo counted in 5s and 10s? Who do you think will solve this problem, Ash or Flo?*

ASSESSMENT CHECKPOINT Are all children capable of reading the word problems? Assess their ability to explain what a problem is asking them to do and what method they will use to solve it. Ask children to provide at least one representation to prove or check their solution. Ensure that all children are using the number of objects in the rows or columns to count in steps.

ANSWERS

Question ❶ : There are 15 cars in the car park.

Question ❷ : There are 16 ice cubes in a full tray.

Question ❸ : Izzy (25) has more counters than Ben (20).

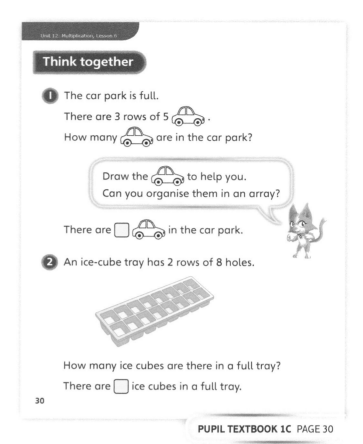

PUPIL TEXTBOOK 1C PAGE 30

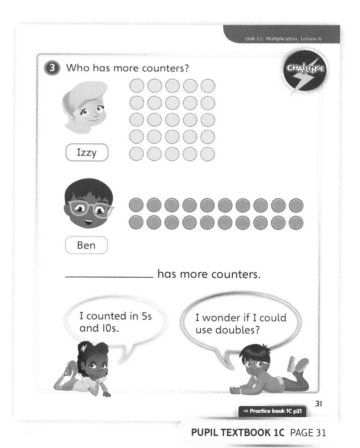

PUPIL TEXTBOOK 1C PAGE 31

Practice

WAYS OF WORKING Independent thinking

IN FOCUS Questions **1** and **2** scaffold children in their use of the number line as the more efficient method of showing multiplication. Encourage children to use this method to show their working in the questions that follow.

STRENGTHEN If children are struggling to match the pictures in question **2** to the number lines, provide them with a concrete version of the problem, such as an enlarged copy they could cut out. Children can arrange the shapes as they wish to help them match the shapes to the number lines. Ask: *Can you arrange the shapes into an array? Which number line does your array link to?*

DEEPEN Question **4** offers children an opportunity to develop their algebraic thinking. Ask: *What do you know about the shapes? How can you find what one circle is worth? Do you need to double the number you know or find out what number has been doubled to get the missing number?*

ASSESSMENT CHECKPOINT As long as children's reading ability allows them to access the word problems they should be able solve them using the concepts they have been taught through this unit. They should confidently demonstrate their understanding and ability to use arrays, number lines and doubles to solve the problems given.

ANSWERS Answers for the **Practice** part of the lesson appear in the separate **Practice and Reflect answer guide**.

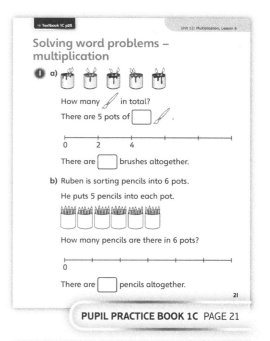

PUPIL PRACTICE BOOK 1C PAGE 21

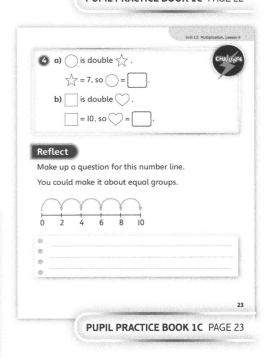

PUPIL PRACTICE BOOK 1C PAGE 22

Reflect

WAYS OF WORKING Independent thinking

IN FOCUS Discuss with children some ideas of what the problem could be about. Once children have had time to discuss and think about the types of question they could write, give them time to write their own. Ask children if their question works with the number line. Can they prove it?

ASSESSMENT CHECKPOINT Look for children to be demonstrating their understanding of word problems through designing their own. Their question should require the person solving it to find 5 groups of 2.

ANSWERS Answers for the **Reflect** part of the lesson appear in the separate **Practice and Reflect answer guide**.

After the lesson ⏸

- Were children able to confidently use the number line to solve multiplication word problems?
- Were there any words that children found tricky that limited their ability to solve the problems?
- How will you cement their understanding of these words for future lessons?

PUPIL PRACTICE BOOK 1C PAGE 23

End of unit check

Don't forget the *Power Maths* unit assessment grid on p26.

WAYS OF WORKING Group work – adult led

IN FOCUS Question **1** assesses children's abilities to identify equal groups.

Question **2** assesses whether children can differentiate between the number of groups and the number of items in each group.

Question **3** assesses whether children can skip count in 10s to find 4 groups of 10.

Question **4** assesses children's understanding of arrays and their related vocabulary.

Question **5** assesses children's understanding of doubles. It requires children to find both double and half of a given number.

Think!

WAYS OF WORKING Pair work

IN FOCUS This question assesses children's understanding of arrays. It is important to note that Joe, Sara and Poppy are all correct in their own way. To make sure children realise this, ask:
- *Can you explain why each child has said what they did?*
- *Can you create the array? Can you use it to demonstrate each child's thinking?*
- *Is any one child correct or incorrect? Explain.*

ANSWERS AND COMMENTARY Children will demonstrate mastery in this question by realising that each child is correct. They will be able to explain why each child has said what they have and demonstrate each child's thinking using appropriate representations.

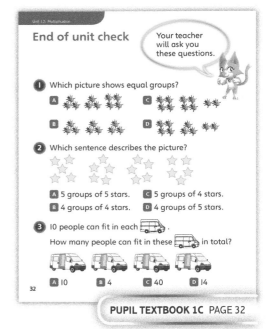

PUPIL TEXTBOOK 1C PAGE 32

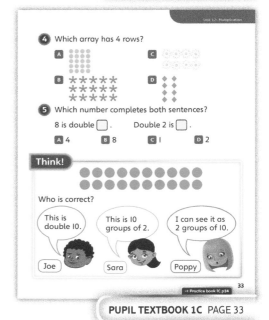

PUPIL TEXTBOOK 1C PAGE 33

Q	A	WRONG ANSWERS AND MISCONCEPTIONS	STRENGTHENING UNDERSTANDING
1	B	Choosing A, C or D would suggest that children are unsure of what the term 'equal groups' means.	**Finding and making equal groups:** Give children a collection of countable objects. Ask: *Can you sort these into equal groups of X?* For children who find this tricky, provide grids of the required group size to arrange the objects into. Ask: *What do you notice about each group? How can you tell they are equal?*
2	D	Choosing A, B or C could suggest that children are unsure of the distinction between the number of groups and the number of items in each group.	
3	C	Choosing A may indicate that children haven't recognised that they need 4 groups of 10; B suggests that children have not recognised that each van represents 10 people.	
4	D	Choosing A or C suggests that children are muddling the vocabulary associated with arrays (rows and columns). Choosing B suggests inaccurate counting.	**Understanding arrays:** Provide flashcards with the vocabulary of arrays. Encourage children to find arrays in their environment and to describe the elements of their arrays with appropriate mathematical vocabulary.
5	A	Choosing B, C or D would indicate that children are unsure about doubles and how to find them.	

My journal

WAYS OF WORKING Independent thinking

ANSWERS AND COMMENTARY

Children may record answers such as:
- Joe is right because there are 2 groups of 10. When there is the same number twice it means there is double that number.
- Sara is right because the columns in the array show 10 groups of 2.
- Poppy is right because the rows in the array show 2 groups of 10.

If the children are struggling to find why any of the children are correct, ask:
- *What do you know about doubles? Does anything you know match what you can see in the picture?*
- *Can you see any groups of 10 or 2 in the picture?*
- *Does the number of groups match what the children have said? How do you know?*

PUPIL PRACTICE BOOK 1C PAGE 24

Power check

WAYS OF WORKING Independent thinking

ASK
- *Do you think you are more confident at solving multiplication problems now?*
- *Do you think you would be able to recognise arrays elsewhere?*
- *How confident are you that you could find doubles of numbers up to 10? 20? 50? 100?*

Power play

WAYS OF WORKING Independent thinking

IN FOCUS Use this **Power play** to assess children's ability to find arrays. Children should be able to find arrays within the grid and colour them. If children are struggling to begin finding arrays, ask: *Could you make an array with 5 rows using this grid? What would be the problem if you made a 4 by 10 array? Should you start with a big array or a small one? Why?*

ANSWERS AND COMMENTARY If children are unable to solve the **Power play** it will be important to first diagnose whether this is because they are unsure about how to create an array or whether it is because they cannot find a way to fit them into the grid provided. If it is the case that children are unsure how to create arrays, provide them with the opportunities mentioned in the **Strengthen** sections throughout the unit to help secure their understanding.

PUPIL PRACTICE BOOK 1C PAGE 25

After the unit

- How could you implement children's skills of finding doubles into the wider curriculum? Could you give them opportunities to find doubles of numbers up to and beyond 100?
- How will you use the learning and multiplicative reasoning children have developed in this unit to support their understanding in the unit on division that follows?

Strengthen and **Deepen** activities for this unit can be found in the *Power Maths* online subscription.

Unit 13
Division

Don't forget to watch the Unit 13 video!

Mastery Expert tip! "While teaching this unit I tried to refer back to children's learning in multiplication as much as possible as the two operations are so closely linked. It really helped children develop a deep conceptual understanding and improved their multiplicative reasoning!"

WHY THIS UNIT IS IMPORTANT

In this unit, children will develop their understanding of division. Children are introduced to the concept of equal groups, represented in various concrete, pictorial and abstract ways, including the number line.

The unit then looks at division in the context of sharing equally. Children will share a given number of objects equally across a given number of groups to find out how many are in each group. Children will be encouraged to make links between the two types of division in order to strengthen their conceptual understanding.

Finally, children will use their understanding of division to solve simple word problems. A secure understanding of equal groups and sharing, and the ability to apply it in more abstract contexts, will prepare children for more formal work on division later, and develop their multiplicative reasoning.

WHERE THIS UNIT FITS

→ Unit 12: Multiplication
→ **Unit 13: Division**
→ Unit 14: Halves and quarters

This unit builds on children's work on multiplication in Unit 12. Unit 13 focuses on the division of whole numbers, while Unit 14 will introduce children to halves and quarters.

Before they start this unit, it is expected that children:

• can group objects into sets
• can compare two numbers
• recognise where numbers are equal and unequal.

ASSESSING MASTERY

Children who have mastered this unit will be able to make a given number of equal groups from a given total, or share a given total equally among a given number of groups. They will be able to confidently use concrete resources and pictures to represent their method of division and will be able to explain clearly, using the appropriate vocabulary, which type of division they have used. They will also be able to record both types of division using a number line. Children will use their conceptual understanding to solve word problems, explaining fluently what they have done.

COMMON MISCONCEPTIONS	STRENGTHENING UNDERSTANDING	GOING DEEPER
Children may incorrectly share a number into groups of (for example) 4 when asked to share between 4 groups (or vice versa).	Give children plenty of practice in both types of division using different numbers and different contexts. Ask: *How many groups are there? How many items are there in each group?*	Give children clues to a number. For example: *My number can be shared into 2 equal groups. When I find groups of 5 there are 2 of them. What is my number?*
Children may not recognise equal groups because they do not look exactly the same.	Ask children to sort and group irregularly-shaped objects, such as fruit and vegetables or different coloured counters. Ask: *This counter is red, not yellow. Does this change the number of counters in the group?*	Children could also be encouraged to come up with similar puzzles of their own.

Unit 13
Division

WAYS OF WORKING

Use these pages to introduce the unit focus to children. You can use the characters to explore different ways of working too.

STRUCTURES AND REPRESENTATIONS

Array: An array is a visual representation of multiplication and division. Arrays are an excellent tool for showing equal groups within a number. While specific use is not made of them in this unit, some of the pictorial representations are arranged as arrays.

Number line: A number line helps children to represent their skip counting. It will help children count on and back from a given starting point and help them identify patterns and groups within the count.

```
0  1  2  3  4  5  6  7  8  9  10
```

KEY LANGUAGE

There is some key language that children will need to know as part of the learning in this unit:

→ equal groups, same, different
→ share, sharing equally
→ fairly
→ total, altogether, each
→ division

Unit 13
Division

In this unit we will ...
⚡ Make equal groups
⚡ Share amounts equally
⚡ Solve word problems

Counters can help us show groups. Can you use counters to find how many groups of 2 flowers there are?

34

PUPIL TEXTBOOK 1C PAGE 34

We will need some maths words. Which of these are new?

equal groups   share

We can also use a number line to help us. Can you put these into groups of 5? How many groups are there?

```
0 1 2 3 4 5 6 7 8 9 10 11 12 13 14 15 16 17 18 19 20
```

35

PUPIL TEXTBOOK 1C PAGE 35

Making equal groups ❶

Learning focus

In this lesson, children will develop their understanding of equal groups. They will recognise when groups are equal and when they are not, and how many equal groups are needed to make a whole number.

Small steps

→ Previous step: Solving word problems – multiplication
→ **This step: Making equal groups (1)**
→ Next step: Making equal groups (2)

NATIONAL CURRICULUM LINKS

Year 1 Number – Multiplication and Division

Solve one-step problems involving multiplication and division, by calculating the answer using concrete objects, pictorial representations and arrays with the support of the teacher.

ASSESSING MASTERY

Children can recognise when groups are equal and when they are not. Children can say how many equal groups make a whole number and model the groups using different representations.

COMMON MISCONCEPTIONS

Children may not recognise groups as being equal because they do not look exactly the same. Show children groups of children who are wearing different clothes. Ask:
• *How many children are in each group?*
• *Does what the children are wearing change the number of children in each group? Explain why not.*

Children may transpose the numbers describing the number of groups and the amount each group represents. For example, children may label 5 groups of 2 as 2 groups of 5. Ask children to count how many items are in each group, and also to circle each group of items and count how many groups they have circled. Ask:
• *Can you explain how many groups of items you have, in a sentence?*

STRENGTHENING UNDERSTANDING

Children could practise the skill of sharing into equal groups through normal classroom activities and routines (for example, sharing snacks, sharing resources or grouping children into small teams).

GOING DEEPER

Ask children to investigate how many ways they could share a number of children into different equal groups. Challenge children further by stating that there needs to be an even number of equal groups. For example, ask: *You are going to play some games of football. There are 12 children. How many ways could you split the children into teams? Why would three teams of four children not work for our games of football?*

KEY LANGUAGE

In lesson: equal, group, different, altogether

STRUCTURES AND REPRESENTATIONS

Arrays

RESOURCES

Optional: counters or other countable objects (toy people, toy animals or pictures of these, interlocking cubes), printed rectangles to represent tables, printed circles to represent groups, paper clips

 In the eTextbook of this lesson, you will find interactive links to a selection of teaching tools.

Before you teach ⏸

• What elements of the previous unit on multiplication could be used to enhance children's learning in this lesson?
• How will you incorporate these into the lesson?

Discover

WAYS OF WORKING Pair work

ASK

- Question ❶ a): *How can you tell if the groups are equal?*
- Question ❶ a): *Which group is the biggest? Which is the smallest?*
- Question ❶ b): *How can you represent groups of 2 children?*
- *Can you make different equal groups using the number of children in the picture?*

IN FOCUS Question ❶ encourages children to explore sharing 10 into groups. Ask them to investigate into what equal groups they can share 10. Discuss what happens when sharing 10 into groups of 4. What do children notice?

ANSWERS

Question ❶ a): The groups have different numbers of children. The children are not in equal groups.

Question ❶ b): There are 5 groups of 2 children.

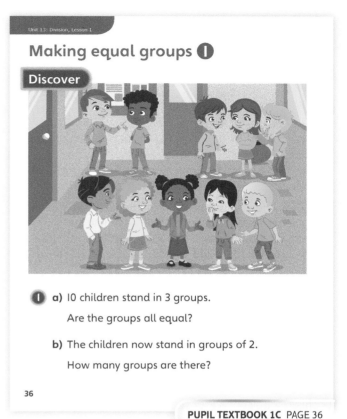

Making equal groups ❶

Discover

❶ a) 10 children stand in 3 groups.

Are the groups all equal?

b) The children now stand in groups of 2.

How many groups are there?

36

PUPIL TEXTBOOK 1C PAGE 36

Share

WAYS OF WORKING Whole class teacher led

ASK

- Question ❶ a): *Were the children in equal groups? How did you prove your thinking?*
- Question ❶ b): *How did you represent the equal groups of 2?*
- *Did you find any other equal groups?*

IN FOCUS Use question ❶ b) to ensure children are confident when observing and explaining the difference between, for example, 5 groups of 2 and 2 groups of 5: show children representations of the two sets of groups and discuss the similarities and differences.

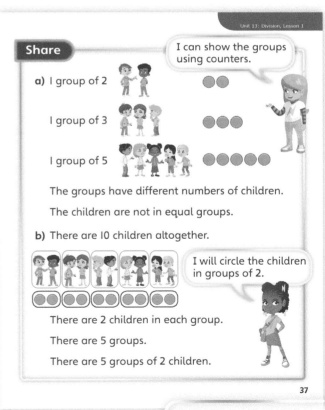

Share

a) 1 group of 2

1 group of 3

1 group of 5

The groups have different numbers of children.

The children are not in equal groups.

b) There are 10 children altogether.

I will circle the children in groups of 2.

There are 2 children in each group.

There are 5 groups.

There are 5 groups of 2 children.

I can show the groups using counters.

37

PUPIL TEXTBOOK 1C PAGE 37

Think together

WAYS OF WORKING Whole class teacher led (I do, We do, You do)

ASK

- *How could you represent the groups?*
- Question ❶ : *Can you share the children into equal groups of 4?*
- Questions ❶ and ❷ : *How many children will be in each of the groups? How do you know?*

IN FOCUS These questions help children develop the vocabulary needed to support their reasoning and mathematical discussion. Make sure all children are given the opportunity to try and say the full sentences, shown in this section, that describe the equal groups.

Questions ❶ and ❷ are designed to help tackle the misconception of confusing group size and number of groups. Separating the different elements into their own individual sentences before putting them together as one description will help cement children's understanding of each concept.

STRENGTHEN Give children concrete representations of the 12 children (toy people, or something more abstract like counters) to support them in answering in question ❶. You could also give them printed rectangles to represent the tables, so that children can arrange the toys or counters around them. Ask: *Can you arrange the children into equal groups around the three tables?*

DEEPEN Extend question ❸ by encouraging children to explore the similarities and differences between 3 groups of 5 and 5 groups of 3. Ask: *How are 3 groups of 5 the same as 5 groups of 3? How are they different? Can you show me what you have noticed using different representations?*

ASSESSMENT CHECKPOINT Assess whether children can share counters or other concrete objects into equal groups. Can they describe the groups accurately, stating both the number of groups and the number of items in each group?

ANSWERS

Question ❶ : There are 3 groups.

There are 3 groups of 4 children.

Question ❷ : There are 4 groups.

There are 3 children in each group.

There are 4 groups of 3 children.

Question ❸ : Molly has made the most groups.

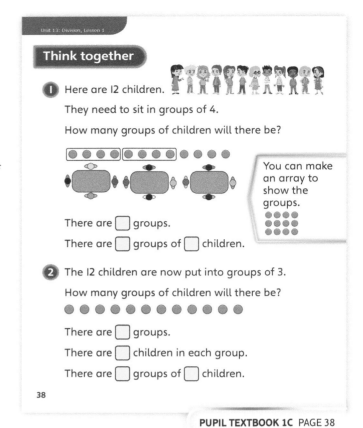

PUPIL TEXTBOOK 1C PAGE 38

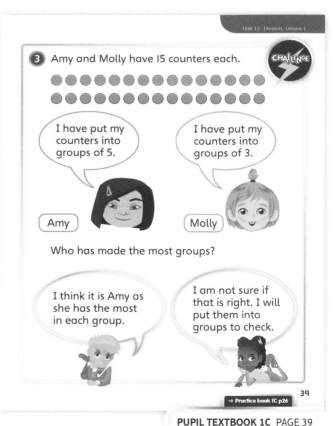

PUPIL TEXTBOOK 1C PAGE 39

Practice

WAYS OF WORKING Independent thinking

IN FOCUS Questions **1** and **2** are designed to support children in finding equal groups independently. Encourage them to draw around the groups they are making to help structure their thinking and to cement the link between the pictorial representation and the written sentences.

Question **4** will help children recognise that, while groups look different, they may still be equal. Children could be encouraged to build the shapes with cubes themselves.

STRENGTHEN If children find grouping the objects tricky, give them concrete resources to share into equal groups. You could give children who need further support printed circles to represent the groups; children can then arrange the resources in the circles. For example for question **1** a), ask: *Can you show me how you would share the eight horses into equal groups of two?*

DEEPEN Give children more 2 by 6 grids and challenge them to find as many different solutions to question **5** as they can. Ask: *Which solution has the most groups? Can you explain why?*

ASSESSMENT CHECKPOINT Assess whether children can recognise equal groups and explain how they know they are equal.

Use question **5** to assess whether children can find different equal groups within a given number. Are they beginning to understand that, as a number is shared into more groups, the number each group represents decreases?

ANSWERS Answers for the **Practice** part of the lesson appear in the separate **Practice and Reflect answer guide**.

Reflect

WAYS OF WORKING Independent thinking

IN FOCUS The **Reflect** activity is best presented in a concrete way. Give children 18 paper clips each and allow them time to make the chains before discussing the answer. How did children find the activity? You could also ask children to explore whether Jed could use all 18 paper clips to make chains of other equal lengths.

ASSESSMENT CHECKPOINT Check whether children can fluently share the paper clips into chains of three. Listen to children's justifications of their method: they should talk about sharing or grouping and describe how they ensured that each chain had the correct number of paper clips in it.

ANSWERS Answers for the **Reflect** part of the lesson appear in the separate **Practice and Reflect answer guide**.

After the lesson ⏸

- Were children able to see the link between, for example, 3 lots of 5 and 5 lots of 3?
- Did any children make the link between this lesson and their understanding of arrays?

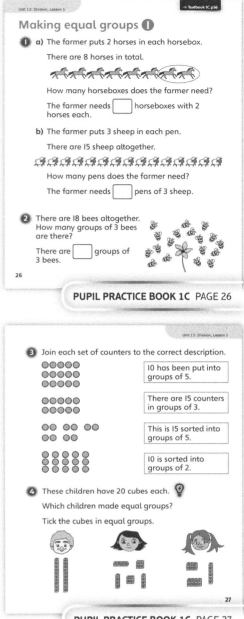

PUPIL PRACTICE BOOK 1C PAGE 26

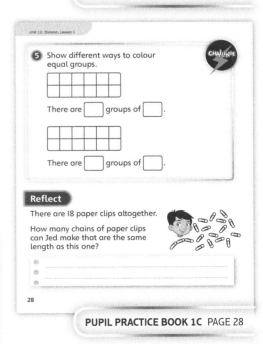

PUPIL PRACTICE BOOK 1C PAGE 27

PUPIL PRACTICE BOOK 1C PAGE 28

Making equal groups ❷

Learning focus

In this lesson, children will consolidate their learning and understanding about finding equal groups. They will practise finding and making equal groups in different contexts and record these on a number line.

Small steps

→ Previous step: Making equal groups (1)
→ **This step: Making equal groups (2)**
→ Next step: Sharing equally (1)

NATIONAL CURRICULUM LINKS

Year 1 Number – Multiplication and Division

Solve one-step problems involving multiplication and division, by calculating the answer using concrete objects, pictorial representations and arrays with the support of the teacher.

ASSESSING MASTERY

Children can recognise when groups are equal and when they are not. Children can say how many equal groups make a whole number and model the groups using a number line.

COMMON MISCONCEPTIONS

This lesson follows on from what children learned in the previous lesson and therefore the misconception from Lesson 1 may still be present around not recognising groups as being equal because they do not look exactly the same. Children may also still transpose the numbers describing the number of groups and the amount each group represents.

Children may confuse how to record the equal groups on a number line. You may find they jump along the number line in steps relating to how many equal groups there are, not what number each group represents (for example, for 2 groups of 5, they jump to 2 on the number line). Encourage children to make the groups using resources or pictures.

Ask:
• *How many objects are in the first group? Can you show that in a single jump along the number line?*
• *How will you use the number line to show the second group?*

STRENGTHENING UNDERSTANDING

Children could practise counting back along a number line in equal jumps. Draw a large number line on the floor and tell children what number to start at. Ask: *Can you find out how many jumps you would need to make to get back to zero if you jumped (for example) two at a time?*

GOING DEEPER

Give children simple word problems to solve. For example: *Alana had 30 stickers. She gave each of her friends five stickers each. How many people did she share the stickers between?*

KEY LANGUAGE

In lesson: equal, group

STRUCTURES AND REPRESENTATIONS

Arrays, number line

RESOURCES

Optional: counters or other countable objects (balls, shoes, rulers, sticks, pens, or pictures of these)

 In the eTextbook of this lesson, you will find interactive links to a selection of teaching tools.

Before you teach

• Were there any misconceptions from the previous lesson that you need to consider before beginning this lesson?
• What learning opportunities will you offer to help overcome these misconceptions so they do not limit the progress made?

Discover

WAYS OF WORKING Pair work

ASK

- *How many ping pong balls can you count?*
- *How could you represent the equal groups of 5? Could you use an array?*
- *How many boxes would you need for 10 balls? 15? 20? Is there a pattern?*

IN FOCUS Question **1** provides a good opportunity to recap children's learning from the previous lesson. Be sure to discuss the key vocabulary needed to describe equal groups.

ANSWERS

Question **1** a): 2 boxes are needed for 10 balls.

Question **1** b): 3 boxes are needed for 15 balls.

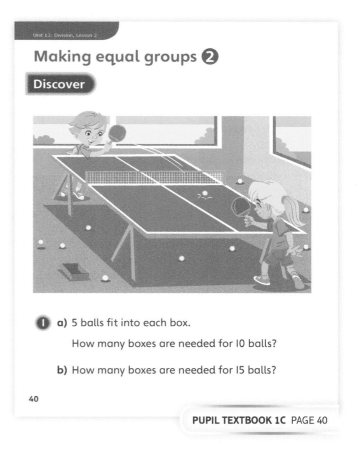

Making equal groups **2**

Discover

1 a) 5 balls fit into each box.

How many boxes are needed for 10 balls?

b) How many boxes are needed for 15 balls?

40

PUPIL TEXTBOOK 1C PAGE 40

Share

WAYS OF WORKING Whole class teacher led

ASK

- Question **1** a): *How did you show the equal groups? Did you do the same as Astrid? Explain your ideas.*
- Question **1** a): *How does the number line make the groups clear?*
- Question **1** a): *Why did Flo start at 10 on her number line?*
- Question **1** b): *Can you explain how the number line matches the groups shown in the picture?*
- *Will the number line work if you count the other way?*

IN FOCUS Use question **1** to introduce children to the concept of counting backwards or forwards along a number line in order to find the number of groups required.

DEEPEN Encourage children to share different totals into different numbers of equal groups. You could use real-life contexts, such as grouping children into work groups or teams; while some children are being grouped in different ways, other children could observe the groupings and draw the related picture or number line.

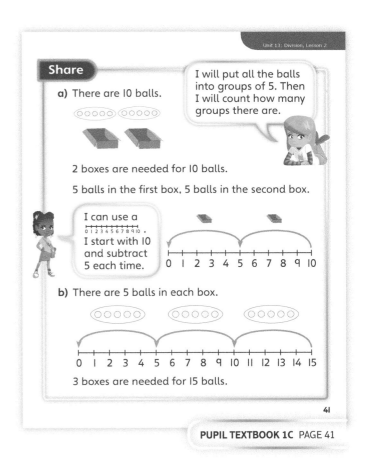

Share

a) There are 10 balls.

I will put all the balls into groups of 5. Then I will count how many groups there are.

2 boxes are needed for 10 balls.

5 balls in the first box, 5 balls in the second box.

I can use a number line. I start with 10 and subtract 5 each time.

b) There are 5 balls in each box.

3 boxes are needed for 15 balls.

41

PUPIL TEXTBOOK 1C PAGE 41

Think together

Whole class teacher led (I do, We do, You do)

ASK

- *What do you need to know before you can share things into equal groups?*
- *What size will each equal group be? How do you know?*
- *How will you represent the equal groups?*
- *Where will you begin skip counting on the number line? Why?*

IN FOCUS Use these questions to ensure children are not confusing group size and the number of groups when sharing a number into equal groups. Discuss the differences between, for example, 5 groups of 6 and 6 groups of 5. Question ❸ requires children to clearly demonstrate their understanding of these concepts.

STRENGTHEN To strengthen children's understanding of the link between the concrete, pictorial and abstract representations of equal groups, encourage children to first make the equal groups with concrete resources, then draw the groups and finally arrange their drawings along a number line. Ask: *Can you explain what is the same about the representations?*

DEEPEN Deepen children's understanding by asking them to prove to you that their answers are correct. When children are working on question ❸, challenge them to explain how Ash's comment is helpful.

ASSESSMENT CHECKPOINT Assess whether children can fluently find equal groups and make them using concrete and pictorial representations. Are children becoming more confident at linking the groups to the number line and explaining how these representations are communicating the same concepts in different ways?

ANSWERS

Question ❶ : 6 boxes are needed to fit all the balls.

Question ❷ : There are 6 groups of 2 bats.

Question ❸ : There are 40 counters in the bag.

There are 10 counters in each group.

There are 4 groups.

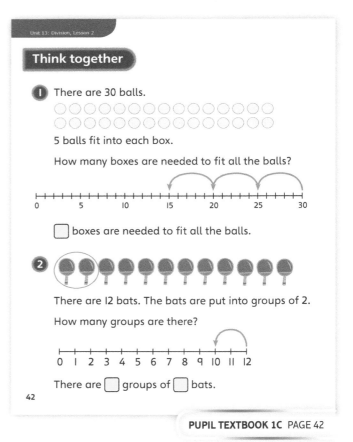

PUPIL TEXTBOOK 1C PAGE 42

PUPIL TEXTBOOK 1C PAGE 43

Practice

WAYS OF WORKING Independent thinking

IN FOCUS Questions **1** and **2** present children with two representations for each context: encourage children to circle the shoes or counters and draw the jumps on the number line, rather than choosing just one method. This will help to cement their conceptual understanding.

STRENGTHEN If children struggle with question **2**, discuss with them why the questions are difficult. Agree that the counters shown represent the paintbrushes and rulers in the questions. Ask: *Can you circle the groups of paintbrushes using the counters? What would a group look like on the number line?*

DEEPEN Extend question **3** by asking children how many flower patterns Ella could make if the flower had no leaves (each flower pattern would require 8 sticks rather than 10). Ask: *Can you share 40 into equal groups of eight? What other equal groups can you share 40 into?*

In question **4**, children should spot that the number of groups is always half the number of people. Challenge children to explain how they can use the pattern to find the number of groups for any number of people (that are in multiples of 2).

ASSESSMENT CHECKPOINT Assess whether children can confidently make concrete and pictorial representations of equal groups and link these to a number line. Can they use a number line to find how many equal groups of a given size there are in a given total?

ANSWERS Answers for the **Practice** part of the lesson appear in the separate **Practice and Reflect answer guide**.

Reflect

WAYS OF WORKING Independent thinking

IN FOCUS The **Reflect** question requires children to share 30 pens into equal groups of 10. Allow children to use resources and draw pictures in order to create the representations they need to find the equal groups, before explaining their work in writing. They could then share their ideas with a partner or the class. What different representations did children use? Ask: *Can you convince your partner that you have chosen the clearest representations?*

ASSESSMENT CHECKPOINT Children should find that there are 3 groups of 10 pens. Assess how confidently children use the methods covered in the last two lessons. Can they fluently explain how they found the answer, using appropriate vocabulary?

ANSWERS Answers for the **Reflect** part of the lesson appear in the separate **Practice and Reflect answer guide**.

After the lesson

- Were there any misconceptions in this lesson that surprised you?
- Can you explain why children demonstrated these misconceptions? How will you plan for them next time you teach this unit?

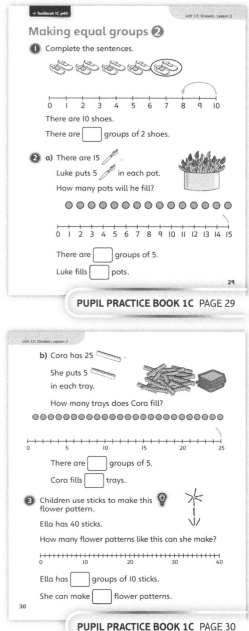

PUPIL PRACTICE BOOK 1C PAGE 29

PUPIL PRACTICE BOOK 1C PAGE 30

PUPIL PRACTICE BOOK 1C PAGE 31

Sharing equally ❶

Learning focus

In this lesson, children will develop their understanding of 'sharing' as a model of division. They will share a number of objects into equal groups.

Small steps

→ Previous step: Making equal groups (2)
→ **This step: Sharing equally (1)**
→ Next step: Sharing equally (2)

NATIONAL CURRICULUM LINKS

Year 1 Number – Multiplication and Division

Solve one-step problems involving multiplication and division, by calculating the answer using concrete objects, pictorial representations and arrays with the support of the teacher.

ASSESSING MASTERY

Children can recognise and explain sharing as 'one each' shared to each group over and over again until the total amount has been exhausted. Children can use this concept to share numbers into equal groups and solve simple problems.

COMMON MISCONCEPTIONS

Children may confuse finding 'groups of a certain number' with 'sharing between a number of groups'. Show children two pictures, one of a number shared into equal groups of 3 and one of the same number shared into 3 groups. Ask:
- *What is the same and different about these two pictures?*
- *Which picture shows the number shared into 3 equal groups? How do you know?*
- *How has the number been shared in the other picture?*

STRENGTHENING UNDERSTANDING

Children could practise this skill of equal sharing through games and role play. For example, they could share out the counters between players in a board game or they could role-play a party, sharing the slices of a cake between all the party goers.

GOING DEEPER

Ask children to pick two digit cards and make a 2-digit number. When children have made their numbers, ask them to explore what equal groups they can share their number into, and what equal groups do not work. Challenge children to prove their ideas.

KEY LANGUAGE

In lesson: share, equally, same amount, group

Other language to be used by the teacher: fairly

RESOURCES

Optional: counters or other countable objects or pictures of these, playing cards, marbles, printed circles to represent groups, digit cards

 In the eTextbook of this lesson, you will find interactive links to a selection of teaching tools.

Before you teach ❶❶

- How will you make the difference between 'finding groups of a certain number' and 'sharing between groups of a certain number' explicit in the lesson?
- Are all children secure with the idea of equal groups?

Discover

Pair work

ASK

- *How many pizzas is the chef making?*
- *Can he share the ingredients fairly across all the pizzas?*
- *How many pieces of each topping will each pizza have? How do you know?*
- *How could you represent your sharing to prove your ideas?*

IN FOCUS Question ❶ introduces the concept of sharing equally. You could ask children to describe a time when they have shared. Why is it important to share? How do they make sure they share fairly with their friends? Such discussion is likely to lead to the idea of sharing out 'one each' until the total is exhausted.

ANSWERS

Question ❶ a): There are 2 🗨 on each pizza.

Question ❶ b): There are 3 🍍 on each pizza.

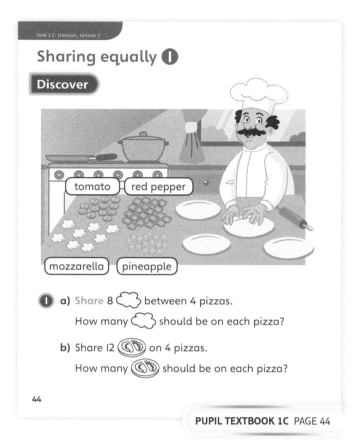

PUPIL TEXTBOOK 1C PAGE 44

Share

WAYS OF WORKING Whole class teacher led

ASK

- Question ❶ a): *How did you share the mozzarella cheese fairly?*
- Question ❶ a): *How did you represent the sharing?*
- Question ❶ a): *How can you describe the sharing in a sentence? Can you think of another way to describe it?*

IN FOCUS To facilitate a practical approach to question ❶, you could give children toy (or paper) pizzas and toppings to share between them.

DEEPEN Challenge children to explore whether they could share 6 mushrooms easily between 4 pizzas. Some children may begin to make the link with simple fractions.

PUPIL TEXTBOOK 1C PAGE 45

Think together

Whole class teacher led (I do, We do, You do)

ASK

• *How do you know how many equal groups you are sharing into?*
• *What else do you need to know?*
• *What patterns do you notice?*
• *How could you check your sharing?*

IN FOCUS The scenario in question **1** results in 4 equal groups of 4, offering an opportunity for discussion. What do children notice about the number of groups and the size of the groups? Can they explain why this has happened?

STRENGTHEN If children struggle to share out the pizza toppings using the pictures in the **Pupil textbook**, give them concrete representations in the form of toy (or paper) pizzas and toppings, or printed circles and counters. When they have shared out the toppings using the representations, ask them to show you what they have done using the picture in the **Pupil textbook**.

DEEPEN Question **3** requires children to share between two, rather than between four as previously in this lesson. Deepen the investigation by asking children to investigate different ways of sharing the pizza slices. For example, could the pizza be shared equally between three people? Could it be shared equally between five people? You could challenge them to find all the ways the pizza could be shared fairly.

ASSESSMENT CHECKPOINT Assess whether children can explain what is meant by sharing and how to share into equal groups. Can they share different numbers into different sized groups and represent this in both a concrete and a pictorial manner?

ANSWERS

Question **1** : There are 4 🔲 on each pizza.
　　　　　　　Now there are 4 groups of 4.

Question **2** : 20 ☁ are shared between 4 pizzas.
　　　　　　　There are 5 ☁ on each pizza.
　　　　　　　Now there are 4 groups of 5.

Question **3** : Sam and Mo get 6 slices each.

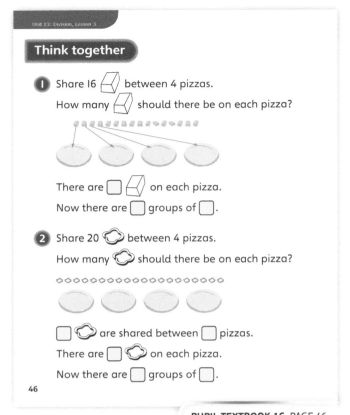

PUPIL TEXTBOOK 1C PAGE 46

PUPIL TEXTBOOK 1C PAGE 47

Practice

WAYS OF WORKING Independent thinking

IN FOCUS Questions ❶ and ❷ use pictorial representations to support children's reasoning about the sharing required. Encourage children to repeat the completed sentences to themselves or to a partner: this will help cement their use and understanding of the key vocabulary.

Question ❸ b) offers an excellent opportunity for children to develop their reasoning. Ask children to explain what each statement means and then decide which statement is true. Can they prove that they are correct?

STRENGTHEN If children struggle to share the pictures in questions ❶ and ❷ into equal groups, discuss with them how they represented the objects to be shared earlier in the lesson and ask: *What could you do this time to make the sharing easier?* Guide them towards drawing the cars in the boxes and circling the dinosaurs.

DEEPEN Challenge children to make up their own puzzle similar to question ❹ .

ASSESSMENT CHECKPOINT Assess whether children are fluent at sharing when given a total number and a number of groups to share into. Can they represent the sharing in both a concrete and a pictorial manner?

ANSWERS Answers for the **Practice** part of the lesson appear in the separate **Practice and Reflect answer guide**.

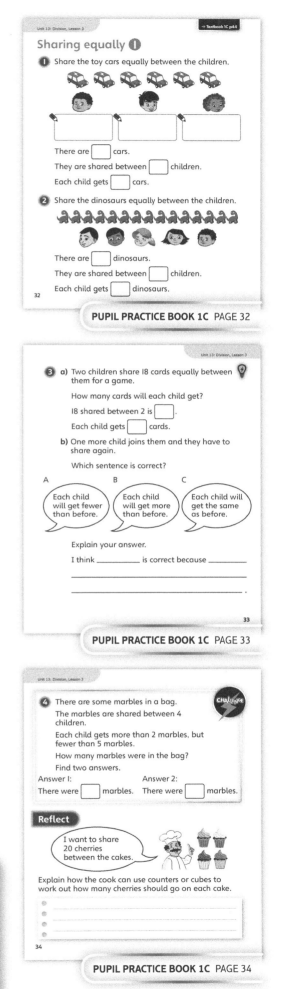

PUPIL PRACTICE BOOK 1C PAGE 32

PUPIL PRACTICE BOOK 1C PAGE 33

Reflect

WAYS OF WORKING Independent thinking

IN FOCUS The **Reflect** question requires children to share 20 cherries between 4 cakes. Allow children to use resources and draw pictures in order to carry out the sharing, before writing their explanation for the chef. They could then share their ideas with their partner or the class. Did all children use the counters or cubes in the same way? Having heard other children's explanations, would they change their own explanation for the chef in any way?

ASSESSMENT CHECKPOINT Assess the quality of children's explanations of how to share the cubes or counters into 4 equal groups.

ANSWERS Answers for the **Reflect** part of the lesson appear in the separate **Practice and Reflect answer guide**.

After the lesson

- Were children able to share numbers into equal groups, reliably?
- Could children explain why some numbers could be shared into certain equal groups and why some could not?
- What real-life contexts could you use to give children practice in these skills?

PUPIL PRACTICE BOOK 1C PAGE 34

Sharing equally ②

Learning focus

In this lesson, children will consolidate their understanding about sharing into equal groups and link this to finding equal groups. They will practise sharing into equal groups in different contexts.

Small steps

→ Previous step: Sharing equally (1)
→ **This step: Sharing equally (2)**
→ Next step: Solving word problems – division

NATIONAL CURRICULUM LINKS

Year 1 Number – Multiplication and Division

Solve one-step problems involving multiplication and division, by calculating the answer using concrete objects, pictorial representations and arrays with the support of the teacher.

ASSESSING MASTERY

Children can recognise and explain sharing as 'one each' shared over and over again until the total amount has been exhausted. Children can use this concept to share numbers into equal groups and solve simple problems.

COMMON MISCONCEPTIONS

Following on from the previous lesson, children may still confuse finding 'groups of a certain number' with 'sharing between a certain number of groups'. When asked to share a total into 3 groups, for example, children may begin counting groups of 3. Show children two pictures, one of a number shared into equal groups of 3 and one of the same number shared into 3 groups. Ask:

- *What is the same and what is different about these two pictures?*
- *Which picture shows the number shared into 3 equal groups? How do you know?*
- *How has the number been shared in the other picture?*

Children may also share inaccurately, neglecting to ensure that they find equal groups. Ask:

- *What is the same about each of the groups? What is different?*
- *Should there be any differences between the groups? Explain your ideas.*

STRENGTHENING UNDERSTANDING

Give children opportunities to play games like the one shown in the **Discover** section of the lesson. Children should share out counters and pieces when setting up the board, making sure everyone has an equal number. Discuss how children can share counters fairly, and how they can check that everyone has their fair share.

GOING DEEPER

Deepen children's understanding and reasoning by asking questions such as: *True or false: I can always share any number between two.* Can they prove their thinking? Can they find a number that does not work?

KEY LANGUAGE

In lesson: share, equally, each, group

Other language to be used by the teacher: fairly

RESOURCES

Optional: counters or other countable objects

 In the eTextbook of this lesson, you will find interactive links to a selection of teaching tools.

Before you teach

- Before linking the two contexts of division, are there any misconceptions that need to be dealt with from last lesson?
- Which context do you think children are most comfortable with? How will this affect the lesson you teach?

Discover

Pair work

ASK

- *How many counters are there?*
- *How many equal groups will the children share the counters into? How do you know?*
- *Can you show me how you have shared the counters?*
- *Could two people play the game and share the counters fairly? Could five people play? Explain your answer.*
- *Why does each child get more counters if fewer children are playing?*

IN FOCUS Use question ❶ to recap children's learning from the previous lesson. Be sure to discuss the key vocabulary needed to describe sharing into equal groups. Children could model the sharing using real counters.

ANSWERS

Question ❶ a): Each child gets 3 counters.

Question ❶ b): Each child gets 4 counters.

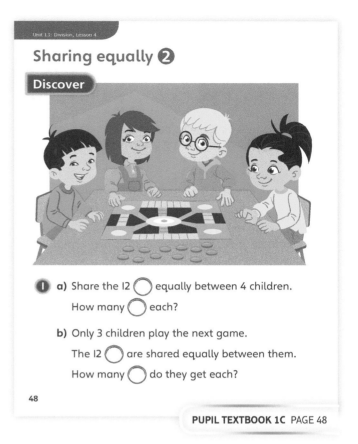

PUPIL TEXTBOOK 1C PAGE 48

Share

WAYS OF WORKING Whole class teacher led

ASK

- *How did you share the counters? Did your method match Flo's or Astrid's?*
- *How are the methods shown the same and different?*
- *Which method do you think is clearest to use? Why?*
- *Which method is sharing and which is finding equal groups?*

IN FOCUS Use the two parts of question ❶ to reiterate the similarities and differences between 4 groups of 3 and 3 groups of 4. Help children notice that these two types of division result in the same numerical solution (12 shared into 4 equal groups gives 3 in each group; 12 shared into groups of 4 gives 3 equal groups). Discuss the differences between questions that require children to share and those that require them to find equal groups. For example, compare question ❶ a) with the question 'Some children share 12 counters equally between them. They each get 3 counters. How many children are there?'

DEEPEN Children could also investigate how many counters are needed when different numbers of children are playing. Discuss the fact that there are multiple solutions.

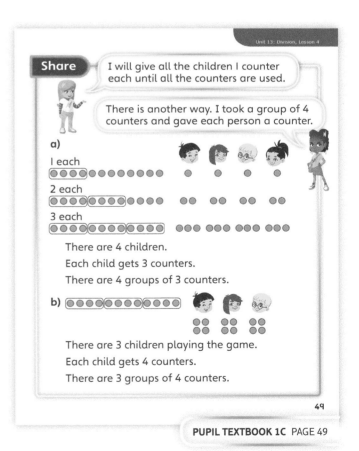

PUPIL TEXTBOOK 1C PAGE 49

Think together

Unit 13: Division, Lesson 4

Think together

WAYS OF WORKING Whole class teacher led (I do, We do, You do)

ASK

- *What do you need to know before you can begin sharing?*
- Question **1** a): *Are you finding groups of 2 or sharing into 2 groups?*
- *How can you show the sharing?*
- *How will you represent the objects in the question?*

IN FOCUS Use these questions to further reinforce the link between the two types of division. Discuss with children which method is most appropriate for the question they are currently working on. Can they explain why?

STRENGTHEN If children struggle to share out the objects using the pictures in the **Pupil textbook**, give them counters or other countable objects to put into groups. Agree with children that they first need to count out the right number of counters. Then ask: *How will you use the counters to show how the objects are shared?*

DEEPEN Question **3** requires children to write a sentence stating how many marbles each child gets; this will deepen their use of vocabulary. Extend the question by asking children to also write an explanation of how they found the solution.

ASSESSMENT CHECKPOINT Assess whether children are fluent at sharing when given a total number and a number of groups to share into. Use question **3** to assess children's ability to use the appropriate vocabulary. Can they confidently explain the link between the two types of division (equal groups and sharing)?

ANSWERS

Question **1** : They each get 6 counters.

There are 2 groups of 6 counters.

Question **2** : There are 5 books on each shelf.

Question **3** : The children each get 5 marbles.

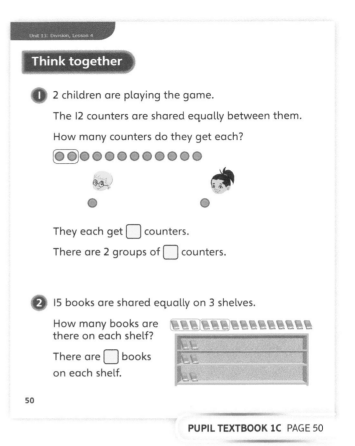

1 2 children are playing the game.

The 12 counters are shared equally between them.

How many counters do they get each?

They each get ☐ counters.

There are 2 groups of ☐ counters.

2 15 books are shared equally on 3 shelves.

How many books are there on each shelf?

There are ☐ books on each shelf.

50

PUPIL TEXTBOOK 1C PAGE 50

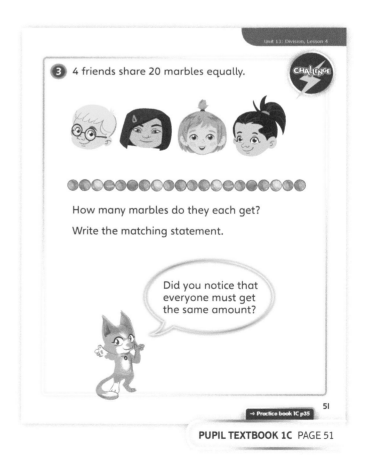

3 4 friends share 20 marbles equally.

CHALLENGE

How many marbles do they each get?

Write the matching statement.

Did you notice that everyone must get the same amount?

51

→ Practice book 1C p35

PUPIL TEXTBOOK 1C PAGE 51

Practice

Independent thinking

IN FOCUS Questions **1** to **3** will reinforce the link between finding equal groups and sharing into equal groups. Encourage children to experiment with both concepts to reinforce and cement the link. If a child uses only one method of division, ask them how they could show the sharing in a different way. Can they use concrete resources or the picture in the **Pupil Practice Book** to show you?

Question **4** requires children to show their understanding of what it means to share items equally between 3 groups. Note that Ben has shared his sweets equally, but he has made 5 equal groups (of 3), not 3 equal groups. Prompt children to explain Ben's mistake by asking: *Where has Ben gone wrong? What would you say to him to help him see his mistake?*

STRENGTHEN Encourage children to use concrete resources to show the sharing in questions **1** and **2**. Ask: *How many equal groups will you be sharing into? How many objects are you sharing between the equal groups?*

DEEPEN Challenge children to make up their own puzzle similar to question **5** .

ASSESSMENT CHECKPOINT Use questions **1** to **3** to determine whether children are confidently making informed choices as to which type of division they wish to use to solve a problem. Can they explain how the two methods are similar and different and use this understanding to explain their reasoning?

ANSWERS Answers for the **Practice** part of the lesson appear in the separate **Practice and Reflect answer guide**.

Reflect

WAYS OF WORKING Independent thinking

IN FOCUS The **Reflect** question requires children to share 8 cubes between 4 people. Allow children to use resources and draw pictures in order to carry out the sharing, before writing their explanation. They could then share their ideas with their partner. Did they both choose to solve the problem in the same way? If not, how are the methods similar and how are they different?

ASSESSMENT CHECKPOINT Assess whether children can clearly explain their method. They should be able to explain how they approached the question and justify their method, using the appropriate vocabulary and any concrete, pictorial or abstract representations they need to support their ideas.

ANSWERS Answers for the **Reflect** part of the lesson appear in the separate **Practice and Reflect answer guide**.

After the lesson ⏸

- How confident were children at recognising the link between the two types of division?
- How effective was your explanation of the link between the two types of division? How would you improve your explanation next time you teach this lesson?

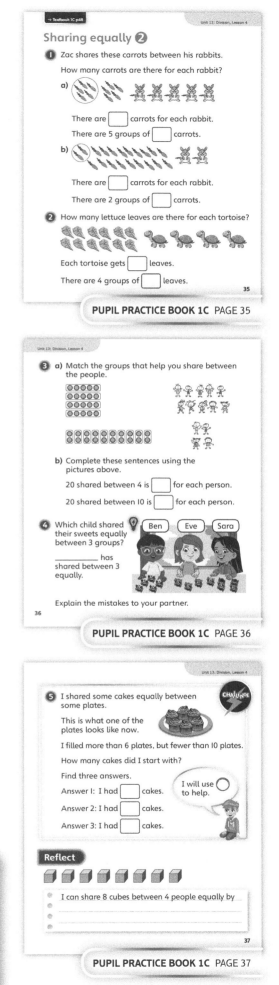

PUPIL PRACTICE BOOK 1C PAGE 35

PUPIL PRACTICE BOOK 1C PAGE 36

PUPIL PRACTICE BOOK 1C PAGE 37

Solving word problems – division

Learning focus

In this lesson, children will use all the strategies they have learned to solve simple word problems based around division. Children will revisit their understanding of finding equal groups and sharing through these questions.

Small steps

→ Previous step: Sharing equally (2)
→ **This step: Solving word problems – division**
→ Next step: Finding halves (1)

NATIONAL CURRICULUM LINKS

Year 1 Number – Multiplication and Division

Solve one-step problems involving multiplication and division, by calculating the answer using concrete objects, pictorial representations and arrays with the support of the teacher.

ASSESSING MASTERY

Children can read and understand a word problem that involves division. Children can explain what the problem is asking them to do and can use an appropriate method to represent and solve it.

COMMON MISCONCEPTIONS

Children who struggle to read or understand the written vocabulary may misunderstand the problem and therefore muddle their working out. Support children by providing word banks or flash cards with pictorial representations of the words children are likely to use in this lesson. Ask:
- *Which word are you finding tricky in this question?*
- *Can you find it in the word bank? What does it mean?*

STRENGTHENING UNDERSTANDING

Introduce children to word problems through role play. For example, ask children to prepare for a party. Ask questions such as: *There are 6 people coming to the party. We have 18 slices of cake. How many slices of cake will each guest receive?*

GOING DEEPER

Encourage children to make up their own word problems for their partner to solve. Specify that the word problem should involve sharing equally or finding equal groups. Ask children to show how they would expect someone to solve their problem. Use the opportunity to emphasise different methods; for example, ask: *Can it be solved using a number line?*

KEY LANGUAGE

In lesson: division, share, equally, group

Other language to be used by the teacher: fairly

STRUCTURES AND REPRESENTATIONS

Arrays, number line

RESOURCES

Optional: counters or other countable objects, blank number lines, handouts with further word problems linked to the scenario seen in **Discover**, word bank or flash cards with pictorial representations of words used in this lesson.

 In the eTextbook of this lesson, you will find interactive links to a selection of teaching tools.

Before you teach

- Were children capable of solving word problems involving multiplication?
- Were there any misconceptions or weaknesses that need to be addressed in this lesson?

Discover

ASK

- *How many of each animal are there?*
- *Could you share the horses between the 3 pens? Could you share the sheep between the 3 pens? Explain.*
- *How can you show the sharing?*
- *Could you show your solution using grouping?*

IN FOCUS Use question ① to discuss how word problems are presented and what makes them different from other problems children have solved before. Take the opportunity to recap the two types of division children have studied over the previous four lessons. Can they use both methods confidently and explain their reasoning?

ANSWERS

Question ① a): 5 pens are needed for the sheep.

Question ① b): Each horse gets 4 carrots.

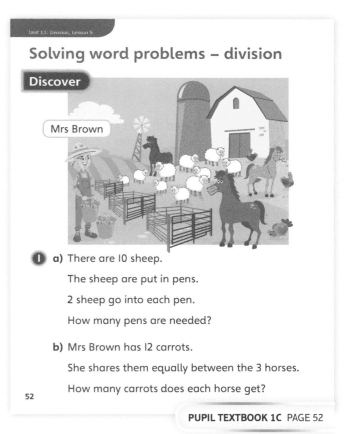

Solving word problems – division

Discover

① a) There are 10 sheep.

The sheep are put in pens.

2 sheep go into each pen.

How many pens are needed?

b) Mrs Brown has 12 carrots.

She shares them equally between the 3 horses.

How many carrots does each horse get?

52

PUPIL TEXTBOOK 1C PAGE 52

Share

ASK

- *What information did you need to know before you could answer the questions?*
- *Who used grouping to find the solutions? How did you show the grouping?*
- *Was it clearer to use sharing or grouping for this question? Explain why.*
- *Question ① b): Did anyone do the same as Astrid? Could you have found the solution another way? Explain.*

IN FOCUS Use question ① a) to discuss how a number line can be used to show sharing or grouping. Give children further practice in using a number line by asking them, for example, how many pens would be needed for 12 sheep, and counting the number of sheep that go into each pen.

STRENGTHEN To develop children's familiarity with word problems, give them handouts with further word problems linked to the scenario used here. For example: Mrs Brown has 15 carrots. She shares them equally between 5 horses. How many carrots does each horse get?

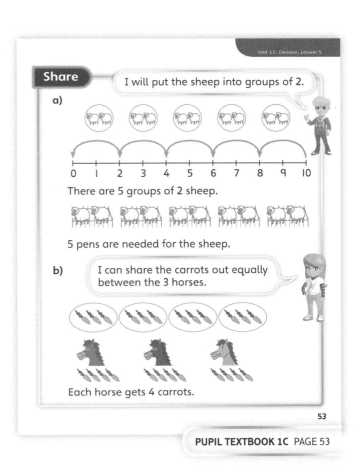

Share

I will put the sheep into groups of 2.

a)

There are 5 groups of 2 sheep.

5 pens are needed for the sheep.

b) I can share the carrots out equally between the 3 horses.

Each horse gets 4 carrots.

53

PUPIL TEXTBOOK 1C PAGE 53

Think together

Whole class teacher led (I do, We do, You do)

ASK
- *What information do you need to find the solution?*
- *How will you show the sharing into equal groups?*
- *Question* ① : *How does the number line help show the sharing?*

IN FOCUS Use questions ① and ② to ensure children can confidently choose an appropriate representation for their working. Discuss with children how they could approach each question, encouraging them to try different methods and discussing their preferences.

STRENGTHEN If children struggle with question ② , offer them counters or other countable objects to represent the biscuits. Discuss how they can show the sharing. Can they link the sharing they have done to a number line? You could give them a partially completed number line (as in question ①) to support them in this.

DEEPEN To deepen understanding, encourage children to give evidence to support their ideas. Ask:
- *How could you show your thinking in a picture?*
- *Could you prove this with resources?*

Extend question ③ further by asking:
- *Could Mrs Brown buy 40 apples exactly if they came in bags of 3?*
- *Which numbers of apples in a bag work if you want to buy 40 apples exactly? Which numbers do not? Can you explain why?*

ASSESSMENT CHECKPOINT Use questions ① and ② to assess how confidently children can read and understand a word problem. Can they explain what the problem is asking them to do and what method they will use to solve it?

ANSWERS

Question ① : She needs 4 boxes for 20 eggs.

Question ② : Each child gets 5 biscuits.

Question ③ : Mrs Brown needs 8 bags with 5 apples in.

Mrs Brown needs 4 bags with 10 apples in.

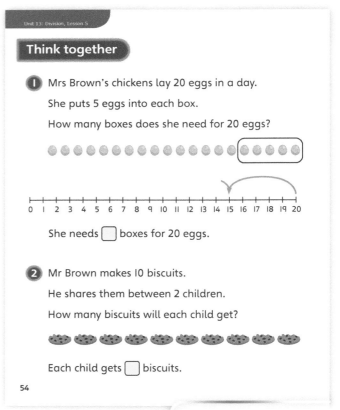

Think together

① Mrs Brown's chickens lay 20 eggs in a day.

She puts 5 eggs into each box.

How many boxes does she need for 20 eggs?

She needs ☐ boxes for 20 eggs.

② Mr Brown makes 10 biscuits.

He shares them between 2 children.

How many biscuits will each child get?

Each child gets ☐ biscuits.

54

PUPIL TEXTBOOK 1C PAGE 54

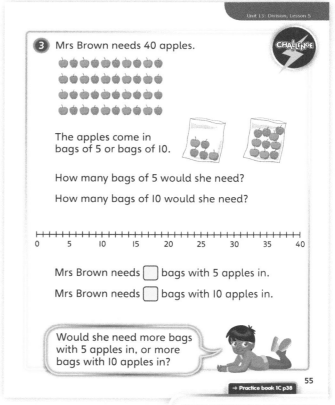

③ Mrs Brown needs 40 apples.

The apples come in bags of 5 or bags of 10.

How many bags of 5 would she need?

How many bags of 10 would she need?

Mrs Brown needs ☐ bags with 5 apples in.

Mrs Brown needs ☐ bags with 10 apples in.

Would she need more bags with 5 apples in, or more bags with 10 apples in?

55

→ Practice book 1C p38

PUPIL TEXTBOOK 1C PAGE 55

Practice

WAYS OF WORKING Independent thinking

IN FOCUS Questions **1** and **2** are designed to test how efficiently children can find solutions, choosing their own representations to help them. If necessary, encourage children to use number lines to show their thinking.

STRENGTHEN Give children who struggle to visualise the scenario in question **3** counters or other countable objects to represent the teddy bears; they could draw the shelves on a piece of paper. Discuss with them what the question is asking them to find out and how they could show what the question describes in order to find the solution.

DEEPEN Question **4** allows children to develop their ability to justify their ideas and convince others they are correct. Develop these skills further by asking them what they would say to someone who didn't agree with them. How would they prove that their reasoning is correct? Alternatively, challenge them to prove that their answer is correct in two different ways.

ASSESSMENT CHECKPOINT Use questions **1** and **2** to determine whether children can read and solve simple word problems. They should confidently demonstrate their understanding of equal sharing, making equal groups and using number lines to solve the problems given.

ANSWERS Answers for the **Practice** part of the lesson appear in the separate **Practice and Reflect answer guide**.

Reflect

WAYS OF WORKING Independent thinking and paired work

IN FOCUS The **Reflect** question asks children to review the questions they have answered in this lesson. Give children the opportunity to independently evaluate their work. They could then share their thoughts with their partner. Did they agree on which question was the hardest? Can they explain what in particular they found difficult? Can they help each other with the questions they found difficult?

ASSESSMENT CHECKPOINT Use children's discussion of the methods used, and any difficulties they encountered, to assess their understanding of the concepts covered in the word problems. Can they use appropriate vocabulary confidently and fluently?

ANSWERS Answers for the **Reflect** part of the lesson appear in the separate **Practice and Reflect answer guide**.

After the lesson

- Were there any words that children found tricky that limited their ability to solve the problems?
- How will you cement their understanding of these words for future lessons?
- What percentage of the class were able to fluently use both methods of division to solve the problems? Were the class more confident in one way than the other when working independently?

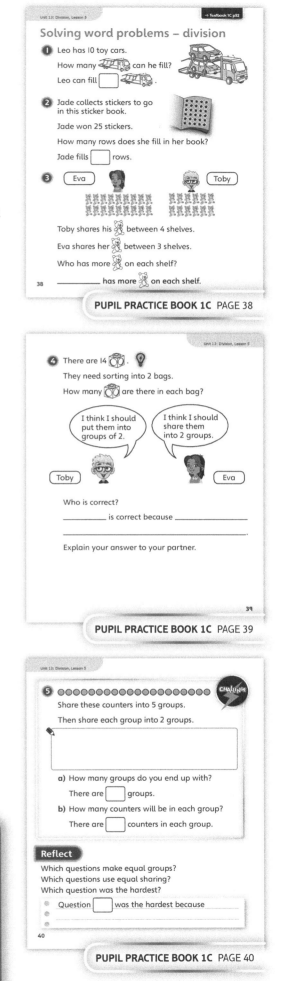

PUPIL PRACTICE BOOK 1C PAGE 38

PUPIL PRACTICE BOOK 1C PAGE 39

PUPIL PRACTICE BOOK 1C PAGE 40

End of unit check

Don't forget the *Power Maths* unit assessment grid on p26.

WAYS OF WORKING Group work – adult led

IN FOCUS Question **2** assesses children's understanding of the number line as a model of division, as well as their ability to share a given total between a given number of groups.

Questions **3** and **4** assess children's ability to read and understand word problems involving division.

Think!

WAYS OF WORKING Pair work or small groups

IN FOCUS This question probes children's understanding of the sharing model of division. It will assess their understanding of how the total amount and number of groups affect the number each group represents. Ask: *Are the boys or the girls correct? How could you find out?*

Check children understand the key words listed at the bottom of the page.

Encourage children to think through or discuss what they notice about how many teddy bears each girl and boy gets, and why this is, before writing their answer in **My journal**.

ANSWERS AND COMMENTARY Children who have mastered this unit will be able to make equal groups of a given number from a given total, or share a given total equally among a given number of groups, clearly explaining what they have done using resources, pictures and the appropriate vocabulary. They will be able to record both types of division using a number line.

PUPIL TEXTBOOK 1C PAGE 56

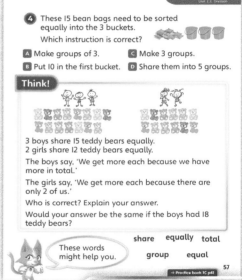

PUPIL TEXTBOOK 1C PAGE 57

Q	A	WRONG ANSWERS AND MISCONCEPTIONS	STRENGTHENING UNDERSTANDING
1	B	C suggests that the child has either transposed the numbers in their answer or misunderstood the question, finding 3 groups instead of groups of 3.	Show children pairs of pictures showing items shared into, for example, 3 groups of 5 and 5 groups of 3. Ask children to tell you what is the same and what is different about the pictures. Ask them to complete a set of sentences for each group: *There are ☐ groups. There are ☐ items in each group. There are ☐ groups of ☐ items.*
2	D	B suggests that the child looked for 5 equal groups rather than equal groups of 5. A or C suggest that the child may be unsure of how to accurately skip count along a number line.	
3	B	A suggests that the child has not read the question carefully. C suggests that the child has confused the number of groups with group size (also question 4: A, D).	Strengthen children's understanding of the use of a number line to represent division by working through a division problem in a concrete way. Once children have grouped or shared the objects, arrange them along a printed number line. Ask: *Can you draw a jump for each group of objects?*
4	C	B could suggest a lack of understanding regarding 'sorting equally'. The child may be unable to see the link between 'sharing equally' and 'sorting equally'.	

My journal

WAYS OF WORKING Independent thinking

ANSWERS AND COMMENTARY

The girls are correct because they have 6 teddy bears each while the boys only have 5.

Discuss why the boys are wrong to think that having more teddy bears in total means you get more each – it depends on how many you are sharing between.

If children struggle to decide who is correct, ask:
- *How many teddy bears do the boys have to share between them?*
- *How many teddy bears do the girls have to share between them?*
- *How many children are sharing the teddy bears in each case?*
- *What resources or pictures could you use to help share the teddy bears?*

Children may need intervention support before they are introduced to simple fractions in Unit 14 or before they encounter division again in Year 2 Unit 5.

Power check

WAYS OF WORKING Independent thinking

ASK
- *How confident do you feel using a number line to answer division questions now?*
- *Do you think you have improved at solving division word problems? How do you know?*

Power puzzle

WAYS OF WORKING Pair work or small groups

IN FOCUS Use this **Power puzzle** to assess children's ability to share a number into equal groups. Children should recognise that they need to first find out the total number of dots and then consider what equal groups they can make using that number.

ANSWERS AND COMMENTARY If children can complete the **Power puzzle**, and can correctly describe what they have done ('I have split the dots into 2 groups of 4', for example), this suggests that they have a secure understanding of sharing and equal groups.

If children are unable to create equal groups, is this because they are unable to divide the total amount, or are they simply unable to work out where to draw the lines? If they are struggling to divide the total amount, give them counters to represent the dots and ask: *What equal groups can you find in this number of counters? Can you find a way of making those groups in the picture?* These children may need further concrete practice in grouping and sharing before returning to more abstract questions.

After the unit ⏸
- How did the learning opportunities you offered children over the course of this unit develop their multiplicative reasoning?
- How did you develop children's ability to use the unit-specific vocabulary? How will you continue to develop their use of it beyond the unit?

→ Textbook 1C p56

End of unit check

My journal

3 boys share 15 teddy bears equally.
2 girls share 12 teddy bears equally.

The boys say, 'We get more each because we have more in total.'

The girls say, 'We get more each because there are only 2 of us.'

Who is correct? Explain your answer.

Would your answer be the same if the boys had 18 teddy bears?

These words might help you.

group   equal

share   equally

total

41

PUPIL PRACTICE BOOK 1C PAGE 41

Unit 13: Division

Power check

How do you feel about your work in this unit?

Power puzzle

Liam drew two straight lines to split these dots into equal groups.

Draw two straight lines in each box so that the counters are split into equal groups.

42

PUPIL PRACTICE BOOK 1C PAGE 42

Strengthen and **Deepen** activities for this unit can be found in the *Power Maths* online subscription.

Unit 14
Halves and quarters

Mastery Expert tip! "I found that lots of open-ended questions encouraged my class to think deeper about halves and quarters. This definitely had an impact on their understanding of the unit."

Don't forget to watch the Unit 14 video!

WHY THIS UNIT IS IMPORTANT

This unit is important as children will learn how to find halves and quarters of both shapes and groups of objects. It lays the foundations for later learning about fractions and therefore the foundations need to be secure.

WHERE THIS UNIT FITS

→ Unit 13: Division
→ **Unit 14: Halves and quarters**
→ Unit 15: Position and direction

This unit builds on simple sharing completed in earlier units during the year. The unit focuses on strategies to find halves and quarters and ends on applying the skills learned to solve word problems. Following this unit, children will move on to learning about position and direction – including half and quarter turns.

Before they start this unit, it is expected that children:

• can share objects into 2 groups
• can share objects into 4 groups
• know the importance of equal sharing
• have a simple understanding of what splitting an object in half means.

ASSESSING MASTERY

Children who have mastered this unit will be able to use efficient strategies to find halves and quarters of shapes and groups of objects. Children will work accurately and confidently to find equal parts and they will know how the equal parts relate to the whole. Children will be able to work in reverse: being told what a quarter is and calculating what the whole would be. Finally, children will use the correct vocabulary and reasoning when explaining their methods, particularly when solving word problems.

COMMON MISCONCEPTIONS	STRENGTHENING UNDERSTANDING	GOING DEEPER
Children may not understand the concept of equal parts.	Do practical sharing activities such as cutting cake or dividing sweets between friends.	Ask children to think of where they can find halves and quarters in everyday life.
Unequal sharing is common, such as not giving the same amount to each group.	Represent fractions with drawings and apparatus (tables and counters work well).	Ask children to explain methods of halving and quartering to deepen thinking.
Children may think quarters always look identical and not allow for different layouts.	Show children different ways to find quarters. Compare these ways.	Ask children to start with a half or a quarter and find out what the whole should be.

Go through the unit starter pages of the **Pupil Textbook** with children. Talk through the key learning points (that the characters mention) and the key vocabulary.

It will help to represent halves and quarters visually on shapes.

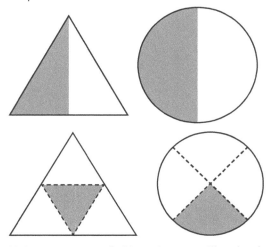

Lining up groups of objects in rows will make sharing easier.

There is some key language that children will need to know as a part of the learning in this unit.

→ half, halves, quarter

→ equal

→ share, split

→ part, whole

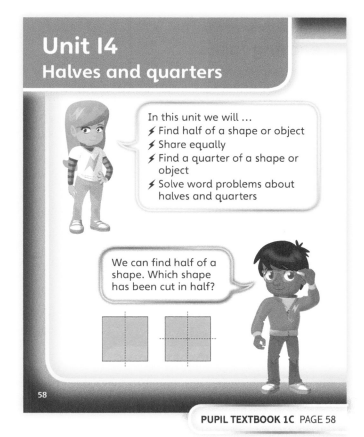

PUPIL TEXTBOOK 1C PAGE 58

PUPIL TEXTBOOK 1C PAGE 59

Finding halves ❶

Learning focus

In this lesson, children will recognise what a half is. They will apply their knowledge by halving shapes and objects.

Small steps

→ Previous step: Solving word problems – division
→ **This step: Finding halves (1)**
→ Next step: Finding halves (2)

NATIONAL CURRICULUM LINKS

Year 1 Number – Fractions

Recognise, find and name a half as one of two equal parts of an object, shape or quantity.

ASSESSING MASTERY

Children can confidently find half of shapes and objects. Children can explain their method of finding half.

COMMON MISCONCEPTIONS

Children may not understand the concept of equal parts. Ask:
• *Show a cake unfairly split in two. If you have this part and I have the other part, do we have the same amount?*

STRENGTHENING UNDERSTANDING

Some children may need some support when halving objects into equal parts. Cutting or folding paper shapes with children in intervention groups would work well to strengthen understanding.

GOING DEEPER

To deepen understanding give children half of a shape (irregular shapes could be used here). Ask children to draw the other half to create a whole and then ask them to explain their methodology.

KEY LANGUAGE

In lesson: halves, half, share, equal, split, whole, part, more than, less than
Other language to be used by the teacher: fair, unfair

STRUCTURES AND REPRESENTATIONS

Diagrams of shapes, half shaded, to promote visual understanding of what a half is

RESOURCES

Mandatory: shapes

Optional: mirrors

 In the eTextbook of this lesson, you will find interactive links to a selection of teaching tools.

Before you teach ⏸

• How did the previous division lesson go?
• How many children will need support with halving equally?
• Could you create a classroom display to reinforce key vocabulary and concepts?

Discover

WAYS OF WORKING Pair work

ASK

- Question ❶ a): *Is it equal if one gardener has a tiny piece and the other gardener has the rest?*
- Question ❶ b): *What is the new word on this page? Does anyone know what it means?*

IN FOCUS Listen carefully to children's discussions in pairs for question ❶ a). Do children understand how to divide the garden into **equal** parts? The notion of fairness might form part of the discussion.

Question ❶ b) introduces children to some key vocabulary, including a new word: 'halves'. Having a display will lead to children discovering what it means.

ANSWERS

Question ❶ a): Accept an answer in which children say that the gardeners each need the same or an equal amount of the flower bed.

Question ❶ b): The first square (blue) and the last square (pink) are split into halves.

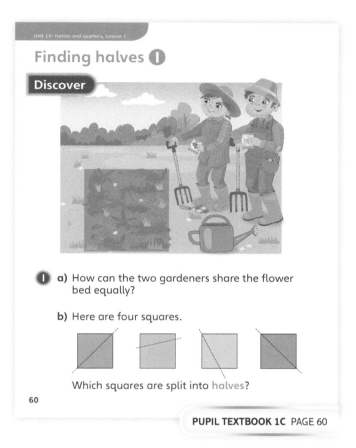

Finding halves ❶

Discover

❶ a) How can the two gardeners share the flower bed equally?

b) Here are four squares.

Which squares are split into halves?

60

PUPIL TEXTBOOK 1C PAGE 60

Share

WAYS OF WORKING Whole class teacher led

ASK

- Question ❶ a): *Why is there more than one way to split the garden into halves?*
- Question ❶ b): *Why are the two parts not equal in the orange and green squares?*
- Question ❶ b): *Where would you move the line to make it equal?*

IN FOCUS Look at question ❶ b) together. Once children have discussed which squares have been split into two equal halves, ask children if they can think of any other possible ways to split the squares into equal halves (splitting vertically down the middle and horizontally through the middle).

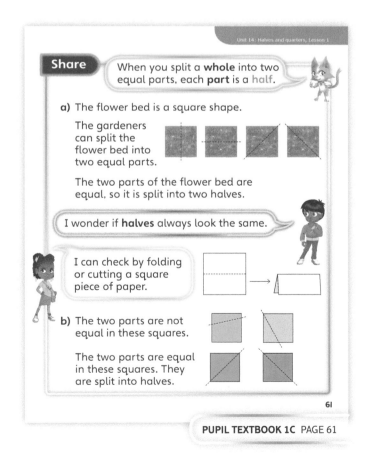

Share

When you split a **whole** into two equal parts, each **part** is a **half**.

a) The flower bed is a square shape.

The gardeners can split the flower bed into two equal parts.

The two parts of the flower bed are equal, so it is split into two halves.

I wonder if **halves** always look the same.

I can check by folding or cutting a square piece of paper.

b) The two parts are not equal in these squares.

The two parts are equal in these squares. They are split into halves.

61

PUPIL TEXTBOOK 1C PAGE 61

Think together

Whole class teacher led (I do, We do, You do)

ASK

- Question **1** : *If the rectangles were chocolate cakes, what would be the fairest way to share them? What would be the most unfair?*
- All questions: *How could you check your answers?*

IN FOCUS Look at question **2** and ask children to share their thoughts. Some children may think shape B looks like it is half shaded because the line is through half of the height of the shape. However, make sure children see that the size of the top half of the shape is not equal to the bottom half of the shape because it 'curves in'. Checking with a mirror is a good strategy here.

STRENGTHEN To strengthen learning in this section, run an intervention, in which shapes (on paper) are folded to find halves.

DEEPEN Ask children to think of real-life situations in which finding half of something is important, such as cutting a cake or half-time in a football match.

ASSESSMENT CHECKPOINT Question **2** will allow you to assess if children can recognise half of a shape. Do children know by sight which shapes have equal halves or do they need to spend more time working it out, perhaps using paper?

Question **3** will allow you to assess if children can apply their knowledge of halves to length.

ANSWERS

Question **1** : B, C

Question **2** a): A, F

Question **2** b): B

Question **2** c): C, D, E

Question **3** : They could fold the string in half or use a measuring instrument.

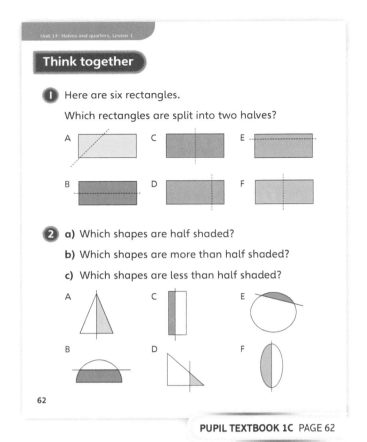

PUPIL TEXTBOOK 1C PAGE 62

PUPIL TEXTBOOK 1C PAGE 63

Practice

WAYS OF WORKING Independent thinking

IN FOCUS For all questions in this section, it would be useful to discuss with the whole class the importance of using a ruler in mathematics. Ask: *What could happen in question ❶, if a ruler is not used? Would drawing the lines 'free-hand' be accurate? Would you get two equal parts?*

STRENGTHEN To strengthen understanding, make a matching game for children to revise halves following this **Practice** section. Cut a range of shapes in half and then jumble them up. Children can then find the pairs.

DEEPEN Children could find halves of lengths of objects around the classroom. Ask them to measure something using string (a table for instance). Children can cut the string to the same length as the object and then fold the string in half to find the middle (half the length).

ASSESSMENT CHECKPOINT Question ❺ should help you decide if children have grasped what equal parts look like and what more and less than a half looks like.

ANSWERS Answers for the **Practice** part of the lesson appear in the separate **Practice and Reflect answer guide**.

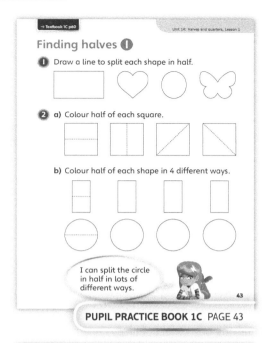

PUPIL PRACTICE BOOK 1C PAGE 43

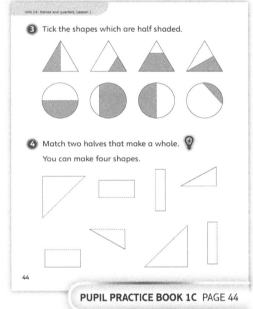

PUPIL PRACTICE BOOK 1C PAGE 44

Reflect

WAYS OF WORKING Independent thinking

IN FOCUS This question requires children to look very carefully at the shapes to identify the odd one out. The circle is the correct answer. To reinforce learning, trace the shape, cut out the smaller piece, and show children that it is smaller by placing the traced piece on top of the bigger piece.

ASSESSMENT CHECKPOINT This question will allow you to assess whether children can identify half of a range of shapes.

ANSWERS Answers for the **Reflect** part of the lesson appear in the separate **Practice and Reflect answer guide**.

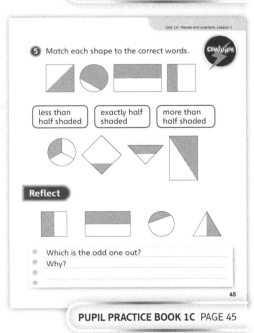

PUPIL PRACTICE BOOK 1C PAGE 45

After the lesson ⏸

- Which children need to strengthen their understanding?
- Do these children need more activities around practical halving?
- Will the key vocabulary need to be recapped at the start of the next lesson?

Finding halves ②

Learning focus

In this lesson, children will find half of groups of objects using their knowledge of sharing between two.

Small steps

→ Previous step: Finding halves (1)
→ **This step: Finding halves (2)**
→ Next step: Finding quarters (1)

NATIONAL CURRICULUM LINKS

Year 1 Number – Fractions

Recognise, find and name a half as one of two equal parts of an object, shape or quantity.

ASSESSING MASTERY

Children can confidently divide objects into two equal groups: making the link between the previous lesson and this lesson, halving one object or shape and halving a group of objects or shapes. Children can recognise that the total group is the 'whole' and each smaller group is 'half' and, furthermore, can count each smaller group to check they are equal.

COMMON MISCONCEPTIONS

Unequal sharing might happen in this lesson. Children often do 'one for me, one for you, one for me' and so on. However, sometimes children may make the mistake of doing 'one for me, one for you, one for you, one for me, one for you'.

STRENGTHENING UNDERSTANDING

Work with a group of children who need strengthening and ask them to hold up their hands and show you a number of fingers. Then ask them to put half their fingers down. Repeat with different numbers.

GOING DEEPER

Ask children to halve nine counters. This will really get them thinking about the left-over counter. See if some children suggest (from Lesson 1) that this left-over counter could be split in half.

KEY LANGUAGE

In lesson: half, halves, each, how many?, share, equal, parts, split, whole, group

Other language to be used by the teacher: fair, unfair, unequal

STRUCTURES AND REPRESENTATIONS

Counters to visually represent groups of objects, bar model

RESOURCES

Mandatory: counters

Optional: sorting hoops

 In the eTextbook of this lesson, you will find interactive links to a selection of teaching tools.

Before you teach

- How can you make links between Lesson 1 and Lesson 2?
- Do you have enough counters ready?
- Should key words be recapped?

Discover

WAYS OF WORKING Pair work

ASK

• Question **1** a): *Should you count the total amount of apples first?*
• Question **1** b): *How could you use counters to help you share?*

IN FOCUS Ensure there are counters available for children who need support with their counting skills and prompt them to use them too. This is particularly important for question **1** b) in which children are required to work backwards: they should place 2 counters on each donkey in the **Pupil Textbook** to work out the original amount in the bag.

ANSWERS

Question **1** a): Each horse gets 4 apples.

Question **1** b): There were 4 apples in Paul's bag.

Finding halves ❷

Discover

1 **a)** Salma gives half of her apples to each horse.

How many apples does each horse get?

b) Paul has some apples in a bag.

He gives 2 apples to each donkey.

There are no more apples in the bag.

How many apples were in Paul's bag?

64

PUPIL TEXTBOOK 1C PAGE 64

Share

WAYS OF WORKING Whole class teacher led

ASK

• Question **1** a): *How can you check that you have shared into equal parts?*
• Question **1** a): *Why is it useful to cross out the apples after you have counted them?*
• Question **1** b): *Why is it important to know that there are two donkeys?*

IN FOCUS Question **1** a) in the **Pupil Textbook** shows the good practice of crossing out objects after counting them. Talk to children about why this is important when finding half – children should understand that it stops them counting an object more than once.

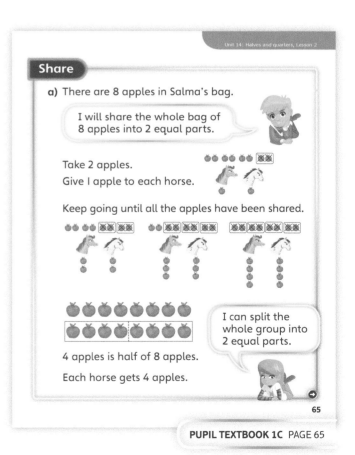

Share

a) There are 8 apples in Salma's bag.

I will share the whole bag of 8 apples into 2 equal parts.

Take 2 apples.
Give I apple to each horse.

Keep going until all the apples have been shared.

I can split the whole group into 2 equal parts.

4 apples is half of 8 apples.

Each horse gets 4 apples.

65

PUPIL TEXTBOOK 1C PAGE 65

Think together

WAYS OF WORKING Whole class teacher led (I do, We do, You do)

ASK

- Question ❶ : *What do the counters represent?*
- Question ❷ : *What are you looking out for in each picture?*
- Question ❸ : *Can you explain your halving strategy to your partner?*

IN FOCUS Look at question ❸ a) together. Ask children how the apples have been represented in the ten frame. Talk through the fact that the apples, represented as counters, have been arranged in two rows of five – making it easy to 'cut' the whole amount in half. Reinforce that half of 10 is 5. Reinforce that two lots of 5 is 10.

STRENGTHEN To strengthen understanding, do some sharing games in which groups of counters are shared equally between two children.

DEEPEN Tell children that a certain number is half of an amount of counters. Ask children to find out how many counters the whole would have been. Repeat with different amounts.

ASSESSMENT CHECKPOINT Question ❸ will let you assess whether children can halve different amounts, represent this in a visual structure and then write it as a number sentence.

ANSWERS

Question ❶ : Half of 8 carrots is 4 carrots.
　　　　　　Each donkey gets 4 carrots.

Question ❷ : Groups A and D have been shared into halves.

Question ❸ a): Half of 10 apples is 5 apples.

Question ❸ b): Half of 12 apples is 6 apples.

Question ❸ c): Half of 10 carrots is 5 carrots.

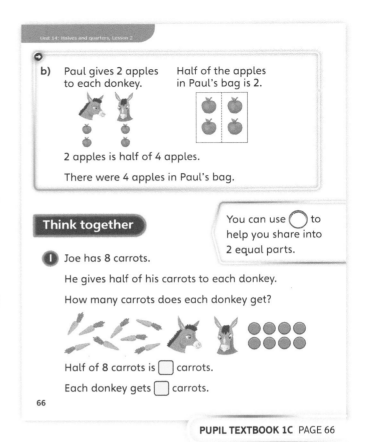

b) Paul gives 2 apples to each donkey.

Half of the apples in Paul's bag is 2.

2 apples is half of 4 apples.

There were 4 apples in Paul's bag.

Think together

You can use ◯ to help you share into 2 equal parts.

❶ Joe has 8 carrots.

He gives half of his carrots to each donkey.

How many carrots does each donkey get?

Half of 8 carrots is ☐ carrots.

Each donkey gets ☐ carrots.

66

PUPIL TEXTBOOK 1C PAGE 66

❷ Which groups of apples have been shared into halves?

A　　B　　C　　D

❸ Complete the sentences.

a)

Half of 10 apples is ☐ apples.

b)

Half of ☐ _____ is ☐ _____.

c)

Half of ☐ carrots is 5 carrots.

67

→ Practice book 1C p46

PUPIL TEXTBOOK 1C PAGE 67

Practice

WAYS OF WORKING Pair work

IN FOCUS Question **2** d) requires children to colour half of the smiley faces – however the smiley faces are not placed in a uniform manner. Children will need to work out a way of halving these without counting a smiley face more than once. A good idea would be to use two colours here.

STRENGTHEN This is a good opportunity to mark children's work and identify those children in need of strengthening. Go through the questions with children and ask them to check their answers, perhaps using counters to help them with this. Ask: *Is each group equal? Have you found half?*

DEEPEN Repeat the activity in question **3** of the **Think together** section from the **Pupil Textbook**. This time, however, ask children to show their workings on a bar model.

ASSESSMENT CHECKPOINT Question **5** will allow you to assess children's problem-solving skills when finding halves of amounts. Children who can work this out independently are likely to have mastered the lesson.

ANSWERS Answers for the **Practice** part of the lesson appear in the separate **Practice and Reflect answer guide**.

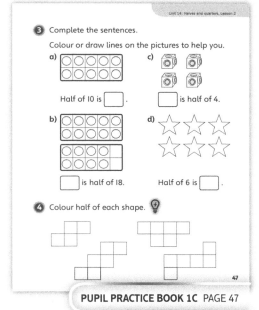

PUPIL PRACTICE BOOK 1C PAGE 46

PUPIL PRACTICE BOOK 1C PAGE 47

Reflect

WAYS OF WORKING Whole class

IN FOCUS The **Reflect** question will allow children to draw on their knowledge from this lesson and Lesson 1 on the different methods of finding half. To finish this lesson, ask the class to stand and sort themselves into two halves. Even if you have an odd number of children, it will be interesting to see what happens.

ASSESSMENT CHECKPOINT This **Reflect** exercise will allow you to check children's understanding of the methods they use to halve a group of objects. Note if they are using appropriate mathematical vocabulary.

ANSWERS Answers for the **Reflect** part of the lesson appear in the separate **Practice and Reflect answer guide**.

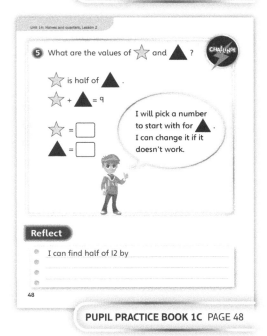

PUPIL PRACTICE BOOK 1C PAGE 48

After the lesson ⏸

- How many children mastered the lesson?
- Did children make links between Lesson 1 and Lesson 2?
- What methods did children use to find half of groups of objects?

Finding quarters ❶

Learning focus

In this lesson, children will recognise what a quarter is. They will apply their knowledge by finding quarters of shapes.

Small steps

→ Previous step: Finding halves (2)
→ **This step: Finding quarters (1)**
→ Next step: Finding quarters (2)

NATIONAL CURRICULUM LINKS

Year 1 Number – Fractions

Recognise, find and name a quarter as one of four equal parts of an object, shape or quantity.

ASSESSING MASTERY

Children can confidently find a quarter of each shape and explain their method. Secure children can do the inverse too: be given a quarter of a shape and work out the original.

COMMON MISCONCEPTIONS

Children may think that all quarters must look the same (because they are equal parts). However, this is not always true.

There can also be the misconception of thinking that a quarter of a number is 4 because a quarter is split into four parts.

STRENGTHENING UNDERSTANDING

Give children different paper shapes and ask them to fold them into quarters. This practical work will strengthen understanding.

GOING DEEPER

Provide children with a range of irregular shapes on paper and ask them to find a quarter. They will begin by folding, but realise that the parts are not equal. Discuss this and come up with strategies to find quarters.

KEY LANGUAGE

In lesson: quarters, split, equal, parts, whole, more than, less than

STRUCTURES AND REPRESENTATIONS

Shaded shapes are used throughout this lesson

RESOURCES

Mandatory: paper shapes

Optional: multilink cubes

 In the eTextbook of this lesson, you will find interactive links to a selection of teaching tools.

Before you teach

- How will you introduce the new word 'quarter'?
- How many children mastered halving in the last lesson?
- How will you link halving to quartering?

Discover

Unit 14: Halves and quarters, Lesson 3

WAYS OF WORKING Pair work

ASK

- Question ① a): *Can you see that the two boards are both split into four equal parts – but in different ways?*
- Question ① b): *Why is the first board **not** split into quarters?*

IN FOCUS In question ① b), children are introduced to a new word 'quarters'. Some children will use inference from the clues provided to discover the meaning whilst others may need some prompting.

ANSWERS

Question ① a): Both boards are split into 4 equal parts.

Question ① b): The second and third boards are split into quarters.

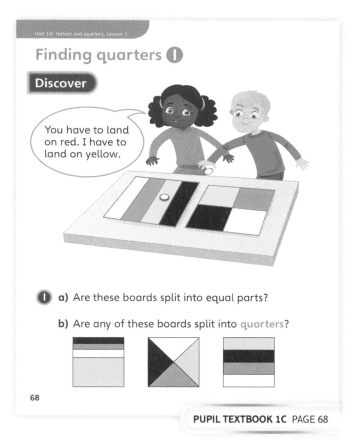

Finding quarters ①

Discover

You have to land on red. I have to land on yellow.

① **a)** Are these boards split into equal parts?

b) Are any of these boards split into quarters?

68

PUPIL TEXTBOOK 1C PAGE 68

Share

WAYS OF WORKING Whole class teacher led

ASK

- Question ① a): *Can you see the different ways you can find one quarter?*
- Question ① a): *Can you remind me what the word 'equal' means?*
- Question ① b): *Which parts are the same, which parts are different?*

IN FOCUS Question ① b) is very important in visually representing quarters. Make clear reference to the fact that the parts must be equal or they cannot be quarters.

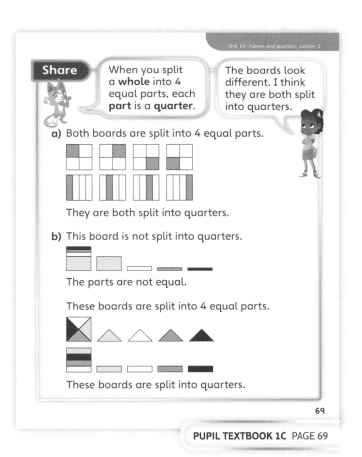

Share

*When you split a **whole** into 4 equal parts, each **part** is a **quarter**.*

The boards look different. I think they are both split into quarters.

a) Both boards are split into 4 equal parts.

They are both split into quarters.

b) This board is not split into quarters.

The parts are not equal.

These boards are split into 4 equal parts.

These boards are split into quarters.

69

PUPIL TEXTBOOK 1C PAGE 69

Think together

Whole class teacher led (I do, We do, You do)

ASK

- Question **1** : *How many parts should there be?*
- Question **2** : *What is the difference between how the circles have been split? Are both circles showing quarters?*
- Question **2** : *Shape 'D' looks unusual. Should all the quarters be the same shape?*

IN FOCUS Question **2** looks at how a shape can be split into four quarters, where each of the quarters need not be identical. Discuss with children the concept of halving, then halving again – link to Lesson 1 in which shapes were halved in different ways.

STRENGTHEN For question **3**, have multilink cubes ready for those who need it to work out the answer.

DEEPEN Question **3** looks at the inverse of finding quarters: reasoning from the part to the whole. This is a good way to explore the concept in more depth. Give children opportunities to solve similar problems and explain their solutions.

ASSESSMENT CHECKPOINT For question **1** , if a child says A is in quarters – they need to be reminded that, even though the parts are equal, counting the total number of parts is vital.

Question **2** will allow you to assess children's understanding of quarters. If they spot that C is split into quarters, they are likely to have mastered recognising quarters.

ANSWERS

Question **1** : B and D are split into quarters.

Question **2** : B and C are split into quarters.

Question **3** : The shape could be 12 cubes in any continuously connected formation that includes 4 right angles, for example an open square.

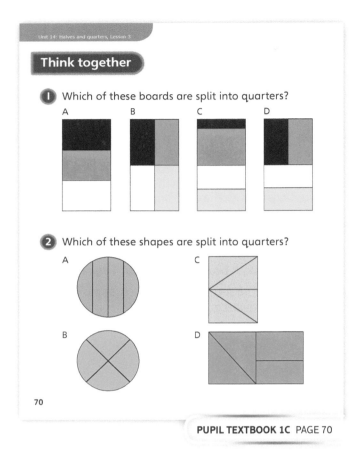

Think together

1 Which of these boards are split into quarters?

A   B   C   D

2 Which of these shapes are split into quarters?

A   C

B   D

70

PUPIL TEXTBOOK 1C PAGE 70

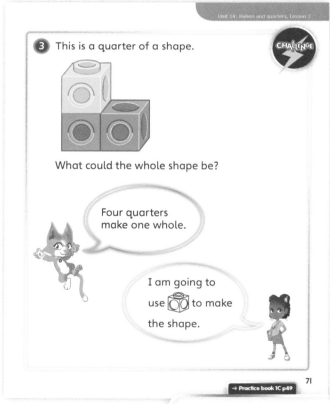

3 This is a quarter of a shape.

CHALLENGE

What could the whole shape be?

Four quarters make one whole.

I am going to use ⬚⬚ to make the shape.

71

→ Practice book 1C p49

PUPIL TEXTBOOK 1C PAGE 71

Practice

WAYS OF WORKING Pair work

IN FOCUS Question **2** has four rectangles at the end. Encourage children to quarter them in a range of different ways.

For question **3**, the first shape only has three parts and they are unequal. Discuss this with children and see if they realise they can split the larger section to make four equal parts altogether.

STRENGTHEN Print some similar shapes to the ones in question **3** onto a sheet of paper (enlarge them and include the dividing lines). Ask children to cut the shapes out, count the parts and then see if they are equal in size. This will help children revise their strategies.

DEEPEN To deepen understanding, get children to do some more work with quartering irregular shapes (this will call upon estimation skills too). A good idea would be to see if children can show one quarter of each letter of the alphabet.

ASSESSMENT CHECKPOINT Question **5** will allow you to assess whether children can split irregular shapes into quarters in different ways.

ANSWERS Answers for the **Practice** part of the lesson appear in the separate **Practice and Reflect answer guide**.

Reflect

WAYS OF WORKING Independent thinking

IN FOCUS Ash's question prompts children to think of other ways to split the rectangle into quarters. This will deepen children's understanding – the realisation will be that shapes can be quartered in a range of different ways.

ASSESSMENT CHECKPOINT This **Reflect** question will allow you to assess which children can show quarters on a shape without scaffolding, and can reason why.

ANSWERS Answers for the **Reflect** part of the lesson appear in the separate **Practice and Reflect answer guide**.

After the lesson ⏸

- Do you need to schedule some same-day intervention for certain children?
- Do children understand that quarters do not always look identical?
- Could you do some artwork in which stamps are used; such as making four-part patterns?

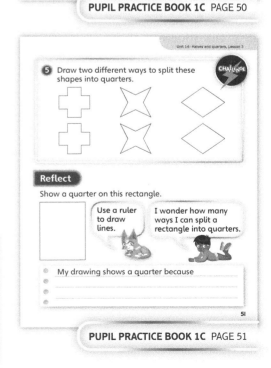

PUPIL PRACTICE BOOK 1C PAGE 49

PUPIL PRACTICE BOOK 1C PAGE 50

PUPIL PRACTICE BOOK 1C PAGE 51

Finding quarters ②

Learning focus

In this lesson, children will find a quarter of a small quantity using equal sharing.

Small steps

→ Previous step: Finding quarters (1)
→ **This step: Finding quarters (2)**
→ Next step: Solving word problems – halves and quarters

NATIONAL CURRICULUM LINKS

Year 1 Number – Fractions

Recognise, find and name a quarter as one of four equal parts of an object, shape or quantity.

ASSESSING MASTERY

Children can securely find a quarter of a small quantity by sharing between four and using mental strategies to do this. Children can describe capacity using the vocabulary 'quarter full'.

COMMON MISCONCEPTIONS

Care should be taken if using the 'quarter is a half of a half' explanation – this may generate a misconception about repeated halving for all fractions later on. Ask:
• *Can you use the repeated halving method to split something into five groups?*

STRENGTHENING UNDERSTANDING

To strengthen understanding, practise sharing counters between four children. Focus on giving each child a counter in order and checking that each child has the same amount at the end to ensure all children have shared equally.

GOING DEEPER

Ask children to find a quarter of various quantities (real-life examples). For instance, children could find one quarter of 8 litres or 16 kg.
You could also ask children to draw what one and a quarter might look like.

KEY LANGUAGE

In lesson: quarter, whole, quarter full, split, share, equal, more than, less than, exactly

Other language to be used by the teacher: fair, unfair, unequal, capacity

STRUCTURES AND REPRESENTATIONS

Children will use counters or draw dots to support their sharing

RESOURCES

Mandatory: counters

 In the eTextbook of this lesson, you will find interactive links to a selection of teaching tools.

Before you teach

• Are children confident with finding quarters of shapes?
• How will you link the previous lesson to this one?
• Could you show children some real-life examples of finding one quarter of a small quantity (sharing fruit, grouping children)?

Discover

WAYS OF WORKING Pair work

ASK

- Question ① a): *How do you find a quarter of a group of objects?*
- Question ① a): *Do you remember finding half of a group of objects – could this help?*
- Question ① b): *What strategy could you use to solve this and find the whole?*

IN FOCUS For question ①, look carefully at the sharing strategies children use. As in the previous lesson, children may try to cut each orange into 4 pieces. Some children will count each one – watch if they make any markings such as dots.

ANSWERS

Question ① a): Each child gets 2 oranges.

Question ① b): The whole is 12 oranges.

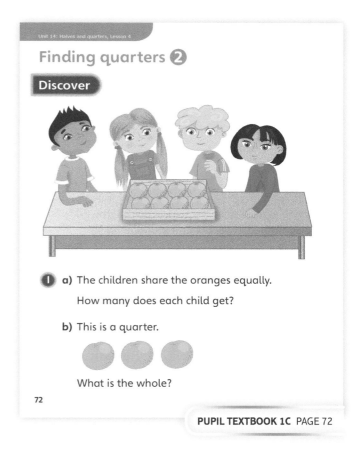

Share

WAYS OF WORKING Whole class teacher led

ASK

- Question ① a): *Can you think of any other way of splitting this group into quarters?*
- Question ① a): *What if the 8 oranges were arranged in a line? Where would you split these into quarters?*
- Question ① a): *If you had to split 16 oranges into quarters, what shape could you arrange them into?*
- Question ① b): *Why does the grid have four parts?*

IN FOCUS Question ① b) has a grid of four squares to show children a visual strategy to find the answer. If children found this challenging, they could repeat the question (but start with 4 oranges) and draw their own grid.

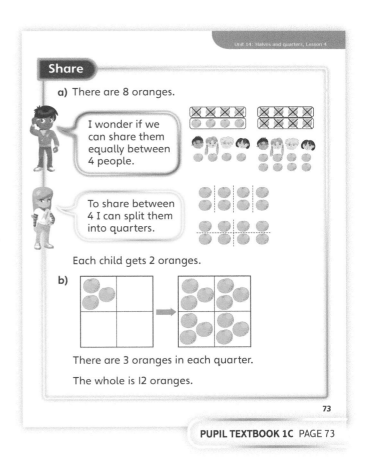

Think together

WAYS OF WORKING Whole class teacher led (I do, We do, You do)

ASK

- Question ❶ : *Can you show me how you would work these out using a drawing?*
- Question ❸ a): *Is that one quarter full? Why not?*

IN FOCUS In question ❶ b) because the cherries are in rows of four, children may intuitively circle the groups of four. This will provide a good class discussion point – the difference between sharing between 4 and grouping in 4s.

STRENGTHEN Some children may need support with their sharing strategies. Model sharing counters or making dots on paper.

DEEPEN Do some work linking halves to quarters. Children could find one half and then one quarter of 20 and then see how the answers relate to one another.

Ask children if they know how many quarters make a half. Can they draw a visual representation of this?

ASSESSMENT CHECKPOINT Question ❸ will allow you to see which children can apply their knowledge of finding quarters to capacity.

ANSWERS

Question ❶ a): 1 orange is a quarter of 4 oranges.

Question ❶ b): 5 cherries is a quarter of 20 cherries.

Question ❷ a): A quarter of 12 plums is 3 plums.

Question ❷ b): The whole is 16 pears.

Question ❸ a): More than a quarter full

Question ❸ b): A quarter full

Question ❸ c): More than a quarter full

Question ❸ d): A quarter full

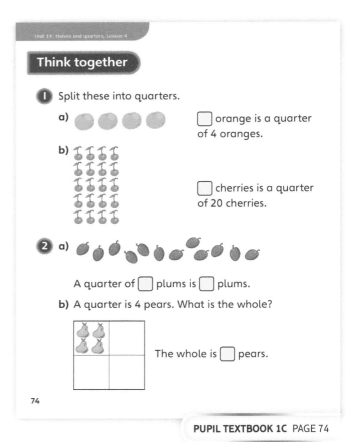

PUPIL TEXTBOOK 1C PAGE 74

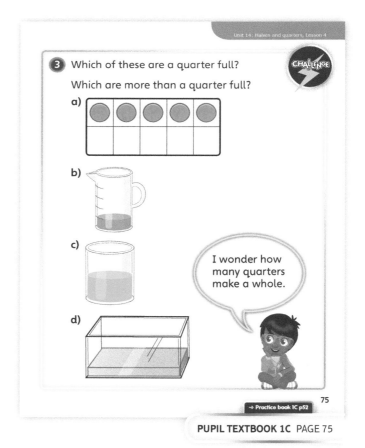

PUPIL TEXTBOOK 1C PAGE 75

Practice

WAYS OF WORKING Independent thinking or pair work

IN FOCUS Question **5** requires children to have a solid understanding of how to find a quarter of a small quantity. Children will need to realise that Ben is incorrect – giving 4 sweets to someone does not mean that 4 is a quarter. Encourage children to include in their answer what number of sweets Ben would have to give to Meg, if he was giving her one quarter (the answer being 5).

STRENGTHEN For question **4**, encourage children to draw dots to represent the numbers visually. This will make the questions easier to comprehend.

DEEPEN Mark question **6** with children. Ask children to create a similar problem involving symbols and quartering.

ASSESSMENT CHECKPOINT Question **5** will allow you to assess children's understanding of finding a quarter. Children should be able to explain their strategy and the reason why Ben is incorrect.

ANSWERS Answers for the **Practice** part of the lesson appear in the separate **Practice and Reflect answer guide**.

Reflect

WAYS OF WORKING Whole class

IN FOCUS Ask the class to discuss their answers to the **Reflect** question in pairs first. Then ask children to come to the board and write how they would find a quarter of 12. Afterwards, see if any children can improve the answer – they can come to the board and edit using a different coloured pen. Repeat until you have an excellent explanation of how to find a quarter of 12.

ASSESSMENT CHECKPOINT The **Reflect** question will tell you if children have grasped the method and vocabulary associated with finding quarters of small quantities.

ANSWERS Answers for the **Reflect** part of the lesson appear in the separate **Practice and Reflect answer guide**.

After the lesson ⏸

- Could you set a home learning activity in which children have to find quarters of small quantities?
- Do you need to re-model any sharing strategies?
- Are children ready for word problems?

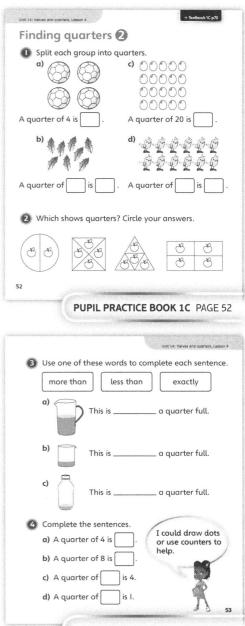

PUPIL PRACTICE BOOK 1C PAGE 52

PUPIL PRACTICE BOOK 1C PAGE 53

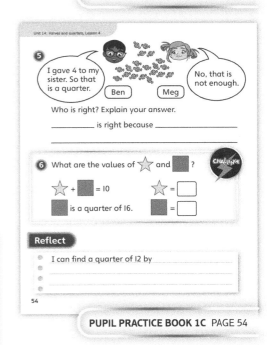

PUPIL PRACTICE BOOK 1C PAGE 54

Solving word problems – halves and quarters

Learning focus

In this lesson, children will apply the knowledge they have acquired over the unit to solve word problems.

Small steps

→ Previous step: Finding quarters (2)
→ **This step: Solving word problems – halves and quarters**
→ Next step: Describing turns

NATIONAL CURRICULUM LINKS

Year 1 Number – Fractions

- Recognise, find and name a half as one of two equal parts of an object, shape or quantity.
- Recognise, find and name a quarter as one of four equal parts of an object, shape or quantity.

ASSESSING MASTERY

Children can work methodically and efficiently to solve word problems. Children can explain their solutions effectively and can check their answers by using a different method.

COMMON MISCONCEPTIONS

Children may confuse halves and quarters. Ask:
- *Do you remember the difference between finding halves and finding quarters?*

Children may split each object into halves or quarters, rather than sharing them. Ask:
- *If you have more than one object, how should you halve or quarter them?*

STRENGTHENING UNDERSTANDING

Go through some word problems with children who need strengthening. Ask: *Which words give you clues? Can you draw the problem?*

GOING DEEPER

Children can deepen their learning by thinking of their own word problems. Challenge them to think of a problem in which 16 cakes must be halved and then quartered.

KEY LANGUAGE

In lesson: half, quarter, half full, quarter full, compare, part, whole, split

Other language to be used by the teacher: share, capacity

STRUCTURES AND REPRESENTATIONS

Counters and drawings are used to represent finding halves and quarters

Ordering items in rows and columns is a useful way to represent them

RESOURCES

Mandatory: counters

 In the eTextbook of this lesson, you will find interactive links to a selection of teaching tools.

Before you teach

- Which children will need support comprehending the questions? How can you provide that support?
- Would it be useful to highlight key words in the problems?

Discover

WAYS OF WORKING Pair work

ASK

- *How many bread rolls were there to start with?*
- *How would you teach the family to cut the cake?*
- *Question ❶ a): How many people are there altogether? Why do you need to know that?*
- *Question ❶ b): Which glass might be a quarter full? How does it look different?*

IN FOCUS This section will get children thinking carefully about the family's statements and discussing the mathematics involved. Prompt children to think about and discuss all of the speech bubbles – and not just to answer questions ❶ a) and ❶ b).

ANSWERS

Question ❶ a): 2 people are vegetarians.

Question ❶ b): Glass B is half full.

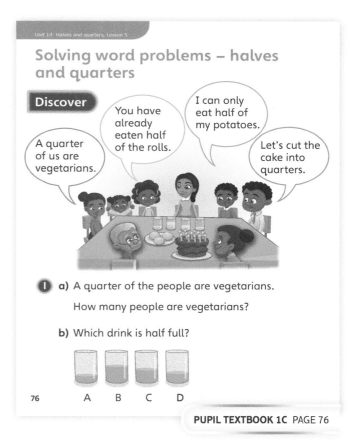

PUPIL TEXTBOOK 1C PAGE 76

Share

WAYS OF WORKING Whole class teacher led

ASK

- *Question ❶ a): What was your strategy to find a quarter?*
- *Who can remind us of what 'part' and 'whole' mean?*

IN FOCUS All answers in this section demonstrate understanding of how the number of parts relates to the context of the problem and how different methods can be used.

Question ❶ b) is a good reminder of what half looks like in terms of capacity. It is also a good visual reminder that two halves make a whole.

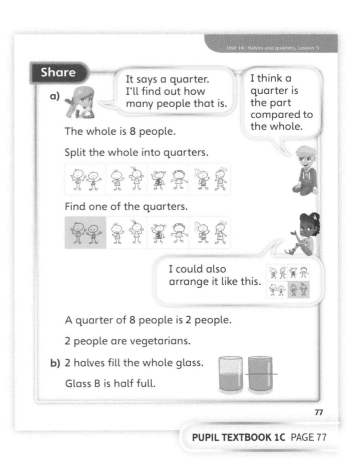

PUPIL TEXTBOOK 1C PAGE 77

Think together

Think together

WAYS OF WORKING Whole class teacher led (I do, We do, You do)

ASK

- Question ❷ : *Are the parts all equal?*
- Question ❸ a): *What diagram could you draw to help you?*

IN FOCUS Question ❷ is a good example of the need to check the answer. Ask children if they know all the parts are equal, and if so how. You could prompt them to trace each piece and cut, to see if they are the same size.

STRENGTHEN Run intervention exercises in which children draw the word problems – visually representing the maths involved.

Another option would be to make the problems practical through role play, using things such as food items.

DEEPEN Ask children to look at question ❷. Ask: *How many pieces has cake A been cut into? If the cake was chopped into 4 equal pieces it would be quarters. What do you think it is called if it is chopped into 8 equal pieces?*

Question ❸ cements children's understanding of parts and wholes. Children reason from the part to the whole, rather than simply following a method to break a whole into a certain number of parts. This kind of reasoning is a good indicator of deep understanding. You could further deepen understanding by presenting children with similar problems.

ASSESSMENT CHECKPOINT Question ❷ will allow you to assess children's knowledge of halving and quartering. Assess if children spot that C, E and F are not equal parts. The rounded edges on these cakes mean they are not completely equal. However, it is possible for a shape to be divided into quarters in the same way as for cake F (if F had square corners), i.e. each respective half of the shape is halved. This is a good discussion point.

ANSWERS

Question ❶ : Half of 12 🥔 is 6 🥔

Question ❷ : Cake B is cut into halves.

　　　　　　Cake D is cut into quarters.

Question ❸ a): There were 6 rolls on the plate.

Question ❸ b): There were 12 candles on the cake.

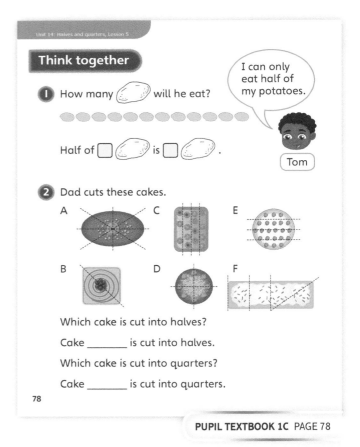

PUPIL TEXTBOOK 1C PAGE 78

PUPIL TEXTBOOK 1C PAGE 79

Practice

WAYS OF WORKING Pair work

IN FOCUS Question ② requires children to find half and then a quarter of 20 pebbles. It is a good opportunity to show children that 4 quarters makes a whole, 2 halves make a whole; and 1 half and 2 quarters makes a whole. Get children to show their workings by drawing dots and stripes on the stones.

STRENGTHEN Question ④ will be quite a challenge for some children. Encourage children to colour the circles and triangles that Michael uses. Then compare this amount with the ones in the picture.

DEEPEN Children can create their own halving and quartering problems. Can children make a two-step problem in which 16 has to be halved then quartered?

ASSESSMENT CHECKPOINT Question ② will allow you to assess if children can understand and show the relationship between the whole, halves and quarters.

ANSWERS Answers for the **Practice** part of the lesson appear in the separate **Practice and Reflect answer guide**.

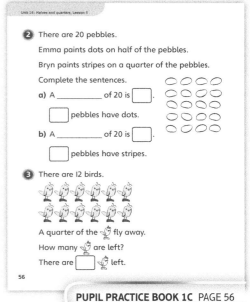

PUPIL PRACTICE BOOK 1C PAGE 55

PUPIL PRACTICE BOOK 1C PAGE 56

Reflect

WAYS OF WORKING Pair work

IN FOCUS This **Reflect** question is a useful opportunity for children to reflect on the lesson in pairs. Look at the feedback from children after it is written – this could signpost any children that need further intervention.

ASSESSMENT CHECKPOINT The **Reflect** question will allow you to assess not only who needs more support, but also who needs their confidence building.

ANSWERS Answers for the **Reflect** part of the lesson appear in the separate **Practice and Reflect answer guide**.

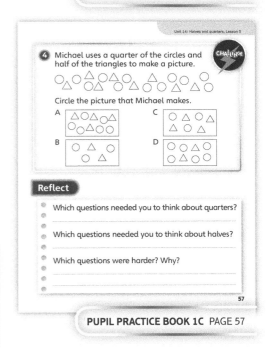

PUPIL PRACTICE BOOK 1C PAGE 57

After the lesson ⏸

- What intervention groups could you run?
- Are children ready for the end of unit check?
- Who is lacking in confidence with fractions?

End of unit check

Don't forget the *Power Maths* unit assessment grid on p26.

WAYS OF WORKING Group work, adult led

IN FOCUS Look at question ❶ with some children you want to assess in more detail. Can children tell you why they have chosen the answer they have? Can they say why the other answers are **not** cut into halves?

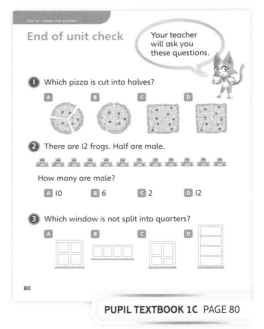

PUPIL TEXTBOOK 1C PAGE 80

Think!

WAYS OF WORKING Pair work or small groups

IN FOCUS This question will encourage children to think deeply. They should be able to share the strawberries between four, but will have two left over. Observe what they do with the left-over strawberries. Encourage children to think through or discuss this section before writing their answer in **My journal**.

ANSWERS AND COMMENTARY Children will demonstrate mastery in this section by finding half of a group of objects and recognising that they must share equally. They will also demonstrate mastery by solving word problems about halves and quarters, and will know what 'part' and 'whole' mean.

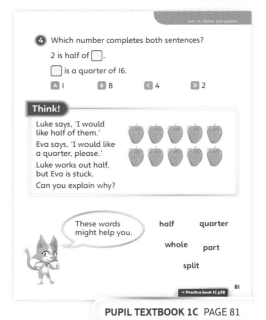

PUPIL TEXTBOOK 1C PAGE 81

Q	A	WRONG ANSWERS AND MISCONCEPTIONS	STRENGTHENING UNDERSTANDING
1	C	Choosing B suggests that the child does not understand that the parts must be equal.	Children may need to do some intervention in which they undertake extra sharing activities with counters. Vocabulary practice might be needed – this could be a good home learning opportunity. Some children may need to practise reading questions carefully.
2	B	C indicates the child has counted the number of groups formed after sharing.	
3	C	Children may not read the question carefully and therefore look for the windows that are split into quarters, rather than the odd one out.	
4	C	Answering B may show that children have not remembered the difference between halves and quarters.	

My journal

Independent thinking

It is easier for Luke because you can share the strawberries equally into two halves.

It is harder for Eva because you cannot share the strawberries equally into quarters. There will be two left over.

Children may know the correct answer, but may find it challenging to write the reason why. Support them with vocabulary and structuring an answer including examples.

PUPIL PRACTICE BOOK 1C PAGE 58

Power check

Independent thinking

- *What can you do now that you could not do at the start of the unit?*
- *What do you know now that you did not at the start of the unit?*
- *Can you write down what new words you have learned and what they mean?*

Power puzzle

Pair work or small groups

How can children start the puzzle? It is useful if you remind children to carefully count the total number of boxes in each grid and then find half to shade. Observe whether children use their fingers to calculate half or whether they make marks on the grids.

Some children could also shade a quarter using a different colour.

Look at whether the correct number of boxes have been shaded. Children should not be doing the same pattern twice. Children should recognise that each box represents a part of a whole and that shading any boxes within the shape which amount to half of the total will be correct, whether the shaded boxes are next to each other or not.

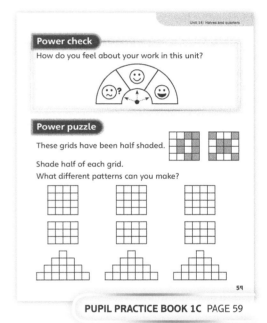

PUPIL PRACTICE BOOK 1C PAGE 59

After the unit ⏸

- Which children need further support with fractions?
- Are all children ready for the next unit?
- Which teaching strategies helped children master this unit?

Strengthen and **Deepen** activities for this unit can be found in the *Power Maths* online subscription.

Unit 15
Position and direction

Don't forget to watch the Unit 15 video!

Mastery Expert tip! "I found that taking children outside to give and follow instructions really helped to secure their understanding of the vocabulary used in this unit."

WHY THIS UNIT IS IMPORTANT

This unit gives a practical application to children's learning from the previous unit on fractions. They will learn to describe rotations as quarter, half, three-quarter and whole turns, and will combine turns with lateral movement to give and follow route instructions. Children will also learn to describe the position of an object in relation to other objects, using the words 'above', 'below', 'left', 'right' and 'between'.

Children will develop these skills further in Year 2, when they will be introduced to the terms 'clockwise' and 'anticlockwise' and will follow more complex routes. The ability to identify fractions of a turn will also provide children with the groundwork for telling the time in Unit 17. Following a sequence of instructions will develop children's procedural fluency, in preparation for future units involving number and, in particular, calculations.

WHERE THIS UNIT FITS

→ Unit 14: Halves and quarters
→ **Unit 15: Position and direction**
→ Unit 16: Numbers to 100

In this unit, children will apply their knowledge of fractions to contextual and practical problems. Being able to identify and describe position and movement will help children to develop their spatial awareness and reasoning. Unit 16 will look at numbers to 100.

Before they start this unit, it is expected that children:
- can give and follow a simple series of instructions with two or three steps
- understand the concept of a whole, halves and quarters, especially in relation to a circle
- understand 'turn' as rotation around a point.

ASSESSING MASTERY

Children who have mastered this unit will be able to describe the direction and fraction of a turn using the words 'left' and 'right', and 'quarter', 'half', 'three-quarters' and 'whole'. They will be able to identify and describe a route to a desired goal, and to give and follow a series of instructions. They will also be able to describe the position of an object in relation to one or more other objects using the words 'left', 'right', 'above', 'below' and 'between'.

COMMON MISCONCEPTIONS	STRENGTHENING UNDERSTANDING	GOING DEEPER
Children may confuse left and right when describing turns, particularly if the object is oriented differently from them.	Give children objects they can rotate. Ask them to turn their object left and right, with the object in different orientations. You could label the sides of the object 'left' and 'right' to support them.	Ask children to draw a treasure map on a grid or create one in the playground, with objects to avoid. Challenge them to write a series of instructions to reach the treasure for their partner to follow.
Children may not understand quarter and half turns and the relationship between them.	Give children paper circles folded into quarters. Children could colour a quarter, half, three-quarters and whole turns in both directions, and use the results as a reference throughout the unit.	

Unit 15: Position and direction

WAYS OF WORKING

Draw children's attention to the vocabulary on the page. Discuss what they think the words mean in the context of position and direction. Can children use the vocabulary to describe the arrows? Can they use the vocabulary to describe the positions of the animals?

STRUCTURES AND REPRESENTATIONS

Although there are no set mathematical structures and representations for this unit, curved arrows can be used to illustrate the direction and fraction of a turn.

KEY LANGUAGE

There is some key language that children will need to know as part of the learning in this unit:

→ turn, position, direction

→ half turn, quarter turn, three-quarter turn, whole turn

→ left, right, in between

→ forwards, backwards

→ above, below

→ top, middle, bottom

→ up, down

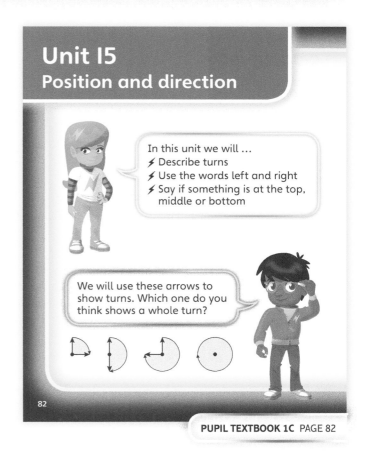

PUPIL TEXTBOOK 1C PAGE 82

PUPIL TEXTBOOK 1C PAGE 83

Describing turns

Learning focus

In this lesson, children will learn to describe turns as quarter, half, three-quarter or whole turns.

Small steps

→ Previous step: Solving word problems – halves and quarters
→ **This step: Describing turns**
→ Next step: Describing positions (1)

NATIONAL CURRICULUM LINKS

Year 1 Geometry – Position and Direction

Describe position, direction and movement, including whole, half, quarter and three-quarter turns.

ASSESSING MASTERY

Children can describe the turn of an object using the words 'quarter', 'half', 'three-quarter' and 'whole'. Children can recognise that a half turn will result in facing the same way regardless of which direction they turn in and that a quarter turn in one direction will give the same result as a three-quarter turn in the opposite direction.

COMMON MISCONCEPTIONS

Children may not have secure understanding of quarters and halves. Ask children to stand up and do a quarter turn or a turn towards the window. Ask:

• *How much have you turned? How many quarters in a half? How many quarters in a whole?*

STRENGTHENING UNDERSTANDING

Ask children to carry out the rotations in the problems practically, either using objects or turning themselves, so that they develop a conceptual understanding of quarter and half turns. Provide children with paper circles and ask them to fold them into half and half again. They can colour in a quarter, half and three-quarters and keep the result as a reference for use throughout the lesson.

GOING DEEPER

Challenge children to complete a series of turns. Ask them to rotate and stop to face different directions and then record the turns they completed. Extend by going beyond a whole turn or changing which direction they turn in within a series of turns.

KEY LANGUAGE

In lesson: half turn, facing, turn, quarter turn, three-quarter turn, position, whole turn

Other language to be used by the teacher: direction

RESOURCES

Optional: Paper circles, colouring pencils, objects to rotate

 In the eTextbook of this lesson, you will find interactive links to a selection of teaching tools.

Before you teach

• Are children secure with halves and quarters?
• What practical opportunities will you provide within the lesson?
• Would children benefit from having the key vocabulary displayed?

Discover

WAYS OF WORKING Pair work

ASK

- Question ❶ a): *Can you draw which way David turned? Compare with your friends. What do you notice?*
- Question ❶ b): *What turn would David have to do to get back to facing the rock?*

IN FOCUS Question ❶ b) requires children to apply what they have learned in the previous unit on fractions to describing turns. There are two possible answers depending on which direction David turns.

ANSWERS

Question ❶ a): David is facing the 🌳.

Question ❶ b): David could have made either a quarter turn or a three-quarter turn depending on which direction he turned.

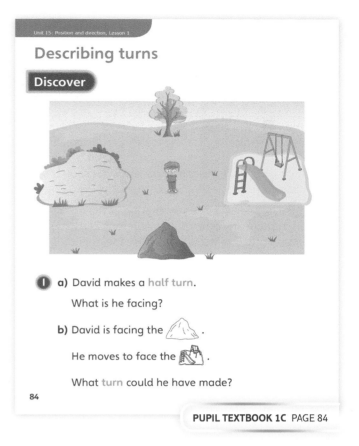

Describing turns

Discover

❶ a) David makes a **half turn**.

What is he facing?

b) David is facing the 🗻.

He moves to face the 🛝.

What **turn** could he have made?

84

PUPIL TEXTBOOK 1C PAGE 84

Share

WAYS OF WORKING Whole class teacher led

ASK

- *How could David get from facing the rock to facing the pond?*
- *If David is facing the pond, what could he be facing if he made a quarter or three-quarter turn?*

IN FOCUS Question ❶ a) illustrates that the end result of a half turn is the same regardless of which direction David turns. Discuss whether or not we need to state the direction of the turn for half turns. Question ❶ b) illustrates that with quarter and three-quarter turns, knowing the direction of the turn is vital in order to determine the end position. This is in contrast to half turns.

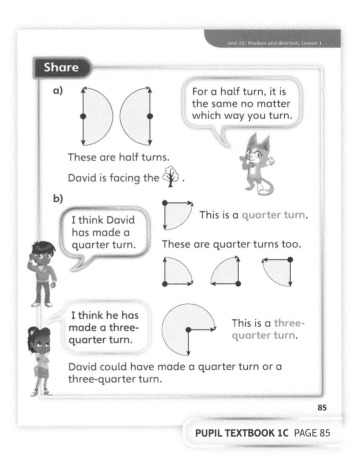

Share

a)

These are half turns.

David is facing the 🌳.

For a half turn, it is the same no matter which way you turn.

b)

I think David has made a quarter turn.

This is a **quarter turn**.

These are quarter turns too.

I think he has made a three-quarter turn.

This is a **three-quarter turn**.

David could have made a quarter turn or a three-quarter turn.

85

PUPIL TEXTBOOK 1C PAGE 85

Think together

Unit 15: Position and direction, Lesson 1

Think together

WAYS OF WORKING Whole class teacher led (I do, We do, You do)

ASK

· Question **2** : *What turn would the ladybird have to make for each of the pictures? Is there more than one possible answer?*

· Question **3** : *Do you need to know which direction Laura turned?*

IN FOCUS Question **2** looks at rotation of the object in isolation, without any other points of reference. Some children may find it difficult to visualise the orientation of the ladybird after its rotation.

STRENGTHEN For question **2** , provide children with a toy ladybird to rotate as described. This will help them to visualise the end position. For question **3** , provide children with a paper circle folded in half. They can then draw Laura in the middle and the house at one end of the crease. This will help them determine the position of the tree.

DEEPEN Have four children sitting around a table so that each child is sitting in one of the four quadrants. Place a programmable toy in the centre facing one child. This child then says the name of one of the other children and describes the turn that the toy has to make in order to face him or her. The first child then inputs the instructions to make the toy face the named child. It is then the turn of the child that the toy is now facing. If no programmable toy is available, children can manually turn an item such as a toy car.

ASSESSMENT CHECKPOINT Question **2** will determine if children understand the vocabulary of quarter turn and if they take into account the direction of the turn (shown by the arrow). Question **3** will determine if children understand the concept of a half turn and understand that knowing the direction of the turn does not affect the end position.

ANSWERS

Question **1** : David is facing the 🛝 .

Question **2** : Option A shows the new position of the 🐞 .

Question **3** : The 🌳 is in the top square.

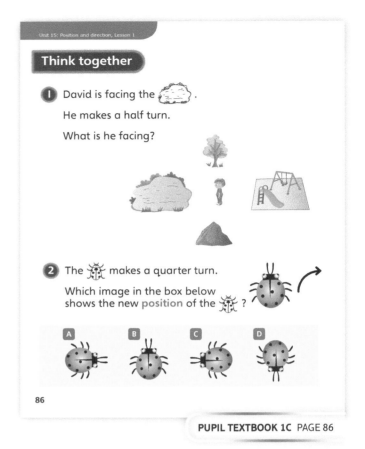

1 David is facing the ☁ .

He makes a half turn.

What is he facing?

2 The 🐞 makes a quarter turn.

Which image in the box below shows the new **position** of the 🐞 ?

A   B   C   D

86

PUPIL TEXTBOOK 1C PAGE 86

3

Laura is facing the 🏠 .

She makes a half turn.

She is facing the 🌳 .

Which box is the 🌳 in?

What happens if Laura makes a **whole turn**? Where is she facing?

→ Practice book 1C p60

87

PUPIL TEXTBOOK 1C PAGE 87

Practice

IN FOCUS Question **3** requires children to know that a half is equivalent to two quarters. Children need to apply their learning from the previous unit in order to answer the question and to justify their decision.

STRENGTHEN Provide children with objects so they can physically carry out the turns described in the problems. If they are struggling to understand the vocabulary, provide them with labelled visual images of quarters and halves such as circles with the different fractions shaded in.

DEEPEN Extend question **4** by asking children to write a series of instructions with two or more steps. Their partner then needs to work out the direction they will be facing at the end. They could begin by physically following the instructions on a compass drawn on the playground and then move on to using the compass drawn in question **4** .

ASSESSMENT CHECKPOINT Use question **2** to assess whether children can identify what turn has been made by looking at the start and end position. Use question **4** to assess whether children can follow instructions for rotation from different starting points.

ANSWERS Answers for the **Practice** part of the lesson appear in the separate **Practice and Reflect answer guide**.

Reflect

IN FOCUS The **Reflect** part of the lesson requires children to illustrate a chosen turn. In order to do this, they need to be able to visualise it for themselves, which requires a secure understanding. To describe it to a partner, children need to be able to use the mathematical vocabulary accurately.

ASSESSMENT CHECKPOINT Assess whether children have a secure understanding of quarter, half, three-quarter and whole turns and whether they can use the correct vocabulary.

ANSWERS Answers for the **Reflect** part of the lesson appear in the separate **Practice and Reflect answer guide**.

After the lesson ⏸

- Are children secure with quarter, half, three-quarter and whole turns?
- Can children use the correct vocabulary to describe a turn?

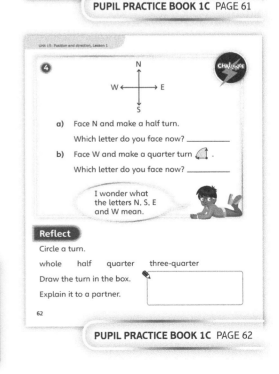

PUPIL PRACTICE BOOK 1C PAGE 60

PUPIL PRACTICE BOOK 1C PAGE 61

PUPIL PRACTICE BOOK 1C PAGE 62

Describing positions ❶

Learning focus

In this lesson, children will describe direction and lateral movement. They will learn how to follow and give instructions in order to reach a given goal.

Small steps

→ Previous step: Describing turns
→ **This step: Describing positions (1)**
→ Next step: Describing positions (2)

NATIONAL CURRICULUM LINKS

Year 1 Geometry – Position and Direction

Describe position, direction and movement, including whole, half, quarter and three-quarter turns.

Year 1 Non-statutory guidance

Pupils use the language of position, direction and motion, including: left and right, top, middle and bottom, on top of, in front of, above, between, around, near, close and far, up and down, forwards and backwards, inside and outside.

ASSESSING MASTERY

Children can use the correct vocabulary associated with rotation and lateral movement in order to describe a route. Children can follow instructions to get to a given goal and identify left and right turns regardless of the orientation of the object.

COMMON MISCONCEPTIONS

Children may confuse left and right. They may not be able to reliably identify their own left and right or they may struggle to identify an object's left and right when its orientation is different from theirs. Ask:
• *Who can hold up their left* [or right] *hand? Who can point to my left* [or right] *hand?*

STRENGTHENING UNDERSTANDING

Provide practical opportunities for children to carry out the problems. Having objects that children can rotate can help them to identify the direction and fraction of a turn.

GOING DEEPER

Children could apply what they have learned to creating their own problems for each other to solve. For example, they could make up a treasure map with a set of instructions for their partner to follow from the starting point to the treasure.

KEY LANGUAGE

In lesson: left, right, forwards, quarter turn, half turn, three-quarter turn, whole turn

Other language to be used by the teacher: direction, facing, backwards

RESOURCES

Optional: objects for children to physically rotate and move, skipping ropes, PE cones, vocabulary prompts showing key words with pictures to illustrate them, blank 5×5 grids

 In the eTextbook of this lesson, you will find interactive links to a selection of teaching tools.

Before you teach ❚❚

• Are children secure describing the fraction of a turn?
• How will you support children who struggle to identify left and right?

Discover

Pair work

ASK

- *In which direction does Anna walk?*
- *How did you work out which direction Anna had to turn?*

IN FOCUS Question ❶ b) requires children to begin to link together instructions in order to get to a desired goal. They also need to determine the direction of the turns using the words 'left' and 'right'. When Anna gets to the final cone, she is no longer facing the same way as the viewer. Some children may, therefore, struggle to determine which direction she has to turn.

ANSWERS

Question ❶ a): Anna will make a quarter turn right.

Question ❶ b): Walk forwards. Make a quarter turn left. Walk forwards.

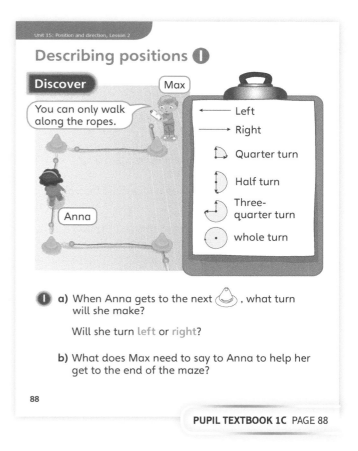

PUPIL TEXTBOOK 1C PAGE 88

Share

WAYS OF WORKING Whole class teacher led

ASK

- *From the last cone, what movements would Anna need to make to complete a square?*
- *What movements has Anna already made?*
- *How can Anna go back the way she came?*

IN FOCUS The **Pupil Textbook** includes pictures of a left turn and a right turn to help children answer question ❶ a). This is an opportunity to get children to carry out left and right turns in order to secure their understanding. They could also practise determining their partner's direction of turn when facing them, as they then need to consider it from their partner's perspective as opposed to their own.

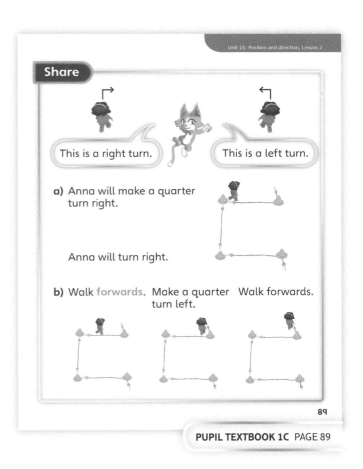

PUPIL TEXTBOOK 1C PAGE 89

Think together

WAYS OF WORKING Whole class teacher led (I do, We do, You do)

ASK

- Question **1** : *Which of the movements do you know Anna definitely did not start with?*
- Question **2** : *Is there more than one possible answer for any of the instructions?*
- Question **3** : *How can you keep track of which way you are facing?*

IN FOCUS Question **3** requires children to follow a series of instructions. They need to keep track of which direction they are facing after the turn in order to complete the route. Some children may interpret moving forwards as moving up the grid regardless of their current orientation.

STRENGTHEN For question **2** , you could set up a course that replicates Anna's. Children can then carry out Anna's movements before completing the instructions. They could label their left and right hands as prompts.

DEEPEN Challenge children to create their own route using the map in question **3** . They should visit two or more of the items. They could then ask a partner to test out their instructions.

ASSESSMENT CHECKPOINT Use question **2** to assess whether children can apply the correct vocabulary. Can they determine the correct direction of the turn after Anna's orientation changes?

Question **3** will determine whether children can follow a series of instructions in order to reach a desired goal. It will also highlight which children recognise left and right.

ANSWERS

Question **1** : Walk 4 steps forwards.
Make a quarter turn left.
Walk 3 steps forwards.

Question **2** : First walk 5 steps forwards.
Then make a quarter turn left
(or three-quarter turn right).
Next walk 3 steps forwards.
After that make a quarter turn left
(or three-quarter turn right).
Finally walk 8 steps forwards.

Question **3** : You end up at ▯▯ .

Think together

1 Describe Anna's route. Put the sentences in the correct order using I, 2 and 3.

Finish

Walk 3 steps forwards. ☐

Make a quarter turn left. ☐

Walk 4 steps forwards. ☐

Start

2 Complete the sentences to describe Anna's route.

Finish   Start

First walk ☐ steps _____ .

Then make a _____ turn _____ .

Next walk ☐ steps _____ .

After that make a _____ turn _____ .

Finally walk ☐ steps _____ .

forwards	left	right
quarter turn	half turn	three-quarter turn

90

PUPIL TEXTBOOK 1C PAGE 90

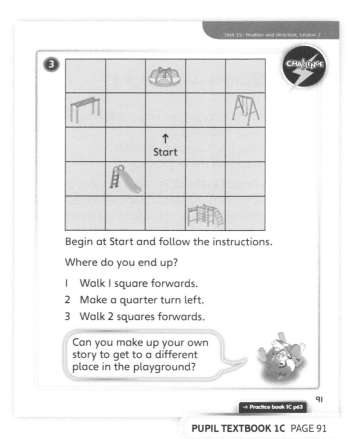

3

Begin at Start and follow the instructions.

Where do you end up?

I   Walk I square forwards.

2   Make a quarter turn left.

3   Walk 2 squares forwards.

Can you make up your own story to get to a different place in the playground?

91

→ Practice book 1C p63

PUPIL TEXTBOOK 1C PAGE 91

Practice

WAYS OF WORKING Pair work

IN FOCUS Question **4** requires children to give instructions to reach a desired goal. Note that the duck has to go past a junction in order to make the correct turn. Some children may think that once they reach a junction, an action such as a turn has to take place, and they will therefore turn towards the tree. Encourage children to look carefully at the picture and plan the route before answering the question.

STRENGTHEN Have vocabulary prompts showing the key words, with pictures to illustrate them, for children to refer to. Some children may still need practical opportunities to secure their understanding of rotation and linear movement. They could go outside on the playground and give each other simple instructions to follow.

DEEPEN Give children a blank 5×5 grid each. Challenge them to create a treasure map with a start point and an X for the end point, and obstacles to avoid (water, pirates, quicksand and so on). Then ask them to plan a route to get to the treasure safely.

ASSESSMENT CHECKPOINT Use question **3** to assess whether children can select and put instructions in order to get to a desired goal. Use question **4** to assess whether they can select the appropriate vocabulary to complete instructions.

Question **5** will determine whether children can identify the direction and fraction of a turn.

ANSWERS Answers for the **Practice** part of the lesson appear in the separate **Practice and Reflect answer guide**.

Reflect

WAYS OF WORKING Whole class

IN FOCUS The **Reflect** part of the lesson is designed to help secure children's understanding of the direction and fraction of turns. It draws on their learning from the previous unit on fractions as well as Lesson 1 of this unit, while incorporating their understanding of left and right.

ASSESSMENT CHECKPOINT This activity will determine whether children can recognise left and right as well as quarter, half and three-quarter turns.

ANSWERS Answers for the **Reflect** part of the lesson appear in the separate **Practice and Reflect answer guide**.

After the lesson

- Can you create a PE activity in which children can apply their learning from this lesson?
- How many children can confidently and correctly apply the vocabulary used in this lesson?
- Were children able to adjust their perception of left and right as the orientation of the object they were observing changed?

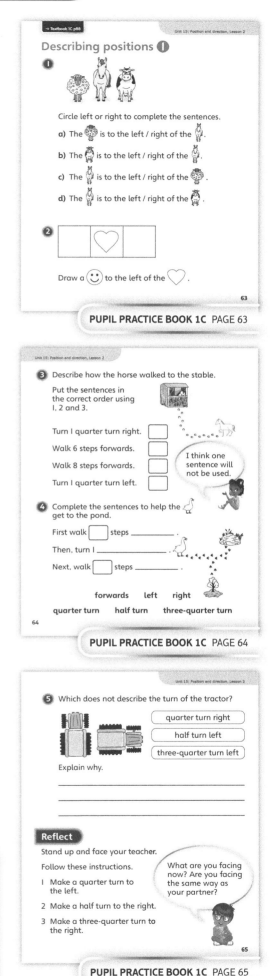

PUPIL PRACTICE BOOK 1C PAGE 63

PUPIL PRACTICE BOOK 1C PAGE 64

PUPIL PRACTICE BOOK 1C PAGE 65

Describing positions ❷

Learning focus

In this lesson, children will describe the position of an object based on its relation to other objects. They will apply their knowledge of left and right from the previous lesson.

Small steps

→ Previous step: Describing positions (1)
→ **This step: Describing positions (2)**
→ Next step: Counting to 100

NATIONAL CURRICULUM LINKS

Year 1 Geometry – Position and Direction

Describe position, direction and movement, including whole, half, quarter and three-quarter turns.

Year 1 Non-statutory guidance

Pupils use the language of position, direction and motion, including: left and right, top, middle and bottom, on top of, in front of, above, between, around, near, close and far, up and down, forwards and backwards, inside and outside.

ASSESSING MASTERY

Children can describe the position of one object in relation to other objects using the words 'left', 'right', 'above' and 'below'. They can adapt their description of position when relating it to a different object.

COMMON MISCONCEPTIONS

Children may confuse above and below. Ask:
• *Can you place your pencil below or above your book? What is above or below your desk?*

Children may also still confuse left and right. Ask:
• *Who is sitting to the left of you? Who is sitting to the right of you? Is the window to the left or right of you?*

STRENGTHENING UNDERSTANDING

Give children construction equipment and ask them to follow instructions such as: *Put the blue cube above the red cube. Place the green cube to the right of the yellow cube.*

GOING DEEPER

Give pairs of children multilink cubes. Ask one child in each pair to make a simple design, without showing it to their partner. Using the key vocabulary, they should then give instructions to their partner; their partner should attempt to make the design without showing it to the first child. When they have finished, children can compare their designs to see if they match.

KEY LANGUAGE

In lesson: above, position, top, middle, bottom, below, up, down, in between

Other language to be used by the teacher: left, right

RESOURCES

Optional: construction equipment, multilink cubes, vocabulary prompts showing key words with pictures to illustrate them, blank 2×3 grids, cubes or counters

 In the eTextbook of this lesson, you will find interactive links to a selection of teaching tools.

Before you teach

• Are children secure identifying left and right?
• Do children need practice in identifying position before the lesson?

Discover

WAYS OF WORKING Pair work

ASK

- *Did you come up with a different answer from your partner? Who is correct?*
- Question ❶ b): *How many ways can you think of to describe the position of the teddy bear?*

IN FOCUS Question ❶ b) requires children to describe the position of the teddy bear. There are a number of ways of doing this: establish that the description changes depending on what we choose to relate the position of the teddy bear to.

ANSWERS

Question ❶ a): The 📚 are above the 🦕.

Question ❶ b): The 🧸 is on the bottom shelf.

The 🧸 is below the 🎯.

The 🧸 is to the right of the 🤖.

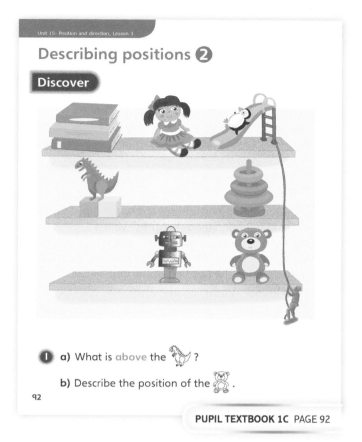

Describing positions ❷

Discover

❶ a) What is above the 🦕?

b) Describe the position of the 🧸.

92

PUPIL TEXTBOOK 1C PAGE 92

Share

WAYS OF WORKING Whole class teacher led

ASK

- Question ❶ b): *Is the teddy bear below the slide?*
- *How would you describe the position of the blocks?*
- *Can you describe the position of the rings in relation to two different objects?*

IN FOCUS Question ❶ b) highlights how the position of the teddy bear can be described in different ways. Discuss with children how the position of other objects can also be described in different ways. Emphasise that, as the point of reference changes, the description of the position also changes.

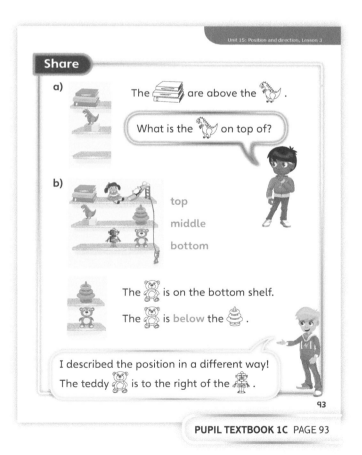

Share

a) The 📚 are above the 🦕.

What is the 🦕 on top of?

b) top
middle
bottom

The 🧸 is on the bottom shelf.

The 🧸 is below the 🎯.

I described the position in a different way!
The teddy 🧸 is to the right of the 🤖.

93

PUPIL TEXTBOOK 1C PAGE 93

Think together

Whole class teacher led (I do, We do, You do)

ASK

- *What different words can you think of to describe position?*
- *What objects can you describe the position of by looking at the rings?*
- *Question ❸ : How many different ways can you think of to describe the position of the doll?*

IN FOCUS Question ❷ introduces the words 'up' and 'down'. Children need to understand that these words are being used to describe movement, not position. Question ❸ introduces the phrase 'in between', prompting children to describe the position of the doll in relation to two items at once.

STRENGTHEN Take three different coloured cubes or counters and arrange them in different ways, each time asking children to describe the position of a particular colour. Give children construction equipment or multilink cubes so they can practically explore position for themselves. Have vocabulary prompts showing the key words, with pictures to illustrate them, for children to refer to.

DEEPEN Ask children to explore which objects they can and cannot relate to the position of the doll in question ❸ , in order to find as many ways as they can to describe its position. Ask: *How could you describe the position of the doll in relation to the dinosaur or the rings?*

ASSESSMENT CHECKPOINT Use question ❸ to assess how confidently children can describe the position of an object in different ways, including in relation to more than one item.

ANSWERS

Question ❶ : The books are on the top shelf.

Question ❷ : The 🐧 is going down the slide.

The 🐿 is climbing up the rope.

Question ❸ : Both children are correct.

The position of the doll can be described in many different ways, including:

The 👧 is on the top shelf.

The 👧 is to the right of the 📚 .

The 👧 is to the left of the 🛝 .

The 👧 is in between the 📚 and the 🛝 .

Unit 15: Position and direction, Lesson 3

Think together

❶ Look at the 📚 .

Which shelf are they on?

The 📚 are on the _____ shelf.

❷ Complete the sentences.

The 🐧 is going _____ the slide.

The 🐿 is climbing _____ the rope.

up　　down　　**bottom**　　**middle**　　**top**

94

PUPIL TEXTBOOK 1C PAGE 94

❸ Describe the position of the 👧 .　CHALLENGE

The 👧 is on the top shelf.

The 👧 is to the right of the 📚 .

Are the two children correct?

Are there other ways you can describe the position of the doll?

I can write a sentence using in between. The 👧 is in between the 📚 and the 🛝 .

95

→ Practice book 1C p66

PUPIL TEXTBOOK 1C PAGE 95

Practice

Pair work

IN FOCUS Question **3** requires children to think of three ways to describe the position of the socks. They therefore need to consider at least three different points of reference and think carefully about the vocabulary of position.

STRENGTHEN Give each child a blank 2×3 grid and six cubes or counters of different colours. Tell children where to place each cube or counter, giving one instruction at a time. For example: *Place the red cube in the middle of the top row. Now place the green cube to the left of the red cube.* Once all squares are filled, support children in describing the position of different-coloured cubes or counters.

DEEPEN Extend question **3** by asking children to try to use all the words that they know to describe position. Are there any words they cannot use?

Give pairs of children two blank 2×3 grids and six cubes or counters of different colours. Ask one child to place the counters or cubes on their grid, keeping it hidden from their partner. The second child should then ask questions that require only yes or no answers in order to place their counters or cubes in the same positions as the first child's. They can then compare to their grids to see if they match.

ASSESSMENT CHECKPOINT Use question **4** to assess children's understanding of the vocabulary of position. Can they follow descriptions of position to identify specific letters?

ANSWERS Answers for the **Practice** part of the lesson appear in the separate **Practice and Reflect answer guide**.

Reflect

Pair work

IN FOCUS The **Reflect** part of the lesson requires children to think carefully about how best to describe the position of a shape so that their partner can identify it. It highlights the importance of clear descriptions with correct language so another person can follow it. Note that there are two cuboids, meaning that 'below the cuboid' and 'left of the cuboid' could each refer to either of two shapes: children will need to take this into account, for example relating the position of the cone to the rectangle rather than the cuboid, or describing it as 'between one of the cuboids and the rectangle'.

ASSESSMENT CHECKPOINT This activity will determine whether children can correctly use and understand all the vocabulary related to position.

ANSWERS Answers for the **Reflect** part of the lesson appear in the separate **Practice and Reflect answer guide**.

After the lesson ⏸

- Are children secure with left and right, and above and below?
- Were children clear and concise in their descriptions of position?

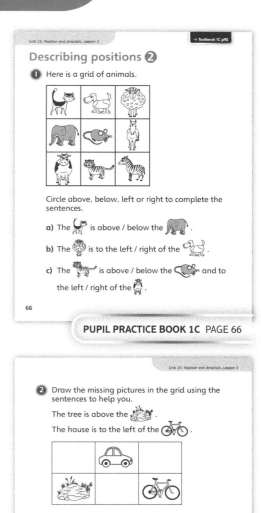

PUPIL PRACTICE BOOK 1C PAGE 66

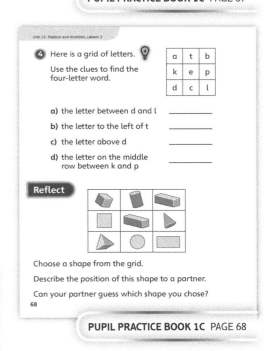

PUPIL PRACTICE BOOK 1C PAGE 67

PUPIL PRACTICE BOOK 1C PAGE 68

End of unit check

> Don't forget the *Power Maths* unit assessment grid on p26.

WAYS OF WORKING Group work – adult led

IN FOCUS Questions ❶ and ❷ will identify whether children understand the vocabulary associated with describing position in relation to other objects.

Questions ❸ and ❹ will identify whether children understand and can apply the vocabulary used to describe the direction and fraction of a turn.

Think!

WAYS OF WORKING Pair work or small groups

IN FOCUS

- This question can be used to assess whether children can identify and describe routes to a specific goal.
- Children should use the words at the bottom of the page in their answers. Ask: *What other words related to position and direction do you need to use?*
- Encourage children to think through or discuss different possible routes before writing their answer in **My journal**. You could challenge them to find the longest or shortest route, or to find all the possible routes. You could ask: *Can the mouse visit every square only once?*

ANSWERS AND COMMENTARY Children who have mastered the concepts in this unit will be able to accurately describe linear and rotational movement, and the position of objects, using the words 'forwards', 'backwards', 'left', 'right', 'quarter', 'half', 'three-quarter', 'whole', 'above', 'below' and 'between'. They will be able to follow a series of descriptions or instructions related to position and direction, and give accurate and concise instructions and descriptions.

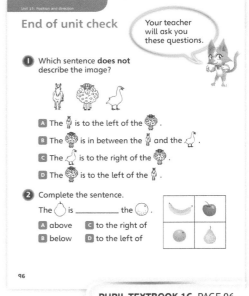

PUPIL TEXTBOOK 1C PAGE 96

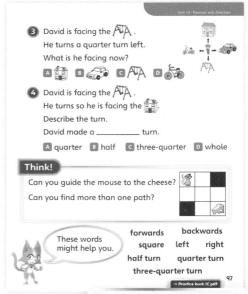

PUPIL TEXTBOOK 1C PAGE 97

Q	A	WRONG ANSWERS AND MISCONCEPTIONS	STRENGTHENING UNDERSTANDING
1	D	A or C suggests that children are not secure with identifying left and right (also question 2 D). B suggests that children have not understood the question.	Give children practical opportunities to practise the key language. For example, ask them to follow instructions such as 'Make a quarter turn to your right' or answer questions such as 'Face the window. What turn have you made?' Similarly, ask children to create a simple design using different coloured multilink cubes by following instructions such as 'Put the red cube to the right of the blue cube' or give them a completed design and ask them to describe the position of different cubes.
2	C	A or B suggests that children do not understand positional language.	
3	B	D suggests that children have confused left and right, perhaps because of David's orientation.	
4	B	Any wrong answer suggests that children are not secure with fractions of turns (also question 3 A, C).	

My journal

WAYS OF WORKING Independent thinking

ANSWERS AND COMMENTARY There are four possible paths:
- Go forwards 1 square; make a quarter turn right; go forwards 2 squares; make a quarter turn left; go forwards 1 square
- Make a quarter turn right; go forwards 1 square; make a quarter turn left; go forwards 2 squares; make a quarter turn right; go forwards 1 square
- Go forwards 1 square; make a quarter turn right; go forwards 1 square; make a quarter turn left; go forwards one square; make a quarter turn right; go forwards 1 square
- Make a quarter turn right; go forwards 1 square; make a quarter turn left; go forwards 1 square; make a quarter turn right; go forwards 1 square; make a quarter turn left; go forwards 1 square

If children are still experiencing difficulties, carry out the problem on a grid drawn on the playground with a child as the mouse. As the child moves towards the cheese, encourage them to describe each movement they make. Have prompts (such as circles shaded to represent different fractions of a turn and pictorial representations of left and right) available if necessary.

Power check

WAYS OF WORKING Independent thinking

ASK
- *How happy do you feel about following or giving instructions for a route?*
- *Can you use the vocabulary you learned in this unit to describe the position of something to a friend?*

Power puzzle

WAYS OF WORKING Pair work or small groups

IN FOCUS Use the **Power puzzle** to see if children have a secure understanding of the vocabulary relating to position. Can they apply this knowledge to solve a problem? Make sure children understand that they need to determine the names of the unlabelled children from the clues given. Carefully read each clue to children, emphasising the key vocabulary describing position. Ask children to work in pairs, and tell them that they must both agree before they label each child: this will encourage children to justify their decisions.

ANSWERS AND COMMENTARY

	Maya	Molly
Anya	Katie	Bob
Hassan	Shaan	

If children are successful in completing the puzzle, this suggests that they have mastery in their understanding of positional language. If children are unsuccessful, then they may still be confusing some of the vocabulary.

After the unit ⏸

- Are children secure in their understanding of the vocabulary relating to position?
- Can you find opportunities to use positional language in everyday situations, such as asking children to find resources or organising and tidying the classroom?

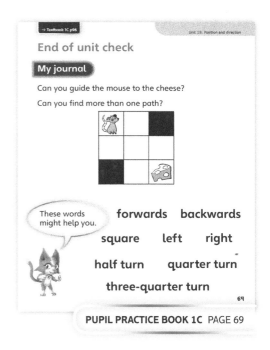

→ Textbook 1C p96

End of unit check

My journal

Can you guide the mouse to the cheese?

Can you find more than one path?

These words might help you. **forwards   backwards**

square   left   right

half turn   quarter turn

three-quarter turn

PUPIL PRACTICE BOOK 1C PAGE 69

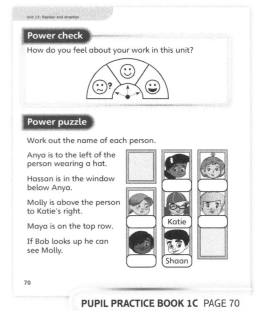

Unit 15: Position and direction

Power check

How do you feel about your work in this unit?

Power puzzle

Work out the name of each person.

Anya is to the left of the person wearing a hat.

Hassan is in the window below Anya.

Molly is above the person to Katie's right.

Maya is on the top row.

If Bob looks up he can see Molly.

Katie

Shaan

PUPIL PRACTICE BOOK 1C PAGE 70

Strengthen and **Deepen** activities for this unit can be found in the *Power Maths* online subscription.

Unit 16
Numbers to 100

Don't forget to watch the Unit 16 video!

Mastery Expert tip! "When teaching this unit, I made sure that when children met a more abstract representation, like the part-whole model or the bar model, I always had a matching concrete representation to support it. It really helped secure children's understanding of what they were learning."

WHY THIS UNIT IS IMPORTANT

In this unit, children will develop their understanding of, and ability to manipulate, numbers to 100. They will investigate patterns in 2-digit numbers, specifically 1 more and 1 less, and 10 more and 10 less, before moving on to partition numbers and identify the place value of digits within a number.

Children will then use their knowledge and understanding of place value to first compare two 2-digit numbers, and then three or more numbers up to 100.

Finally, children will explore number bonds to 100. Children will link number bonds to 100 with number bonds to 10, and this will develop a strong conceptual understanding of number bonds to 100 that children will take into their future mathematics. A secure understanding of 2-digit numbers will support children's understanding of, and ability to work with, numbers and the number system.

WHERE THIS UNIT FITS

→ Unit 15: Position and direction
→ **Unit 16: Numbers to 100**
→ Unit 17: Time

This unit builds on children's previous number work, in particular Unit 9: Numbers to 50 and Unit 3: Addition and subtraction within 10 (1), in which they explored number bonds to 10. Unit 16 focuses on the structure of 2-digit numbers and number bonds to 100. Unit 17 will focus on time.

Before they start this unit, it is expected that children:
• recognise and can use ten frames
• recognise and can use different representations of 10 and 1
• can count forwards and backwards in 10s and 1s from 0.

ASSESSING MASTERY

Children who have mastered this unit will be able to confidently count forwards and backwards, to and from 100. They will be able to confidently discuss the patterns found when counting in 10s and 1s, and show them using multiple representations. Children will be able to partition 2-digit numbers using concrete resources, the part-whole model and the place value grid. They will show understanding of the place value of each digit in a number and use this to fluently compare and order numbers. Finally, children will be able to find and use number bonds to 100, using their knowledge of number bonds to 10 to help them.

COMMON MISCONCEPTIONS	STRENGTHENING UNDERSTANDING	GOING DEEPER
Children may write the full tens number in a place value grid, rather than the number of tens.	Encourage children to describe the number 40, for example, as '4 tens' as well as saying '40'. They could play snap using cards showing both ways of describing each multiple of 10.	Give children riddles that require an understanding of place value. For example: *My number has 6 tens and 7 ones. What could my number be?*
Children may forget to align the start of their concrete or pictorial representations of numbers when comparing them, thereby skewing the comparison.	Offer children something that provides a clear starting point for their comparisons, such as the edge of a page or a blank number line.	

WAYS OF WORKING

Use these pages to introduce the unit focus to children. You can use the characters to explore different ways of working too.

STRUCTURES AND REPRESENTATIONS

Ten frame: This model will help children visualise 10. It can be used to help them count in 10s and to recall number bonds to 10.

Number line: A number line helps children represent the order of numbers. It can be used to help children count on and back from a given starting point and help them identify patterns within the count.

Number track: Like a number line, a number track helps children represent the order of numbers. A number track can support children in counting and in comparing and ordering numbers.

100 square: This model will help children visualise 100, and see patterns such as those created when counting one more or one less, or ten more or ten less.

Place value grid: The place value grid helps children to record and describe how a number is 'made'. This representation can empower children to more efficiently describe, compare and order numbers.

Part-whole model: This model helps children understand that two or more parts combine to make a whole. It also helps to strengthen children's understanding of number bonds.

Bead string: The bead string offers children the opportunity to manipulate different numbers. In this unit, it is used to represent numbers up to 100 and to show different ways in which 100 can be partitioned.

Bar model: The bar model enables children to represent a problem more easily. In the context of this unit, it is used to show number bonds to 100.

KEY LANGUAGE

There is some key language that children will need to know as part of the learning in this unit:

→ 100 square, number square

→ place value grid

→ pattern, same, different

→ less than, fewer, smaller, less, (<)

→ greater than, larger, bigger, more, (>)

→ equal to, (=)

→ greatest, biggest

→ fewest, smallest

→ tens, ones, place value, partition

→ how many?, count

→ number bonds

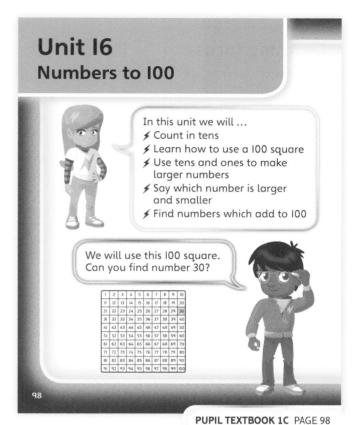

PUPIL TEXTBOOK 1C PAGE 98

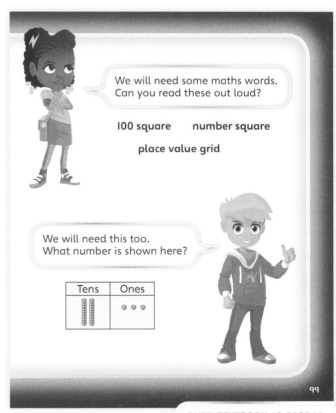

PUPIL TEXTBOOK 1C PAGE 99

Counting to 100

Learning focus

In this lesson, children will develop their ability to count to numbers up to 100 by counting 10s and 1s using multiple representations.

Small steps

→ Previous step: Describing positions (2)
→ **This step: Counting to 100**
→ Next step: Exploring number patterns

NATIONAL CURRICULUM LINKS

Year 1 Number – Number and Place Value

- Count, read and write numbers to 100 in numerals; count in multiples of 2s, 5s and 10s.
- Identify and represent numbers using objects and pictorial representations including the number line, and use the language of: equal to, more than, less than (fewer), most, least.
- Count to and across 100, forwards and backwards, beginning with 0 or 1, or from any given number.

ASSESSING MASTERY

Children can count reliably to 100, forwards and backwards. Children can identify missing numbers in a sequence and can continue a count from any 1- or 2-digit number. Children can use multiple representations to support their counting and reasoning.

COMMON MISCONCEPTIONS

Children may miscount when counting the next ten (for example, saying 78, 79, 70-10 (seventy-ten)). If children are making this mistake, provide a number line or number track and count with them. When you reach the potential next ten, ask:
- *Can you read that number? How is it different from the numbers that came before it?*

Children may miscount when counting through a lot of numbers. Encourage children to count in 10s. Ask:
- *Can you think of a quicker, more efficient, way to count?*

STRENGTHENING UNDERSTANDING

Mimic the scenario in the **Discover** section. Children could go outside and litter pick for the school or community and deliver their pickings when they have 10. Alternatively, children could be sent on a nature hunt and asked to find 10 leaves each. Ask: *How many collections of 10 do we have? Can we count the leaves in 10s? How many would we have if you found 4 more leaves?*

GOING DEEPER

Children may be able to count up in 10s from 0, and recognise the pattern associated with this skill. Deepen their thinking by asking children if they can count in 10s from a number other than 0. Ask: *Can you count from 13 to 53? Do you notice any patterns when you count in 10s?*

KEY LANGUAGE

In lesson: count, how many (more)?, tens, all number names from 0–100

Other language to be used by the teacher: ones

STRUCTURES AND REPRESENTATIONS

Ten frame, number line, number track

RESOURCES

Mandatory: counters

Optional: large printed ten frames, countable objects such as buttons

 In the eTextbook of this lesson, you will find interactive links to a selection of teaching tools.

Before you teach ⏸

- Are children confident grouping 10 objects?
- What real-life contexts can you use to enhance the learning in this lesson?

Discover

Pair work

ASK

- *How many pieces of litter can you see on the ground?*
- *Can Gaby deliver her litter now? How much more should she pick up? Is there enough?*

IN FOCUS Use question ❶ a) to discuss children's counting methods. Focus on efficient methods such as counting up in 10s. Use the park manager's instruction as a way in to discussing this point.

ANSWERS

Question ❶ a): Children should have counted out 52 counters. Look for a clear explanation of how children counted.

Question ❶ b): Gaby needs to collect 8 more pieces of litter.

Share

Whole class teacher led

ASK

- Question ❶ a): *Why do you think Astrid keeps losing count?*
- Question ❶ a): *Is Flo's idea a good one?*
- Question ❶ b): *How can you prove how many more pieces of litter Gaby needs to pick up? Could you prove it another way?*
- *At what point did you need to begin counting in 1s?*

IN FOCUS Use the ten frames and number line in question ❶ a) to reinforce the idea of counting in 10s. Agree that it helps us quickly proceed through a counting sequence, and reduces the risk of mistakes. Reinforce the correct names of the tens numbers.

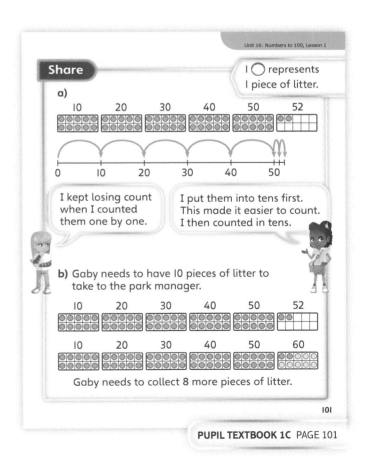

129

Think together

Whole class teacher led (I do, We do, You do)

ASK

- Question **1** : *How could you represent the number?*
- Question **1** : *What will you show on the number line?*
- Question **2** : *How many flowers are in each bunch? How can you use that to help you count?*
- Question **2** : *What do you need to do with the single flowers?*

IN FOCUS Questions **1** and **2** encourage children to recognise that counting in 10s first is an efficient method of counting a large number of items. Question **2** requires children to copy and label the number line in order to reach the answer.

STRENGTHEN If children find counting the flowers tricky, provide them with large printed ten frames so they can create the number themselves. Ask: *How many ten frames do you think you will need? How will you show the last flowers that are not in a bunch of 10?*

DEEPEN When children are working on question **3**, encourage them to explain their reasoning and give proof to demonstrate their understanding. Ask: *How can you show that there is a mistake? What would the picture look like if the first boy was correct?*

ASSESSMENT CHECKPOINT Assess whether children can recognise different representations of 2-digit numbers. They should recognise that counting in 10s and then 1s is more efficient than just counting in 1s, and should demonstrate this skill in their own counting.

ANSWERS

Question **1** : There are 36 🍄.

Question **2** : There are 78 🌾.

Question **3** a): There are 76 sweets, not 67.

Question **3** b): 52 is missing from the number track.

Question **3** c): The second 65 on the number line should be 69.

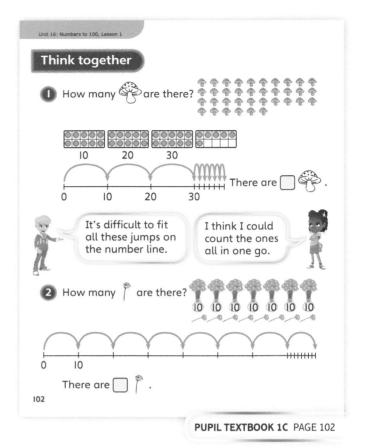

PUPIL TEXTBOOK 1C PAGE 102

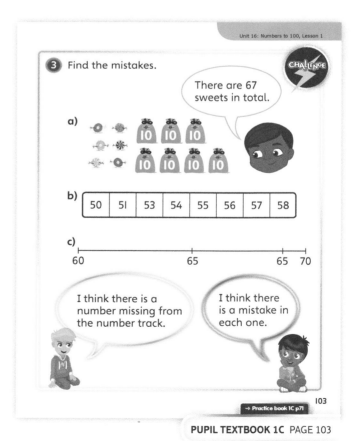

PUPIL TEXTBOOK 1C PAGE 103

Practice

WAYS OF WORKING Independent thinking

IN FOCUS Question **1** provides a good opportunity for children to use concrete resources to independently group objects into 10s to help them count. Give children 36 counters or other countable objects each to manipulate, explaining that these represent the buttons on the page.

Question **4** develops children's ability to use their counting skills to count forwards and backwards.

STRENGTHEN Encourage children to recognise that they could count the counters in question **3** a) more efficiently in 10s, rather than counting them individually. Ask: *What do the frames represent? Could you use the ten frames to help you count quickly?* For question **3** b), ask: *Can you count in 10s this time? How could you change the counters so you can count them more easily?*

DEEPEN For question **5** , use Ash's comment to discuss whether there is more than one way of approaching the puzzle. Ask: *What do you have to do to complete a dot-to-dot? Are there two ways of solving this? Can you count in 10s here?*

ASSESSMENT CHECKPOINT Assess whether children are counting forwards and backwards with confidence. Use questions **1** to **3** to check they understand the benefit of counting in 10s and then 1s. Can they explain why this is more efficient than counting in 1s?

ANSWERS Answers for the **Practice** part of the lesson appear in the separate **Practice and Reflect answer guide**.

PUPIL PRACTICE BOOK 1C PAGE 71

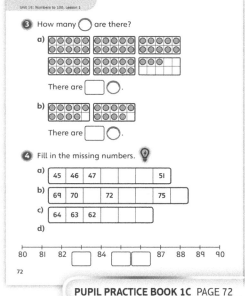

PUPIL PRACTICE BOOK 1C PAGE 72

Reflect

WAYS OF WORKING Pair work

IN FOCUS The **Reflect** part of the lesson requires children to count from 34 to 62. Discuss with children whether there is a quick way of doing this. Ask: *Where should you begin counting? What should you count first? When you get to the next ten, could you make the rest of your counting quicker? What should you count in when you get to 60?*

ASSESSMENT CHECKPOINT Children should be able to recognise when they need to count in 1s and when it is more efficient to count in 10s. This should also be the case when counting backwards.

ANSWERS Answers for the **Reflect** part of the lesson appear in the separate **Practice and Reflect answer guide**.

After the lesson ⏸

- Were children more confident at counting forwards or backwards?
- Could children confidently explain why counting in 10s is more efficient?

PUPIL PRACTICE BOOK 1C PAGE 73

Exploring number patterns

Learning focus

In this lesson, children will investigate the patterns created by counting 1 more, 1 less or 10 more, 10 less. They will use a 100 square to help them investigate these patterns.

Small steps

→ Previous step: Counting to 100
→ **This step: Exploring number patterns**
→ Next step: Partitioning numbers (1)

NATIONAL CURRICULUM LINKS

Year 1 Number – Number and Place Value

• Count, read and write numbers to 100 in numerals; count in multiples of 2s, 5s and 10s.
• Given a number, identify one more and one less.

ASSESSING MASTERY

Children can use a 100 square to spot patterns. They can recognise and explain the patterns that are created when counting 1 more or 1 less and 10 more or 10 less, and can relate these patterns to the rows and columns on the 100 square.

COMMON MISCONCEPTIONS

When using the 100 square, children may get stuck when they reach the end of a row, not knowing where to go next. Ask:
• *What number do you think comes next? Can you see that anywhere on the 100 square?*

It may help to have a number track or number line available, matching the numbers children are counting, to support their recognition of what number comes next.

STRENGTHENING UNDERSTANDING

Introduce children to counting on a 100 square through playing games. For example, they could play Snakes and Ladders using a board arranged like a 100 square (with the lowest number in each row on the left). This will help them begin to recognise how a 100 square works.

Similarly, you could introduce children to the concept of 10 more or 10 less and 1 more or 1 less by playing games using spinners (instead of dice) with those options written on them.

GOING DEEPER

If children are secure with the patterns on a 100 square, challenge them to investigate what patterns they can find if the length of each row is changed. For example, what patterns can they see if each row has only five numbers in it? Ask: *Are the patterns the same in this number grid? How have they changed? Can you find any new patterns?*

KEY LANGUAGE

In lesson: pattern, **100 square**, column, tens, **number square**, more, less

Other language to be used by the teacher: row, ones

STRUCTURES AND REPRESENTATIONS

100 square

RESOURCES

Mandatory: 100 square

Optional: number tracks, number lines

 In the eTextbook of this lesson, you will find interactive links to a selection of teaching tools.

Before you teach ⏸

• Are children confident counting forwards and backwards in 10s?
• How will you use this lesson to develop children's resilience when problem solving?

Discover

ASK

- *What are the children making?*
- *How are the numbers arranged? Can you spot any patterns?*
- *What do you predict the last number will be?*

IN FOCUS Use the picture and question ❶ to encourage children to spot patterns. Do not feel limited to counting on and back in 10s and 1s, as recognising any patterns will help children get ready for spotting the patterns discussed during the lesson.

ANSWERS

Question ❶ a): The children need to put 27 next.

Question ❶ b): 36 will go below 26 on the 100 square.

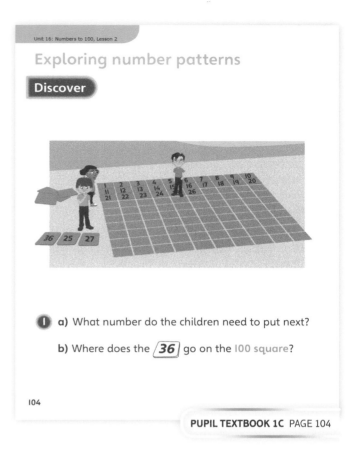

Exploring number patterns

Discover

❶ **a)** What number do the children need to put next?

b) Where does the **36** go on the 100 square?

104

Share

ASK

- Question ❶ a): *Did you find the next number in the same way as Dexter?*
- Question ❶ b): *Can you explain the pattern that Flo is talking about?*
- Question ❶ b): *Can you show whether this pattern applies to all the columns?*

IN FOCUS Use the completed 100 square in ❶ b) to discuss the pattern Flo sees and how it relates to the concept of 10 more and 10 less. Agree that it is helpful for this question because 36 is 10 more than 26. You could also use the completed 100 square to discuss what the pattern of 1 more and 1 less looks like, taking the opportunity to assess whether children know where to go when they reach the end of the row.

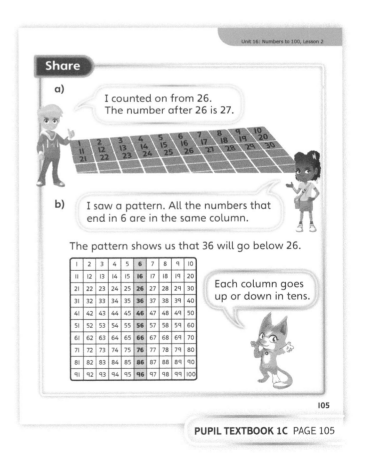

Share

a) I counted on from 26. The number after 26 is 27.

b) I saw a pattern. All the numbers that end in 6 are in the same column.

The pattern shows us that 36 will go below 26.

1	2	3	4	5	6	7	8	9	10
11	12	13	14	15	16	17	18	19	20
21	22	23	24	25	26	27	28	29	30
31	32	33	34	35	36	37	38	39	40
41	42	43	44	45	46	47	48	49	50
51	52	53	54	55	56	57	58	59	60
61	62	63	64	65	66	67	68	69	70
71	72	73	74	75	76	77	78	79	80
81	82	83	84	85	86	87	88	89	90
91	92	93	94	95	96	97	98	99	100

Each column goes up or down in tens.

105

Think together

WAYS OF WORKING Whole class teacher led (I do, We do, You do)

ASK

- *How can you use a 100 square to find 1 more?*
- *Choose a number between 1 and 99. How many more is the number below your number on the 100 square? How many less is the number above your number?*
- *How will you find a number more than one space away?*

IN FOCUS Questions ❶ and ❷ give children the opportunity to practise using the patterns found on the 100 square; question ❷ provides an opportunity to discuss different ways of finding the same numbers.

STRENGTHEN If children are finding question ❷ tricky, consider giving them a complete number square. Ask them to find the part of the 100 square shown in the question. Ask: *How can you use this to help you?*

DEEPEN The questions posed by Dexter and Ash in question ❸ offer a good opportunity for children to demonstrate their reasoning. Challenge children to explain to Ash how to use the 100 square to count on from 8. Can they write a sentence explaining how?

ASSESSMENT CHECKPOINT Use questions ❷ and ❸ to assess whether children can recognise and describe the patterns shown on a 100 square. Children should be able to confidently explain how those patterns can help them count forwards and backwards in 10s and 1s.

ANSWERS

Question ❶ : One more than 43 is 44.

One less than 43 is 42.

Question ❷ : Numbers 45, 56, 65, 75 and 79 are covered.

Question ❸ :

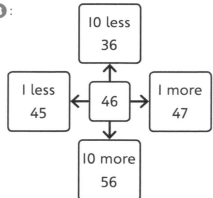

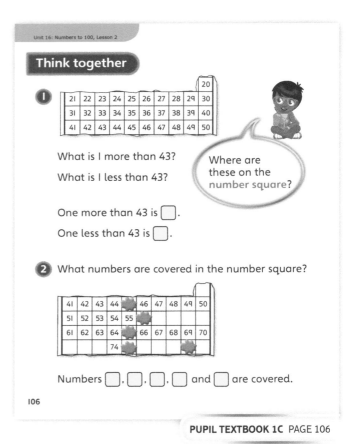

PUPIL TEXTBOOK 1C PAGE 106

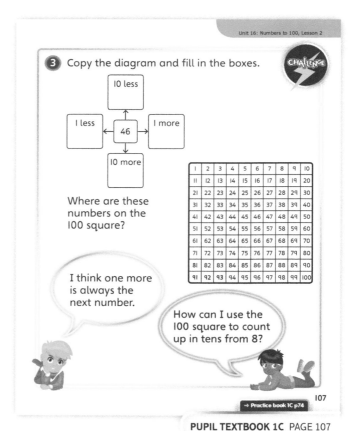

PUPIL TEXTBOOK 1C PAGE 107

Practice

WAYS OF WORKING Independent thinking

IN FOCUS Question ❶ secures children's understanding of the complete 100 square before they go on to solve problems using only parts of it in question ❷ ; encourage children to describe where the parts came from and how they know.

When children are working on question ❺ , ask: *How could you use the 100 square to help you solve this? Can you match this question to a part of the 100 square?*

STRENGTHEN If children are struggling with question ❸ , give them a 100 square they can write on. Ask them to circle the number they are starting at, then ask them what is 1 more or 1 less than that number. Can they follow the pattern and show it on the 100 square?

DEEPEN Question ❹ is a good opportunity to develop children's reasoning. Before children solve the problem, ask them to predict what they will see and to explain their predictions. After they have solved the problem, ask: *Did the solution match your prediction? Can you explain why?*

ASSESSMENT CHECKPOINT Assess children's confidence in using the 100 square. Do children recognise that columns count in 10s and rows count in 1s? Can children explain the patterns and how they can help them to count?

ANSWERS Answers for the **Practice** part of the lesson appear in the separate **Practice and Reflect answer guide**.

Reflect

WAYS OF WORKING Independent thinking

IN FOCUS The **Reflect** part of the lesson offers children an opportunity to demonstrate a secure understanding of the 100 square. Ask questions such as: *What row will the number 15 appear in? How do you know?*

ASSESSMENT CHECKPOINT Assess whether children can visualise the patterns seen on a 100 square. For example, to find 46, do they count along to 6, then down in 10s to 46? Alternatively, do they count down the tens column to 40, then count on in 1s to 46? Whatever method children choose, expect them to explain their reasoning clearly.

ANSWERS Answers for the **Reflect** part of the lesson appear in the separate **Practice and Reflect answer guide**.

After the lesson ⏸

- Were children confident using the 100 square?
- Did children demonstrate any surprising misconceptions?
- Did this lesson sufficiently challenge children's problem-solving ability?

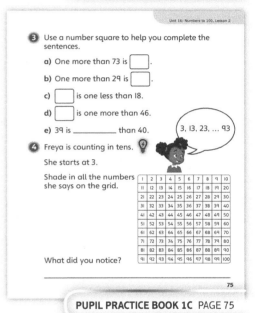

PUPIL PRACTICE BOOK 1C PAGE 74

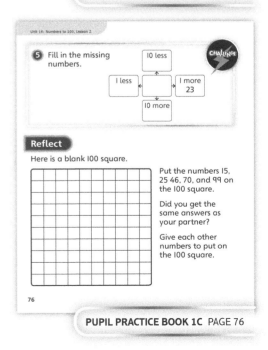

PUPIL PRACTICE BOOK 1C PAGE 75

PUPIL PRACTICE BOOK 1C PAGE 76

Partitioning numbers ①

Learning focus

In this lesson, children will consolidate their understanding of counting numbers in 10s and 1s and will learn to partition numbers, representing this on a place value grid.

Small steps

→ Previous step: Exploring number patterns
→ **This step: Partitioning numbers (1)**
→ Next step: Partitioning numbers (2)

NATIONAL CURRICULUM LINKS

Year 1 Number – Number and Place Value

Identify and represent numbers using objects and pictorial representations including the number line, and use the language of: equal to, more than, less than (fewer), most, least.

Year 2 Number – Number and Place Value

Recognise the place value of each digit in a 2-digit number (tens, ones).

ASSESSING MASTERY

Children can use different representations of numbers to fluently partition them into their tens and ones. They can use a place value grid to clearly and more efficiently record their partitioning.

COMMON MISCONCEPTIONS

When working with Base 10 equipment, children will sometimes put more than 10 ones in the ones column. Although it is possible to partition a number in this way (for example, 36 = 20 + 16), it leads to confusion about place value and digits. For example, children may write 36 as 216 (2 tens and 16 ones). Ask:
• *How many ones have you put in the ones column? If you have counted 10 ones, where could you put them instead?*

When recording their partitioning in a place value grid, children may record the tens as the full tens number, rather than the number of tens. For example, they may write 36 as 30 tens and 6 ones, rather than 3 tens and 6 ones. Ask:
• *What does the number 36 look like on the 100 square? Can you make the number with cubes? How many groups of 10 are there?*

STRENGTHENING UNDERSTANDING

Strengthen understanding by providing children with practical opportunities to group amounts into 10s and 1s. For example, can they sort classroom resources into groups of 10? How many extra are left after grouping? So how many do they have altogether?

GOING DEEPER

Deepen children's ability to partition numbers by asking them to partition a number in a different way. Children can work systematically to find all the different ways to partition a given number.

KEY LANGUAGE

In lesson: partition, how many?, how many more?, count, tens, ones, exchange, **place value grid**

Other language to be used by the teacher: column, digits

STRUCTURES AND REPRESENTATIONS

Number line, place value grid, ten frames

RESOURCES

Mandatory: Base 10 equipment

Optional: bead strings, interlocking cubes, blank place value grids, 100 square, pictures of Base 10 equipment (tens and ones)

 In the eTextbook of this lesson, you will find interactive links to a selection of teaching tools.

Before you teach ⏸

• How will you make sure children have sufficient opportunities to work with concrete and pictorial representations of the place value grid?
• What resources will you provide to help children demonstrate their thinking?

Discover

ASK

- *What data is the girl recording?*
- *Do you recognise anything in the picture from any other lessons? Can you use that to count the sunny days more quickly?*
- *How many more days until there have been 50 days of sun?*

IN FOCUS Use the picture in question ❶ to recap children's learning from the previous lesson. Children should recognise the grid as a 100 square. Discuss how children can use this to help them count more quickly, linking the picture to counting in 10s and 1s.

ANSWERS

Question ❶ a): There have been 36 days of ☼.

Question ❶ b): There are 3 full rows of 10.

There are 6 more ☼.

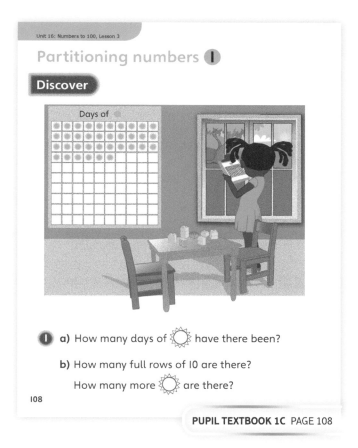

Share

ASK

- Question ❶ a): *Whose method is more efficient, Dexter's or Flo's? Did you count the suns in a different way?*
- Question ❶ b): *How are the cubes linked to the 100 square? Could you represent the number in a different way?*
- Question ❶ b): *Can you explain what the place value grid represents?*

IN FOCUS Question ❶ b) introduces children to the place value grid for the first time. Spend time securing their understanding of how to record the tens (3 tens, not 30).

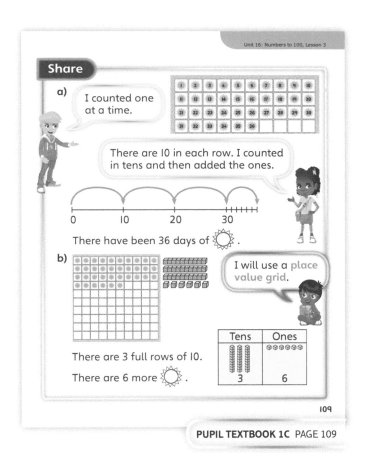

137

Think together

WAYS OF WORKING Whole class teacher led (I do, We do, You do)

ASK

- Question **1** : *How will you count how many days of rain there have been? How can you use the 100 square and number line to help you?*
- Question **2** : *Can you explain to me how to read the place value grid?*
- Question **3** : *How can you use Flo's suggestion to help you?*

IN FOCUS Question **1** uses scaffolding to help children move from using the 100 square to more abstract representations.

STRENGTHEN Question **2** will help develop children's concrete understanding of the place value grid. Give them blank place value grids to fill in with the correct numerals, to support them in making the link with the concrete representation.

DEEPEN Discuss with children the most efficient way of representing the number in question **3** . Use Ash's comment to encourage their thinking: ask them why putting Gaby's number in a place value grid would be useful. What numbers would they write in the grid? Alternatively, show children a place value grid you have completed with the tens filled in incorrectly and ask children to explain your errors.

ASSESSMENT CHECKPOINT Assess whether children can confidently say how many tens and ones make up a number. Use question **2** to determine whether children recognise the place value grid and understand how it represents how many tens and ones there are in a 2-digit number.

ANSWERS

Question **1** : There are 6 rows of 10.

　　　　　　　There are 2 more.

　　　　　　　There have been 62 days of ◯.

Question **2** a): 17

Question **2** b): 45

Question **2** c): 60

Question **2** d): 7

Question **3** : 47

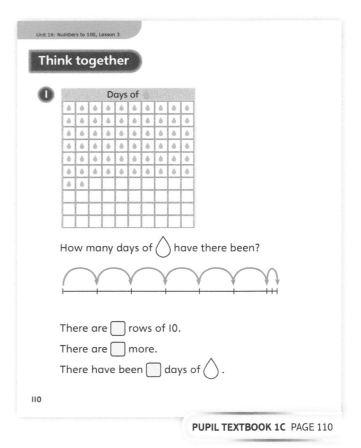

PUPIL TEXTBOOK 1C PAGE 110

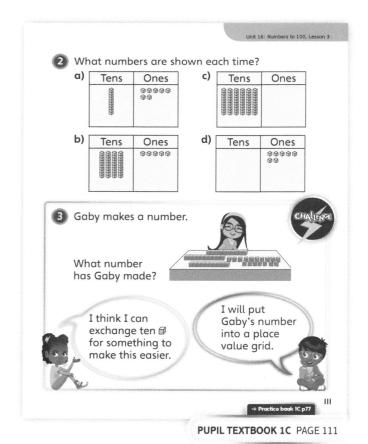

PUPIL TEXTBOOK 1C PAGE 111

Practice

WAYS OF WORKING Independent thinking

IN FOCUS Questions ❶ and ❷ present children with different representations of numbers, with tens and ones in different arrangements. This will help develop children's fluency.

STRENGTHEN For question ❸, give children large blank place value grids on which they can arrange Base 10 equipment. If children have moved beyond the concrete, you could give them pictures of Base 10 equipment (tens and ones). For either option, ask children if they can make the number 45 and how they would arrange the equipment on the place value grid. Can they explain how their representation shows the number 45?

DEEPEN When children are working on question ❹, ask questions to develop children's reasoning. Encourage them to justify their ideas. Ask: *How are you going to represent your number? Could you use any of the representations you have met in the last few lessons? Which representation shows the number most clearly?* You could ask them to draw and make a second number and ask: *Which of the two numbers you have made is the greatest? How do you know?*

ASSESSMENT CHECKPOINT Assess whether children can accurately partition 2-digit numbers. Use question ❹ to check if they can represent their partitioning using multiple representations. Can they use a place value grid and number line to demonstrate their partitioning?

ANSWERS Answers for the **Practice** part of the lesson appear in the separate **Practice and Reflect answer guide**.

Reflect

WAYS OF WORKING Pair work

IN FOCUS When working on the **Reflect** activity, give each partner the opportunity to come up with one of the numbers. Children could move on to making pairs of numbers individually and then discuss how many pairs of numbers are possible.

ASSESSMENT CHECKPOINT Children should be able to confidently partition numbers in different ways. Assess children's reasoning and justification when discussing their chosen number. Have they used the place value grid accurately?

ANSWERS Answers for the **Reflect** part of the lesson appear in the separate **Practice and Reflect answer guide**.

After the lesson ⏸

- Are children confident when explaining the use of the place value grid?
- Did children recognise that an amount can be partitioned in more than one way?

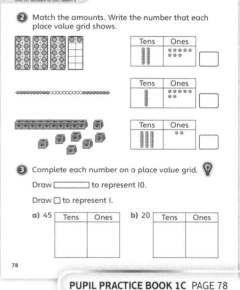

PUPIL PRACTICE BOOK 1C PAGE 77

PUPIL PRACTICE BOOK 1C PAGE 78

PUPIL PRACTICE BOOK 1C PAGE 79

Partitioning numbers ❷

Learning focus

In this lesson, children will consolidate their learning from the previous session on partitioning. They will relate their prior learning to the part-whole model and continue developing their confidence with the place value grid.

Small steps

→ Previous step: Partitioning numbers (1)
→ **This step: Partitioning numbers (2)**
→ Next step: Comparing numbers (1)

NATIONAL CURRICULUM LINKS

Year 1 Number – Number and Place Value

Identify and represent numbers using objects and pictorial representations including the number line, and use the language of: equal to, more than, less than (fewer), most, least.

Year 2 Number – Number and Place Value

Recognise the place value of each digit in a 2-digit number (tens, ones).

ASSESSING MASTERY

Children can partition numbers confidently and fluently, using a place value grid and concrete resources to demonstrate their partitioning. They can link their representations of partitioning to the part-whole model.

COMMON MISCONCEPTIONS

Children may muddle the place value of digits within a number when working with the place value grid or part-whole model. Ask:
• *Which digit tells you how many tens there are in a 2-digit number? Which digit tells you how many ones there are?*

When recording their partitioning in a place value grid, children may write the tens as the full tens number, rather than the number of tens. For example, they may write 43 as 40 tens and 3 ones, rather than 4 tens and 3 ones. Ask:
• *What does the number 43 look like on the 100 square? Can you make the number with cubes? How many groups of 10 are there?*

STRENGTHENING UNDERSTANDING

If children are struggling to partition, ask them to make a number using Base 10 equipment, then to make it again using place value cards. Can they match the tens and the ones in the two representations?

GOING DEEPER

Give children who are able to partition confidently word problems to solve. For example: *10 pens fit in a box. Rachael has 56 pens. How many boxes of 10 can she fill? How many extra pens will she have left over?* Ask children to draw the problem or prove their solution with the representations they have been learning about.

KEY LANGUAGE

In lesson: partition, how many?, in total, place value grid, count, tens, ones

Other language to be used by the teacher: place value, digit, part-whole model

STRUCTURES AND REPRESENTATIONS

Number line, place value grid, part-whole model

RESOURCES

Mandatory: Base 10 equipment, dice

Optional: bead strings, place value cards, blank place value grids, blank part-whole models

 In the eTextbook of this lesson, you will find interactive links to a selection of teaching tools.

Before you teach ⏸

• How can you increase children's confidence in partitioning numbers?
• What concrete and pictorial resources could you supply to help children understand the place value grid and part-whole model?

Discover

WAYS OF WORKING Pair work

ASK

- Question ❶ a): *How many chairs are in each stack? How could you count those chairs efficiently?*
- Question ❶ b): *How many different ways can you think of to represent the number of chairs?*
- Question ❶ b): *Could you represent this number using a place value grid?*

IN FOCUS Use question ❶ to recap what children learned in the previous lesson. Children should be able to demonstrate their ability to represent the number in different ways, particularly within a place value grid.

ANSWERS

Question ❶ a): There are 43 chairs in total.

Question ❶ b):

Tens	Ones
4	3

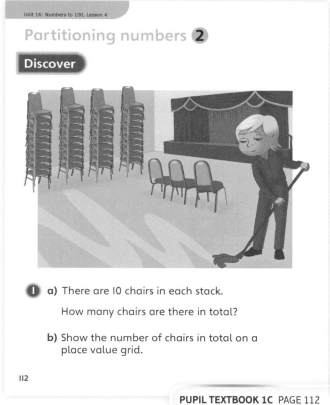

Partitioning numbers ❷

Discover

❶ a) There are 10 chairs in each stack.

How many chairs are there in total?

b) Show the number of chairs in total on a place value grid.

112

PUPIL TEXTBOOK 1C PAGE 112

Share

WAYS OF WORKING Whole class teacher led

ASK

- *How has Flo represented the chairs?*
- Question ❶ a): *How does the number line represent the number?*
- Question ❶ b): *Did your place value grid look the same as Flo's? Explain how they are the same or different.*

IN FOCUS Use question ❶ b) to remind children what they have already learned about the place value grid. Recap why the tens are listed as '4' and not '40', and discuss how the addition number sentence links to the place value grid.

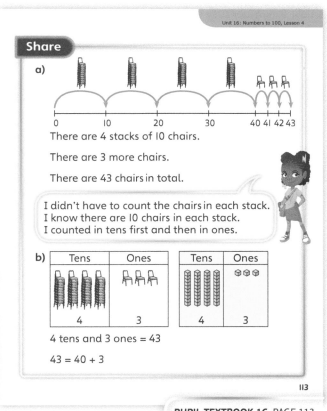

Share

a)

There are 4 stacks of 10 chairs.

There are 3 more chairs.

There are 43 chairs in total.

I didn't have to count the chairs in each stack. I know there are 10 chairs in each stack. I counted in tens first and then in ones.

b)

Tens	Ones
4	3

Tens	Ones
4	3

4 tens and 3 ones = 43

43 = 40 + 3

113

PUPIL TEXTBOOK 1C PAGE 113

Think together

WAYS OF WORKING Whole class teacher led (I do, We do, You do)

WAYS OF WORKING Whole class teacher led (I do, We do, You do)

ASK

- Question ❶ : *How will you count the piles of 10 chairs efficiently?*
- Question ❶ : *What do you need to do to find out how many extra chairs there are?*
- Question ❷ : *Could you represent each number in a place value grid? In a part-whole model?*

IN FOCUS Question ❶ links back to what children have learned in previous lessons, and also helps secure their understanding that 6 tens are equal to 60 (necessary for understanding the place value grid).

Question ❷ begins to link children's understanding of partitioning, and the place value grid, to the part-whole model.

STRENGTHEN For question ❷, it would be beneficial to have all the resources pictured available for children as concrete manipulatives. Ask children to create each number with resources (cubes, place value grid, part-whole model, bead string) and discuss what is the same and what is different about each representation. This will help strengthen children's understanding of the links between the place value grid and the part-whole model.

DEEPEN To further develop children's problem solving skills, ask them how many solutions they think there are to question ❸. When making a pair of numbers, what is the smallest number they can make? What is the biggest?

ASSESSMENT CHECKPOINT Assess children's ability to count in 10s and 1s by asking them to explain to you how the number line in question ❶ represents the number of chairs. Can they relate this to the place value grid?

Use questions ❷ and ❸ to determine whether children have a fluent and confident understanding of how to partition 2-digit numbers. Can they use place value grids effectively? Can they explain how the representation links to the part-whole model?

ANSWERS

Question ❶ : There are 6 stacks of 10 chairs.

There are 8 extra chairs.

There are 68 chairs in total.

Question ❷ a): 52

5 tens and 2 ones = 52

52 = 50 + 2

Question ❷ b): 76

Question ❷ c): 34

Question ❸ : Any pair of numbers made from 86 Base 10 cubes. Astrid made 26 and 60.

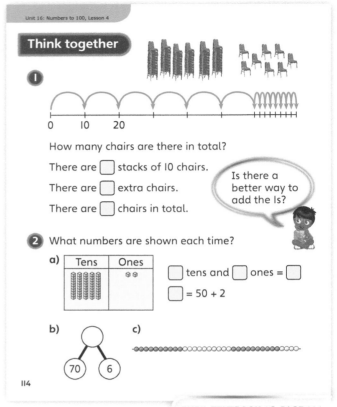

PUPIL TEXTBOOK 1C PAGE 114

PUPIL TEXTBOOK 1C PAGE 115

Practice

WAYS OF WORKING Independent thinking

IN FOCUS Question **1** reinforces children's understanding of place value and that 4 tens are equal to 40, and 5 tens are equal to 50.

Question **2** reinforces children's understanding of the part-whole diagram and place value grid. To strengthen children's understanding of the link between the two representations, encourage them to show each number using the representation not pictured.

STRENGTHEN Question **3** gives children the opportunity to work with place value and partitioning in a more abstract way. If children find this tricky, give them Base 10 equipment so they can make the numbers. These can be arranged on a blank place value grid. Similarly, they could make the numbers using place value cards, then arrange them on a blank part-whole model.

DEEPEN Develop children's reasoning skills by asking them to predict the biggest and smallest number they can make in questions **4** and **5**. Can they explain their predictions? Encourage children to prove that their solutions are correct to a partner, using a variety of resources.

ASSESSMENT CHECKPOINT Assess children's fluency in place value and partitioning. Can children clearly explain their reasoning and prove that their solutions are correct? Children should choose the representations they use to support their ideas based on which they deem to be most effective in the context of the problem.

ANSWERS Answers for the **Practice** part of the lesson appear in the separate **Practice and Reflect answer guide**.

Reflect

WAYS OF WORKING Pair work

IN FOCUS Begin by asking children to complete the **Reflect** activity independently. Then ask them to repeat it, this time using their partner's number. Ask children to discuss what was the same and what was different about their representations of the two numbers. Did they create the numbers in the same way? If not, can they convince their partner that their representation is clearer? Such discussion will develop children's reasoning and justification skills.

ASSESSMENT CHECKPOINT Assess the quality of children's explanations during their discussions with their partner. Do they link their explanation to how clearly their representation demonstrates each number's place value? Children should demonstrate confidence and fluency in whichever representations they choose to use.

ANSWERS Answers for the **Reflect** part of the lesson appear in the separate **Practice and Reflect answer guide**.

After the lesson ⏸

- Do children favour one method of representing the place value of 2-digit numbers?
- If so, how will you ensure that children continue to use the other representations in their work?
- Did children demonstrate confident reasoning when explaining their ideas to their partner?

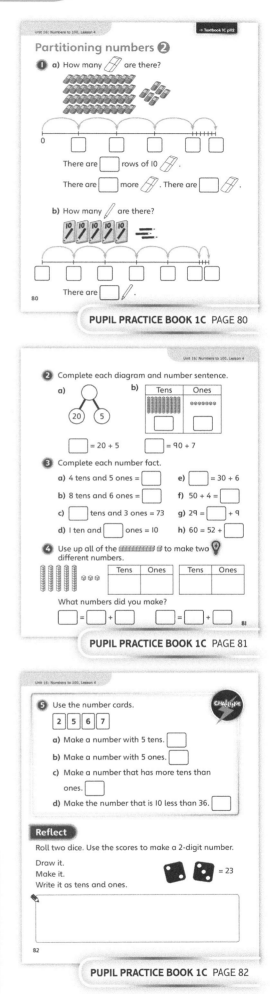

PUPIL PRACTICE BOOK 1C PAGE 80

PUPIL PRACTICE BOOK 1C PAGE 81

PUPIL PRACTICE BOOK 1C PAGE 82

Comparing numbers ①

Learning focus

In this lesson, children will use what they know about place value to compare numbers up to 100. They will demonstrate their comparisons using partitioning and representations of tens and ones.

Small steps

→ Previous step: Partitioning numbers (2)
→ **This step: Comparing numbers (1)**
→ Next step: Comparing numbers (2)

NATIONAL CURRICULUM LINKS

Year 1 Number – Number and Place Value

Identify and represent numbers using objects and pictorial representations including the number line, and use the language of: equal to, more than, less than (fewer), most, least.

ASSESSING MASTERY

Children can use their understanding of partitioning and place value to confidently compare numbers. They can use the correct terminology and signs to represent their comparisons and can evidence their thinking through fluent use of different representations.

COMMON MISCONCEPTIONS

When comparing numbers using concrete resources, children may not align the start of the two representations, thereby skewing their comparison. Provide children with a blank number line to arrange their numbers along. Ask:
• *Where should you start making each number? How will you know if both numbers are starting at the correct point? Why will this help you to compare more accurately?*

STRENGTHENING UNDERSTANDING

You could introduce the concept by comparing heights of objects in the classroom. Children could measure objects to the nearest centimetre and record the measurements. Ask: *What is the tallest? What is the shortest? Can you use what you have learned about place value to help you compare heights?*

GOING DEEPER

Deepen children's understanding of the difference between two 2-digit numbers by asking questions such as: *How much more is 56 than 45? How can you prove the difference? What two numbers can you find that have the biggest difference? What two numbers can you find that have the smallest difference? Is there only one solution?*

KEY LANGUAGE

In lesson: <, >, =, compare, more, fewer, greater than

Other language to be used by the teacher: less than, smaller, equal to, the same

STRUCTURES AND REPRESENTATIONS

Ten frames, place value grids

RESOURCES

Mandatory: Base 10 equipment

Optional: bead strings, blank number lines, blank place value grids

 In the eTextbook of this lesson, you will find interactive links to a selection of teaching tools.

Before you teach ⏸

• Are children confident partitioning a 2-digit number?
• How confident are children at using the signs and vocabulary of comparison?

Discover

WAYS OF WORKING Pair work

ASK

- *What is the same and what is different about Tamsin's and Ray's collections?*
- *Are the two collections easy to compare at the moment?*
- *How could you represent both numbers to make them easier to compare?*

IN FOCUS Use the picture in question ① to begin discussing different representations of 2-digit numbers. Use Ray's collection to recap counting in 10s and discuss the number of tens and ones in the number on Tamsin's bucket. Agree that it is easier to compare two numbers if they are both represented in the same way.

ANSWERS

Question ① a): Ray's

Tamsin's

Question ① b): Tamsin has the most 🐚.

Unit 16: Numbers to 100, Lesson 5

Comparing numbers ①

Discover

① a) Use 🎲 to show the number of 🐚 each child has.

 b) Who has the most 🐚 , Ray or Tamsin?

116

PUPIL TEXTBOOK 1C PAGE 116

Share

WAYS OF WORKING Whole class teacher led

ASK

- Question ① a): *How has each representation been linked to the Base 10 equipment?*
- Question ① b): *How can you use the Base 10 equipment to help you compare the numbers?*
- Question ① b): *Which blocks should you look at first, the tens or the ones?*

IN FOCUS Use question ① to introduce children to the use of Base 10 equipment as a method of comparing numbers. Make sure children are aware that it is important for them to start making both numbers at the same point to ensure that the comparison is clear and fair. You could challenge children to write the comparison with a different sign (such as 41 > 35).

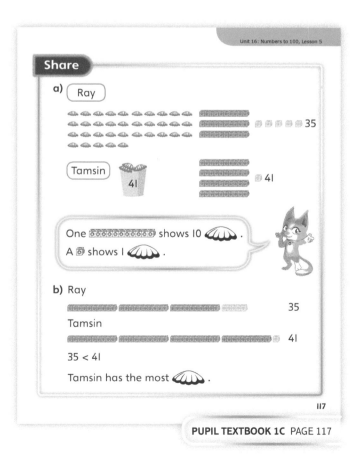

Unit 16: Numbers to 100, Lesson 5

Share

a) Ray

35

Tamsin
41

One [blocks] shows 10 🐚 .
A 🎲 shows 1 🐚 .

b) Ray
35

Tamsin
41

35 < 41

Tamsin has the most 🐚 .

117

PUPIL TEXTBOOK 1C PAGE 117

Think together

WAYS OF WORKING Whole class teacher led (I do, We do, You do)

ASK

- Question ❶ : *How will you begin comparing the numbers? Could you represent the numbers in other ways?*
- Question ❶ : *What does the sign < mean?*
- Question ❷ : *Can you write the comparison in more than one way?*

IN FOCUS In question ❶, children should recognise that the flags are arranged in rows of 10, with the 'extra' ones in the last row for each. Using Flo's comment as inspiration, children could be asked to make and compare the numbers using Base 10 equipment.

STRENGTHEN If children struggle to compare the pairs of numbers in questions ❶ and ❷, encourage them to make the numbers using Base 10 equipment or another concrete resource they feel comfortable with. Depending on the resource, it may be helpful to give children a large blank number line and a reminder that they should start making both numbers at the same point.

DEEPEN Question ❸ requires children to compare two different numbers represented in two different ways. Discuss why Astrid and Flo used the methods they did. How have they made it easier for themselves to compare the two numbers? Challenge children to represent two different numbers in different ways and ask a partner to compare them and complete a number sentence using the < or > sign.

ASSESSMENT CHECKPOINT Assess children's confidence when comparing numbers. Can they use Base 10 equipment to demonstrate their comparisons and relate their reasoning to their knowledge of place value?

ANSWERS

Question ❶ : 42 < 48

　　　　　Tamsin has fewer flags.

Question ❷ a): 64 > 54 or 54 < 64

Question ❷ b): 40 > 38 or 38 < 40

Question ❸ : 38 < 43 or 43 > 38

　　　　　43 is greater than 38.

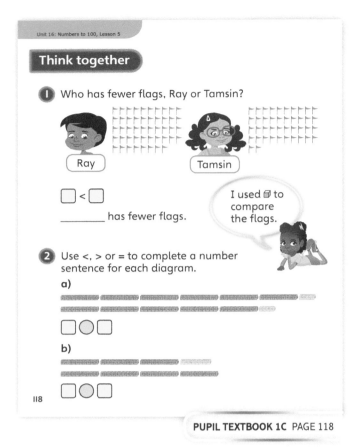

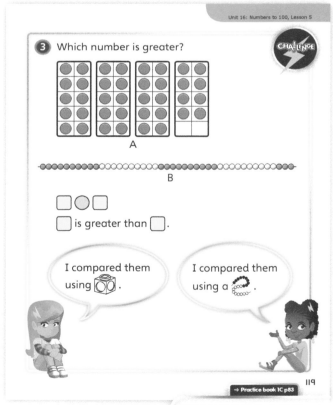

PUPIL TEXTBOOK 1C PAGE 118

PUPIL TEXTBOOK 1C PAGE 119

Practice

WAYS OF WORKING Independent thinking

IN FOCUS Questions ❶ and ❷ require children to compare pairs of numbers represented in different ways. Question ❶ helps children build a sentence explaining the comparison, while question ❷ asks them to complete number sentences using the <, > or = signs; in question ❷ b) and ❷ c) children create the whole number sentence independently.

STRENGTHEN For question ❸, encourage children to recreate the picture using Base 10 equipment on blank place value grids. Once they have done this, ask: *Can you arrange the Base 10 equipment in another way to help you compare the numbers?* Encourage children to arrange the Base 10 equipment along a blank number line. Ask: *Has this made the comparison clearer? What is the same and what is different between this arrangement and how it looked on the place value grid?*

DEEPEN Challenge children to find all the possible answers to question ❺. Ask: *What is the greatest number you can make that is less than 24? What is the greatest number you can make on the ten frame?*

ASSESSMENT CHECKPOINT Assess whether children understand the different representations of numbers shown in the questions. Can they make sensible choices about the representations and methods they use to make comparisons? Can they confidently use the language and signs of comparison to explain their ideas?

ANSWERS Answers for the **Practice** part of the lesson appear in the separate **Practice and Reflect answer guide**.

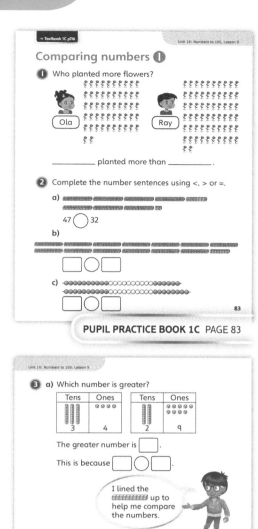

PUPIL PRACTICE BOOK 1C PAGE 83

PUPIL PRACTICE BOOK 1C PAGE 84

Reflect

WAYS OF WORKING Independent thinking

IN FOCUS During the **Reflect** part of the lesson, give children the opportunity to use resources, draw pictures and write down their ideas. They should then explain their work to their partner.

ASSESSMENT CHECKPOINT Children should have come to the conclusion that 72 is greater than 66, or that 66 is less than 72. Either way, they should have chosen an appropriate representation to demonstrate the comparison. Listen to children's reasoning: assess how confidently they use the vocabulary of comparison. Can they convince their partner that they have chosen the clearest representation?

ANSWERS Answers for the **Reflect** part of the lesson appear in the separate **Practice and Reflect answer guide**.

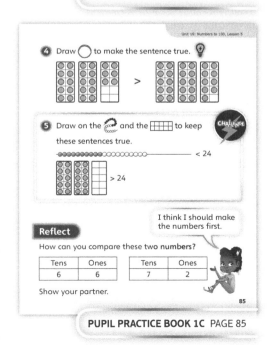

PUPIL PRACTICE BOOK 1C PAGE 85

After the lesson ⏸

- Which representation was most popular for comparing numbers across the class? Which was least popular?
- How will you develop children's use of their least favoured representation to lessen this disparity?

Comparing numbers **2**

Learning focus

In this lesson, children will further consolidate their understanding of how to compare numbers up to 100. They will link their understanding of representations using a place value grid.

Small steps

→ Previous step: Comparing numbers (1)
→ **This step: Comparing numbers (2)**
→ Next step: Ordering numbers

NATIONAL CURRICULUM LINKS

Year 1 Number – Number and Place Value

Identify and represent numbers using objects and pictorial representations including the number line, and use the language of: equal to, more than, less than (fewer), most, least.

ASSESSING MASTERY

Children can compare two 2-digit numbers using their knowledge of tens and ones and can represent their ideas using a place value grid. They can explain which place value column they should compare first and why, fluently using the language and signs of comparison.

COMMON MISCONCEPTIONS

As the representations of numbers become more abstract, children may compare the ones before the tens and so make statements such as '19 > 21'. Ask:
• *Can you make those two numbers using resources? Which is bigger, a ten or a one? Why should you compare tens first? Where do you find the tens digit in a 2-digit number?*

STRENGTHENING UNDERSTANDING

Give children the opportunity to practise comparing numbers through games or role play.

For example, play games in pairs where children can score points. Record the scores using concrete resources (counters, cubes) and also using the abstract numerals. Discuss who has won the game. Ask: *How do you know they scored the most? What can you tell me about their score compared to the other player's?*

Children could role play a scenario in which some objects or sweets have been shared out in two unequal groups. The objects being counted could be put in a bag with the number written on the outside. Ask: *Who has the most? Who has the least? How do you know? How could you check?*

GOING DEEPER

Children who have mastered the concept of comparing numbers could be given the opportunity to plan and film a video tutorial, teaching other children how to compare two 2-digit numbers. Give them a list of the necessary vocabulary, signs and representations that they should use to explain the concept effectively. The videos could be shared on the school website or during the lesson.

KEY LANGUAGE

In lesson: <, >, =, compare, most, tens, ones, greater than, the same, more, less than, digit, between

Other language to be used by the teacher: place value, bigger, equal to, smaller

STRUCTURES AND REPRESENTATIONS

Place value grid, ten frames

RESOURCES

Mandatory: Base 10 equipment

Optional: blank number line, blank place value grid, counters, blank ten frames, bead strings

 In the eTextbook of this lesson, you will find interactive links to a selection of teaching tools.

Before you teach

• How will you ensure children get enough opportunities to reason in this lesson?
• How will you provide children with opportunities to justify their opinions and convince others of the validity of their ideas?

Discover

WAYS OF WORKING Pair work

ASK

- Question ➊ a): *How many letters does Mark have? How many letters does Janet have?*
- Question ➊ a): *What is the same and what is different about the two numbers?*
- Question ➊ b): *Why might it be trickier to compare the number of letters Sue and John have?*
- *How can you show your comparison of the numbers clearly?*

IN FOCUS Begin the discussion of question ➊ with a recap of what children learned in the previous lesson. Can they remember how to use Base 10 equipment to compare the two numbers? Also discuss how the representations of numbers in this picture are more abstract (numerals instead of objects).

DEEPEN You could challenge children to put their comparison for each part into a sentence. Ask: *What mathematical vocabulary will you use?*

ANSWERS

Question ➊ a): Janet has the most ✉ to deliver.

Question ➊ b): John has the most ✉ to deliver.

PUPIL TEXTBOOK 1C PAGE 120

Share

WAYS OF WORKING Whole class teacher led

ASK

- Question ➊ a): *How has Dexter represented the numbers? Did you do the same? Why or why not?*
- Question ➊ a): *Whose method was more efficient, Dexter's or Flo's?*
- Question ➊ b): *Did you do the same as Flo?*
- Question ➊ b): *Did you record the comparison using the same sentence? Could you have written it in a different way?*

IN FOCUS Discuss with children how the place value grid can help them compare the numbers in question ➊, making links to children's prior learning and understanding of comparing numbers. Reinforce the concept that, for example, 6 tens is the same as 60, to help children make links between the Base 10 equipment and more abstract representations, including a place value grid completed with digits instead of pictures.

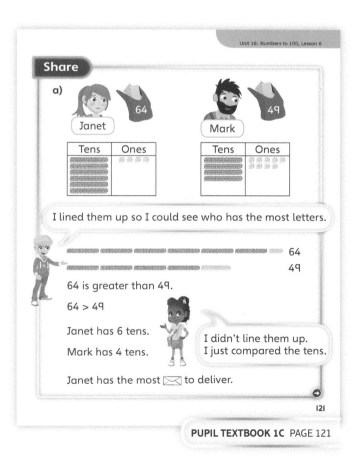

PUPIL TEXTBOOK 1C PAGE 121

Think together

WAYS OF WORKING Whole class teacher led (I do, We do, You do)

ASK

- Question ❶ : *How could you represent the numbers to help you compare them?*
- Question ❶ : *How many tens are there in 38? How many tens are there in 31? Can you use that information alone to compare 38 and 31?*
- Question ❷ : *What can you tell me about the numbers in the sequence 0, 5, 10, 15, 20, …?*

IN FOCUS Question ❷ gives children opportunities to reason about number and demonstrate their fluency. For example, do they recognise that the tens digit of any number they put in the first circle must be 6 or 7? Can they explain why?

STRENGTHEN Encourage children to use Base 10 equipment to create the numbers and arrange them in a blank place value grid. If necessary, remind them again that, for example, 6 tens are equal to 60. If children are still finding comparison tricky, they could arrange their representations of the two numbers along a blank number line, as in previous lessons. Discuss what is the same and what is different about the place value grid and the representation of the numbers along a number line. Ask: *Which representation makes the comparison clearer? Why?*

DEEPEN When children are working on question ❶, ask them when they would be able to use the = sign. Give them a question such as: *What number is missing from this comparison: 38 = ☐ ?* Ask them to prove their ideas.

You could also challenge children to find a number that can go in all three circles in question ❷ (65), and any numbers that do not fit in any of the groups (46, 47, 54, 56, 57).

ASSESSMENT CHECKPOINT Ask children to explain their answers to questions ❶ and ❷ and assess the confidence of their explanations. They should be fluent in the use of the vocabulary and signs of comparison.

ANSWERS

Question ❶ : 38 > 31

31 > 26

26 < 38

Question ❷ : Greater than 60: **64, 65, 67, 74, 75, 76**

Between 58 and 68: **64, 65, 67**

In the sequence that starts 0, 5, 10, 15, 20 …:
45, 65, 75

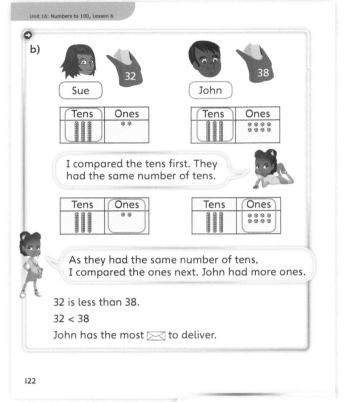

PUPIL TEXTBOOK 1C PAGE 122

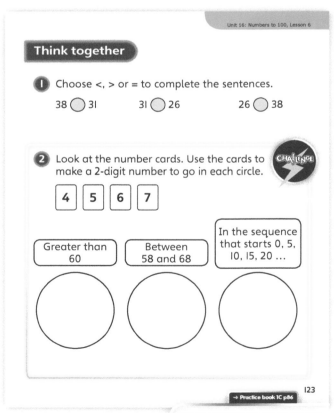

PUPIL TEXTBOOK 1C PAGE 123

Practice

WAYS OF WORKING Independent thinking

IN FOCUS Question ① includes pictorial representations of the numbers children are asked to compare, before they move on to more abstract representations in later questions. You could encourage children to make both pairs of numbers using Base 10 equipment on a blank place value grid to further cement the link.

STRENGTHEN For questions ② and ③, give children Base 10 equipment and blank place value grids so they can make the numbers alongside the abstract representations in the **Pupil Practice book**. Ask: *What is the same and what is different about the two place value grids? Can you show me why one number is bigger than the other?*

DEEPEN Extend question ⑤ by asking children how many solutions they can find for each number sentence. Ask: *Are there any digits that would work in all three number sentences?* (No) *Are there any digits that will not work in any of the number sentences?* (No) Encourage children to use their understanding of all representations used so far to represent their ideas clearly and efficiently.

ASSESSMENT CHECKPOINT Use question ② to assess whether children can use the place value grid to efficiently compare 2-digit numbers. Can they confidently explain how the place value grid links to their knowledge of concrete representations of numbers?

ANSWERS Answers for the **Practice** part of the lesson appear in the separate **Practice and Reflect answer guide**.

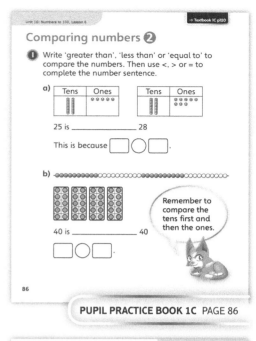

PUPIL PRACTICE BOOK 1C PAGE 86

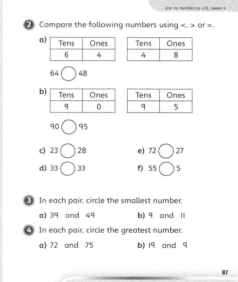

PUPIL PRACTICE BOOK 1C PAGE 87

Reflect

WAYS OF WORKING Independent thinking

IN FOCUS When children have come up with their own solutions to the **Reflect** activity, ask them to share their solutions with a partner. Did they both compare the numbers in the same way? If not, whose method do they think is more efficient?

ASSESSMENT CHECKPOINT Assess whether children can confidently justify their ideas using the correct vocabulary and mathematical signs.

ANSWERS Answers for the **Reflect** part of the lesson appear in the separate **Practice and Reflect answer guide**.

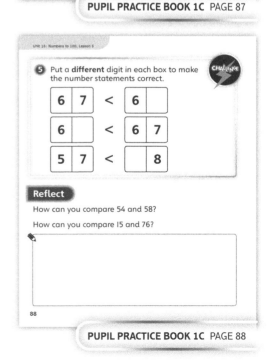

PUPIL PRACTICE BOOK 1C PAGE 88

After the lesson ⏸

- Have the last two lessons ensured that children have a deep, conceptual understanding of comparing numbers?
- Were children able to recognise the more abstract nature of how tens are represented on a place value grid? Does this need recapping? If so, how and when will you recap this learning point?

Ordering numbers

Learning focus

In this lesson, children will use their understanding of comparing numbers to compare and order two or more 2-digit numbers.

Small steps

→ Previous step: Comparing numbers (2)
→ **This step: Ordering numbers**
→ Next step: Bonds to 100 (1)

NATIONAL CURRICULUM LINKS

Year 1 Number – Number and Place Value

Identify and represent numbers using objects and pictorial representations including the number line, and use the language of: equal to, more than, less than (fewer), most, least.

ASSESSING MASTERY

Children can fluently use their understanding of place value to compare the value of more than two numbers and order them from greatest to least, or vice-versa. They confidently use Base 10 equipment and place value grids to justify their ideas and demonstrate their ability to work systematically and efficiently when making their comparisons, comparing two numbers at a time to avoid confusion.

COMMON MISCONCEPTIONS

Children may be unsure about how to compare three or more numbers at once. Provide children with a blank number line to arrange their numbers along. Ask:
• *Where should you put each number? How will this help you compare?*

STRENGTHENING UNDERSTANDING

Provide children with a list of fruit and vegetables. Ask each child to circle all the fruits and vegetables that they like to eat and count how many they like in total. Children could then order the names of the children who like the most fruits and vegetables to who likes the least.

GOING DEEPER

Children could be encouraged to make up simple riddles. For example: *My number is greater than 61 but less than 72. What is my number?* Children could make up three riddles, then share them with a partner who can try to guess their friend's numbers. Once the numbers have been found, ask children to order all three.

KEY LANGUAGE

In lesson: <, >, =, order, smallest, greatest, place value grid, compare, tens, ones, most, the same, less, least, digit

Other language to be used by the teacher: greater than, less than, more, bigger, smaller, equal to, ascending, descending

STRUCTURES AND REPRESENTATIONS

Place value grid, ten frames

RESOURCES

Mandatory: Base 10 equipment

Optional: blank place value grid, bead strings, blank number line

 In the eTextbook of this lesson, you will find interactive links to a selection of teaching tools.

Before you teach ⏸

• How will you ensure children discuss, critique and develop their systematic approach to mathematics?
• How will you ensure children get enough opportunities to record pictorially, as well as with concrete resources and written work?

Discover

Pair work

ASK

- *Who has the bowl that holds the most spoonfuls?*
- *How could you represent the numbers to help you compare them?*
- *Can you order the numbers from greatest to smallest? Can you order them from smallest to greatest?*
- *Which bowl belongs to which child?*

IN FOCUS Question ① builds on children's learning from previous lessons, requiring them to compare and order three numbers. Discuss with children how they can use what they know to help them answer the questions. Children should recognise that they can compare the numbers and should be able to explain how their prior learning will help them do this.

ANSWERS

Question ① a): 25 < 27 < 45

Question ① b):

Maya	⌣	25 🥄
Eshan	⌣	27 🥄
Alisha	⌣	45 🥄

Share

Whole class teacher led

ASK

- Question ① a): *Did anyone represent the problem in the same way as Astrid? Did anyone represent the problem in the same way as Flo? Did anyone use a different representation?*
- Question ① a): *Could you use different comparison signs to compare and order the numbers?*
- *What important vocabulary do you think you will need to use in this lesson?*

IN FOCUS Use question ① a) to discuss the different representations shown, their similarities and differences, and their respective benefits. The picture of the Base 10 equipment could be used to reinforce children's understanding that the representations of the numbers need to start at the same point to ensure the comparisons are accurate. Agree that 45 > 27 > 25 is true, but the question asks children to order the number of spoonfuls from smallest to greatest.

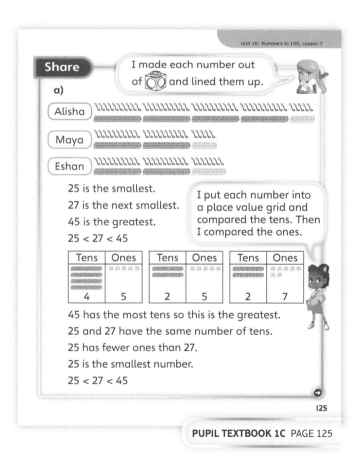

Think together

WAYS OF WORKING Whole class teacher led (I do, We do, You do)

ASK

- Question ❶ : *Can you predict what order the teams will be in when you order the scores?*
- Question ❶ : *How have the numbers been represented? How else could you represent them?*
- Question ❷ : *How does the place value grid make it easy to compare and order the numbers?*
- Question ❷ : *What part of the place value grid should you look at first? Why?*

IN FOCUS Questions ❶ and ❷ include pictures of the three numbers made using Base 10 equipment. Encourage children to make the numbers themselves to further scaffold their comparisons. Ensure children notice that the required order is different in each question.

Discuss how children can ensure their comparisons are organised and systematic. Children should recognise that it is easier to systematically compare one number with each of the others, and then compare the remaining pair, rather than comparing them randomly (for example, compare A and B, then A and C, and finally B and C).

STRENGTHEN If children are struggling to use the place value grids in question ❷ , give them a blank number line to arrange the tens and ones along.

DEEPEN Deepen question ❸ by asking children if the solutions would change if they were allowed to use the same card twice. Can they explain how and why the solutions would change? Can they prove it? Challenge children to make three different numbers (using the same card twice) and to put them into the correct order.

ASSESSMENT CHECKPOINT Use questions ❶ and ❷ to assess whether children can confidently compare three 2-digit numbers, using the representations they have met before. Children should be using the vocabulary associated with ordering numbers (greatest, least, and so on) to explain their comparisons and ordering.

ANSWERS

Question ❶ : Bears (31), Lions (36), Tigers (49)

Question ❷ : 68 > 67 > 40

Question ❸ : Accept any 2-digit number made from 1, 3, 7 and 8.

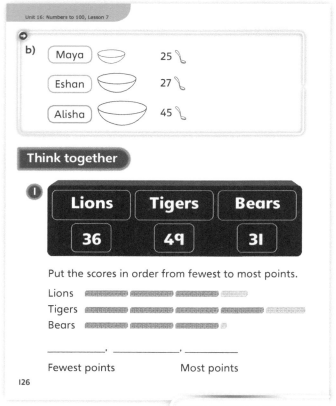

PUPIL TEXTBOOK 1C PAGE 126

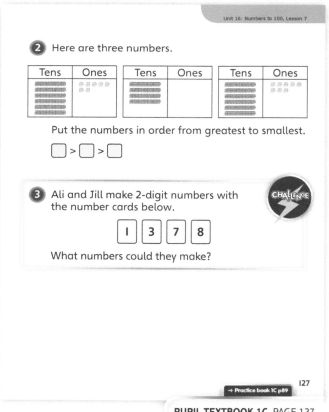

PUPIL TEXTBOOK 1C PAGE 127

Practice

WAYS OF WORKING Independent thinking

IN FOCUS Question ❶ includes a picture of the three numbers made using Base 10 equipment below the abstract representation. Again, children could be encouraged to make the numbers themselves to reinforce their understanding.

STRENGTHEN If children struggle with questions ❸ and ❹, ask how they could represent the numbers. Ask: *Which number looks greatest or smallest? Which should you compare first, the tens or the ones? What order does the question ask you to put the numbers in?*

DEEPEN Extend question ❺ by asking children how many different 2-digit numbers they can make. Challenge them to put them in order from smallest to greatest or from greatest to smallest. Ask: *Is there a quick way to tell where the number is likely to go in the order?*

ASSESSMENT CHECKPOINT Assess whether children can confidently order three 2-digit numbers from greatest to smallest and from smallest to greatest. Do they choose appropriate representations, whether concrete, pictorial or abstract, to help show their comparisons and support their explanations? Can they fluently use the vocabulary and signs of comparison to describe the order?

ANSWERS Answers for the **Practice** part of the lesson appear in the separate **Practice and Reflect answer guide**.

Reflect

WAYS OF WORKING Independent thinking

IN FOCUS During the **Reflect** part of the lesson, encourage children to prove their ideas, using the methods and representations they have been developing and practising over the last few lessons. Once children have found their solution and proof, let them share their ideas with their partner.

ASSESSMENT CHECKPOINT Check whether children are using appropriate vocabulary and representations to explain their ideas. They should demonstrate fluency and conceptual understanding of how to compare and order more than two 2-digit numbers.

ANSWERS Answers for the **Reflect** part of the lesson appear in the separate **Practice and Reflect answer guide**.

After the lesson ⏸

- Were children able to order the four numbers in the **Reflect** section? Did moving beyond three numbers create any issues?
- If so what were they and how will you plan for them in the future?
- How fluent is children's use of the vocabulary associated with comparing and ordering numbers?

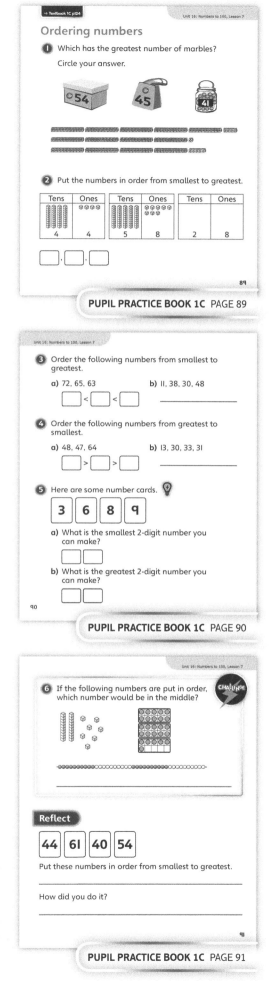

PUPIL PRACTICE BOOK 1C PAGE 89

PUPIL PRACTICE BOOK 1C PAGE 90

PUPIL PRACTICE BOOK 1C PAGE 91

Bonds to 100 ❶

Learning focus

In this lesson, children will use their knowledge of number bonds to 10 to develop their understanding of number bonds to 100.

Small steps

→ Previous step: Ordering numbers
→ **This step: Bonds to 100 (1)**
→ Next step: Bonds to 100 (2)

NATIONAL CURRICULUM LINKS

Year 1 Number – Number and Place Value

Represent and use number bonds and related subtraction facts within 20.

Year 2 Number – Number and Place Value

Recall and use addition and subtraction facts to 20 fluently, and derive and use related facts up to 100.

ASSESSING MASTERY

Children can use their understanding of number bonds to 10 to find number bonds to 100. They can demonstrate their understanding of number bonds through the use of concrete, pictorial and abstract representations, and can write number bonds as addition calculations and as the inverse subtractions.

COMMON MISCONCEPTIONS

Children may find recording the subtraction calculations trickier than the addition. For example, children may write $60 - 40 = 100$. Ask:
• *Where will you start if you are subtracting from 100?*

Give children a representation of 100 (for example, 10 ten frames or a bead string). Ask:
• *Can you show me how much you would have left if you subtracted 40? Can you write that as a number sentence?*

Use this opportunity to talk through recording the subtraction.

STRENGTHENING UNDERSTANDING

To support children's fluency with number bonds, ask them to play a game of snap in which they need to find pairs of tens which total 100. For example, one card could show a picture of 40 represented using ten frames, with the numeral written below. Can children identify the card that creates the number bond to 100?

GOING DEEPER

Give children simple word problems. For each question, encourage children to represent the number bonds to 100 and record them using the methods covered in the lesson. For example:
• *Jo had 100 sweets. She gave 30 of them to her sister. How many did she have left?*
• *Luke is trying to collect 100 stickers. So far, he has 20. How many more does he need?*

If children are confident solving these, they could be challenged to create their own word problem to give to a friend.

KEY LANGUAGE

In lesson: +, –, =, number bond, count, tens, part, whole

Other language to be used by the teacher: zero, ten, twenty, thirty, forty, fifty, sixty, seventy, eighty, ninety, one hundred, add, plus, more, subtract, minus, less

STRUCTURES AND REPRESENTATIONS

Part-whole model, bar model, ten frame, number line

RESOURCES

Optional: blank ten frames, counters, bead strings

 In the eTextbook of this lesson, you will find interactive links to a selection of teaching tools.

Before you teach ⏸

• How confident are children with the concept of addition and subtraction?
• What support will you provide for children who may struggle with the abstract recording?

Discover

WAYS OF WORKING Pair work

ASK

- *How many representations of 100 can you see? Do they show 100 in the same way? Explain.*
- *Question ❶ b): How could Cora write what her counters represent?*
- *Question ❶ b): Do you recognise the empty representations at the bottom of the page? Can you name them and explain how they work?*

IN FOCUS Use question ❶ a) to recap counting efficiently in 10s. Use the two colours of counter to begin discussing the related addition facts. This would be a good opportunity to discuss what would happen if you took 50 away from the hundred, and how you could write the subtraction.

ANSWERS

Question ❶ a): There are 50 ◯ .
                    There are 50 ⬤ .

Question ❶ b):

50 + 50 = 100

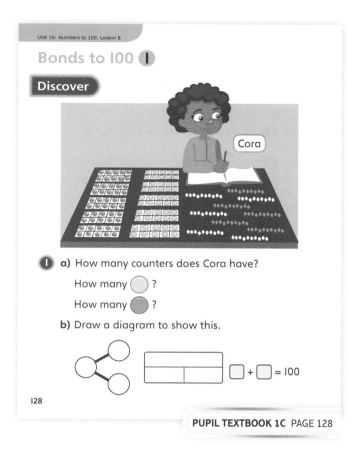

Bonds to 100 ❶

Discover

❶ a) How many counters does Cora have?

How many ◯ ?

How many ⬤ ?

b) Draw a diagram to show this.

☐ + ☐ = 100

128

PUPIL TEXTBOOK 1C PAGE 128

Share

WAYS OF WORKING Whole class teacher led

ASK

- *Question ❶ a): Can you explain how you represented your counting? How is it the same as Astrid's method? How is it different?*
- *Question ❶ a): How do the ten frames link to the number line?*
- *Question ❶ b): Could you complete the part-whole model and bar model in another way? Explain.*
- *Question ❶ b): Can you see a connection between 50 + 50 = 100 and 5 + 5 = 10? Explain.*

IN FOCUS Use Ash's comment in question ❶ b) to help children see the link between number bonds to 10 and number bonds to 100. You could encourage children to find the pattern and predict other number bonds to 100.

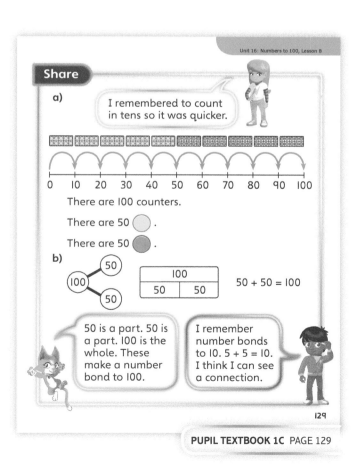

Share

a) I remembered to count in tens so it was quicker.

0 10 20 30 40 50 60 70 80 90 100

There are 100 counters.

There are 50 ◯ .

There are 50 ⬤ .

b)

100 → 50, 50

100	
50	50

50 + 50 = 100

50 is a part. 50 is a part. 100 is the whole. These make a number bond to 100.

I remember number bonds to 10. 5 + 5 = 10. I think I can see a connection.

129

PUPIL TEXTBOOK 1C PAGE 129

Think together

Whole class teacher led (I do, We do, You do)

ASK

- Question **1** : *How can you tell how many more you need to reach 100?*
- Question **1** : *How are the two number lines linked?*
- Question **1** : *Can you write the number bond in another way?*
- Question **2** : *Could you show this number bond using a different representation?*

IN FOCUS Questions **1** and **2** illustrate how number bonds can be shown using various representations. You could use the opportunity to reinforce children's understanding that addition is commutative and that we can write two different addition sentences to represent a number bond (for example, 60 + 40 = 100 and 40 + 60 = 100).

STRENGTHEN If children are struggling to find the number bonds using the pictures on the page, encourage them to make the numbers themselves, initially using the resources pictured and then using any resources they feel comfortable with. Can children use both representations to prove how many tens are on one side of the number bond and how many tens are on the other side?

DEEPEN Ask children if they can write the number bonds in a different way. Children are likely to show the two related additions. Ask: *Can you write a number bond starting with 100?* This will reinforce children's understanding of the related subtraction facts, as well as the addition facts which are the focus of the questions.

ASSESSMENT CHECKPOINT Use question **3** to assess whether children recognise that a number bond is two numbers which create a given number. Can they use both ten frames and bead strings to demonstrate their ability to find number bonds to 100? Can they link their understanding to number bonds to 10?

ANSWERS

Question **1** : 60 + 40 = 100 (or 40 + 60 = 100)

Question **2** a): 20 + 80 = 100 (or 80 + 20 = 100)

Question **2** b): 90 + 10 = 100 (or 10 + 90 = 100)

Question **3** :

10 + 90 = 100	60 + 40 = 100
20 + 80 = 100	70 + 30 = 100
30 + 70 = 100	80 + 20 = 100
40 + 60 = 100	90 + 10 = 100
50 + 50 = 100	100 + 0 = 100

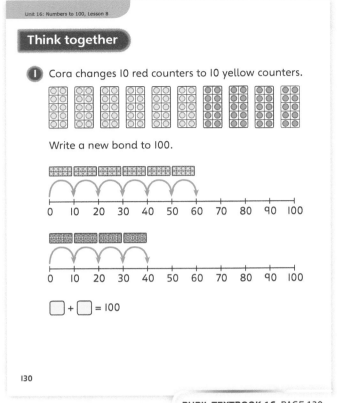

Unit 16: Numbers to 100, Lesson 8

Think together

1 Cora changes 10 red counters to 10 yellow counters.

Write a new bond to 100.

☐ + ☐ = 100

130

PUPIL TEXTBOOK 1C PAGE 130

Unit 16: Numbers to 100, Lesson 8

2 Cora uses the string to make bonds to 100.

Complete the bonds to 100.

a) ☐ + ☐ = 100

b) ☐ + ☐ = 100

3 Use ☐ or string to try and find all of the ten bonds that make 100. **CHALLENGE**

☐ + ☐ = 100   ☐ + ☐ = 100
☐ + ☐ = 100   ☐ + ☐ = 100
☐ + ☐ = 100   ☐ + ☐ = 100
☐ + ☐ = 100   ☐ + ☐ = 100
☐ + ☐ = 100   ☐ + ☐ = 100

How can I make sure I do not miss any bonds?

I wonder if some of these bonds are the same.

→ Practice book 1C p92

131

PUPIL TEXTBOOK 1C PAGE 131

Practice

WAYS OF WORKING Independent thinking

IN FOCUS Question **1** presents children with number bonds using a variety of representations. Again, children could make the numbers themselves, using the pictures as a guide. Children could be encouraged to find both ways of writing the same number bond in an addition sentence, to reinforce their understanding of commutativity.

STRENGTHEN If children find questions **3** and **4** tricky, ask them to make the number bonds using concrete resources. Can they see the missing number using their representation?

DEEPEN Question **5** gives children a good opportunity to deepen their problem-solving skills. If children solve the given puzzle confidently, give them an empty table and some symbols to fill the table with and ask them to create their own similar problems for their partner to solve.

ASSESSMENT CHECKPOINT Assess whether children can confidently find number bonds to 100, using the part-whole model and ten frames.

Use questions **3** and **4** to determine if children understand that a number bond can be represented using a subtraction sentence. Can they give all the related addition and subtraction facts when given a number bond?

ANSWERS Answers for the **Practice** part of the lesson appear in the separate **Practice and Reflect answer guide**.

Reflect

WAYS OF WORKING Pair work

IN FOCUS The **Reflect** part of the lesson asks children to write down as many bonds to 100 as they can. You could challenge children to find as many as they can within a given time limit, if you think your class will engage with this kind of activity in a positive way; it is important that children do not see mathematics as a race. Once children have written down their bonds, they can share their ideas with their partner.

ASSESSMENT CHECKPOINT Assess how children go about writing down the bonds. Do they recognise the pattern inherent in number bonds to 100 (0 + 100, 10 + 90, 20 + 80, and so on)? Do they use their understanding of number bonds to 10 to support their findings?

ANSWERS Answers for the **Reflect** part of the lesson appear in the separate **Practice and Reflect answer guide**.

After the lesson ⏸

- How confident were children with the pattern of number bonds to 100?
- How would you improve this lesson next time?

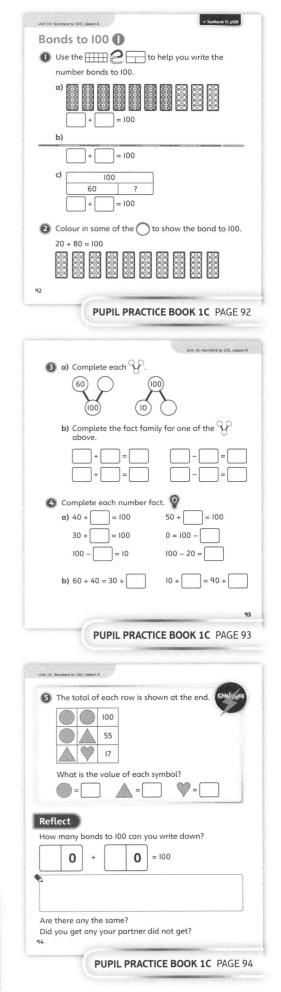

Bonds to 100 ②

Learning focus

In this lesson, children will consolidate their understanding of and ability to find number bonds to 100. They will develop their understanding of the link between number bonds to 10 and number bonds to 100.

Small steps

→ Previous step: Bonds to 100 (1)
→ **This step: Bonds to 100 (2)**
→ Next step: Using before and after

NATIONAL CURRICULUM LINKS

Year 1 Number – Number and Place Value

Represent and use number bonds and related subtraction facts within 20.

Year 2 Number – Number and Place Value

Recall and use addition and subtraction facts to 20 fluently, and derive and use related facts up to 100.

ASSESSING MASTERY

Children can fluently describe and explain the relationship between number bonds to 10 and number bonds to 100. They can use multiple representations to clearly support their understanding and explanations when describing the links between the number bonds.

COMMON MISCONCEPTIONS

In questions where a single counter or object represents 10, children may not recognise this and may assume it represents 1. Ask:

• *Can you read the question to me again? What does it say a counter is worth? How many counters do I have? What would they be worth in total?*

STRENGTHENING UNDERSTANDING

Again, use games of snap to support children's fluency with number bonds. Children may still need cards that show pictorial representations of the numbers, or they may be able to play with cards showing just the numerals.

GOING DEEPER

Challenge children who are fluent at finding number bonds to 100 using multiples of 10 by asking, for example: *Can you find the number bond to 100 from 37? How will you use your number bonds to 10 to help you?* Ask children to show the number bond on a bead string and then use a different representation.

KEY LANGUAGE

In lesson: number bonds, +, −, =

Other language to be used by the teacher: zero, ten, twenty, thirty, forty, fifty, sixty, seventy, eighty, ninety, one hundred, add, plus, more, subtract, minus, less

STRUCTURES AND REPRESENTATIONS

100 square, part-whole model, bar model, ten frame

RESOURCES

Optional: counters, bead strings, Base 10 equipment, 100 squares, blank ten frames, blank part-whole models, interlocking cubes

 In the eTextbook of this lesson, you will find interactive links to a selection of teaching tools.

Before you teach

• Were there any misconceptions in the previous lesson that will need addressing in this lesson?
• How will you adapt your planning to ensure you have time to address the misconceptions again with children?

Discover

Unit 16: Numbers to 100, Lesson 9

Bonds to 100 ❷

WAYS OF WORKING Pair work

ASK

- Question ❶ a): *How can you tell how many stamps Eddie has used?*
- Question ❶ a): *How many stamps does he have altogether?*
- Question ❶ a): *Can you work out how many he has left to use without counting them?*
- Question ❶ b): *What do you notice about the stamps he has printed on the wall?*

IN FOCUS Question ❶ is designed to help children see the similarities and differences between the number bonds to 10 and their partner bonds to 100. Encourage them to see the link between 3 + 7 = 10 and 30 + 70 = 100. You could ask them to show the link using resources or a picture of their own.

ANSWERS

Question ❶ a): Eddie has used 3 of the stamps.
Eddie has not used 7 of the stamps.
3 + 7 = 10

Question ❶ b): 30 squares have stamps in them.
70 squares do not have stamps in them.
30 + 70 = 100

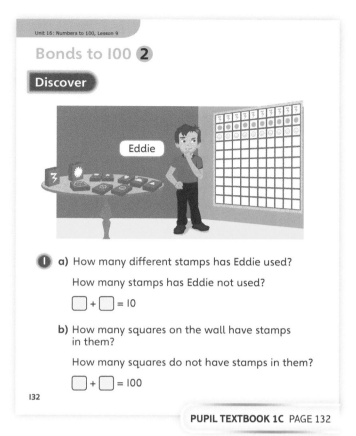

Discover

❶ a) How many different stamps has Eddie used?

How many stamps has Eddie not used?

☐ + ☐ = 10

b) How many squares on the wall have stamps in them?

How many squares do not have stamps in them?

☐ + ☐ = 100

132

PUPIL TEXTBOOK 1C PAGE 132

Share

WAYS OF WORKING Whole class teacher led

ASK

- Question ❶ a): *How did you write the number bond to 10? Can you write it in any other ways?*
- Question ❶ b): *How did you count the tens? Explain your reasoning.*
- Question ❶ b): *Astrid has chosen to use a part-whole model to work out what needs to be added to 30 to make 100. What other ways could she have used?*
- *What links can you see between the number bonds to 10 and 100? Do the pictures on the page make the links clear?*

IN FOCUS Use question ❶ b) to ensure children recognise the links between the two number bonds. Use Ash's comment at the bottom of the page to help children realise how they can use the relationship between number bonds to 10 and number bonds to 100 to help them in the future. Use the part-whole model to reinforce children's ability to find the related subtraction facts, as well as the addition facts that are the focus of the question.

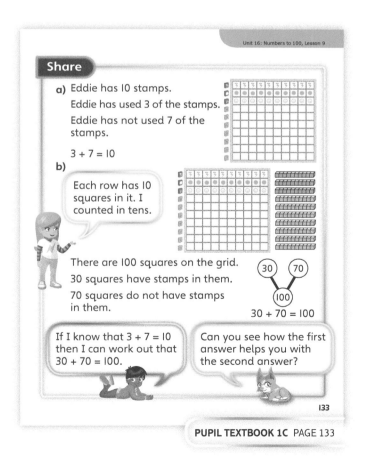

Share

a) Eddie has 10 stamps.
Eddie has used 3 of the stamps.
Eddie has not used 7 of the stamps.

3 + 7 = 10

b)

Each row has 10 squares in it. I counted in tens.

There are 100 squares on the grid.
30 squares have stamps in them.
70 squares do not have stamps in them.

30 ⌒ 70
100
30 + 70 = 100

If I know that 3 + 7 = 10 then I can work out that 30 + 70 = 100.

Can you see how the first answer helps you with the second answer?

133

PUPIL TEXTBOOK 1C PAGE 133

Think together

WAYS OF WORKING Whole class teacher led (I do, We do, You do)

ASK

- Question ❶ : *How will you write the number bond as an addition? Can you write the related subtraction?*
- Question ❶ : *Can you use the number bond to 10 to help you find the number bond to 100? Explain how.*
- Question ❷ : *How do you know which representation matches which set of number bonds?*
- Question ❷ : *Can you use the number bond to 100 to help you find the number bond to 10? Explain how.*

IN FOCUS Questions ❶ and ❷ support children in making the link between number bonds to 10 and number bonds to 100. The representations become increasingly abstract, enabling children to demonstrate fluency and independence when choosing concrete representations to support their understanding.

STRENGTHEN If children struggle with the abstract representations in question ❷ , ask them where they have seen the part-whole model and bar model before and discuss what they show. Ask children to make the numbers using concrete resources, then discuss what is the same and what is different about their representations and the part-whole model or bar model. Can they now use their representations to help them complete the number bonds?

DEEPEN Use Astrid's comment in question ❸ to encourage children to question any assumptions they make when solving problems. Ask: *Is Astrid correct? Explain your answer.* Discuss whether she could be both correct and mistaken at the same time. What advice would children give her?

ASSESSMENT CHECKPOINT Assess whether children can fluently explain the relationships between number bonds to 10 and number bonds to 100. Can they confidently use concrete and pictorial representations to demonstrate the link and make the number bonds?

ANSWERS

Question ❶ : 6 stamps are used.
4 stamps are not used.
6 + 4 = 10

60 squares have stamps in them.
40 squares do not have stamps in them.
60 + 40 = 100

Question ❷ : 1 + 9 = 10
10 + 90 = 100
80 + 20 = 100
8 + 2 = 10

Question ❸ : 60 + 40 = 100 or 40 + 60 = 100

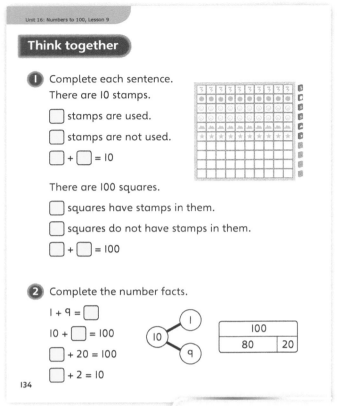

PUPIL TEXTBOOK 1C PAGE 134

PUPIL TEXTBOOK 1C PAGE 135

Practice

WAYS OF WORKING Independent thinking

IN FOCUS Question **4** will reinforce the link between the two sets of number bonds. Encourage children to explain which number bond they will find first and why.

STRENGTHEN If children struggle to identify the correct number bonds in question **3**, encourage them to represent the two numbers on a balloon using Base 10 equipment, by colouring in squares on a 100 square or using counters on ten frames. Then ask if the two numbers total 10 or 100 and how they can tell.

DEEPEN If children answer question **5** successfully, deepen their understanding by asking them to prove their solution using a picture. If children are able to do this, they could be encouraged to try to create their own word problems.

ASSESSMENT CHECKPOINT Assess whether children can find number bonds to 100. Children should be able to explain the link between number bonds to 10 and number bonds to 100, and should use different representations to support their reasoning.

ANSWERS Answers for the **Practice** part of the lesson appear in the separate **Practice and Reflect answer guide**.

Reflect

WAYS OF WORKING Pair work

IN FOCUS The **Reflect** part of the lesson tests children's recall of number bonds to 100. They should be able to explain how they know whether a bond is correct using concrete or pictorial representations and/or with reference to number bonds to 10.

ASSESSMENT CHECKPOINT Assess children's fluency in recognising and naming number bonds to 100. Some children may be able to recall some of the bonds without working them out. All children should recognise any mistakes made and be able to prove their thinking using multiple representations.

ANSWERS Answers for the **Reflect** part of the lesson appear in the separate **Practice and Reflect answer guide**.

After the lesson ▐▐

- How were children's problem-solving abilities improved during this lesson?
- Could you have offered more problem-solving opportunities?

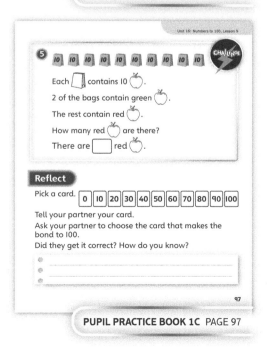

PUPIL PRACTICE BOOK 1C PAGE 95

PUPIL PRACTICE BOOK 1C PAGE 96

PUPIL PRACTICE BOOK 1C PAGE 97

End of unit check

> Don't forget the *Power Maths* unit assessment grid on p26.

WAYS OF WORKING Group work – adult led

IN FOCUS Question **4** assesses children's ability to read and understand a place value grid and use it to compare two numbers. It requires knowledge of the < and > signs.

Question **5** assesses children's fluency with number bonds to 100.

Think!

WAYS OF WORKING Pair work or small groups

IN FOCUS This question requires children to manipulate the number 75 using concrete, pictorial and abstract representations. Children need to recognise the place value of the digits within the number and represent the parts in different ways.

Draw children's attention to the vocabulary at the bottom of the page.

Encourage children to think through or discuss the structure of the number 75 before writing their answer in **My journal**.

ANSWERS AND COMMENTARY Children who have mastered the concepts of this unit will be able to count confidently in 10s and 1s and recognise how many tens and ones there are in any 2-digit number. They will be able to partition 2-digit numbers and compare them using the < and > signs. They will be able to find and use number bonds to 100, using their knowledge of number bonds to 10 to help them.

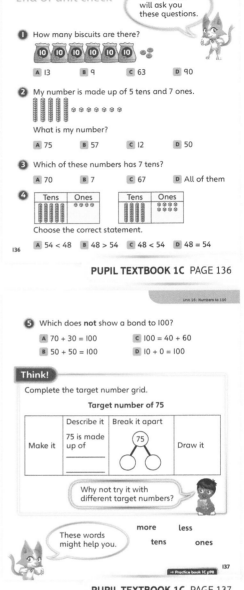

PUPIL TEXTBOOK 1C PAGE 136

PUPIL TEXTBOOK 1C PAGE 137

Q	A	WRONG ANSWERS AND MISCONCEPTIONS	STRENGTHENING UNDERSTANDING
1	C	B suggests that the child has simply counted everything as a one. D suggests that the child has counted everything as a ten.	If children are struggling with the concept of place value, ask them to make a number using a concrete resource and tell you how many full groups of 10 there are, and how many 'extra' ones there are. Encourage them to organise the representation on a blank place value grid. Ask: *How does this show how many tens and ones there are?*
2	B	A suggests that the child has transposed the digits.	
3	A	B, C or D suggests that the child is struggling with place value.	
4	C	Any incorrect answer suggests that the child has either incorrectly compared the numbers or does not have a secure understanding of the < and > signs.	If children struggle to compare numbers, ask them to make two numbers using Base 10 equipment and lay them out along a number line. Can they now see which number is bigger? Then ask them to arrange each representation on a blank place value grid. Ask: *Can you see how the place value grid shows the comparison?*
5	D	C suggests that the child has not recognised this as a number bond because the '100' does not come at the end.	

My journal

Independent thinking

ANSWERS AND COMMENTARY

Children should choose a clear, concrete method (for example, Base 10 equipment, counters, a bead string) to represent 75. They should write that '75 is made up of 7 tens and 5 ones' and complete the part-whole model to show 75 = 70 + 5 (with the parts in either order). Their drawing should clearly represent 75.

Assess how confidently children approach the task. Those who find it difficult may not yet have a secure understanding of place value and will need intervention support before this topic is taught again in Year 2 Unit 1.

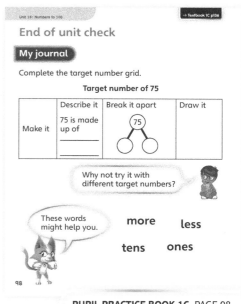

PUPIL PRACTICE BOOK 1C PAGE 98

Power check

WAYS OF WORKING Independent thinking

ASK

- *Do you think you could explain what you have learned about place value to someone else?*
- *How confident do you feel about comparing and ordering numbers?*

Power play

WAYS OF WORKING Pair work or small groups

IN FOCUS Use this **Power play** to see if children can compare two 2-digit numbers or (if playing in groups of three or four) order 2-digit numbers in ascending and descending order. Children who have mastered the concepts involved may be able to spot advantageous combinations of digits that they can choose to help them win the game.

ANSWERS AND COMMENTARY If children are able to play the game confidently and compare and order the numbers fluently, it would suggest that they are confident with place value and comparing numbers. If they are still struggling, they may need to be offered the opportunity to go back to some of the strengthening activities for these two concepts.

PUPIL PRACTICE BOOK 1C PAGE 99

After the unit ⏸

- How could the concepts covered in this unit be taken further in other areas of the curriculum? Comparing and ordering numbers can be implemented easily into PE through comparing scores. How else could these concepts be practised?
- How confidently were children able to apply their understanding of this unit to their reasoning? Were they able to use the vocabulary fluently?

Strengthen and **Deepen** activities for this unit can be found in the *Power Maths* online subscription.

165

Unit 17
Time

Mastery Expert tip! "As a teacher, I am always talking about time, and this means that there are lots of ways to reinforce the learning from this unit outside of lessons. I use the classroom clock a lot when talking about the events of the day, and how long things will take."

Don't forget to watch the Unit 17 video!

WHY THIS UNIT IS IMPORTANT

This unit introduces children to various aspects of time. Children will develop their ability to tell the time by reading an analogue clock or watch, estimating and comparing durations, and carrying out simple calculations involving time. All of these skills have real practical importance in daily life. Despite the popularity of digital displays, the ability to read time 'at a glance' from an analogue display remains a vital skill for children to learn.

In this unit, children strengthen their understanding of the hands of a clock, including the second hand. Children will develop their understanding of units of measurement of time (hours, minutes and seconds). They will use the following vocabulary to develop their understanding of durations of time and the ordering of events in time: 'before', 'after', 'yesterday', 'today', 'tomorrow', 'day', 'week', 'date', 'month', 'year', 'calendar', 'faster or slower', 'longer or shorter' and 'earlier or later'.

Finally, children will use number lines to calculate simple addition and subtraction word problems involving time.

WHERE THIS UNIT FITS

→ Unit 16: Numbers to 100
→ **Unit 17: Time**
→ Unit 18: Money

This unit builds on, and formalises, children's experiences of using various measurements of time in daily life, as well as their prior experience with numbers, calculations, and problem solving.

Before they start this unit, it is expected that children:
- recognise a clock face and a calendar, and understand that they are used to tell the time and day or date, respectively
- can carry out simple addition and subtraction calculations
- can use real-world knowledge and experience to sequence events.

ASSESSING MASTERY

Children who have mastered the work in this unit will be able to work confidently within simple situations involving time, including understanding clocks and calendars. They will be able to tell the time to the half hour using an analogue clock or watch, and use a calendar to say what day of the week a particular date falls on. They will be able to use a range of language to order and estimate the duration of familiar events, and they will be able to solve simple problems involving various units of time.

COMMON MISCONCEPTIONS	STRENGTHENING UNDERSTANDING	GOING DEEPER
Some children may find sequencing events hard and may need support in using the appropriate language (such as 'before' and 'after', 'faster' and 'slower').	The number line is a particularly useful representation of events sequenced in time and can be used to assist with calculations.	Some children will be ready for more advanced language patterns involving several factors: 'the blue car arrived after the yellow car, but before the red one'.
Some children may have little knowledge of important facts (like the sequence of months) and some real-world experiences may be misleading: children may have heard adults say things such as 'We had to wait hours for the bus this morning!'	Make sure that the learning in this lesson is related to real-world experiences wherever possible, and exploit opportunities to talk about times, dates and sequences of events as these arise during the school routine.	Some children will already know the months of the year, days of the week and how to tell the time. The activities in this lesson will allow you to find out how secure this knowledge is. Can they explain what they know, and use it to solve problems?

WAYS OF WORKING

Use these pages to introduce the unit focus to children. You can use the characters to explore different ways of working too.

The rate of progress through this unit will depend to some extent on children's existing knowledge and real-world experiences. You may find it useful to talk through each of the examples here in turn, and try to get an idea of children's current understanding.

STRUCTURES AND REPRESENTATIONS

Clocks: Clocks are used regularly to show how to tell the time and measure durations of time. They are used for demonstration purposes and also as the basis of problems to solve. Various clocks should be used, including analogue wall clocks, watches, stopwatches and sand timers.

Calendars: Calendars are used to show particular dates and the passage of time over periods of days, weeks and months within a year. They indicate the day of the week as well as the number of days within a month and the months of the year.

December

S	M	T	W	T	F	S
				1	2	3
4	5	6	7	8	9	10
11	12	13	14	15	16	17
18	19	20	21	22	23	24
25	26	27	28	29	30	31

KEY LANGUAGE

There is some key language that children will need to know as part of the learning in this unit:

→ before, after
→ faster, slower, shorter, longer, earlier, later
→ yesterday, today, tomorrow
→ day, week, month, year
→ Monday, Tuesday, Wednesday, Thursday, Friday, Saturday, Sunday
→ calendar, date
→ minute hand, hour hand, second hand
→ o'clock, half past
→ second, minute, hour

Unit 17
Time

In this unit we will …
⚡ Say if things happen before or after
⚡ Use a calendar
⚡ Tell time to the hour and the half hour
⚡ Compare time
⚡ Solve time word problems

This is a calendar. Can you use it to find how many days are in a week?

138

PUPIL TEXTBOOK 1C PAGE 138

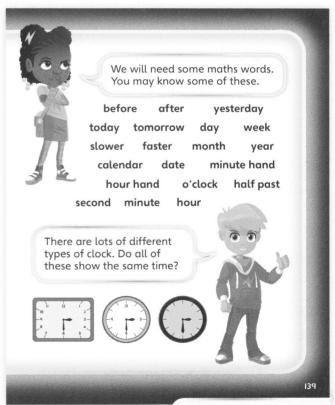

We will need some maths words. You may know some of these.

before   after   yesterday
today   tomorrow   day   week
slower   faster   month   year
calendar   date   minute hand
hour hand   o'clock   half past
second   minute   hour

There are lots of different types of clock. Do all of these show the same time?

139

PUPIL TEXTBOOK 1C PAGE 139

Using before and after

Learning focus

In this lesson, children will use a range of language to sequence events in chronological order.

Small steps

→ Previous step: Bonds to 100 (2)
→ **This step: Using before and after**
→ Next step: Using a calendar

NATIONAL CURRICULUM LINKS

Year 1 Measurement – Time

Sequence events in chronological order using language (for example, before and after, next, first, today, yesterday, tomorrow, morning, afternoon and evening).

ASSESSING MASTERY

Children can use a range of language, especially 'before' and 'after', but also 'yesterday', 'today', 'tomorrow' and the days of the week, to describe the order of a series of events, including events in their own daily routine. Children can make sensible suggestions about things that might have happened before or after a given event.

COMMON MISCONCEPTIONS

Children may have problems with sequencing. Earlier work on number and measurement will probably already have identified children who find sequencing particularly difficult, but it is sensible to use this lesson as a further check. Ask:
• *What will we do before lunch? What will we do after?*

STRENGTHENING UNDERSTANDING

Where children find it difficult to handle the 'information content' of a number of events, make some simple cards to represent the events – arranging a set of cards makes less demand on working memory than trying to sort events 'in your head'. In addition, some children may not know the sequence of days of the week so this lesson is a good time to check that this knowledge is secure.

GOING DEEPER

The language patterns used in this lesson are very simple, but form the basis for more complex forms that some children may be ready for. For example, ask: *Can you tell me what clubs run on the days that are after Tuesday and before Friday?* Make sure that children understand that we are talking about one set of days that meets both conditions (Wednesday and Thursday).

KEY LANGUAGE

In lesson: before, after, yesterday, today, tomorrow, days of the week, Sunday, Monday, Tuesday, Wednesday, Thursday, Friday, Saturday

Other language used by the teacher: next, first, last, morning, afternoon, evening

STRUCTURES AND REPRESENTATIONS

Number lines

RESOURCES

Optional: cards to represent events (pictorially)

 In the eTextbook of this lesson, you will find interactive links to a selection of teaching tools.

Before you teach ⏸

• Are children confident sequencing numbers?
• What resources will you provide for children who are still developing this skill?

Discover

Unit 17: Time, Lesson 1

WAYS OF WORKING Pair work

ASK

- *These pictures show Maya's day. What is the first thing that happens in the morning?*
- *Is this a school day? How can you tell?*
- *What is the last thing that you see Maya doing?*

IN FOCUS This activity features a set of pictures that are organised in 'comic strip' format to represent a series of activities taking place on one school day. The pictures are arranged in chronological order – before, during and after school.

ANSWERS

Question ❶ a): Before school, Maya wakes up, gets dressed, eats her breakfast, brushes her teeth and walks to school.

Question ❶ b): After school, Maya leaves school, plays outside, goes to bed and reads a book.

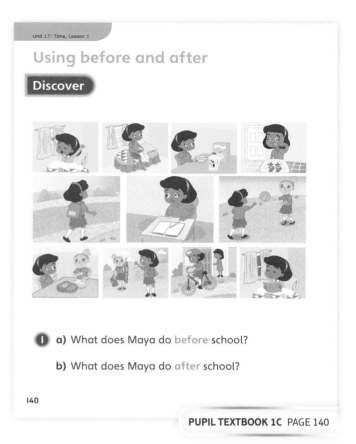

Using before and after

Discover

❶ a) What does Maya do before school?

b) What does Maya do after school?

140

PUPIL TEXTBOOK 1C PAGE 140

Share

WAYS OF WORKING Whole class teacher led

ASK

- *Look at what Astrid says. Which is the first picture that shows Maya at school?*
- *Flo worked out the question another way – she thought about the things that Maya would have to do before school, and the things that she could only do after school. Can you do it that way?*

IN FOCUS The fact that the pictures are set out in order means that either of the methods described here will work; if the pictures were in a random order, we would only have the 'common sense' method that Flo used. This might be ambiguous in some cases – for example, it could be argued that Maya could have gone out on her bike before school. However, the point of this activity is to get the children thinking in terms of 'before, during and after', and using the corresponding language.

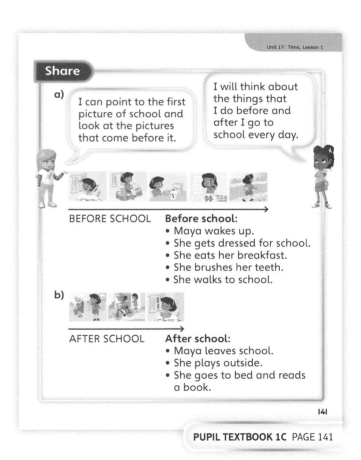

Share

a) I can point to the first picture of school and look at the pictures that come before it.

I will think about the things that I do before and after I go to school every day.

BEFORE SCHOOL

Before school:
- Maya wakes up.
- She gets dressed for school.
- She eats her breakfast.
- She brushes her teeth.
- She walks to school.

b)

AFTER SCHOOL

After school:
- Maya leaves school.
- She plays outside.
- She goes to bed and reads a book.

141

PUPIL TEXTBOOK 1C PAGE 141

Think together

ASK

- *Look at question* ❷ *. What is this girl doing? Why is she doing it?*
- *Question* ❷ *: What do you think might have happened after she watered the plant?*
- *Question* ❷ *: What would have happened before?*

IN FOCUS Question ❸ uses the days of the week. Apart from knowing the names of the days, the question makes use of the patterns 'before or after day X' to mean *all* of the preceding or following days that week, and 'the day before or after day X' to mean the day immediately preceding or following it.

STRENGTHEN There will be plenty of opportunities in children's daily routine to reinforce the sequence of day names, and the use of the key vocabulary related to chronological order. You could make a point of asking questions using this vocabulary, like: *What are you doing tomorrow afternoon? What was the weather here like yesterday?*

You could also get a week's weather forecast for your local area, and ask children to talk about the predictions.

DEEPEN The basic language patterns used in this lesson can naturally be extended to others that are more precise or longer term. For example, ask children: *What did you do yesterday afternoon? What will you do in three days' time?*

ASSESSMENT CHECKPOINT Use question ❸ to check that children know the names of the days of the week. For example, ask: *It was raining on the day after Wednesday, what day was that?* You can also check understanding of 'yesterday, today and tomorrow'. Ask: *Let's imagine that today is Wednesday. What is the weather like today? What was it like yesterday? What about tomorrow?*

ANSWERS

Question ❶ : Joe gets changed before he plays football and drinks some water after he plays football.

Question ❷ : There are many possible answers. For example, the 'before' scene could involve the girl planting a seed, or filling up the watering can, or simply the plant in a pot in need of water. The 'after' scene could show a taller plant, a flower blooming, or the girl putting the watering can away.

Question ❸ a): Before Tuesday, the weather was sunny.

Question ❸ b): On the day after Wednesday, there was thunder and rain.

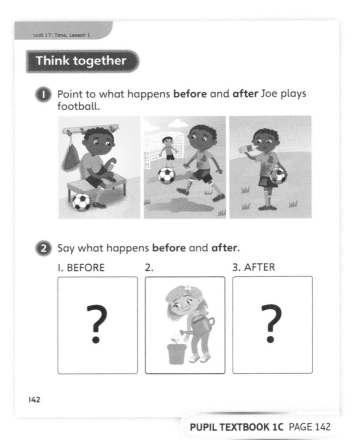

Unit 17: Time, Lesson 1

Think together

❶ Point to what happens **before** and **after** Joe plays football.

❷ Say what happens **before** and **after**.

1. BEFORE   2.   3. AFTER

142

PUPIL TEXTBOOK 1C PAGE 142

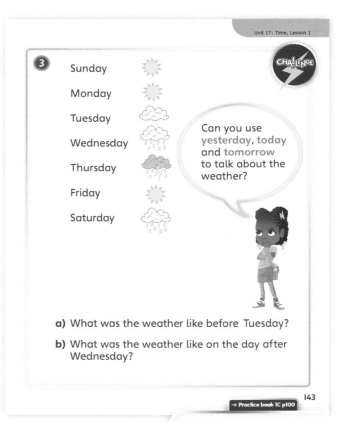

❸ Sunday
Monday
Tuesday
Wednesday
Thursday
Friday
Saturday

Can you use yesterday, today and tomorrow to talk about the weather?

a) What was the weather like before Tuesday?

b) What was the weather like on the day after Wednesday?

→ Practice book 1C p100

143

PUPIL TEXTBOOK 1C PAGE 143

Practice

WAYS OF WORKING Independent thinking

IN FOCUS Question ③ involves using 'before' and 'after' in conjunction with the names of the days of the week. Doing this with the sequence of day names available in print is a stepping stone towards being able to step through the day names, in either order, purely mentally.

STRENGTHEN The sequence of questions in this section follows some of the stages that children will need to go through in developing their understanding: first understanding the logical order of events, then labelling these with simple markers like 'before' and 'after', and then using a broader range of relationships and language to describe more complicated situations. For example, 'If today was Saturday, then tomorrow would be Sunday'. Where children find this work difficult, investigate at what stage in this learning sequence the problems first occur.

DEEPEN The arrangement of the day names in question ④ is similar in structure to a number line. Use this structure to show children some useful analogies such as how 'adding one' is similar to 'one day after' or 'tomorrow'.

ASSESSMENT CHECKPOINT Questions ① and ② involve using real-life experience to order events in time. Check that children can make sense of all of these situations; they should be straightforward, but some children may not be aware that chicks hatch from eggs and they may not have had the practical experience of posting a letter.

ANSWERS Answers for the **Practice** part of the lesson appear in the separate **Practice and Reflect answer guide**.

Reflect

WAYS OF WORKING Pair work

IN FOCUS This activity asks children to tell a story of what might have happened before and after the situation illustrated. Children are natural story tellers, so encourage imaginative responses.

ASSESSMENT CHECKPOINT Check that children's explanations distinguish between events occurring before and after the illustration. There is an element of cause and effect here: how did the girl get into the unfortunate situation shown? What should happen next?

ANSWERS Answers for the **Reflect** part of the lesson appear in the separate **Practice and Reflect answer guide**.

After the lesson ⏸

- Are children confident in using the names of the days of the week?
- Did children have difficulty using the basic patterns of 'before' and 'after'?
- Are children confident with more complex relationships such as 'the day after tomorrow'?

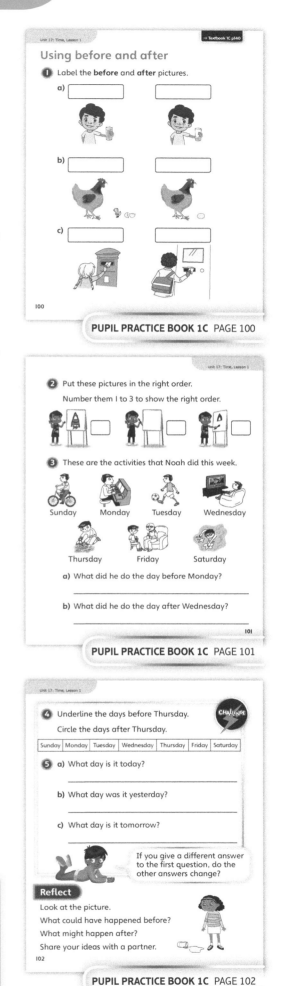

PUPIL PRACTICE BOOK 1C PAGE 100

PUPIL PRACTICE BOOK 1C PAGE 101

PUPIL PRACTICE BOOK 1C PAGE 102

Using a calendar

Learning focus

In this lesson, children use a calendar to read and record information related to days and dates.

Small steps

→ Previous step: Using before and after
→ **This step: Using a calendar**
→ Next step: Telling time to the hour

NATIONAL CURRICULUM LINKS

Year 1 Measurement – Time

Recognise and use language relating to dates, including days of the week, weeks, months and years.

ASSESSING MASTERY

Children can use a calendar to identify and record events on a particular day, and can find the day of the week that a particular date falls on. Children can say a date in the form, for example 'Sunday the 9th of November', and read and understand dates given in the form 'Sunday 9 November'.

COMMON MISCONCEPTIONS

Some children may find the number of sequences that come together to produce a calendar – month names, day names, and the numerical sequence of dates – difficult. They will need time and practice to make sense of this complexity. Ask:
• *What can you tell by looking at a calendar?*

STRENGTHENING UNDERSTANDING

Build on children's existing understanding and experience, using calendars to record key events such as leisure activities, birthdays and holidays. Help children to reflect on the structure of the calendar, in particular how each row represents a week, usually starting on a Sunday. You may find it useful to have a large calendar in the classroom and use it to record the dates of key events.

GOING DEEPER

There is a lot more to learn about the calendar, and some children will be ready to go further. Encourage children to memorise the sequence of month names, understanding that months have different numbers of days, eventually learning the number of days in each month ('Thirty days hath September…'), and understanding leap years.

KEY LANGUAGE

In lesson: day, week, date, calendar, month, year, day names (Sunday, Monday, …), month names (January, February, …), number day in the month, day of the week, today, yesterday, tomorrow

STRUCTURES AND REPRESENTATIONS

Calendars

RESOURCES

Optional: a range of printed and digital calendars

 In the eTextbook of this lesson, you will find interactive links to a selection of teaching tools.

Before you teach

• Do children know the sequence of day names?
• Is there a calendar in your classroom? If so, how do you use it?
• Do children know the sequence of month names? How can you strengthen children's knowledge of month names?

Discover

WAYS OF WORKING Pair work

ASK

- *Aisha is looking at a calendar. Which month does the calendar show?*
- *What are these words written at the top of the calendar, underneath the word 'November'?*
- *What day of the week was the 1st November?*

IN FOCUS This activity involves reading a calendar, and identifying the dates and days of the week on which particular events occur. The point here is to make sure that children are aware that the calendar is more than just an unstructured list of days – it incorporates information about which month we are in, and which day of the week each date falls on.

ANSWERS

Question ❶ a): Aisha's birthday is on Sunday 19 November.

Question ❶ b): Aisha visits the dentist on a Monday. The date is 13 November.

Using a calendar

Discover

This is my birthday!

❶ a) When is Aisha's birthday?

b) On what **day** of the **week** does Aisha visit the dentist? What **date** is this?

144

PUPIL TEXTBOOK 1C PAGE 144

Share

WAYS OF WORKING Whole class teacher led

ASK

- *In these little calendars, we have just got one letter for the days of the week. Do you still know which is which? Why are there two Ts and two Ss?*
- *Where would you look on a calendar to find out what month is shown?*
- *Once you have found the date that you are looking for, how do you find out what day of the week it is?*

IN FOCUS Ensure that children are clear about the difference between the idea of a date (which is a number), and the day of the week (which is a day name). Talk about how these are used in everyday life. For example, you may use day names when you are talking about events that are happening soon or events that recur: *What are you doing on Thursday? What evening does the club meet?* For events planned further in the future, we tend to use dates: *Remember, Sports Day is the 10th July.*

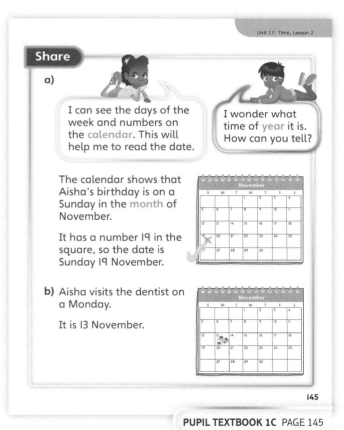

Share

a)

I can see the days of the week and numbers on the **calendar**. This will help me to read the date.

I wonder what time of **year** it is. How can you tell?

The calendar shows that Aisha's birthday is on a Sunday in the **month** of November.

It has a number 19 in the square, so the date is Sunday 19 November.

b) Aisha visits the dentist on a Monday.

It is 13 November.

145

PUPIL TEXTBOOK 1C PAGE 145

Think together

WAYS OF WORKING **WAYS OF WORKING** Whole class teacher led (I do, We do, You do)

ASK

- In question **1**, what month is Charlie looking at? Can you see where he has marked his birthday?
- It says 'M' above Charlie's birthday. What day of the week does this mean?
- Can you say Charlie's birthday in full – with the date, the day of the week, and the name of the month?

IN FOCUS Question **3** introduces a full calendar for a complete year. You may wish to use a 'real' calendar for the current year instead. Ensure that children understand the order of the months – 'across first, then down'. You could ask a range of further questions here. For example, ask: *What day of the week is your birthday? What about Christmas? How many months start on a Monday?*

STRENGTHEN Some children may find the density of information in the full calendar overwhelming. Try working with one 'layer' of information at a time – perhaps just finding a month at first, then a date within a month, and then finding the day of the week for a date.

DEEPEN Children with a secure understanding of the work in this section could start to look at the structure of the calendar in more depth. Ask: *Which days have 31 days? What happens to February in a leap year? If I know today's date, how can I use the calendar to find the date in a week's time?*

ASSESSMENT CHECKPOINT Check that children are familiar with the sequence of month names, even if they have not yet memorised the complete sequence, and check that they can read and locate the months in the calendar. If you are confident that they can find months reliably, check that children can read up from a date to a day of the week, and that they can distinguish between the days with the same initial letters (Tuesday and Thursday, Saturday and Sunday).

ANSWERS

Question **1** : Charlie's birthday is Monday 18 April.

Question **2** : Izzy should draw a cross in the square on the calendar marked '8'.

Question **3** : In the calendar shown, there are four Mondays in June.

PUPIL TEXTBOOK 1C PAGE 146

PUPIL TEXTBOOK 1C PAGE 147

Practice

WAYS OF WORKING Independent thinking

IN FOCUS Question ③ features a number of simple practical tasks related to the calendar: recording a day in the month and identifying a day of the week. These tasks can be practised outside of lessons, by using a classroom calendar.

STRENGTHEN Where children need more practice with the tasks in this section, you may want to suggest to parents and carers that they discuss the 'family calendar' with their child – regularly recording and talking about upcoming events, and discussing what dates and days of the week they fall on.

DEEPEN Children who are confident with the work here could be challenged to carry out more complicated date calculations, including those that go beyond the information shown. For example, given the December calendar shown in question ③ , can children work out what day of the week 1 January the following year falls on? What about 1 February?

ASSESSMENT CHECKPOINT Question ② allows you to assess how children work through all of the key steps in using a calendar that are covered in this lesson: identifying a month, reading the date and looking up the day of the week. This sequence of tasks needs to be carried out in order, even if some of the steps are carried out very quickly. If children find this question difficult, try to identify at which step the problem first occurs.

ANSWERS Answers for the **Practice** part of the lesson appear in the separate **Practice and Reflect answer guide**.

Reflect

WAYS OF WORKING Pair work

IN FOCUS In this lesson, the calendar has been used in a number of ways, including marking an event, locating a marked event, reading a month, finding a date and looking up the days of the week. The **Reflect** activity provides a chance to reflect on the various uses of the calendar which have been introduced.

ASSESSMENT CHECKPOINT Responses here will help to indicate which aspects were significant to each child, and should help you to identify those children who are still becoming familiar with the structure of the calendar.

ANSWERS Answers for the **Reflect** part of the lesson appear in the separate **Practice and Reflect answer guide**.

After the lesson ⏸

- Will children have opportunities to continue to use calendars as part of their regular school routine?
- Are children familiar with the sequence of month names? Have they committed these to memory?

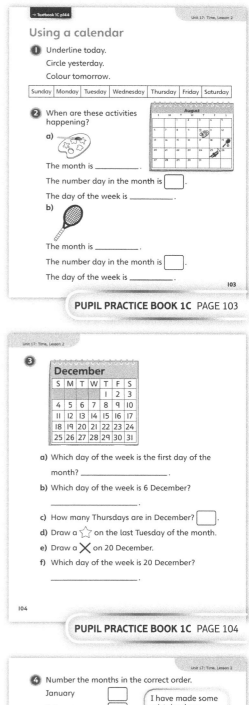

PUPIL PRACTICE BOOK 1C PAGE 103

PUPIL PRACTICE BOOK 1C PAGE 104

PUPIL PRACTICE BOOK 1C PAGE 105

Telling time to the hour

Learning focus

In this lesson, children will use an analogue clock face to read a time to the hour, that is a whole number of hours ('something o'clock').

Small steps

→ Previous step: Using a calendar
→ **This step: Telling time to the hour**
→ Next step: Telling time to the half hour

NATIONAL CURRICULUM LINKS

Year 1 Measurement – Time

Tell the time to the hour and half past the hour and draw the hands on a clock face to show these times.

ASSESSING MASTERY

Children can tell the time using an analogue clock set to a 'whole hour' and they know that all such times are 'something o'clock'. Children can understand the importance of distinguishing between the hour hand and the minute hand, they know that the hour hand is the shorter one, and they are starting to relate the time shown on a clock to times of the day and familiar events.

COMMON MISCONCEPTIONS

Children may encounter many potential problems in starting to tell the time: they may confuse the minute and hour hands, or find it difficult to understand that there are two distinct scales (hours and minutes) arranged in a circular fashion around the clock face. More fundamentally, some children may have only a rudimentary familiarity with times of the day – 'home time' being a more fundamental idea than '3 pm'. Ask:
• What time do you start school? What time do you go home?

STRENGTHENING UNDERSTANDING

Some children will benefit from additional practice, perhaps using a model clock to indicate a range of times. This could easily be turned into a simple game: make some cards, with a time written on each one, deal the cards face down, then turn them up one card at a time, and score one point for each time that is made successfully on the model clock.

GOING DEEPER

Some children may already be able to tell the time to the nearest hour or better. Challenge confident children to draw their own clock faces to show particular times. This is a very useful exercise that encourages children to think carefully about the angular spacing of the numbers around the clock face.

KEY LANGUAGE

In lesson: minute hand, o'clock, hour hand, minute, hour

Other language used by the teacher: longer, shorter

STRUCTURES AND REPRESENTATIONS

Clock faces

RESOURCES

Optional: printed clock faces, model clocks, real clocks, cards with times written on

 In the eTextbook of this lesson, you will find interactive links to a selection of teaching tools.

Before you teach ⏸
• Can any children already tell the time?
• Do any children wear a watch? Digital or analogue?
• Do you have a classroom clock? Do you use it as part of your classroom routine?

Discover

Pair work

ASK

- Question ❶ a): *Look at the picture. How are you going to work out what time it is now?*
- Question ❶ a): *How many hands can you see on the clock? Do you know how to use them to work out what the time is now?*
- Question ❶ b): *How do you know what time the party starts?*

IN FOCUS This activity features a familiar activity where children might be keen to tell the time. Point out the clock on the wall, and make sure that the children understand that they will need to use both the information on the clock and the facts provided in the question to reach a solution.

ANSWERS

Question ❶ a): The clock says that the time is 3 o'clock.

Question ❶ b): At 5 o'clock, the minute hand will be in the same position (pointing straight up to the 12), but the hour hand will be pointing at the 5.

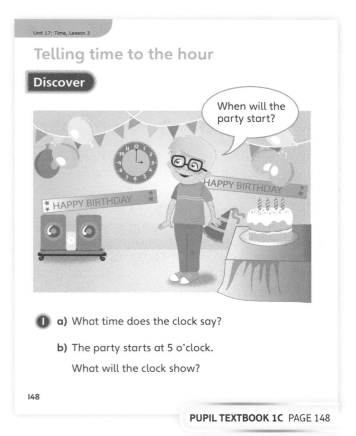

Telling time to the hour

Discover

When will the party start?

❶ a) What time does the clock say?

b) The party starts at 5 o'clock.

What will the clock show?

148

PUPIL TEXTBOOK 1C PAGE 148

Share

Whole class teacher led

ASK

- *Look at Ash's question. Why are there two hands on the clock? What are they called?*
- *Start by looking at o'clock times – one o'clock, two o'clock, and so on. Where will the minute hand be pointing when it is an o'clock time?*
- *Astrid says that she knows how to draw a clock face for the other o'clock times. Would you know how to do it?*

IN FOCUS The key ideas to communicate to children here are:

- The clock has two hands – a minute hand and an hour hand. The hour hand is the shorter one.
- You do not need to worry too much about the minute hand at first. All you need to know is that when it is pointing straight up, it is one of the o'clock times.
- When the minute hand is pointing straight up, the hour hand tells us 'what o'clock' it is.

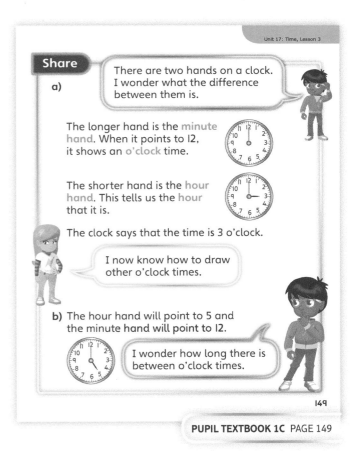

Share

a) There are two hands on a clock. I wonder what the difference between them is.

The longer hand is the minute hand. When it points to 12, it shows an o'clock time.

The shorter hand is the hour hand. This tells us the hour that it is.

The clock says that the time is 3 o'clock.

I now know how to draw other o'clock times.

b) The hour hand will point to 5 and the minute hand will point to 12.

I wonder how long there is between o'clock times.

149

PUPIL TEXTBOOK 1C PAGE 149

Think together

Unit 17: Time, Lesson 3

WAYS OF WORKING Whole class teacher led (I do, We do, You do)

ASK

- *Look at the questions ❶ and ❷. Both of these times are 'something o'clock'. How do you know that?*
- *Which of the hands on the clock is the hour hand?*
- *How can you use the hour hand to work out what the times are?*

IN FOCUS In questions ❶ and ❷, the key ideas are to distinguish between the minute and hour hand, then to recognise that the minute hand pointing straight up indicates 'something o'clock', and finally that the hour hand indicates 'what o'clock' it is.

STRENGTHEN If children find questions ❶ and ❷ difficult, check each stage of the process for telling the time to the nearest hour. Can children consistently distinguish between the minute and hour hands? Can they associate the minute hand pointing straight up with 'something o'clock'? Can they use the hour hand to determine what the hour is?

DEEPEN The very simple clock faces used in these questions are designed to be as easy to read as possible. Real clocks may not be quite so simple. Try finding pictures of clocks with more complicated faces, for example, Big Ben. Can children explain how these work?

ASSESSMENT CHECKPOINT Check that children can correctly read the time on the clock faces shown in questions ❶ and ❷. If in doubt, set further examples of the same kind to help children practise each stage of the process for telling time carefully.

ANSWERS

Question ❶ : The time is 7 o'clock.

Question ❷ : The time is 2 o'clock.

Question ❸ : Paul has drawn the hour hand wrongly. The time he has drawn is really 11 o'clock.

Maria has got the minute and hour hands mixed up.

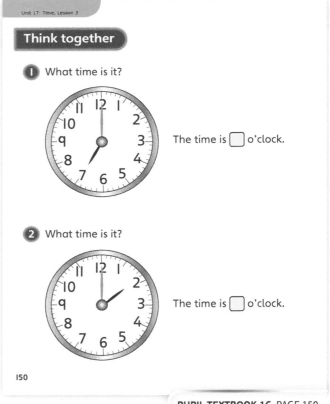

PUPIL TEXTBOOK 1C PAGE 150

PUPIL TEXTBOOK 1C PAGE 151

Practice

WAYS OF WORKING Independent thinking

IN FOCUS Question ❶ provides some straightforward examples that cover the main content of the lesson. Ensure that children know what is required. They can simply draw lines to show which clock face goes with each of the times.

STRENGTHEN Some children may benefit from additional practice with reading or writing the time to the nearest hour, using either printed clock faces or a demonstration clock.

DEEPEN Question ❷ features a wider variety of clock faces. Ask children to investigate what other watch and clock faces are available. Can they tell the time with other designs of clock face?

ASSESSMENT CHECKPOINT Use question ❸ to check that children can draw their own clock faces to represent each of the times shown. Make sure that they draw the minute hand pointing straight up, and clearly longer than the hour hand, which should be pointing at the correct hour. If there are mistakes with any of these points, ask children to explain what they did, in order to try to work out the exact step where they are going wrong.

ANSWERS Answers for the **Practice** part of the lesson appear in the separate **Practice and Reflect answer guide**.

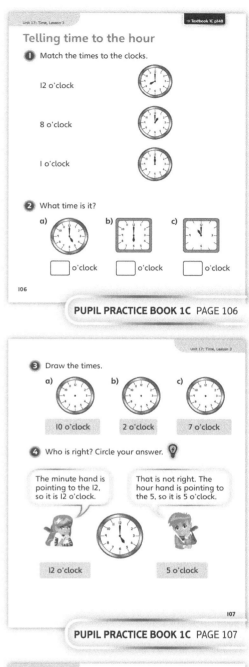

PUPIL PRACTICE BOOK 1C PAGE 106

PUPIL PRACTICE BOOK 1C PAGE 107

Reflect

WAYS OF WORKING Pair work

IN FOCUS In this question, children need to sketch a clock face showing a time of 4 o'clock. This is quite challenging, as it involves drawing a reasonably accurate picture of a clock with the numbers 1–12 in approximately the correct positions, before going on to draw recognisable minute and hour hands in the correct positions.

ASSESSMENT CHECKPOINT Look out for the main features of a correct answer: the minute hand pointing straight up, with a shorter hour hand pointing at the number 4, which should be in the right general position on the clock face. Children with a sounder grasp of this material may be able to position all of the numbers in approximately the correct positions around the clock face.

ANSWERS Answers for the **Reflect** part of the lesson appear in the separate **Practice and Reflect answer guide**.

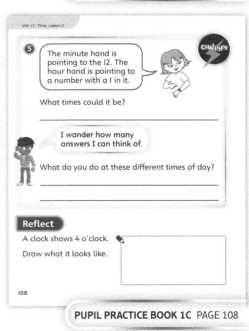

PUPIL PRACTICE BOOK 1C PAGE 108

After the lesson ⏸

- How will you build further practice into the daily classroom routine, perhaps using the classroom clock?
- Can children already tell the time to greater levels of precision?

179

Telling time to the half hour

Learning focus

In this lesson, children will use an analogue clock face to tell the time to the nearest half hour ('something o'clock', or 'half past something').

Small steps

→ Previous step: Telling time to the hour
→ **This step: Telling time to the half hour**
→ Next step: Writing time

NATIONAL CURRICULUM LINKS

Year 1 Measurement – Time

Tell the time to the hour and half past the hour and draw the hands on a clock face to show these times.

ASSESSING MASTERY

Children can distinguish between the minute and hour hands of an analogue clock or watch. Children can use the position of the minute hand to identify times that are 'something o'clock' and 'half past something', and they can use the position of the hour hand to identify the hour.

COMMON MISCONCEPTIONS

Some children may have difficulty in deciding which number the hour hand has just passed. Ask:
• *Where is the hour hand? Which numbers is it between? Which number has it already passed? So, you know it is half past something – but half past what hour?*

STRENGTHENING UNDERSTANDING

Some children may be less familiar with the idea of 'half past the hour'. Try to use descriptive language to support understanding, for example: *'The time is half past 8. That means that we have already gone past 8 o'clock, but it is not 9 o'clock yet; it is exactly half way between 8 o'clock and 9 o'clock.'*

GOING DEEPER

Some children may already know how to tell time to the nearest minute, and may be able to read a wide range of analogue and digital clock faces. You could encourage them to think more deeply about the relative positions of the hands on a clock. Ask: *How can you tell whether the position of the hands on a clock is real or made up? Which positions are never allowed?*

KEY LANGUAGE

In lesson: half past, hour, minute, hand, half way, between

STRUCTURES AND REPRESENTATIONS

Analogue clock face, marked with the numbers 1–12

RESOURCES

Optional: printed clock faces for children to complete, demonstration analogue clock face, marked with numbers 1–12.

 In the eTextbook of this lesson, you will find interactive links to a selection of teaching tools.

Before you teach

• Are children confident in telling the time to the hour?
• Are there any routine events in the day that happen at 'half past something', and that could be used as examples?

Discover

Unit 17: Time, Lesson 4

WAYS OF WORKING Pair work

ASK

- *What time does the teacher say that the assembly starts?*
- *Can you see the minute hand on the classroom clock in the picture? Where is it pointing?*
- *How long does it take for the minute hand to go around once? What will happen to the hour hand in the same time?*

IN FOCUS This activity uses a familiar setting to introduce the idea of times that are 'half past something'. Children may already be familiar with the spoken form of this pattern; the activity asks them to relate this to the display on an analogue clock face.

ANSWERS

Question **1** a): The time now is half past 9.

Question **1** b): When it is time for assembly, the minute hand will be pointing straight down (at the 6), and the hour hand will be half way between the 10 and 11.

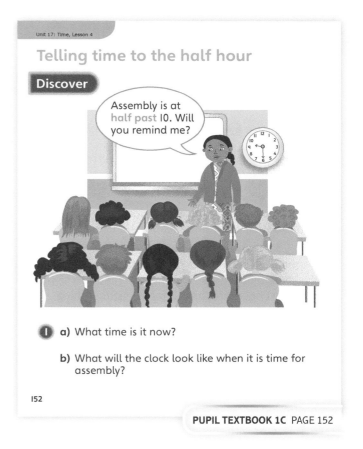

Telling time to the half hour

Discover

> Assembly is at **half past 10**. Will you remind me?

1 a) What time is it now?

b) What will the clock look like when it is time for assembly?

152

PUPIL TEXTBOOK 1C PAGE 152

Share

WAYS OF WORKING Whole class teacher led

ASK

- *Remember, the clock has two hands – the hour hand, and the minute hand. How do you tell which is which?*
- *Which way are the hands of the clock moving? Is it this way [indicate clockwise], or this way [indicate anticlockwise]?*
- *We already know how to spot times which are 'something o'clock'. How can you use the minute hand to spot times that are 'half past something'?*

IN FOCUS The amount of information involved in this part of the lesson may be quite daunting. Get children to focus on the key ideas in the following order:

- You already know that the minute hand pointing straight up indicates 'something o'clock'.
- Now you are finding out what happens when the minute hand is pointing straight down: these are 'half-past something' times.
- You find out the 'something' by looking at the hour hand – the time is half past *the hour that the hour hand has just passed*. You also need to know which way the hour hand is turning (clockwise).

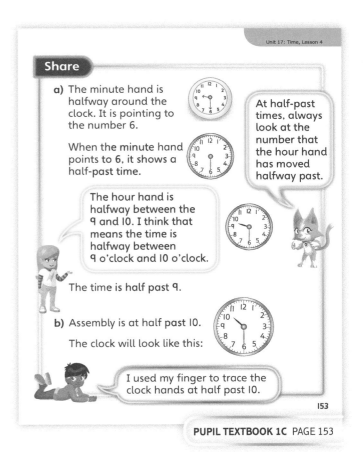

Share

a) The minute hand is halfway around the clock. It is pointing to the number 6.

When the minute hand points to **6**, it shows a half-past time.

> At half-past times, always look at the number that the hour hand has moved halfway past.

> The hour hand is halfway between the 9 and 10. I think that means the time is halfway between 9 o'clock and 10 o'clock.

The time is half past 9.

b) Assembly is at half past 10.

The clock will look like this:

> I used my finger to trace the clock hands at half past 10.

153

PUPIL TEXTBOOK 1C PAGE 153

Think together

Whole class teacher led (I do, We do, You do)

ASK

- *Look at question ① . How do you know that this must be a 'half-past' time?*
- *Question ① : It is half past an hour. How will you decide what the hour is?*
- *Can you do the same with question ② ?*

IN FOCUS Questions ① and ② provide opportunity for further discussion and consolidation where needed.

STRENGTHEN Where children find the step to telling the time to the nearest half hour difficult, try to work out exactly where they are going wrong. Can they tell the time to the nearest hour? Are they correctly distinguishing between the hour and minute hands? Are they finding the correct hour?

The additional support or practice that children may need will depend on the stage where their difficulty arises. For example, if they are consistently choosing the wrong hour, try reinforcing the idea of 'clockwise', perhaps using a demonstration clock.

DEEPEN Discuss with children that very early clocks only had an hour hand and that the minute hand was a later invention. Ask children to think about how they would tell the time on a clock that only had an hour hand.

ASSESSMENT CHECKPOINT Question ③ can be used to check understanding by analysing some common errors that arise when moving on to telling time to the half hour. Check that children do not confuse the hour and minute hands, and that they use their understanding of 'clockwise' to correctly identify the hour.

ANSWERS

Question ① : The time is half past 11.

Question ② : The time is half past 1.

Question ③ : Sidra has drawn the hands the wrong way around. The minute hand should point to the 6 and the hour hand should be half way between the 8 and the 9.

Filip has drawn half past 1; the hour hand should be half way between the 2 and the 3.

PUPIL TEXTBOOK 1C PAGE 154

PUPIL TEXTBOOK 1C PAGE 155

Practice

WAYS OF WORKING Independent thinking

IN FOCUS Question ③ asks children to draw the stated times on a series of clock faces. Remind children of all the key ideas so far: the minute hand is longer than the hour hand; the minute hand points straight down for a 'half-past' time; the hour hand is correctly placed between two numbers for a 'half-past' time.

STRENGTHEN Where children find it difficult to identify the correct hour, give them some printed clock faces and ask them to draw in the hour hand only, for a number of 'half-past' times. This additional practice can be used as a means of reinforcing the idea of 'clockwise'. Ask: *Which way is the hour hand moving? So, which number has it gone past? Which number will it get to next?*

DEEPEN Question ⑤ could be used to ask children questions such as: *Why can't the minute hand point to 6 and the hour hand point to 2?* Children could start to reason that the hour hand has to be pointing half way between two numbers when the minute hand is pointing to 6.

ASSESSMENT CHECKPOINT Use question ③ to check children's understanding of the importance of distinguishing between the minute and hour hands. If this proves difficult, you could try looking at a variety of different clock faces and identifying the hour and minute hands in each case.

ANSWERS Answers for the **Practice** part of the lesson appear in the separate **Practice and Reflect answer guide**.

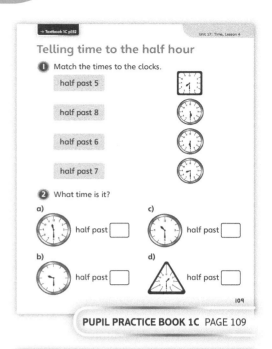

PUPIL PRACTICE BOOK 1C PAGE 109

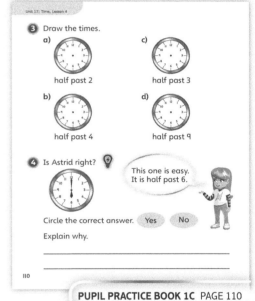

PUPIL PRACTICE BOOK 1C PAGE 110

Reflect

WAYS OF WORKING Pair work

IN FOCUS Children could draw a clock face, or attempt a written description. You might like to explain to children that they do not need to put all of the possible detail into a picture, and they should focus on the main information.

ASSESSMENT CHECKPOINT Drawing an accurate clock face is challenging at this stage, so look out for attempts where the intention is clear: the minute hand will be straight down, and the hour hand will be between the 7 and 8, even if the numbers are not in the correct position on the clock face.

ANSWERS Answers for the **Reflect** part of the lesson appear in the separate **Practice and Reflect answer guide**.

After the lesson ⏸

- Does this lesson open up more possibilities to reinforce children's learning by talking about the timing of a wider variety of events in the school day?
- How will you use the classroom clock when talking about time?

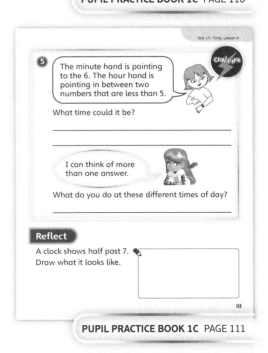

PUPIL PRACTICE BOOK 1C PAGE 111

Writing time

Learning focus

In this lesson, children will estimate, measure, read and record durations of time measured in hours, minutes and seconds.

Small steps

→ Previous step: Telling time to the half hour
→ **This step: Writing time**
→ Next step: Comparing time

NATIONAL CURRICULUM LINKS

Year 1 Measurement – Time

Measure and begin to record the following: time (hours, minutes, seconds).

ASSESSING MASTERY

Children can suggest a suitable unit of measurement (hours, minutes or seconds) for the duration of familiar events. Children can suggest suitable instruments (for example, a stop watch or a sand timer) to measure durations of time.

COMMON MISCONCEPTIONS

Some children may not have a secure idea of the durations of the various units of time. All of the units in this lesson are commonly used in informal ways that may be very different from the more formal uses that we are introducing here. Ask:
• *Have you ever heard someone say something like, 'I'll do it in a second, when I'm off the phone', or 'Hurry up – we've been waiting hours for you to get ready!'?*

STRENGTHENING UNDERSTANDING

Some simple games involving time can be used to help children get an idea of the duration of the various units of time. For example, ask children to close their eyes. Start a timer (preferably a digital timer shown on the classroom board or display screen) and ask children to open their eyes when they think that one minute has gone by, and write down the time shown on the display.

GOING DEEPER

More confident children may be interested in using a range of more precise measuring instruments, including digital and analogue stopwatches. This can naturally lead to the idea of 'parts of a second', measured using fractions or decimals. At this stage we can just say, if asked, that the stopwatch can be used to measure some very accurate times, and we will learn more about this later.

KEY LANGUAGE

In lesson: how long?, seconds, minute, hour, sixty (60), second hand, estimate, timer, measure, fastest, shortest, slowest, longest

STRUCTURES AND REPRESENTATIONS

Clock faces

RESOURCES

Mandatory: stop watches, sand timers or other suitable timing devices, to time intervals of up to several minutes

 In the eTextbook of this lesson, you will find interactive links to a selection of teaching tools.

Before you teach
• What timing devices do you have available?
• Will children be confident with the language patterns and vocabulary of 'how long?', 'hours', 'minutes' and 'seconds'?
• Does your classroom clock have a second hand?

Discover

Unit 17: Time, Lesson 5

WAYS OF WORKING Pair work

ASK

- *What are the children at the start line going to do? How long do you think it might take them? Who is timing them? How?*
- *What is this person doing to the fence? How long do you think that would take?*
- *What are the children going to do on the bench? How long do you think that would take them?*

IN FOCUS This activity uses a familiar context to introduce examples of events that could reasonably be measured in hours, minutes or seconds. The point is not to look for particularly accurate or precise estimates, but rather to identify examples of each of the different units arising naturally from a range of events.

ANSWERS

Question **1** a): Time is measured in seconds, minutes and hours. We could measure how long each of the events would take with a stop clock or other suitable timer.

Question **1** b): Walking along the ⌗ might take a short time, measured in seconds (for example, 5 seconds or thereabouts). Running around the ⬭ might take a longer time, probably measured in minutes (for example, 2 minutes). Painting the ⦚ might take a longer time still, probably measured in hours (for example, 4 hours).

Share

WAYS OF WORKING Whole class teacher led

ASK

- *Flo's clock has got a second hand, which is useful when we want to measure short amounts of time. How can you tell which hand is the second hand of a clock?*
- *What units do we use to measure how long it takes to run around the track?*
- *Painting the fence takes the longest time. How would you measure that? What units would you use?*

IN FOCUS Introducing the second hand might be a little confusing for some children. It is probably less familiar than the hour and minute hands and the language may confuse – the second hand is the third hand! Second hands also vary in appearance – the minute hand is always longer than the hour hand, but there is no simple convention to distinguish the second hand. Try to use a running clock to demonstrate the use of the second hand. This helps to make clear its purpose (timing things that happen in a short amount of time) and makes it easier to tell which hand is the second hand, as it is the one that you can clearly see moving.

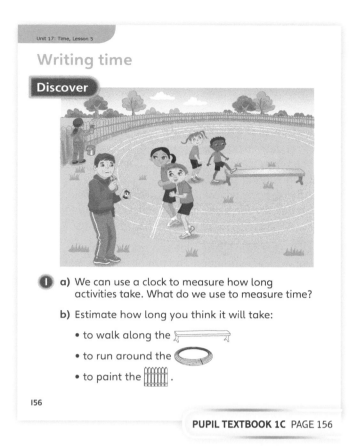

Writing time

Discover

1 a) We can use a clock to measure how long activities take. What do we use to measure time?

b) Estimate how long you think it will take:
- to walk along the ⌗
- to run around the ⬭
- to paint the ⦚ .

156

PUPIL TEXTBOOK 1C PAGE 156

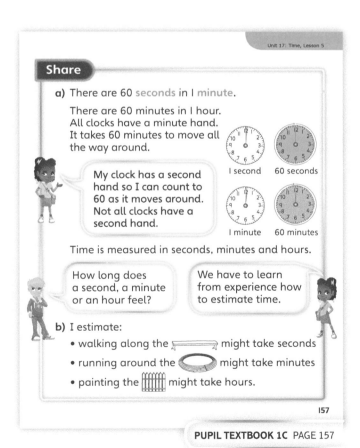

Share

a) There are 60 seconds in 1 minute.

There are 60 minutes in 1 hour. All clocks have a minute hand. It takes 60 minutes to move all the way around.

1 second   60 seconds

My clock has a second hand so I can count to 60 as it moves around. Not all clocks have a second hand.

1 minute   60 minutes

Time is measured in seconds, minutes and hours.

How long does a second, a minute or an hour feel?

We have to learn from experience how to estimate time.

b) I estimate:
- walking along the ⌗ might take seconds
- running around the ⬭ might take minutes
- painting the ⦚ might take hours.

157

PUPIL TEXTBOOK 1C PAGE 157

Think together

Whole class teacher led (I do, We do, You do)

ASK

- *Look at question* **1** *. How long do you think it would take you to do ten star jumps?*
- *What units would you use to say the time it would take – hours, minutes or seconds?*
- *Question* **2** *asks which of the activities would be measured in minutes. Are there any of these that would definitely take hours? Are there any that you could do in seconds?*

IN FOCUS Question **3** provides an opportunity for some practical work in estimation and timing. Ensure that there are suitable measuring devices available, for example, stop watches or sand timers with a known duration. Discuss the units and measuring devices that will be appropriate before children actually start on the practical work. The idea is that there is no point measuring something in minutes if it is likely to be completed in less than a minute.

STRENGTHEN Children will need practical experience of measuring time if they are to develop a good understanding of the duration of the various units – what an hour, minute and second 'feel like'. The activities in this lesson can provide experience of timing events measured in seconds or minutes. For longer periods of time, think about using the routine of the school day by saying: *In two hours' time, it will be time to go home.*

DEEPEN The measurement work here (in question **3**) follows a pattern of deciding on a unit of measurement and then using a suitable device to time the event. Some children may wish to try taking this a step further by making and then checking an estimate of the duration for an event. For example, ask: *How long do you think it will take you to walk across the playground? Write down your estimate, and then find out the actual time that it takes.*

ASSESSMENT CHECKPOINT When learning about other aspects of measurement (such as weight or capacity), we start by using non-standard units (like cubes or cups). Notice that when dealing with time, we have gone straight to using the standard units of hours, minutes, and seconds. Use question **2** to check that children understand when minutes are likely to be a sensible unit of measurement. Notice that there is quite a range of everyday events that fall into this category, and you could ask for further examples: *Can you tell me some other things that might take a few minutes?*

ANSWERS

Question **1** : It would take seconds to do ten star jumps.

Question **2** : Reading a book might take minutes, although a longer book would take hours.

Writing your name should take seconds rather than minutes.

Playtime would be measured in minutes.

Question **3** a): Saying the alphabet should take seconds.

Question **3** b): Reading five pages of a book will probably take a few minutes.

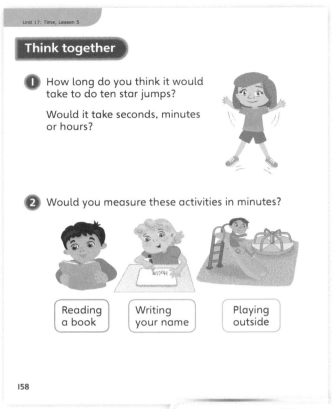

Think together

1 How long do you think it would take to do ten star jumps?

Would it take seconds, minutes or hours?

2 Would you measure these activities in minutes?

Reading a book

Writing your name

Playing outside

158

PUPIL TEXTBOOK 1C PAGE 158

Unit 17: Time, Lesson 5

3 a)

How long does it take you to say the alphabet?

A, B, C, D...

I will measure this in _____ .

It takes me ☐ _____ to say the alphabet.

b)

How long does it take you to read five pages of a book?

I will use a timer to measure how long it takes.

I will measure this in _____ .

It takes me ☐ _____ to read five pages of a book.

→ Practice book 1C p112

159

PUPIL TEXTBOOK 1C PAGE 159

Practice

WAYS OF WORKING Independent thinking

IN FOCUS Question **1** is a simple opportunity to relate the ideas of different units of measurement of time to some familiar activities. Children should be able to draw upon their real-world experience of the activities shown to decide which units of measurement are suitable in each case.

STRENGTHEN You may wish to suggest other 'one minute experiments' that children could carry out, if you want to reinforce the idea of 'how long a minute is'. For example, ask: *How many pencils can you sharpen in one minute?*

DEEPEN Question **5** provides a starting point for further practical experiments involving measurements of time. You might wish to vary the way the experiments are set up; rather than seeing how many times something can be done in a set interval, children could be asked to estimate the time that it will take to complete a certain number of repetitions. For example, ask: *How long will it take for you to undo and then tie up your shoelaces 10 times?*

ASSESSMENT CHECKPOINT Use question **4** to check that children understand that there are 60 seconds in a minute. If this causes problems, look at the markings on the dial of a clock or stopwatch and point out how the second hand 'ticks' around the dial in seconds.

ANSWERS Answers for the **Practice** part of the lesson appear in the separate **Practice and Reflect answer guide**.

Reflect

WAYS OF WORKING Pair work

IN FOCUS This activity invites children to reflect on some familiar events that could be completed in one minute, or one hour. It is important that children understand that we are not looking for any kind of precise timings in this activity, we just want examples of things that would sensibly fit into the time intervals stated.

ASSESSMENT CHECKPOINT Check that children can suggest at least one sensible event for each time interval. If children need a prompt here, you could ask them to think about events in their daily routine: *What will you do at lunchtime, or after school?*

ANSWERS Answers for the **Reflect** part of the lesson appear in the separate **Practice and Reflect answer guide**.

After the lesson ⏸

- Do children have a reasonable idea of how long an hour, minute and second are?
- Can children suggest sensible units for measuring the duration of familiar events?
- Can children distinguish between the hour, minute and second hands on a watch or clock?

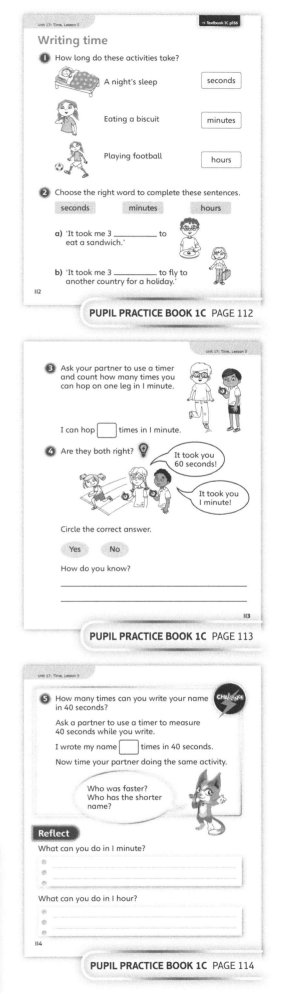

PUPIL PRACTICE BOOK 1C PAGE 112

PUPIL PRACTICE BOOK 1C PAGE 113

PUPIL PRACTICE BOOK 1C PAGE 114

Comparing time

Learning focus

In this lesson, children will learn to use mathematical reasoning, language patterns, and the vocabulary needed to compare time durations.

Small steps

→ Previous step: Writing time
→ **This step: Comparing time**
→ Next step: Solving word problems – Time

NATIONAL CURRICULUM LINKS

Year 1 Measurement – Time

Compare, describe and solve practical problems for: time (for example, faster, slower, earlier, later).

ASSESSING MASTERY

Children can use language patterns and vocabulary like 'faster than' and 'slower than' to compare the duration of events. They can use their knowledge of numbers to say which of two durations (measured in seconds or minutes) is the longer.

COMMON MISCONCEPTIONS

Children may find the logical relationships and language patterns involved in this work difficult. They will need to be able to associate processes that are 'faster' and 'slower' with durations that are 'shorter' and 'longer' respectively. It is important to practise these language patterns so that children recognise and learn the relevant connections. Ask:
• *What would happen if you tidy the room faster? Would the time you spend tidying be longer or shorter?*

STRENGTHENING UNDERSTANDING

As with all aspects of measurement and comparison, it is possible to reduce everything to a set of numbers and just compare those. However, while this is ultimately a useful approach, it is important not to do this prematurely; children also need to appreciate what they are doing when they compare times. Try to relate time comparisons to familiar ideas, including 'finishing earlier', 'working faster', 'getting there first', and so on.

GOING DEEPER

There are links here to subtraction, considered as the difference between two numbers. While it is important that children have a deep understanding of the quantities that they are measuring, much of the power of mathematics comes from the fact that the same techniques (like subtraction) can be used in a wide variety of analogous situations. It is worth discussing this important idea. For example, ask: *Once you have decided what the important numbers are, do you need to work out how to compare them? Or do you already know how to do that?*

KEY LANGUAGE

In lesson: faster, slower, longer, shorter, less, more, greater, smaller, left

Other language used by the teacher: earlier, later

STRUCTURES AND REPRESENTATIONS

Cubes and counters to represent times (durations), number lines

RESOURCES

Mandatory: interlocking cubes, counters

 In the eTextbook of this lesson, you will find interactive links to a selection of teaching tools.

Before you teach ⏸

• As with any measurement, durations can be represented in a variety of ways – including cubes, counters, number lines and numbers.
• Which representations will you use, and why?

Discover

WAYS OF WORKING Pair work

ASK

- *Look at what the teacher is saying here. How long did it take the class to tidy the room yesterday?*
- *Was that a long time, or a short time? Do you think that they should be able to do it more quickly?*
- *Question ❶ b): George tidied his desk in one minute. How many seconds is that?*

IN FOCUS This activity uses a familiar scenario to get children to think about ideas of 'faster' and 'slower'. The stated time for tidying the classroom is a long one – children should be able to apply some real-world knowledge here, and reason that it should be possible to tidy a classroom in less than 20 minutes.

ANSWERS

Question ❶ a): Any time shorter than 20 minutes.

Question ❶ b): 30 seconds is faster than 1 minute.

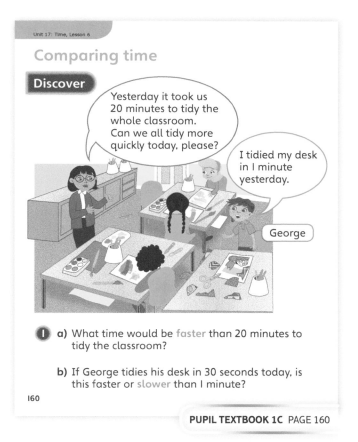

Comparing time

Discover

"Yesterday it took us 20 minutes to tidy the whole classroom. Can we all tidy more quickly today, please?"

"I tidied my desk in I minute yesterday."

George

❶ **a)** What time would be faster than 20 minutes to tidy the classroom?

b) If George tidies his desk in 30 seconds today, is this faster or slower than I minute?

160

PUPIL TEXTBOOK 1C PAGE 160

Share

WAYS OF WORKING Whole class teacher led

ASK

- *Question ❶ a): Dexter has made a chain of cubes to show what 20 minutes looks like. What does each of the cubes stand for?*
- *Question ❶ a): The chain of 19 cubes is shorter than the chain of 20 cubes, so 19 minutes is faster than 20 minutes. What other times would be faster than 20 minutes?*

IN FOCUS This activity uses a concrete representation, in the form of cubes, to represent durations of time and facilitate comparison. You can use the cubes in a more structured way, where the cube on the left represents the first minute that elapsed, and the rightmost cube represents the final minute of the tidying process. With this interpretation, children can line the chains up on the left, and then look at the right-hand ends to see which chain finishes first.

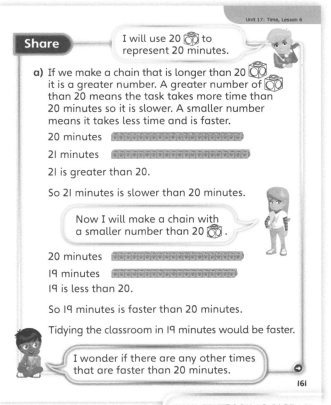

Share

"I will use 20 ⬚ to represent 20 minutes."

a) If we make a chain that is longer than 20 ⬚ it is a greater number. A greater number of ⬚ than 20 means the task takes more time than 20 minutes so it is slower. A smaller number means it takes less time and is faster.

20 minutes

21 minutes

21 is greater than 20.

So 21 minutes is slower than 20 minutes.

"Now I will make a chain with a smaller number than 20 ⬚."

20 minutes

19 minutes

19 is less than 20.

So 19 minutes is faster than 20 minutes.

Tidying the classroom in 19 minutes would be faster.

"I wonder if there are any other times that are faster than 20 minutes."

161

PUPIL TEXTBOOK 1C PAGE 161

Think together

Whole class teacher led (I do, We do, You do)

ASK

- *Look at question* **1** *. If the children started painting at the same time, who would have finished first?*
- *In question* **2** *, the two snails made the same journey. How long did they take? Which one did it faster?*

IN FOCUS Question **2** focuses on the various language patterns related to comparison of durations, and provides a chance to review the relationships concerned. For example, 'Seven is a greater number; it represents more time; it is longer; and it is slower.' It is worth rehearsing all of these patterns and their opposites.

STRENGTHEN Some children may be confused by the relationship between duration and 'speed' (in the sense of 'how quickly an activity was carried out'). Bigger numbers for the duration of an event correspond to lower 'speeds' and vice-versa. If this seems to be an issue, try using cube models to represent the durations, and talk through the various combinations and relationships.

DEEPEN Question **3** can be used to encourage deeper thinking about units and measurements. Some children will realise very quickly that when comparing measurements, 'all we need is the numbers.' This question can serve as a useful reminder that things are not quite so simple: any measurement is a combination of a number and a unit, and we can only make direct comparisons when the units of measurement are the same.

ASSESSMENT CHECKPOINT Check that all of the children understand the relationships between 'longer and shorter', 'faster and slower', and 'greater and smaller (numbers)', and that they can suggest suitable times based on any of these patterns. For example, ask: *It took me 20 minutes to get to school today, but Mrs Jones did it faster. How long might her journey have been?*

ANSWERS

Question **1** : 18 minutes is faster than 24 minutes.

Izzy painted faster.

Question **2** : 7 is a **greater** number than 4.

7 hours is **more time** than 4 hours.

7 hours is **longer** than 4 hours.

One snail took 7 hours. This is **slower** than 4 hours.

Question **3** : No. The first child is correct, because both of her times are measured in seconds, and she has compared them correctly. The second child is wrong because his times used different units; one minute is 60 seconds, so it is slower than 50 seconds.

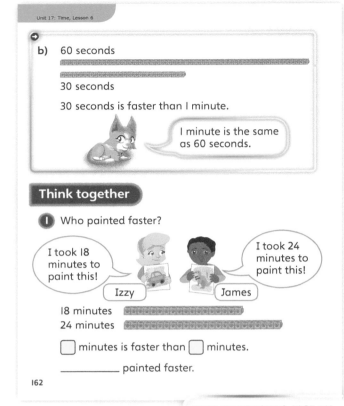

PUPIL TEXTBOOK 1C PAGE 162

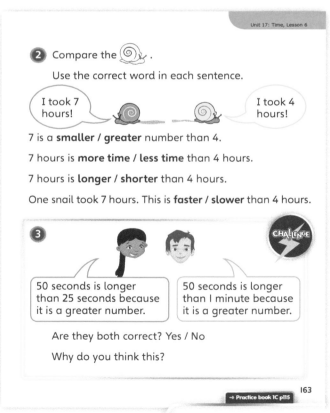

PUPIL TEXTBOOK 1C PAGE 163

Practice

WAYS OF WORKING Independent thinking

IN FOCUS Question ❶ uses all of the main relationships, representations and language patterns from this lesson. Ensure that children understand that the cubes represent the duration, not the distance, for each of the journeys.

STRENGTHEN Where children find it difficult to process the relationships between 'shorter' and 'faster', and so on, try using cube chains to model the situation. For example, in question ❸, make chains of 6, 12, and 2 cubes; align these on the left to show that all of the journeys started at the same time, and then work through all of the language patterns and vocabulary used in the question.

DEEPEN Use question ❹ to explore the idea of time intervals that are subject to conditions which are expressed in the form of an inequality. Challenge children to find all of the times that would meet the conditions in question ❹. This might naturally lead on to the use of fractional parts of an hour, for example 'Amy might have slept for 10 and a half hours.'

ASSESSMENT CHECKPOINT Use question ❷ to check that children understand how to use the duration of an event to decide who completed it faster. Notice how the counters in this question are arranged; they still represent the number of minutes that elapsed, but the simple 'time line' model of the cube chains used in the previous question is no longer available.

ANSWERS Answers for the **Practice** part of the lesson appear in the separate **Practice and Reflect answer guide**.

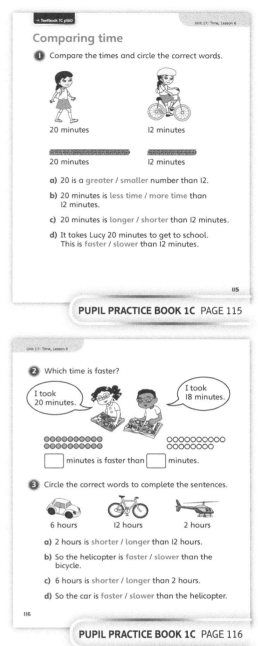

PUPIL PRACTICE BOOK 1C PAGE 115

PUPIL PRACTICE BOOK 1C PAGE 116

Reflect

WAYS OF WORKING Pair work

IN FOCUS This question mixes units to make sure that children are considering the information in the question as a set of measurements, and are not just finding the smallest number.

ASSESSMENT CHECKPOINT If children give an incorrect answer, prompt them to look at the units. Ask: *Look at the question carefully. The first time is 15 seconds; what do the other ones say?* You may also need to ask children how many seconds there are in one minute.

ANSWERS Answers for the **Reflect** part of the lesson appear in the separate **Practice and Reflect answer guide**.

After the lesson ⏸

- Did children understand the relationship between 'faster and slower' and 'shorter and longer'?
- What strategies did children use to compare the numbers? Were children able to do this without referring to concrete or pictorial representations?
- Did children remember to make sure that the units are the same before comparing measurements?

PUPIL PRACTICE BOOK 1C PAGE 117

191

Solving word problems – time

Learning focus

In this lesson, children will use their number knowledge, understanding of time, and reasoning skills to solve a variety of word problems involving time.

Small steps

→ Previous step: Comparing time
→ **This step: Solving word problems – time**
→ Next step: Recognising coins

NATIONAL CURRICULUM LINKS

Year 1 Measurement – Time

- Solve one-step problems that involve addition and subtraction, using concrete objects and pictorial representations, and missing number problems such as $7 = ? - 9$.
- Compare, describe and solve practical problems for: time (for example, faster, slower, earlier, later).

ASSESSING MASTERY

Children can solve simple word problems by finding the sum total of or difference between two time intervals; they can find the amount of time remaining for a task of fixed duration, or calculate the (clock) time at some period in the future. Children can relate addition and subtraction to the ideas of 'later' and 'earlier'.

COMMON MISCONCEPTIONS

Children may be confused by the variety of representations needed in this lesson, including 'time as duration', 'clock time', and calculating with time. The use of clear and well-chosen representations is an important way to ensure that children can identify the aspects that are being worked on in any problem. Ask:
- *What are you being asked to think about in this question? Is there a picture that would make it easier to think about?*

STRENGTHENING UNDERSTANDING

The main representation that will be used in this lesson is the number line, which can be thought of as a 'time line' in this context. This is a powerful tool, and can be used to locate particular events in time (essentially placing a 'dot' on the line), to read the order of events, and to determine durations, by counting the steps between start and end times. Encourage children to use their own sketched number lines throughout this lesson.

GOING DEEPER

Some children may already be able to replace (or at least supplement) the paper number line with 'the number line in my head'. Where children are able to answer some of the questions correctly without writing much down, ask them to explain and think about the methods they were using.

KEY LANGUAGE

In lesson: how long?, minute, number bond, altogether, left, second, faster, slower, hour

STRUCTURES AND REPRESENTATIONS

Number line, clock faces, counters

RESOURCES

Optional: number lines, counters, cubes

 In the eTextbook of this lesson, you will find interactive links to a selection of teaching tools.

Before you teach

- Are children confident with sequencing events in time, using ideas such as 'earlier' and 'later'?
- What strategies will you expect children to use when carrying out additions and subtractions?
- Will children benefit from having any resources available, for example counters or number lines?

Discover

Pair work

ASK

- *What is the chef cooking here? Have you ever seen a pancake being cooked?*
- *The pancake has been cooking for 5 minutes already, and the first side is done. What happens next?*
- *How long does the chef cook the pancake on the other side?*

IN FOCUS Ensure that children understand the scenario presented in the picture: the pancake needs to be cooked on both sides. The pancake has already been cooking for 5 minutes. The first side is cooked, so the chef flips the pancake over. The pancake is then cooked for a further 3 minutes on the other side.

ANSWERS

Question ❶ a): It takes 8 minutes to cook a 🥞.

Question ❶ b): It takes 6 minutes to make a ☕.

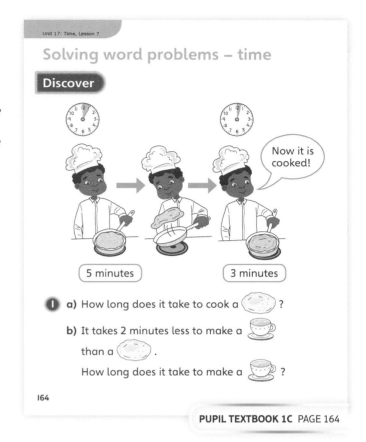

PUPIL TEXTBOOK 1C PAGE 164

Share

WAYS OF WORKING Whole class teacher led

ASK

- *Question ❶ a): Astrid is using a number line to work out the total amount of time needed. Where does she start?*
- *Question ❶ a): How many steps did Astrid move along the number line?*
- *Question ❶ b): The time taken to make a cup of tea has been worked out two different ways. Can you explain them?*

IN FOCUS There are several approaches to the calculation here, each with its own advantages and disadvantages. The number line is a good tool for addition and subtraction problems. It is, however, quite a time-consuming approach and in simple cases children may be happy to replace it with a 'mental number line', which is itself a powerful cognitive model and tool.

Flo uses a known number fact. This is clearly a good and powerful idea, but should not be rushed; children will tend to make this step for themselves as they build familiarity with the number system.

The use of counters in question ❶ b) may help some children. This representation is based on the idea of counting a collection of objects, which should be a familiar picture. Note, however, that the ten frame lacks the structure of the number line, which incorporates an implicit notion of chronological order.

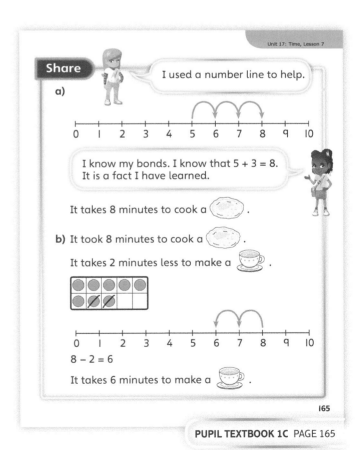

PUPIL TEXTBOOK 1C PAGE 165

Think together

WAYS OF WORKING Whole class teacher led (I do, We do, You do)

ASK

- *Look at question ❶. There is another pancake; is the cooking time the same as the previous one?*
- *How would you work out the answer? Would you use a number line like this? Would anyone do it a different way?*
- *Look at question ❷. Is this going to be another addition calculation, or a subtraction? How can you tell?*

IN FOCUS Question ❶ follows exactly the same format as the question from the previous activity. Make sure that the children understand why the number line was drawn, and how it can be used to find the answer. Check to see whether any children would have done the question in any other way, perhaps using counters or known number facts to carry out the calculation.

STRENGTHEN Some children may benefit from the additional step of starting from zero on the number line and marking the first period of time before adding on the second one. This corresponds to a less efficient 'count all' strategy, rather than the 'count on' approach modelled in the text. However, this may help some children to understand that we are finding the total duration of two successive events.

DEEPEN In question ❷, encourage children to develop and explain their own methods for solving this type of problem, or to make up similar problems of their own. Understanding how to manage the complexity of problems like this one is an important skill in its own right.

ASSESSMENT CHECKPOINT Check that children understand that the first two questions have exactly the same structure, and that any similar problem could be tackled in the same way. This is a good example of a powerful mathematical problem-solving idea: recognising the structure of a problem allows a whole set of examples to be 'compressed down' to a common arithmetic procedure. Ask: *Question ❷ is about running, and that is not the same thing as cooking a pancake. But what **is** the same about the two questions?*

ANSWERS

Question ❶ : 4 + 5 = 9.

Zac takes 9 minutes to cook his 🥞.

Question ❷ : Hassan takes 14 minutes altogether.

This means Abbie takes 11 minutes.

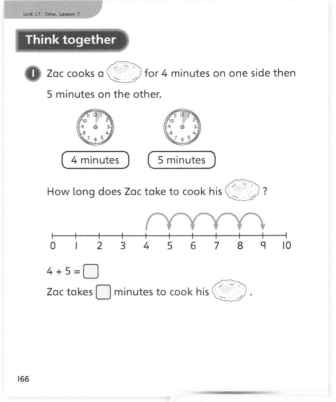

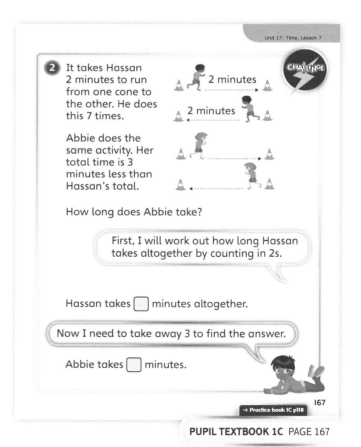

Practice

WAYS OF WORKING Independent thinking

IN FOCUS Question ❷ requires a subtraction. This is a good opportunity to spot any children who are just 'number spotting', and who might assume that the question is another addition problem, simply because the previous ones were. Notice that there is nothing inherently wrong with reducing a problem to a calculation – this is a required step in every question. The problem arises when this is done prematurely, and children guess the calculation without considering the problem context.

STRENGTHEN Where children find this work difficult, try to find out which stage of the problem-solving process is going wrong: Are they finding it difficult to make sense of the situation and work out what calculations are needed? In this case, try to find a representation of the problem that makes more sense. Are children finding it difficult to carry out the calculations? In this case, try using other representations or resources to support the calculations.

DEEPEN Question ❹ introduces another type of problem, involving calculations on a clock. More confident children may be interested in exploring these further; interesting questions arise when the question requires calculations to go past 12 o'clock.

ASSESSMENT CHECKPOINT Check that children know how to use the number line to carry out the subtraction required in question ❷ . Where other strategies are used, make sure that the children concerned can explain their approach.

ANSWERS Answers for the **Practice** part of the lesson appear in the separate **Practice and Reflect answer guide**.

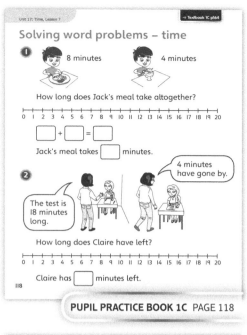

PUPIL PRACTICE BOOK 1C PAGE 118

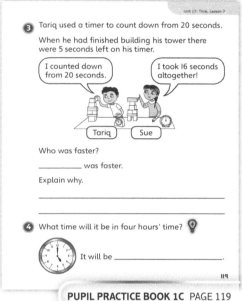

PUPIL PRACTICE BOOK 1C PAGE 119

Reflect

WAYS OF WORKING Pair work

IN FOCUS This activity provides an opportunity for children to record some of their main learning points from the lesson. They can discuss this with their partner before writing their answer.

ASSESSMENT CHECKPOINT Look out for any reflections that relate real-world situations and contexts to the calculations that were needed. For example, some children may explain that problems involving 'earlier' tend to be subtractions, while those involving 'later' usually require addition.

ANSWERS Answers for the **Reflect** part of the lesson appear in the separate **Practice and Reflect answer guide**.

After the lesson ⏸

- How confident are children in deciding for themselves what calculations are needed to solve a problem?
- What calculation strategies did you observe? Are children developing more compact or efficient approaches?

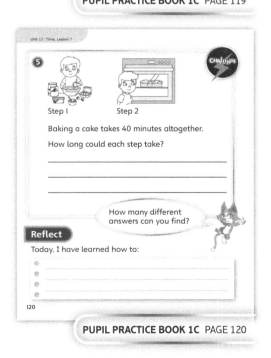

PUPIL PRACTICE BOOK 1C PAGE 120

195

End of unit check

> Don't forget the *Power Maths* unit assessment grid on p26.

WAYS OF WORKING Group work – adult led

IN FOCUS Question **1** assesses children's ability to recognise the months of the year and their chronological order.

Question **2** assesses children's ability to recognise dates on a calendar and work out on which day of the week they fall, given a specific calendar.

Question **3** assesses children's ability to recognise times on an analogue clock. It will require children to understand the terminology of 'X o'clock'.

Question **4** assesses children's ability to find times earlier or later and tell the time to the half hour. It will require children to understand the terminology of 'X o'clock' and 'half past X'.

Question **5** assesses children's ability to compare durations of time and assess which one is longer or shorter and therefore which time is quicker or slower.

Think!

WAYS OF WORKING Pair work or small groups

IN FOCUS Use this section to remind children of the importance of distinguishing carefully between the hour and minute hands.

ANSWERS AND COMMENTARY Children who have mastered this unit will be able to work confidently within simple situations involving time, including understanding clocks and calendars. They will be able to tell the time to the half hour using an analogue clock or watch, and use a calendar to say what day of the week a particular date falls on. They will be able to use a range of language to order and estimate the duration of familiar events, and they will be able to solve simple problems involving various units of time.

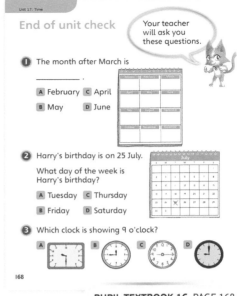

Unit 17: Time
End of unit check
Your teacher will ask you these questions.

1. The month after March is
_____ .
A February   C April
B May   D June

2. Harry's birthday is on 25 July.
What day of the week is Harry's birthday?
A Tuesday   C Thursday
B Friday   D Saturday

3. Which clock is showing 9 o'clock?
A   B   C   D

168

PUPIL TEXTBOOK 1C PAGE 168

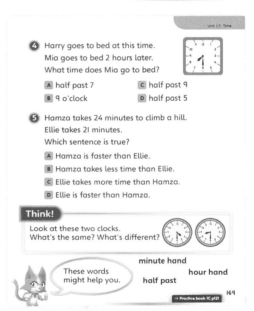

4. Harry goes to bed at this time.
Mia goes to bed 2 hours later.
What time does Mia go to bed?
A half past 7   C half past 9
B 9 o'clock   D half past 5

5. Hamza takes 24 minutes to climb a hill.
Ellie takes 21 minutes.
Which sentence is true?
A Hamza is faster than Ellie.
B Hamza takes less time than Ellie.
C Ellie takes more time than Hamza.
D Ellie is faster than Hamza.

Think!
Look at these two clocks.
What's the same? What's different?

These words might help you.
minute hand
hour hand
half past

→ Practice book 1C p121

169

PUPIL TEXTBOOK 1C PAGE 169

Q	A	WRONG ANSWERS AND MISCONCEPTIONS	STRENGTHENING UNDERSTANDING
1	C	Children may choose D if they simply read down the column, which might indicate a lack of familiarity with the sequence of month names.	Build clock-reading and calendar activities into the daily routine of the classroom wherever possible and ensure that you focus on the core techniques required. For example, when telling the time, ask children: *Which hand on the clock should you look at first? So, what does that tell you? What do you need to do next?* When using a calendar, ask children: *Where is today on the calendar? What day of the week is it? What will the date be in a week's time?*
2	A	Choosing C indicates that children do not appreciate the fact that two days' names start with T.	
3	D	Children may choose B if they do not correctly identify the hour and minute hands.	
4	C	Choosing D would indicate a confusion between the concepts of before and after.	
5	D	Any incorrect answer here might indicate that children do not fully understand the connection between the ideas of faster or slower and shorter or longer.	

My journal

WAYS OF WORKING Independent thinking

ANSWERS AND COMMENTARY

What's the same?
• Both of the clocks show half past the hour.
• Both of the minute hands are pointing straight down at the 6.

What's different?
• The hour hands are in different positions.
• The first clock shows half past 4, and the second one shows half past 7.

Notice that children could point out features related to the position of the hands on the clock faces, or to the times that are shown (or some combination of both aspects).

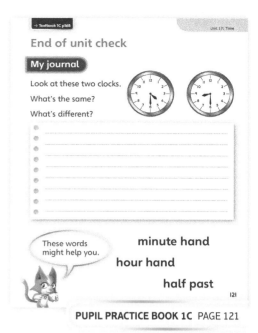

PUPIL PRACTICE BOOK 1C PAGE 121

Power check

WAYS OF WORKING Independent thinking

ASK

• *Could you tell the time before you started this unit?*
• *What about now?*
• *How much do you think you have learned?*
• *How confident do you feel about telling the time?*
• *How confident do you feel about reading dates on a calendar?*

Power puzzle

WAYS OF WORKING Pair work or small groups

IN FOCUS This puzzle will assess children's recognition of written times and their ability to convert them into times shown on a clock face.

Each pair of children will need a demonstration clock for this activity – make sure that it has a working gear mechanism that keeps the hands properly synchronised.

ANSWERS AND COMMENTARY Look out for any disagreements about what times are shown on the clocks. The most likely errors children may make are choosing the wrong hour with the 'half-past' times, and confusion between the hour and minute hands.

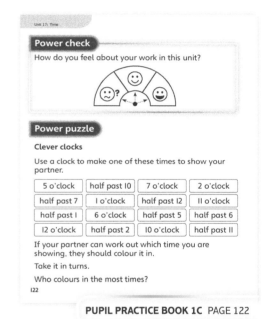

PUPIL PRACTICE BOOK 1C PAGE 122

After the unit ⏸

• Are children now telling the time and using a calendar confidently?
• Did the 'before and after' activities suggest that children had problems with sequencing events?

Strengthen and **Deepen** activities for this unit can be found in the *Power Maths* online subscription.

Unit 18
Money

Don't forget to watch the Unit 18 video!

Mastery Expert tip! "My class really enjoyed this work; we talked a lot about what the coins and notes are worth, and what you could buy with them. I like to use real coins (rather than plastic ones) wherever possible, but this is not essential."

WHY THIS UNIT IS IMPORTANT

This unit focuses on recognising coins and banknotes, and understanding their relative and absolute values. This work has obvious practical significance, in that it is clearly important that children develop familiarity with money in a range of everyday settings. Less obvious is the importance of money as a context for developing fundamental ideas about measurement – the value of a coin or note depends on both the numerical value assigned to it, and the unit (pounds or pence) that is involved. There is also a degree of abstraction involved; notes and coins are compared according to an assigned value, rather than any inherent property such as size or weight.

WHERE THIS UNIT FITS

→ Unit 17: Time
→ **Unit 18: Money**

This unit stands alone but draws on the key skills of reading and writing numbers, counting and addition.

Before they start this unit, it is expected that children:
- can read, write and understand whole numbers to 100
- know that money is used to buy things, and that it is measured in pounds and pence/pennies
- can count in 1s, 2s, 5s and 10s (with or without support number lines)
- can compare values using the signs <, > and = .

ASSESSING MASTERY

Children who have mastered this unit will recognise real coins and banknotes and know their value. They will be able to find the total value of a small set of coins or banknotes (counting in 2s, 5s and 10s where appropriate), and to compare the value of two sets of coins or notes. They will know that there are a limited number of denominations for coins and notes.

COMMON MISCONCEPTIONS	STRENGTHENING UNDERSTANDING	GOING DEEPER
Children may think that larger coins (physically) are worth more than smaller ones.	Emphasise the importance of the unit when naming coins and notes – make sure children say, 'a five pence piece', and not just 'a five'.	Ask children to investigate combinations of coins and notes that make particular totals: *What is the smallest number of coins you could use to make 83 pence? What is the smallest number of notes and coins that you could use to make 83 pounds?*
Children may think that larger sets (sets with more items) of coins or notes must be worth more than smaller ones.	Compare the number of items and their value explicitly: *Which pile has got more coins? Which pile is worth more?*	

WAYS OF WORKING

Use these pages to introduce the unit focus to children. How many coins do they recognise? You can use the characters to explore different ways of working too. Practise counting in 2s, 5s and 10s.

STRUCTURES AND REPRESENTATIONS

Real coins and banknotes

Number line: Number lines help children count. They allow children to identify the starting point, the number counted on and the end point.

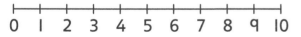

0   1   2   3   4   5   6   7   8   9   10

KEY LANGUAGE

There is some key language that children will need to know as part of the learning in this unit.

→ pound, penny, pennies, pence

→ coins, notes, banknotes

→ £, p

→ greater than, less than, equal, total, altogether

→ <, >, and =, greater than, less than

→ value, worth

Unit 18
Money

In this unit we will ...
⚡ Learn about coins
⚡ Learn about notes
⚡ Count in 1s, 2s, 5s and 10s using coins

Here are some coins. Do you know which is the 5 pence coin?

170

PUPIL TEXTBOOK 1C PAGE 170

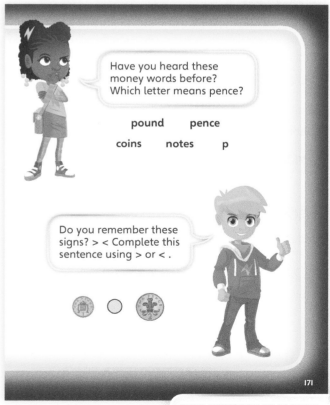

Have you heard these money words before? Which letter means pence?

pound   pence

coins   notes   p

Do you remember these signs? > < Complete this sentence using > or < .

171

PUPIL TEXTBOOK 1C PAGE 171

Recognising coins

Learning focus

In this lesson, children will learn to recognise coins, and become familiar with their relative values.

Small steps

→ Previous step: Solving word problems – time
→ **This step: Recognising coins**
→ Next step: Recognising notes

NATIONAL CURRICULUM LINKS

Year 1 Measurement – Money

Recognise and know the value of different denominations of coins and notes.

ASSESSING MASTERY

Children can recognise all of the coins (1p, 2p, 5p, 10p, 20p, 50p, £1, and £2), and can order them according to value.

COMMON MISCONCEPTIONS

Children may not be familiar with some of the coins – especially the higher denomination ones. If children are not already familiar with the relative values of the coins, they may attempt to sort them by size rather than value; or they may just compare the numerical values shown on the coins, ignoring the denomination (pounds or pence). Ask:
• *Which of these coins is larger (50 pence or 1 pound)? Which one is worth the most?*

STRENGTHENING UNDERSTANDING

Children who are not familiar with the coins will benefit from practising 'naming and selecting'. Ask: *Can you tell me what this coin is? Can you find the 1 pound coin? Choose a coin that is worth more than 10 pence or less than 50 pence.*

GOING DEEPER

Children who grasp this work quickly could make up amounts to 20p using 1p, 2p, 5p and 10p coins and then amounts to £1 or £2 using silver coins. Ask: *How many different ways can you make 15 pence? How many different ways can you make 1 pound with silver coins?*

KEY LANGUAGE

In lesson: pounds, pence, coins, left, right, worth, greater than, less than, value, before, after

Other language to be used by the teacher: amount, most valuable, least valuable, silver, copper, heads, tails

STRUCTURES AND REPRESENTATIONS

Currency

RESOURCES

Mandatory: Coins – either real ones (with numbers not just words), or realistic plastic versions

 In the eTextbook of this lesson, you will find interactive links to a selection of teaching tools.

Before you teach

• Are children familiar with handling money?
• If you use plastic coins are they realistic enough to not confuse children?
• Ensure that the coins you use have the numbers not just the words on their tails side.

Discover

Unit 18: Money, Lesson 1

Recognising coins

Discover

WAYS OF WORKING Pair work

ASK

- *Look at these two trays. What is in them?*
- *Do you know the names of any of the coins?*
- *The list at the bottom of the page shows all of the names: 1p, 2p, 5p, … but how would you say the £ sign?*

IN FOCUS This activity introduces all of the coins in current use. It provides an opportunity to see which coins children already recognise, and the key below the diagram can be used to help name any of the coins that are less familiar.

ANSWERS

Question ❶ a): In the tray are: a 1 pence coin, 2 pence coin, 5 pence coin, 10 pence coin, 20 pence coin, 50 pence coin, 1 pound coin, 2 pound coin.

Question ❶ b): The 🪙 (5p) has been removed from the tray.

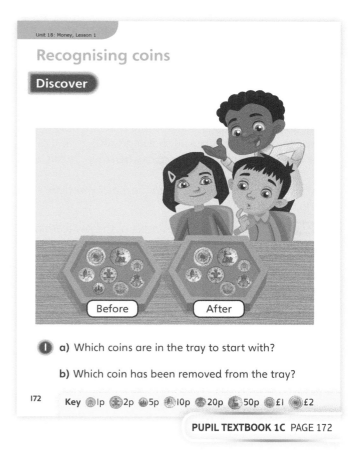

❶ a) Which coins are in the tray to start with?

b) Which coin has been removed from the tray?

172   Key 🪙1p 🪙2p 🪙5p 🪙10p 🪙20p 🪙50p 🪙£1 🪙£2

Share

WAYS OF WORKING Whole class teacher led

ASK

- *How do the colours of the coins help you to see which ones are worth more – or less?*
- *What colour are the most valuable coins? What about the least valuable ones?*
- *What can you say about the silver coins?*
- *Is there a 3 pence coin? Is there a 40 pence coin?*

IN FOCUS Ash's statement about the difference between a 1 pence coin and a 1 pound coin is an important talking point, and should be used to make sure that children understand the relationship between pounds and pence, and that one pound is worth more (is more valuable) than one pence. It is also important that children understand that there are a set number of coins and, for example, there is no 3 pence or 4 pence coin. The numbers are found on the tails side, but some coins only have the words, no numbers. Explain that the side with the Queen's head is called 'heads' and the other side is called 'tails', and this is where they will usually find the value of the coin. Some newer or special edition coins may only have the value in words.

Share The number on the coin tells us how much the coin is worth.

a) There is a:

- 1 pence coin
- 2 pence coin
- 5 pence coin
- 10 pence coin
- 20 pence coin
- 50 pence coin
- 1 pound coin
- 2 pound coin

I wonder what is different between a 1 pence coin and a 1 pound coin.

b) The 🪙 has been removed from the tray.

£5 £10 £20 £50   173

Think together

WAYS OF WORKING Whole class teacher led (I do, We do, You do)

ASK

- *What do you notice about the way that the coins have been put on the table?* (They are all showing 'tails'.)
- *Why is it easier to compare the coins when they are this way up?*
- *Which coins on the table are worth the most? Which are worth the least?*

IN FOCUS Question ③ combines most of the key learning points for this lesson – children have to identify coins from their images, and decide which of each pair is worth the most.

STRENGTHEN Children who are having difficulty recognising coins will benefit from further practice with real or plastic coins. Make sure that children turn them 'tails up' so that they can compare them to the pictures in the book.

DEEPEN Children who grasp this work quickly could be encouraged to think about other possible coin descriptions for question ③ , especially 'double comparisons'.

ASSESSMENT CHECKPOINT Question ② provides a good opportunity to check that children can recognise and name the coins; make up further questions like this to check individual children's understanding.

ANSWERS

Question ① : 1 pence: 2
2 pence: 1
5 pence: 0
10 pence: 3
20 pence: 4
50 pence: 0
1 pound: 2
2 pound: 0

Question ② a): The 1 pence coin is to the left of the 50 pence coin.

Question ② b): The 2 pound coin is to the right of the 50 pence coin.

Question ② c): The 50 pence coin is to the left of the 2 pound coin.

Question ③ a): 2 pence is greater than 1 pence.

Question ③ b): 10 pence is less than 20 pence.

Question ③ c): 50 pence is less than 1 pound.

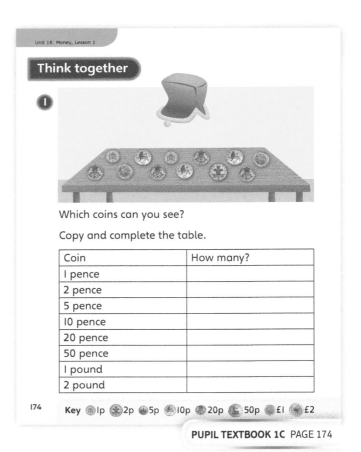

Think together

① Which coins can you see?

Copy and complete the table.

Coin	How many?
1 pence	
2 pence	
5 pence	
10 pence	
20 pence	
50 pence	
1 pound	
2 pound	

174   Key ● 1p ● 2p ● 5p ● 10p ● 20p ● 50p ● £1 ● £2

PUPIL TEXTBOOK 1C PAGE 174

② Complete the sentences.

a) The 1 pence coin is to the left of the _____ .

b) The _____ coin is to the right of the 50 pence coin.

c) The 50 pence coin is to the _____ of the 2 pound coin.

③ Complete the sentences. **CHALLENGE**

Write the value of the coins.

Then choose > (greater than) than or < (less than).

a) ☐ pence is ○ ☐ pence.

b) ☐ pence is ○ ☐ pence.

c) ☐ pence is ○ ☐ pound.

How could I describe a 20 pence coin?

● £5 ● £10 ● £20 ● £50   → Practice book 1C p123   175

PUPIL TEXTBOOK 1C PAGE 175

Practice

WAYS OF WORKING Independent thinking

IN FOCUS Question ④ requires recognition of the coins, an understanding of their relative values, and in part c) the ability to fill in two parts of a three-part relationship.

STRENGTHEN Children who find question ④ difficult could work with a number line to reinforce the idea of the relative value of the coins. Mark the value of each 'pence' coin on a number line, and emphasise the idea that the coin on the right in any pair has the greater value.

DEEPEN Challenge children to find more answers for part c) of question ④. Can they find them all?

ASSESSMENT CHECKPOINT Use question ③ to check that all children are confident with the idea of 'greater than' and 'less than', as applied to the 'pence' coins. (This example allows you to check the basic idea without the added complication of dealing with the 1 pound and 2 pound coins.)

ANSWERS Answers for the **Practice** part of the lesson appear in the separate **Practice and Reflect answer guide**.

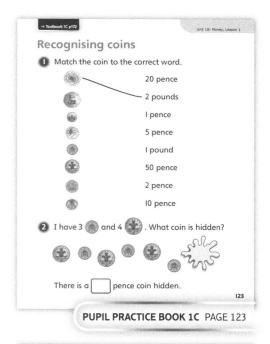

PUPIL PRACTICE BOOK 1C PAGE 123

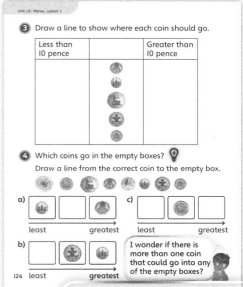

PUPIL PRACTICE BOOK 1C PAGE 124

Reflect

WAYS OF WORKING Pair work

IN FOCUS Encourage children to use a logical series of questions, rather than just guessing. Children could use different kinds of question (for example, about shape or colour), so that they reinforce their coin recognition as well as their understanding of the value of the coins.

ASSESSMENT CHECKPOINT Ask: *Can you always work out what coin your friend chose within three questions?* It can be done – for example, start by asking: *Is it silver?* If it is, ask: *Is it round?* Finally ask about value. If the coin is not silver, ask: *Is it copper?* Then ask about value.

ANSWERS Answers for the **Reflect** part of the lesson appear in the separate **Practice and Reflect answer guide**.

After the lesson ⏸

- Are children able to recognise all of the coins? What opportunities (for example, shopping games) can you provide for extra practice where needed?
- Do children have a good understanding of the 'real-world' value of the coins – that is, what they could actually be used to buy?
- What links can be made with other areas of maths, such as addition and subtraction?

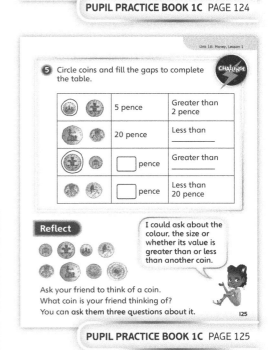

PUPIL PRACTICE BOOK 1C PAGE 125

Recognising notes

Learning focus

In this lesson, children will learn to recognise and compare banknotes.

Small steps

→ Previous step: Recognising coins
→ **This step: Recognising notes**
→ Next step: Counting with coins

NATIONAL CURRICULUM LINKS

Year 1 Measurement – Money

Recognise and know the value of different denominations of coins and notes.

ASSESSING MASTERY

Children can recognise all of the different banknotes, and can arrange them in order of value. Children can compare two banknotes using the words 'less than' or 'greater than'. Children know that there are limited denominations: £5, £10, £20 and £50 and that each banknote has its own colour and size.

COMMON MISCONCEPTIONS

Children may not recognise all the banknotes. Show children a selection of banknotes and ask:
• *Which banknote is this?*
• *What is its value?*

STRENGTHENING UNDERSTANDING

Children who lack a secure grasp of place value may have difficulty when comparing the value of the £5 note with some of the others. It may be useful to refer to the purchasing power of the £5 note in relation to the other notes, to establish that it is the least valuable of them.

GOING DEEPER

Deepen understanding by encouraging children to attempt some harder problems with notes. Ask: *What would one hundred pounds look like? How many different ways could you count out one hundred pounds in notes?*

KEY LANGUAGE

In lesson: notes, banknotes, pound, money, greatest, smallest , least, most , count, >, <

Other language used by the teacher: compare, greater than, less than, worth, value

STRUCTURES AND REPRESENTATIONS

Currency: banknotes

RESOURCES

Mandatory: images of banknotes (real and pretend)

 In the eTextbook of this lesson, you will find interactive links to a selection of teaching tools.

Before you teach

• Have children had experience dealing with banknotes (perhaps in the context of 'play money' in board games)?
• Can children see the connection between the value of some of the coins and the value of the banknotes (5, 10, 20, and 50)?

Discover

Unit 18: Money, Lesson 2

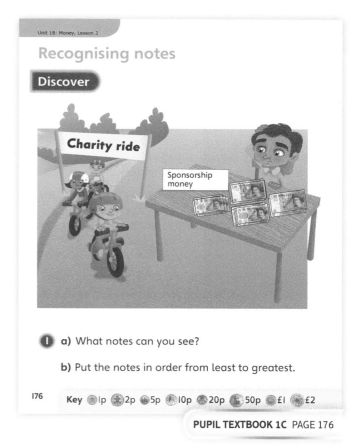

Recognising notes

WAYS OF WORKING Pair work

ASK

- *Can you see the sponsorship money? Are there any coins?*
- *Is it a lot of money? How can you tell?*

IN FOCUS This question should be used to draw out the idea that we are dealing with larger sums of money. Explain that a lot of money has been collected, and that it has been sorted out into piles of banknotes – perhaps to make it easier to count.

ANSWERS

Question ❶ a): There are 5 pound notes, 10 pound notes, 20 pound notes and 50 pound notes on the table.

Question ❶ b): £5, £10, £20, £50

Share

WAYS OF WORKING Whole class teacher led

ASK

- *Which of these notes have you seen in real life?*
- *Can you see the numbers that tell you how much each note is worth?*

IN FOCUS Recognising real notes is an important part of the learning in this lesson. You might like to have some real notes available to show children, especially so that they can see the designs on the other sides, and get an idea of their actual size. Point out that you are showing the 'heads' side of the banknotes – the distinct colour and size of the notes, and the clear numerical markings, should be sufficient to distinguish them, despite the overall similarity of their designs. Remind children of the connection between the value of the silver coins and the value of the banknotes (5, 10, 20 and 50 only).

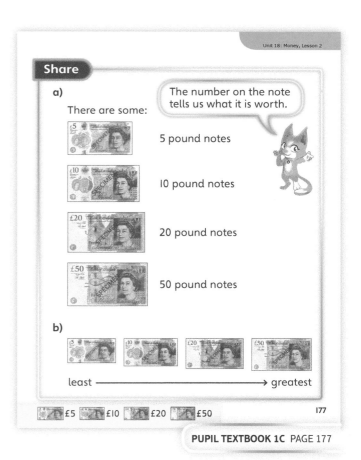

PUPIL TEXTBOOK 1C PAGE 176

PUPIL TEXTBOOK 1C PAGE 177

Think together

WAYS OF WORKING Whole class teacher led (I do, We do, You do)

ASK

- *This is the same sponsorship money – what is different now, though?*
- *Can you see all of the notes now? What will you have to do to find out how many of each note there are?*

IN FOCUS Question ❶ asks children to count how many notes of each kind there are on the table. Make sure everyone understands that the 'How many?' amount that is asked for is the number of notes of each denomination – not the total amount of money.

STRENGTHEN Children who find it difficult to determine the value of a banknote should be encouraged to look for the number in the top left corner (with the Queen's head uppermost). The designs of the notes are deliberately complicated, but the denomination shown clearly in the top left corner is a consistent feature of all of them.

DEEPEN Question ❸ asks children to compare the value of notes. Ask: *What information will you use to decide which one is worth more?* Make the comparisons more challenging by comparing images where the denomination is obscured, or asking questions such as: *Which is worth more – a brown banknote or a red one?*

ASSESSMENT CHECKPOINT Question ❷ should be used to check that children have grasped the key learning point of this lesson, by being able to distinguish and recognise each of the notes.

ANSWERS

Question ❶ : There are five £5 notes.

There are four £10 notes.

There are two £20 notes.

There are three £50 notes.

Question ❷ : The pictures should be matched in the following order £5 – 5 pounds, £10 – 10 pounds, £20 – 20 pounds, and £50 – 50 pounds.

Question ❸   a): <

b): >

c): <

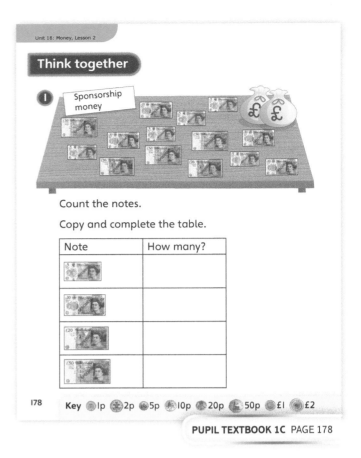

Think together

① Sponsorship money

Count the notes.

Copy and complete the table.

Note	How many?
£5	
£10	
£20	
£50	

178   Key 1p 2p 5p 10p 20p 50p £1 £2

PUPIL TEXTBOOK 1C PAGE 178

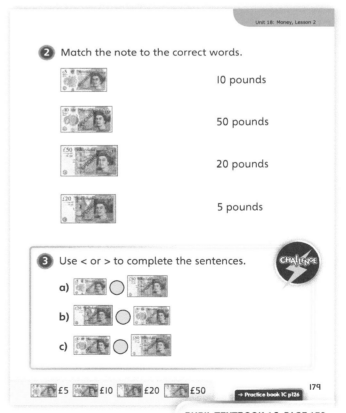

Unit 18: Money, Lesson 2

② Match the note to the correct words.

£5   10 pounds

£10   50 pounds

£50   20 pounds

£20   5 pounds

③ Use < or > to complete the sentences.   CHALLENGE

a) ○

b) ○

c) ○

£5 £10 £20 £50   → Practice book 1C p126   179

PUPIL TEXTBOOK 1C PAGE 179

Practice

WAYS OF WORKING Independent thinking

IN FOCUS Question ④ involves comparing 'notes with notes', as well as 'notes with values'. The extra level of abstraction involved provides an interesting additional challenge.

STRENGTHEN Children who still find it difficult to recognise the notes may benefit from further work with colour images made to the correct relative sizes.

DEEPEN Children who find question ⑤ easy could be asked to draw the sequence of notes with the appropriate inequality sign between each pair. They should notice that the position of the note that is in the wrong order corresponds to an inequality sign that 'changes direction' relative to the others.

ASSESSMENT CHECKPOINT Question ③ provides a good opportunity to check that children can recognise all of the notes; even without the availability of colour as a cue, the designs should be sufficiently distinct to make counting the different denominations reasonably straightforward. Some children might like to think about checking strategies – perhaps counting the total number of notes and making sure that the numbers in the boxes make the same total.

ANSWERS Answers for the **Practice** part of the lesson appear in the separate **Practice and Reflect answer guide**.

Reflect

WAYS OF WORKING Pair work

IN FOCUS The point here is to focus on the denomination of the notes – however realistic the design looks, there is no such thing as a £15 or £30 note.

ASSESSMENT CHECKPOINT This task provides a check on an important piece of real-world knowledge, rather than anything purely mathematical. Children who fail to circle any of the real notes could be shown relevant images in the book; if they indicate that the £15 or £30 notes are real, you could ask them to look back and try to find the matching picture.

ANSWERS Answers for the **Reflect** part of the lesson appear in the separate **Practice and Reflect answer guide**.

After the lesson ⏸

- Are children using visual clues to recognise the notes or are they still reading the numerical values printed on the notes?
- Did children make the connection with the relative values of the coins, knowing that there are a limited number of different denominations?

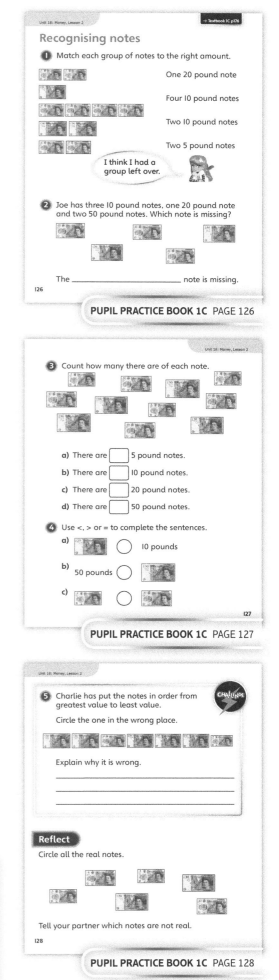

PUPIL PRACTICE BOOK 1C PAGE 126

PUPIL PRACTICE BOOK 1C PAGE 127

PUPIL PRACTICE BOOK 1C PAGE 128

Counting with coins

Learning focus

In this lesson, children will find and compare the total value of small sets of coins.

Small steps

→ Previous step: Recognising notes
→ **This step: Counting with coins**
→ Next step: Counting objects to 100

NATIONAL CURRICULUM LINKS

Year 1 Measurement – Money

- Recognise and know the value of different denominations of coins and notes.
- Count, read and write numbers to 100 in numerals; count in multiples of 2s, 5s and 10s.

ASSESSING MASTERY

Children can recognise coins and use their number skills and knowledge to find the total of a small group of coins of the same kind. They may do this by 'skip counting' in multiples of the coin denomination (for example, counting '5, 10, 15…' to find the total value of a group of 5p coins), or they may use known number facts (for example 'four 2s are eight' to find the value of four 2p coins).

COMMON MISCONCEPTIONS

The most likely confusion in this lesson is likely to arise in moving from counting to calculating – children are expected to compare groups of coins based on their total value, rather than the number of coins in each group. Ask:
- *How many coins are there?*
- *What is their total value?*

STRENGTHENING UNDERSTANDING

Use language patterns that emphasise the idea that we are looking for the total value of each of the groups of coins that we are dealing with in this lesson. For example, be careful to ask: *How much is this group worth?* rather than *How much is this?*

GOING DEEPER

Children who grasp this learning quickly could go on to finding totals of mixed groups of coins. For example, a simple game for pairs could involve one child taking a small collection of mixed coins and challenging a partner to guess the total value, which can then be worked out accurately.

KEY LANGUAGE

In lesson: worth, amount, total, coin, money, altogether, pence, <, >, =, copper

Other language used by the teacher: value, denomination

STRUCTURES AND REPRESENTATIONS

Coins, number lines

RESOURCES

Mandatory: coins – real or realistic plastic

Optional: number lines

 In the eTextbook of this lesson, you will find interactive links to a selection of teaching tools.

Before you teach ⏸

- Do children recognise all of the different coins?
- Is children's understanding of the relative values of the various coins secure?
- Can children count in 2s, 5s and 10s?

Discover

WAYS OF WORKING Pair work

ASK

- *Where are the coins? How have they been arranged on the table?*
- *What sorts of coins can you see? Why do you think they have been put into lines like that?*

IN FOCUS Question ❶ focuses on the key distinction between the number of coins in a group, and the total value of the group. The more coins in a set does not necessarily mean the total value is greater than a group with fewer coins in it. Some children may need number lines or a number square to support their counting in 2s, 5s and 10s.

ANSWERS

Question ❶ a): There are five 1 pence coins.
There is 5 pence altogether.

There are four 2 pence coins.
There is 8 pence altogether.

There are six 5 pence coins.
There is 30 pence altogether.

There are four 10 pence coins.
There is 40 pence altogether.

Question ❶ b): The most coins are in the 5 pence line.

The most money is in the 10 pence line.

Counting with coins

Discover

❶ a) How much money is in each line?

   b) Which line has the most coins?

   Which line has the most money?

180 Key ⊙1p ⊛2p ⊙5p ⊛10p ⊛20p ⊕50p ⊙£1 ⊛£2

PUPIL TEXTBOOK 1C PAGE 180

Share

WAYS OF WORKING Whole class teacher led

ASK

- *Dexter counted the coins in each line. Did you start by doing the same thing?*
- *It is easy to work out the value of the 1 pence pieces. Can you explain why?*
- *You have to do a bit more work for the other lines of coins. Can you explain how Dexter found the total of the line of 2 pence pieces?*

IN FOCUS Part b) of this activity focuses on the distinction between the number of coins in a line (which is a simple count of the coins, disregarding their value) and the total value of the line (which is essentially a multiplication problem, although the actual calculation will most likely be done by repeated addition or 'counting in steps' in this case). This is the key content of the lesson, and it is worth spending some time making sure that the distinction between the number of coins and their total value is clearly understood.

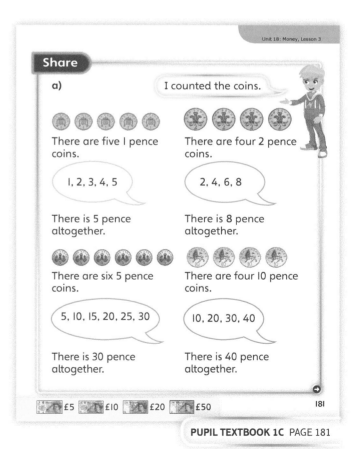

Share

a)   I counted the coins.

There are five 1 pence coins.

1, 2, 3, 4, 5

There is 5 pence altogether.

There are four 2 pence coins.

2, 4, 6, 8

There is 8 pence altogether.

There are six 5 pence coins.

5, 10, 15, 20, 25, 30

There is 30 pence altogether.

There are four 10 pence coins.

10, 20, 30, 40

There is 40 pence altogether.

⊛£5 ⊛£10 ⊛£20 ⊛£50   181

PUPIL TEXTBOOK 1C PAGE 181

Think together

WAYS OF WORKING Whole class teacher led (I do, We do, You do)

ASK

- *What kind of coins are these?*
- *How many of them are there?*
- *What is their total value?*

IN FOCUS In question ❷ , make sure that children understand that it is the total value of the groups of money on each side that is being compared. Notice how the inequality signs are being used in a slightly more demanding context than previously – children have to compare values calculated on the basis of the images shown, rather than numbers that are immediately apparent in the question.

STRENGTHEN Where children find it difficult to compare the total values, support them in using a number line or number square to find each total before then working out the correct inequality or equals sign to use. Provide more examples with fewer coins for children to try in pairs. For example, two 5 pence coins and one 20; one 5 pence coin and four 1 pence or two or three 2 pence coins.

DEEPEN Question ❸ can easily be extended, and will provide a good opportunity to explore number patterns. Ask: *What if Sidra had a different amount of money such as 30 pence, or 12 pence? What coins could she have then? Can you make up some more examples of your own? Can you make 11 pence with just 2 pence coins?*

ASSESSMENT CHECKPOINT Use question ❷ c) to check that children have understood the importance of comparing total values rather than number of coins. There are more 1 pence coins but the 2 pence coins are worth more. Question ❸ tests children's understanding of multiples of 2, 5 and 10.

ANSWERS

Question ❶ : a) There is 50 pence in total.

b) There is 20 pence in total.

c) There is 84 pence in total.

Question ❷ : a) >

b) =

c) <

Question ❸ : Sidra could have 1 pence or 5 pence coins. Children may explain that we cannot count to 15 in 2s or 10s.

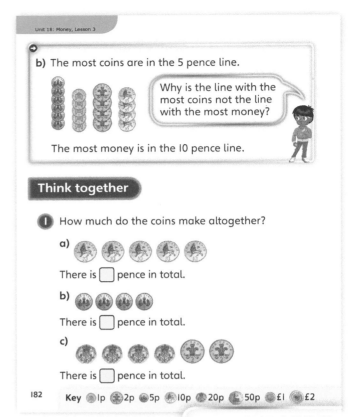

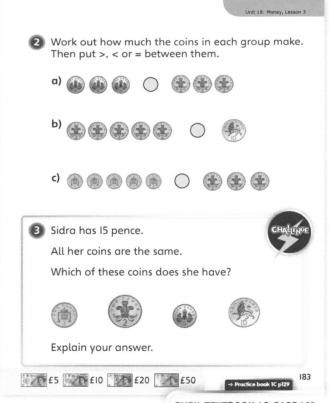

Practice

WAYS OF WORKING Independent thinking

IN FOCUS Question ③ illustrates that, because a 10 pence coin is worth twice the value of a 5 pence, children need twice the number of 5 pence coins to make the same total than they do 10 pence coins.

STRENGTHEN Some children may find the drawing in question ② difficult. Provide apparatus if required; children could make the totals using coins, and then draw around the coins to record their answers.

DEEPEN Questions ⑤ and ⑥ can be extended easily. Children who have a sound grasp of the material in the lesson could be asked: *If Jack only had 5 pence coins, what amounts could he make?* or *If Lucy had 5 copper coins and Pavel had 10 copper coins, and they still had the same amount of money, what coins would they have then?*

ASSESSMENT CHECKPOINT Use question ② to check that children can make totals using coins of different denominations. Question ⑥ tests to see if children can work logically to find a solution. Can they find two solutions?

ANSWERS Answers for the **Practice** part of the lesson appear in the separate **Practice and Reflect answer guide**.

Reflect

WAYS OF WORKING Pair work

IN FOCUS The choice of a total of 20 pence means that any of the coins can be used in this example. You could ask: *What happens if the total amount you want to make is different? Which coin can you always use? How could you tell if you could make the new amount with 2 pence coins?* and so on.

ASSESSMENT CHECKPOINT Children may choose to draw the coins rather than write them out. Children's drawings may be a little hard to follow, especially with the 1 pence and 2 pence coins. If the drawings look wrong, check whether the child's intention was correct by asking them how they decided what to draw.

ANSWERS Answers for the **Reflect** part of the lesson appear in the separate **Practice and Reflect answer guide**.

After the lesson ⏸

- Are children confident in finding the totals of small groups of coins?
- What strategies did you observe children using for finding totals?
- What opportunities will there be for children to work with money outside of formal lessons?

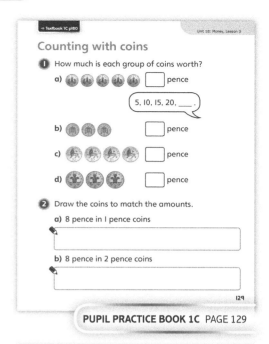

PUPIL PRACTICE BOOK 1C PAGE 129

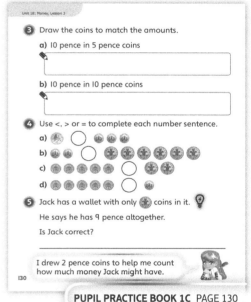

PUPIL PRACTICE BOOK 1C PAGE 130

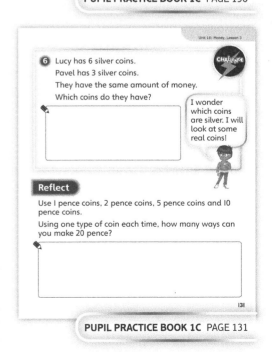

PUPIL PRACTICE BOOK 1C PAGE 131

End of unit check

Don't forget the *Power Maths* unit assessment grid on p26.

WAYS OF WORKING Group work adult led

IN FOCUS Questions ❶ and ❷ check that children recognise coins from their value in pence.

Question ❸ is a good opportunity to check that children can recognise the coin shown, that they understand that the total amount of money is required, and that they can count using the pattern of multiples (2 in this case).

Question ❹ tests whether children know the relative worth of a coin in comparison to the value of other coins.

Question ❺ checks that children know there are only certain denominations of notes (and coins) and that a £25 note is not a real note.

Think!

WAYS OF WORKING Pair work or small groups

IN FOCUS All children will benefit from the practice and reinforcement provided by this activity.

Where appropriate, encourage more systematic ways of working and recording by asking: *How can you be sure that you have found all the ways of doing it? What is the clearest way of writing all this down?*

How many different ways can you find that use one type of coin? Can you make 20 pence just using 5 pence and 10 pence coins? How many different ways can you make 20 pence using just 5 pence and 1 pence coins / 5 pence and 2 pence coins / 10 pence, 2 pence and 1 pence coins?

Ask children to think about how many different types of coin each of the combinations uses. *Can you make 20 pence using at least one of the 1 pence, 2 pence, 5 pence and 10 pence coins?*

ANSWERS AND COMMENTARY Children who have mastered the concepts of this unit will be able to recognise real coins and banknotes, find the total value of a small group of coins and banknotes, compare the value of two groups of coins or notes and make totals with different combinations of coins.

PUPIL TEXTBOOK 1C PAGE 184

PUPIL TEXTBOOK 1C PAGE 185

Q	A	WRONG ANSWERS AND MISCONCEPTIONS	STRENGTHENING UNDERSTANDING
1	B	Where children claim that A (50 pence) or C (£2) are 'worth 20 pence', check that they did not misinterpret the question as asking whether the coins are worth '20 pence or more'.	Children may be less familiar with the higher value coins (£1 and £2); these coins are also 'unusual' in that their values are in pounds rather than pence, and the numerical values are often given in words only (not figures). All of these factors may mean that some children may need a little more practice in dealing with these coins, and it is important not to assume that any hesitancy necessarily reflects significant mathematical difficulties.
2	D	Children who answer A may not understand the difference between pounds and pence (or may have simply misread the question). Answer C could signify a lack of understanding of place value.	
3	B	Children who give answer C may be counting the coins rather than understanding that the total amount of money is required.	
4	B	Answer C may reflect a confusion between 'less than' and 'smaller than'.	
5	C	Other answers indicate that children are not sure of the limited denominations of the notes.	

My journal

WAYS OF WORKING Independent thinking

ANSWERS AND COMMENTARY

Children may start by using just one type of coin, and will often simply draw a collection of coins to represent their answer. More efficient representations will involve writing simple calculations (5 pence + 5 pence + 5 pence + 5 pence = 20 pence). When using more than one type of coin, some children may not appreciate that 'the same coins in a different order' do not in fact represent a new combination. Some children may move towards a tabular form of recording, such as a table with three columns headed 2 pence, 5 pence and 10 pence, where each row of the table shows how many of each coin are used in each combination totalling 20 pence.

Power check

WAYS OF WORKING Independent thinking

ASK

- *Do you think that you know more about money now?*
- *Can you tell quickly which coin is which, or do you have to read what it says on the coin?*
- *The coins are copper, silver or gold coloured. Do you know which is which?*

Power play

WAYS OF WORKING Pair or small group work

IN FOCUS This activity provides a further opportunity for children to use and practise their understanding of coin properties (size, shape, value, colour), as well as developing mental arithmetic approaches and devising efficient sets of questions.

ANSWERS AND COMMENTARY Look out for children whose questions or answers suggest insecure knowledge of coin properties; for example, if we already know that the selected coins are round, there is no point asking whether they are 20 pence pieces. These children may need further practice at handling coins.

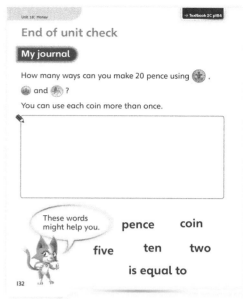

PUPIL PRACTICE BOOK 1C PAGE 132

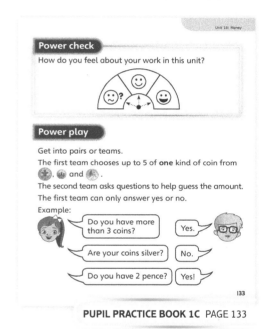

PUPIL PRACTICE BOOK 1C PAGE 133

After the unit ⏸

- Are children confident enough to recognise and use all of the different coins?
- Did you see any unexpected approaches to recording or calculation during this unit?
- What further opportunities will children have to use money?

Strengthen and **Deepen** activities for this unit can be found in the *Power Maths* online subscription.

Published by Pearson Education Limited, 80 Strand, London, WC2R 0RL.

www.pearsonschools.co.uk

Text © Pearson Education Limited 2017
Edited by Pearson, Little Grey Cells Publishing Services and Haremi Ltd
Designed and typeset by Kamae Design
Original illustrations © Pearson Education Limited 2017
Illustrated by Fran and David Brylewski, Nigel Dobbyn, Adam Linley, Nadene Naude and Jorge Santillan at Beehive Illustration;
Emily Skinner at Graham-Cameron Illustration; Paul Higgins at Hunter Higgins Illustrations; and Kamae.
Cover design by Pearson Education Ltd
Back cover illustration © Will Overton at Advocate Art and Nadene Naude at Beehive Illustration.

Series Editor: Tony Staneff
Consultant: Professor Liu Jian

The rights of Tony Staneff, David Board, Julia Hayes, Derek Huby, Neil Jarrett and Timothy Weal to be identified as authors of this work have been asserted by them in accordance with the Copyright, Designs and Patents Act 1988.

First published 2017

20 19 18
10 9 8 7 6 5 4 3 2

British Library Cataloguing in Publication Data
A catalogue record for this book is available from the British Library

ISBN 978 0 435 18980 8

Printed in Great Britain by Ashford Colour Press Ltd.

www.activelearnprimary.co.uk

Note from the publisher
Pearson has robust editorial processes, including answer and fact checks, to ensure the accuracy of the content in this publication, and every effort is made to ensure this publication is free of errors. We are, however, only human, and occasionally errors do occur. Pearson is not liable for any misunderstandings that arise as a result of errors in this publication, but it is our priority to ensure that the content is accurate. If you spot an error, please do contact us at resourcescorrections@pearson.com so we can make sure it is corrected.

COPYMASTERS

Stage 5

Purple Level

Written by
Rose Griffiths

Heinemann is an imprint of Pearson Education Limited, a company
incorporated in England and Wales, having its registered office at Edinburgh
Gate, Harlow, Essex, CM20 2JE. Registered company number: 872828

www.heinemann.co.uk

Heinemann is a registered trademark of Pearson Education Limited

Text © Rose Griffiths 1996, 2005, 2009

First published 1996
Second edition first published 2005
Third edition first published 2009

13 12 11 10 09
10 9 8 7 6 5 4 3

British Library Cataloguing in Publication Data
A catalogue record for this book is available from the British Library.

ISBN 978 0 435912 49 9

Designed and Produced by Debbie Oatley @ room9design
Original illustrations © Pearson Education Ltd 2009
Illustrated by Dan Chernett, Ned Woodman, Keith Sparrow,
Pet Gotohda and Matt Buckley
Printed in the UK by Ashford Colour Press

Acknowledgements
Every effort has been made to contact copyright holders of material
reproduced in this book. Any omissions will be rectified in subsequent
printings if notice is given to the publishers.

Websites
The websites used in this book were correct and up-to-date at the time of
publication. It is essential for tutors to preview each website before using it in
class so as to ensure that the URL is still accurate, relevant and appropriate.
We suggest that tutors bookmark useful websites and consider enabling
students to access them through the school/college intranet.

Contents

Part 1

Sequins	Counting to 500	P1
Tens and hundreds	Addition and subtraction within 300	P2
Refreshments	Arithmetic within 300	P3
Dice sums	Addition within 200	P4, P5
School fair	Using money	P6
Tables superstars	Tables facts within 100	P7, P8
Speedy tables G and H	Mental recall of tables facts	P9
Fractions	Using $\frac{1}{2}$, $\frac{1}{3}$, $\frac{1}{4}$ and $\frac{1}{5}$	P10
Stickers	Multiplication and division within 300	P11, P12
More tables superstars	Tables facts within 100	P13, P14
Nine times table	Nine times table	P15, P16
Multiplying	Multiplication within 300	P17, P18
Crazy golf	Mental addition	P19, P20
Dividing by 2 or 3	Dividing by 2 or 3 within 300	P21, P22
200 Trail	Addition and subtraction within 300	P23–P26
First to £500	Using money	P27–P30 Ⓖ

Part 2

Eight hundred	Counting to 800	P31
Making one hundred	Addition and subtraction to 100	P32, P33
Bags and boxes	Arithmetic within 300	P34, P35
Raffle tickets	Using and spelling numbers to 500	P36, P37
Hundred squares	Addition and subtraction within 500	P38, P39
Speedy tables I and J	Mental recall of tables facts	P40
Hoops	Multiples of 7 to 49	P41, P42
What's the difference?	Subtraction within 500	P43, P44
More raffle tickets	Addition and subtraction within 500	P45, P46
Multiplying	Multiplication within 500	P47, P48
Seven times table	Seven times table	P49, P50
Tenths	Using halves and tenths	P51, P52
Car boot sale	Dividing by 3 within 300	P53, P54
What's missing?	Missing numbers and operations	P55, P56
One hundred bingo	Addition and subtraction to 100	P57, P58 Ⓖ
Forty-nine game	Multiples of 7 to 49	P59, P60

Part 3

One thousand	Counting to 1000	P61
Rounding	Rounding to the nearest 10 or 100	P62–P64
Rough answers	Rounding, using money	P65
Hundred squares	Addition and subtraction within 500	P66, P67
Place value cards	Place value within 1000	P68, P69
Boxes and bones	Arithmetic within 750	P70, P71
Stamps	Arithmetic within 750	P72, P73
More place value cards	Addition within 1000	P74, P75
Eight times table	Eight times table	P76, P77
Add or take away	Addition and subtraction within 750	P78, P79
Speedy tables K and L	Mental recall of tables facts	P80
More multiplying	Multiplication within 750	P81, P82
Halves	Halves and 50 per cent	P83
Holidays	Dividing by 2, 3, 4 or 5 within 750	P84, P85
Rough total game	Rounding, using money	P86, P87 Ⓖ
999 game	Place value within 100	P88, P89 Ⓖ
Eights game	Eight times table	P90, P91, P92 Ⓖ

Ⓖ   Colour versions of these games are included in the Games Pack.

Name: _____ Date: _____

Sequins

There are 500 sequins here.
Colour some of them, to make a pattern.

How many sequins
have you coloured? _____

Ask your partner to check.

Name: _____   Date: _____

Tens and hundreds

Fill in the missing numbers.

$0 + 10 =$ _____
$10 + 10 =$ _____
$100 + 10 =$ _____
$200 + 10 =$ _____

$13 + 10 =$ _____
$227 + 10 =$ _____
$191 + 10 =$ _____

$10 + 206 =$ _____
$10 + 99 =$ _____
$10 + 290 =$ _____

$86 - 10 =$ _____
$210 - 10 =$ _____
$190 - 10 =$ _____

$300 - 10 =$ _____
$200 - 10 =$ _____
$100 - 10 =$ _____

252 is 20 more than 232.

What is 20 more than:

57? _____   73? _____
92? _____   204? _____
194? _____   185? _____

What is 20 less than:

103? _____   211? _____
248? _____   115? _____

— 300
— 290

— 230

— 200

— 180

— 120

— 100

— 70

— 50
— 40

— 20
— 10
— 0

Refreshments

Name: _____ Date: _____

How many cups for £1? _____

How much change? _____

How many cups for £1? _____

How much change? _____

How many sandwiches

for £1? _____

How much change? _____

I had 2 sandwiches and a cup of tea.

How much did it cost? _____

How much change from £5? _____

I had 3 sandwiches and a cup of squash.

How much did it cost? _____

How much change from £5? _____

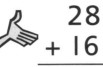

I made up these sums.

 2   8   I   6.

```
  28        82        26        18        21
+ 16      + 61      + 81      + 62      + 86
____      ____      ____      ____      ____

____      ____      ____      ____      ____
```

Which sum had the biggest answer?

I made up these sums.

 7   2   3   5

```
  23        35        73        25        52
+ 75      + 72      + 52      + 37      + 37
____      ____      ____      ____      ____


  27        23        35        32        75
+ 53      + 57      + 27      + 57      + 32
____      ____      ____      ____      ____
```

Which sum had the biggest answer?

Name: _____ Date: _____

Dice sums

Add these
in your head.

5 9. 0 _____		4 3 4 _____	
9. 9. 9. _____		7 6. 8 _____	
7 2 8 _____		1 1 9. _____	

2 0 2 4 8 1 7 5 _____

6. 6. 4 3 1 7 5 8 _____

5 7 2 8 2 4 0 1 _____

8 6. 7 3 1 9. 4 5 _____

6. 9. 7 7 9. 2 3 4 _____

School fair

 I bought these.

How much altogether?

 £1.50  50p  £1.25  30p

_____

 I bought these.

How much altogether?

 95p  95p  95p

_____

How much change from £5? _____

 I bought these.

How much altogether?

 90p  35p  £1.50 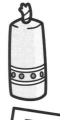 75p

_____

How much change from £10? _____

Text © Rose Griffiths 2009 Pearson Education Ltd **Using money** ◄ Purple Pupil Book Part 1 pages 16 and 17

Name: _____ Date: _____

Tables superstars

Print on card if possible.

Use these cards to practise your tables up to 10 × 10.

$3 \times 9 = 27$

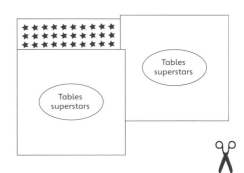

1   Colour the rows of stars in different colours (like the ones on Pupil Book page 18).

2   Cut out the three cards. Write your name on the back of each card.

3   Paperclip the cards to keep them together.

Tables superstars

Tables superstars

Name: _____ **Date:** _____

Tables superstars

3 rows of 6 stars ...

| 3 | × | 6 | = | 18 |

Fill in the missing numbers.

☐ × ☐ = ☐

☐ × ☐ = ☐

☐ × ☐ = ☐

☐ × ☐ = ☐

☐ × ☐ = ☐

☐ × ☐ = ☐

☐ × ☐ = ☐

☐ × ☐ = ☐

Speedy tables G 1 2 3 minute test

Name: _____ Date: _____

3 × 5 = _____	24 ÷ 8 = _____	0 × 4 = _____
6 × 7 = _____	21 ÷ 3 = _____	24 ÷ 4 = _____
4 × 8 = _____	40 ÷ 5 = _____	5 × 6 = _____
10 × 10 = _____	18 ÷ 6 = _____	28 ÷ 7 = _____
9 × 4 = _____	48 ÷ 8 = _____	6 × 9 = _____
7 × 5 = _____	16 ÷ 2 = _____	45 ÷ 9 = _____
3 × 9 = _____	25 ÷ 5 = _____	Score: _____

◄ Purple Pupil Book Part I pages 20 and 21 onwards   Mental recall of tables facts   Text © Rose Griffiths 2009 Pearson Education Ltd

Speedy tables H 1 2 3 minute test

Name: _____ Date: _____

2 × 9 = _____	20 ÷ 4 = _____	4 × 9 = _____
6 × 0 = _____	12 ÷ 3 = _____	24 ÷ 3 = _____
5 × 7 = _____	36 ÷ 6 = _____	6 × 8 = _____
7 × 3 = _____	45 ÷ 5 = _____	15 ÷ 5 = _____
8 × 4 = _____	27 ÷ 9 = _____	7 × 6 = _____
4 × 4 = _____	24 ÷ 6 = _____	54 ÷ 9 = _____
8 × 5 = _____	28 ÷ 4 = _____	Score: _____

Name: ______________________ Date: ____________

Fractions

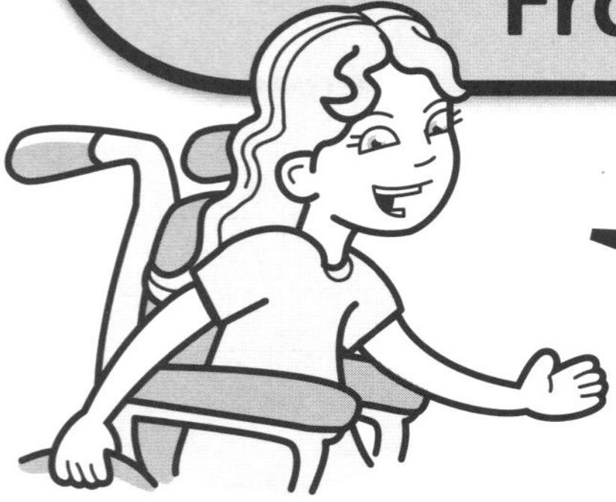

Draw lines to cut up these cakes.

halves | thirds | quarters | fifths

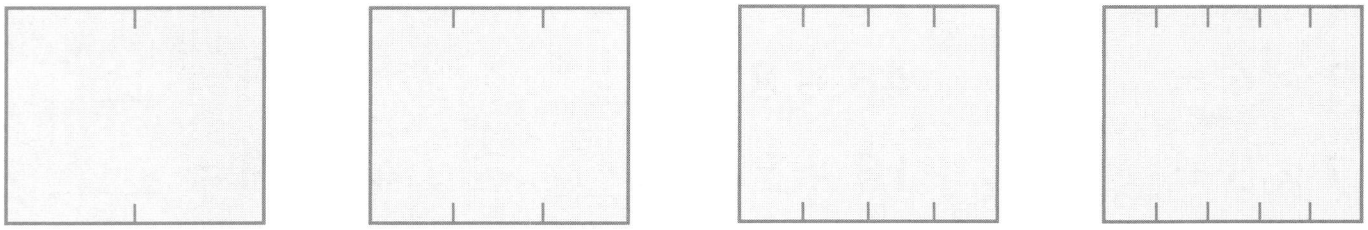

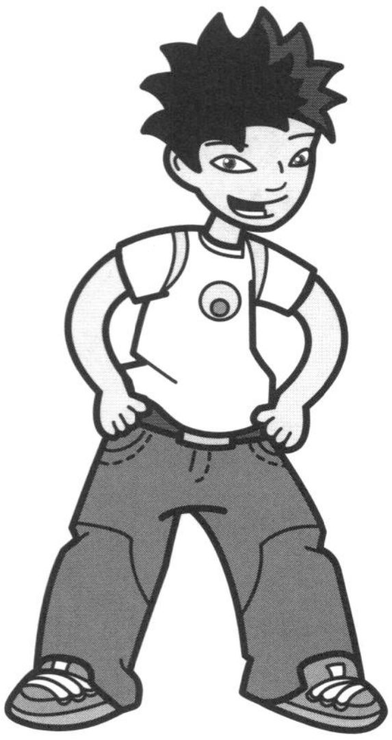

Which is bigger, $\frac{1}{5}$ or $\frac{1}{2}$? ____________

Which is bigger, $\frac{2}{5}$ or $\frac{3}{4}$? ____________

Which is bigger, $\frac{3}{5}$ or $\frac{3}{4}$? ____________

Which is bigger, $\frac{3}{5}$ or $\frac{1}{2}$? ____________

Which is bigger, $\frac{2}{5}$ or $\frac{2}{3}$? ____________

I was hungry!

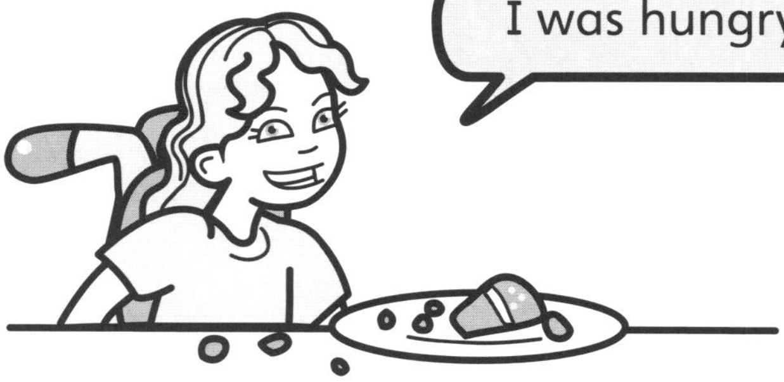

Fill in the missing fractions.

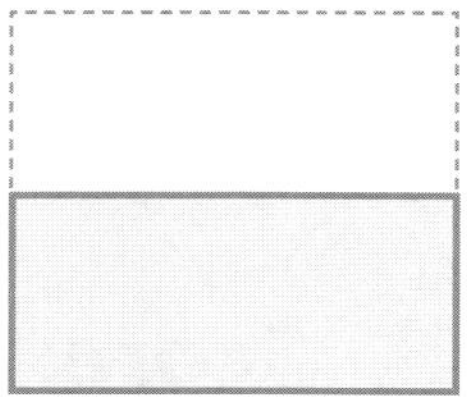

$\frac{1}{2}$ eaten

$\frac{1}{2}$ left

◯ eaten

◯ left

◀Purple Pupil Book Part 1 pages 22 and 23

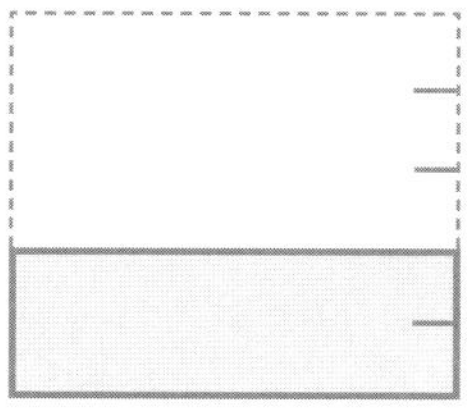

Stickers

5 pets on a sheet of stickers.

How many pets on:

5 sheets? _____   8 sheets? _____

9 sheets? _____   6 sheets? _____

How many sheets for:

15 pets? _____   35 pets? _____

50 pets? _____   20 pets? _____

13	21	36	47
× 5	× 5	× 5	× 5
_____	_____	_____	_____

$5\overline{)55}$ $5\overline{)60}$ $5\overline{)75}$

Stickers

4 fish on a sheet of stickers.

How many fish on:

3 sheets? _____

5 sheets? _____

7 sheets? _____

9 sheets? _____

How many sheets for:

8 fish? _____

32 fish? _____

40 fish? _____

24 fish? _____

16 fish? _____

48 fish? _____

$$\begin{array}{r} 22 \\ \times\ 4 \\ \hline \\ \hline \end{array}$$

$$\begin{array}{r} 17 \\ \times\ 4 \\ \hline \\ \hline \end{array}$$

$$\begin{array}{r} 65 \\ \times\ 4 \\ \hline \\ \hline \end{array}$$

$$\begin{array}{r} 50 \\ \times\ 4 \\ \hline \\ \hline \end{array}$$

$4\overline{)80}$ $4\overline{)84}$ $4\overline{)88}$

More tables superstars

How many 7s make 21?

3

$$7 \overline{)21}^{3}$$

$4 \overline{)24}$

$6 \overline{)36}$

$5 \overline{)5}$

$6 \overline{)12}$

$9 \overline{)54}$

$9 \overline{)36}$

$5 \overline{)30}$

More tables superstars

How many 4s make 9?

2 remainder 1.

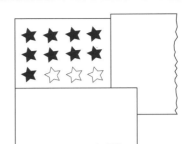

$$4\overline{)9}\;\;^{2\;r.1}$$

$2\overline{)14}$ $2\overline{)15}$ $2\overline{)16}$

$3\overline{)15}$ $3\overline{)16}$ $3\overline{)17}$

$4\overline{)20}$ $4\overline{)22}$ $4\overline{)23}$

$5\overline{)25}$ $5\overline{)27}$ $5\overline{)29}$

$3\overline{)28}$ $5\overline{)40}$ $4\overline{)25}$

$5\overline{)45}$ $2\overline{)19}$ $3\overline{)30}$

$10\overline{)80}$ $10\overline{)86}$ $5\overline{)33}$

Text © Rose Griffiths 2009
Pearson Education Ltd
Tables facts within 100   ◄Purple Pupil Book Part 1 pages 26 and 27

Nine times table

Cut out the eleven tables facts.
Fold along the dotted line and glue flat.

Ask your teacher how to practise with these.

| 5 × 9 | 45 |

| 0 × 9 | 0 | 6 × 9 | 54 |

| 1 × 9 | 9 | 7 × 9 | 63 |

| 2 × 9 | <u>18</u> | 8 × 9 | 72 |

| 3 × 9 | 27 | 9 × 9 | <u>81</u> |

| 4 × 9 | 36 | 10 × 9 | 90 |

Nine times table

Fill in the missing numbers.

10 take away 1	9
20 take away 2	_____
30 take away 3	_____
40 take away 4	_____
50 take away 5	_____
60 take away 6	_____
70 take away 7	_____
80 take away 8	_____
90 take away 9	_____
100 take away 10	_____

1 nine	9
2 nines	_____
3 nines	_____
4 nines	_____
5 nines	_____
6 nines	_____
7 nines	_____
8 nines	_____
9 nines	_____
10 nines	_____

$3 \times 9 = \boxed{}$

$27 \div 3 = \boxed{}$

$\boxed{} \times 9 = 45$

$45 \div 9 = \boxed{}$

$9 \times 8 = \boxed{}$

$72 \div 9 = \boxed{}$

$6 \times 9 = \boxed{}$

$54 \div 6 = \boxed{}$

Multiplying

Use tens and ones. Draw them. Then multiply on paper.

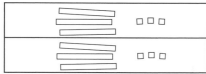 33 times 2

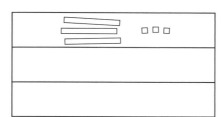 33 times 3

 33 times 4

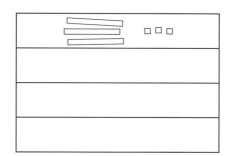

$$\begin{array}{r} 33 \\ \times\ 2 \\ \hline \\ \hline \end{array}$$

$$\begin{array}{r} 33 \\ \times\ 3 \\ \hline \\ \hline \end{array}$$

$$\begin{array}{r} 33 \\ \times\ 4 \\ \hline \\ \hline \end{array}$$

Use tens and ones. __Then__ multiply on paper.

$$\begin{array}{r} 57 \\ \times\ 2 \\ \hline \\ \hline \end{array}$$

$$\begin{array}{r} 90 \\ \times\ 3 \\ \hline \\ \hline \end{array}$$

$$\begin{array}{r} 42 \\ \times\ 5 \\ \hline \\ \hline \end{array}$$

$$\begin{array}{r} 63 \\ \times\ 4 \\ \hline \\ \hline \end{array}$$

$$\begin{array}{r} 38 \\ \times\ 3 \\ \hline \\ \hline \end{array}$$

$$\begin{array}{r} 54 \\ \times\ 5 \\ \hline \\ \hline \end{array}$$

$$\begin{array}{r} 94 \\ \times\ 2 \\ \hline \\ \hline \end{array}$$

 ✔ or ✘

Multiplying

Use tens and ones. Draw them.
Then multiply on paper.

46 times 2   46 times 3   46 times 4

 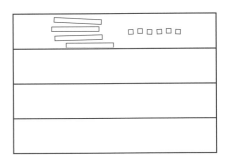

$$\begin{array}{r} 46 \\ \times\ 2 \\ \hline \\ \hline \end{array}$$

$$\begin{array}{r} 46 \\ \times\ 3 \\ \hline \\ \hline \end{array}$$

$$\begin{array}{r} 46 \\ \times\ 4 \\ \hline \\ \hline \end{array}$$

Use tens and ones. <u>Then</u> multiply on paper.

$$\begin{array}{r} 91 \\ \times\ 3 \\ \hline \\ \hline \end{array}$$

$$\begin{array}{r} 79 \\ \times\ 2 \\ \hline \\ \hline \end{array}$$

$$\begin{array}{r} 53 \\ \times\ 4 \\ \hline \\ \hline \end{array}$$

$$\begin{array}{r} 60 \\ \times\ 5 \\ \hline \\ \hline \end{array}$$

$$\begin{array}{r} 66 \\ \times\ 2 \\ \hline \\ \hline \end{array}$$

$$\begin{array}{r} 73 \\ \times\ 4 \\ \hline \\ \hline \end{array}$$

$$\begin{array}{r} 86 \\ \times\ 3 \\ \hline \\ \hline \end{array}$$

 ✔ or ✗

Name:	Date:

Crazy golf

What are our totals?

Crazy Golf

Name: Emma

HOLE	STROKES	HOLE	STROKES
1	4	7	4
2	4	8	4
3	2	9	6
4	6	10	3
5	4	11	5
6	5	12	5
		TOTAL	

Crazy Golf

Name: Shaun

HOLE	STROKES	HOLE	STROKES
1	2	7	5
2	2	8	3
3	5	9	2
4	11	10	3
5	3	11	4
6	2	12	8
		TOTAL	

Crazy Golf

Name: Andy

HOLE	STROKES	HOLE	STROKES
1	3	7	12
2	5	8	3
3	2	9	4
4	1	10	2
5	2	11	4
6	8	12	4
		TOTAL	

Crazy Golf

Name: Kelly

HOLE	STROKES	HOLE	STROKES
1	3	7	7
2	5	8	4
3	4	9	3
4	3	10	7
5	5	11	2
6	3	12	8
		TOTAL	

Crazy Golf

Name: Asha

HOLE	STROKES	HOLE	STROKES
1	3	7	2
2	4	8	4
3	3	9	2
4	3	10	3
5	4	11	4
6	2	12	4
		TOTAL	

Crazy Golf

Name: Frank

HOLE	STROKES	HOLE	STROKES
1	2	7	4
2	5	8	2
3	4	9	3
4	2	10	3
5	6	11	3
6	1	12	5
		TOTAL	

Crazy Golf

Name: Sophie

HOLE	STROKES	HOLE	STROKES
1	3	7	8
2	2	8	2
3	4	9	3
4	3	10	3
5	3	11	4
6	3	12	2
		TOTAL	

Who was the winner?

Name: _____ Date: _____

Crazy golf

Make up these score cards for your partner to add up.
When they finish ✔ or ✘.

What are the totals?

Crazy Golf

Name:

HOLE	STROKES	HOLE	STROKES
1		7	
2		8	
3		9	
4		10	
5		11	
6		12	
		TOTAL	

Crazy Golf

Name:

HOLE	STROKES	HOLE	STROKES
1		7	
2		8	
3		9	
4		10	
5		11	
6		12	
		TOTAL	

Crazy Golf

Name:

HOLE	STROKES	HOLE	STROKES
1		7	
2		8	
3		9	
4		10	
5		11	
6		12	
		TOTAL	

Crazy Golf

Name:

HOLE	STROKES	HOLE	STROKES
1		7	
2		8	
3		9	
4		10	
5		11	
6		12	
		TOTAL	

Crazy Golf

Name:

HOLE	STROKES	HOLE	STROKES
1		7	
2		8	
3		9	
4		10	
5		11	
6		12	
		TOTAL	

Crazy Golf

Name:

HOLE	STROKES	HOLE	STROKES
1		7	
2		8	
3		9	
4		10	
5		11	
6		12	
		TOTAL	

Crazy Golf

Name:

HOLE	STROKES	HOLE	STROKES
1		7	
2		8	
3		9	
4		10	
5		11	
6		12	
		TOTAL	

Who was the winner?

_____

Dividing

Use hundreds, tens and ones to divide by 2.

264 divided by 2

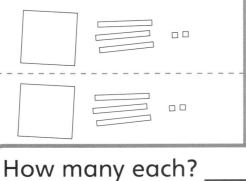

$$2 \quad 6 \quad 4 \quad \div \quad 2 \quad = \quad \rule{2cm}{0.4pt}$$

$2\overline{)264}$

How many each? _____

258 divided by 2

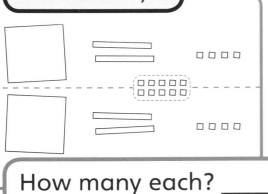

$$2 \quad 5 \quad 8 \quad \div \quad 2 \quad = \quad \rule{2cm}{0.4pt}$$

$2\overline{)258}$

How many each? _____

Use hundreds, tens and ones to help you.

$2\overline{)160}$ $\qquad$ $2\overline{)94}$ $\qquad$ $2\overline{)200}$

$2\overline{)236}$ $\qquad$ $2\overline{)190}$ $\qquad$ $2\overline{)254}$

$2\overline{)152}$ $\qquad$ $2\overline{)298}$ $\qquad$ $2\overline{)300}$

Dividing

Use hundreds, tens and ones to divide by 3.

186 divided by 3

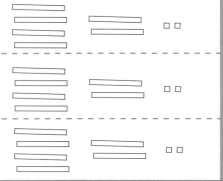

$1\ 8\ 6 \div 3 =$ _____

$3\overline{)186}$

How many each? _____

300 divided by 3

$3\ 0\ 0 \div 3 =$ _____

$3\overline{)300}$

How many each? _____

Choose how to do these.

$3\overline{)195}$ $3\overline{)273}$ $3\overline{)78}$

$3\overline{)111}$ $3\overline{)252}$ $3\overline{)144}$

Dividing by 2 or 3 within 300   ◀ Purple Pupil Book Part I pages 34 and 35

200 Trail

Print these on card. You can use them again.
Colour and cut out the instructions card, two sets of ten cards and game board.
Store in a clear zip-top wallet or in an envelope.
Include three different coloured centimetre cubes (as counters) if possible.

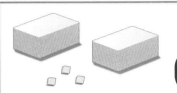

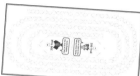

200 Trail

A game for I, 2 or 3 people.

- **Before you start**
  Choose <u>either</u> the adding cards <u>or</u> the taking away cards.
  Shuffle them. Put them in a pile, face down.

  You need a centimetre cube each, as your counter.
  Put it on the 200 Trail board.

- **How to play**

Turn over a card.
Move that many places.
Put the card at the
bottom of the pile.

Your partner checks
your go. Then it is
your partner's turn.

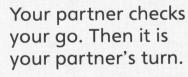

- Shuffle the pile of cards every ten turns, if you want to.
  Keep going until you get to the end of the trail.

◄ Purple Level Pupil Book Part I; **Addition and subtraction within 300**

Text © Rose Griffiths 2009
Pearson Education Ltd

200 Trail

Print these on card. You can use them again.

200 Trail Adding Game	Add two
200 Trail Adding Game	Add four
200 Trail Adding Game	Add ten
200 Trail Adding Game	Add twenty
200 Trail Adding Game	Add thirty

200 Trail Adding Game	Add one
200 Trail Adding Game	Add three
200 Trail Adding Game	Add ten
200 Trail Adding Game	Add twenty
200 Trail Adding Game	Add thirty

200 Trail Taking away Game	Take away 2
200 Trail Taking away Game	Take away 4
200 Trail Taking away Game	Take away 10
200 Trail Taking away Game	Take away 20
200 Trail Taking away Game	Take away 30

200 Trail Taking away Game	Take away 1
200 Trail Taking away Game	Take away 3
200 Trail Taking away Game	Take away 10
200 Trail Taking away Game	Take away 20
200 Trail Taking away Game	Take away 30

200 Trail

sheet 3 of 4
Print these on card. You can use them again.
Colour in and cover with clear plastic if wished, then
cut out both pieces of the board (see Copymaster P26).
Join together with sticky tape.

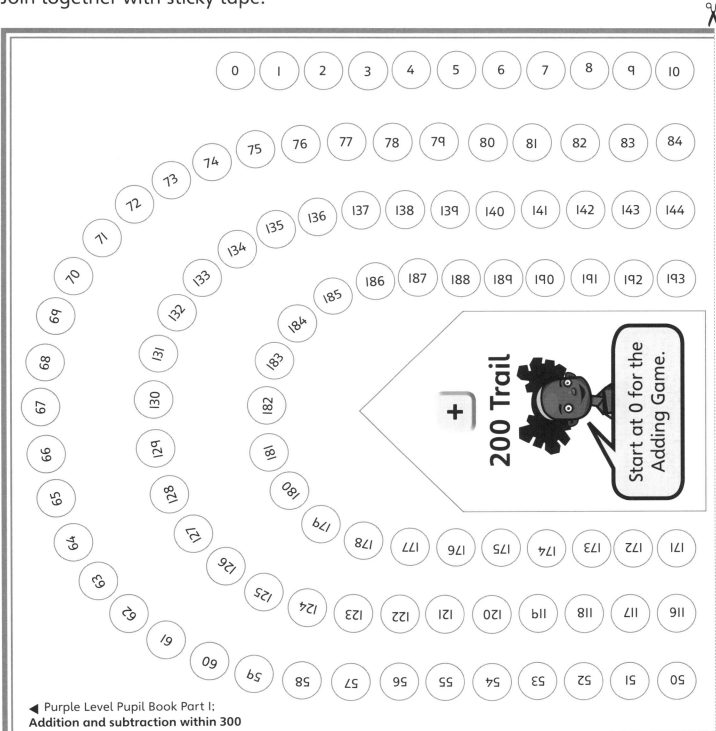

◀ Purple Level Pupil Book Part I;
Addition and subtraction within 300

200 Trail

Print these on card. You can use them again.

Join to the other piece of game board (on Copymaster P25).

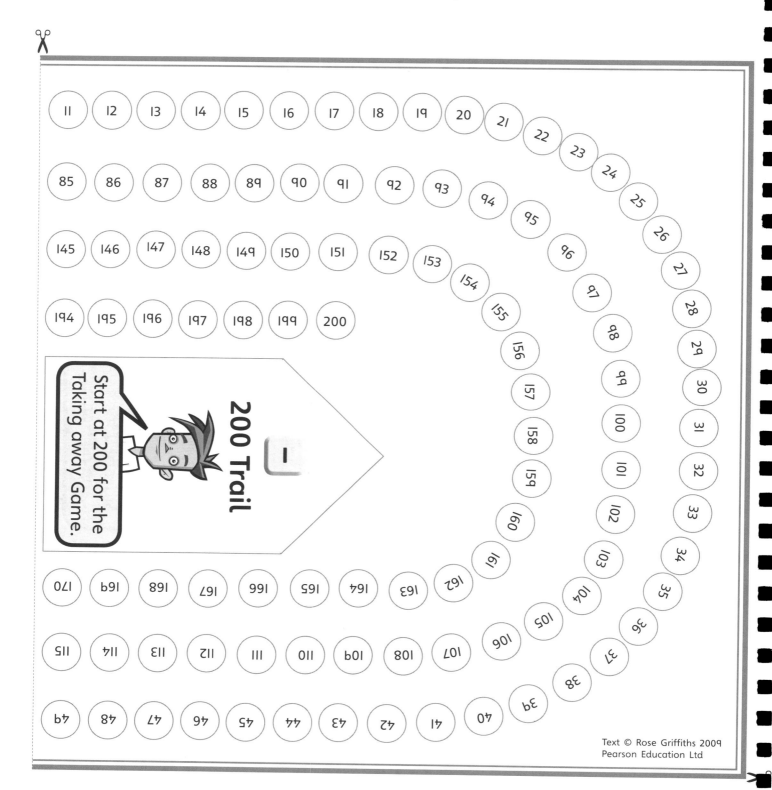

Start at 200 for the Taking away Game.

200 Trail

Text © Rose Griffiths 2009
Pearson Education Ltd

◄Purple Pupil Book Part I: use from
pages 10 and 11 onwards

sheet I of 4
Print these on card. You can use them again.
Colour in and cover with clear plastic, if you wish, then cut out both pieces of the board (see Copymaster P28).
Join together with sticky tape.

£103

£37

£5

£28

First to £500

A game for I, 2 or 3 people.

- **Before you start**
  You need a dice, a counter each,
  up to I5 £100 notes,
  30 £10 notes, and
  30 £1 coins.

Put your counter on the arrow.

£84

◀ Purple Pupil Book Part I;
Using money

£130

£45

£3

First to £500

Print these on card. You can use them again.
Store in a clear zip-top wallet or in an envelope. If possible, include a dice,
3 counters, 30 plastic or card £1 coins, 30 token £10 notes, and 15 token £100 notes (see
Copymasters P29 and P30).

£60

£1

£43

£110

£200

£42

Throw the dice and move
that number of spaces.

Take the amount of
money you land on.

How much money
have you got now?

Now it's your partner's go.

Change ten £1 coins for a £10 note,
or ten £10 notes for a £100 note,
whenever you can.

Keep going until you have £500.

£70

£96

£59

P28
◀ Purple Pupil Book Part 1; use from
pages 16 and 17 onwards

sheet 3 of 4
Print four copies on apricot paper. You can use them again.

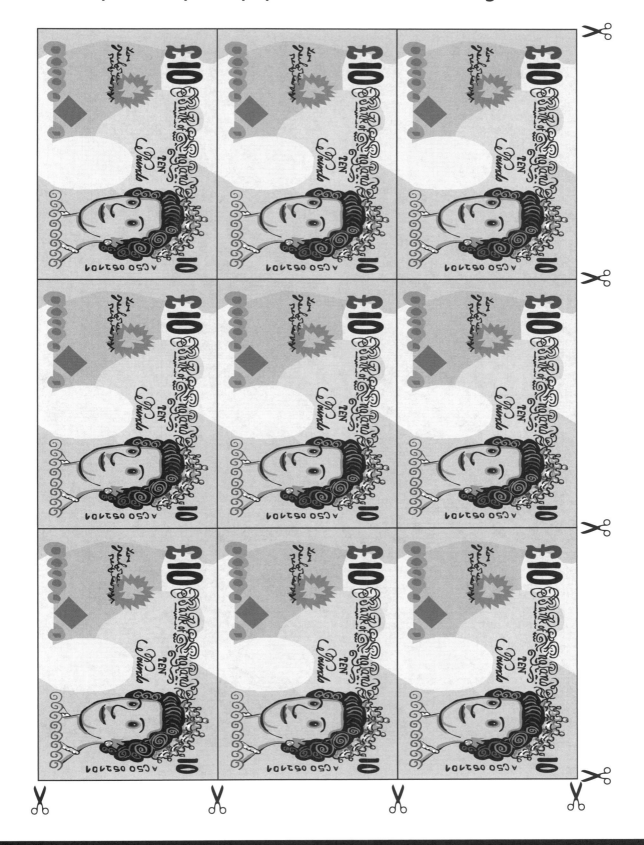

First to £500

Print these on coloured paper (not apricot). You can use them again.

Name: _____   Date: _____

Eight hundred

How many in each box?

431

_____

_____

_____

_____

_____

_____

_____

_____

_____

I've got (48)   How many more to make [100]?

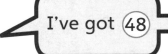

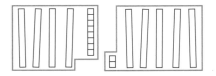

$48 + \boxed{52} = 100$

Make each number with tens and ones. Draw them.

Fill in the missing numbers.

(76)

$76 + \boxed{} = 100$

$100 - 76 = \boxed{}$

(38)

$38 + \boxed{} = 100$

$100 - 38 = \boxed{}$

(53)

$53 + \boxed{} = 100$

$100 - 53 = \boxed{}$

(81)

$81 + \boxed{} = 100$

$100 - 81 = \boxed{}$

(67)

$67 + \boxed{} = 100$

$100 - 67 = \boxed{}$

(19)

$19 + \boxed{} = 100$

$100 - 19 = \boxed{}$

Making one hundred

Check my sums.
✔ or ✗

45	92	36	100	89
+ 55	+ 18	+ 64	+ 0	+ 11
100	100	100	100	100

14	28	55	73	46
+ 84	+ 82	+ 35	+ 27	+ 55
100	100	100	100	100

Complete.

$100 - 70 = \rule{2cm}{0.4pt}$ $100 - 74 = \rule{2cm}{0.4pt}$

$100 - 80 = \rule{2cm}{0.4pt}$ $100 - 83 = \rule{2cm}{0.4pt}$

$100 - 30 = \rule{2cm}{0.4pt}$ $100 - 31 = \rule{2cm}{0.4pt}$

$100 - 20 = \rule{2cm}{0.4pt}$ $100 - 25 = \rule{2cm}{0.4pt}$

$100 - 40 = \rule{2cm}{0.4pt}$ $100 - 47 = \rule{2cm}{0.4pt}$

$100 - 50 = \rule{2cm}{0.4pt}$ $100 - 59 = \rule{2cm}{0.4pt}$

$100 - 90 = \rule{2cm}{0.4pt}$ $100 - 92 = \rule{2cm}{0.4pt}$

$100 - 60 = \rule{2cm}{0.4pt}$ $100 - 66 = \rule{2cm}{0.4pt}$

$100 - 10 = \rule{2cm}{0.4pt}$ $100 - 18 = \rule{2cm}{0.4pt}$

$100 - 0 = \rule{2cm}{0.4pt}$ $100 - 2 = \rule{2cm}{0.4pt}$

Bags and boxes

How many envelopes in 5 boxes?

_____

How many tissues in 3 boxes?

_____

Fill in the missing numbers.

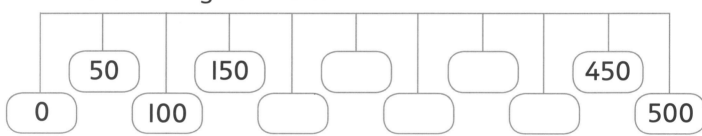

| 50 | 150 | | | 450 | |
| 0 | 100 | | | | 500 |

100 + 25 = _____	250 + 50 = _____	50
175 + 25 = _____	250 + 150 = _____	× 4
275 + 25 = _____	300 + 50 = _____	_____
350 + 25 = _____	350 + 100 = _____	
400 + 25 = _____	350 + 150 = _____	50
475 + 25 = _____	400 + 50 = _____	× 7
		_____
350 − 25 = _____	500 − 50 = _____	150
300 − 25 = _____	500 − 150 = _____	× 2
200 − 25 = _____	500 − 250 = _____	_____

Text © Rose Griffiths 2009
Pearson Education Ltd

Arithmetic within 500

◀ Purple Pupil Book Part 2 pages 42 and 43
Copymaster P35

Name: _____   **Date:** _____

Bags and boxes

 Look at this bank bag.

 How many make £20?

_____

 How many make £10?

_____

 How many make £10?

_____

THE RAPID BANK

NO MIXED COIN PLEASE

£20 IN — POUND COIN
£10 SILVER IN — 50p OR 20p
£5 SILVER IN — 10p OR 5p
£1 BRONZE IN — 2p OR 1p

RE-USABLE BAG ♻
PLEASE RETURN

 How many make £5?

_____

 How many make £5?

_____

 How many make £1?

_____

 How many make £1?

_____

Cut out these tickets.
Use them with copymaster P37.

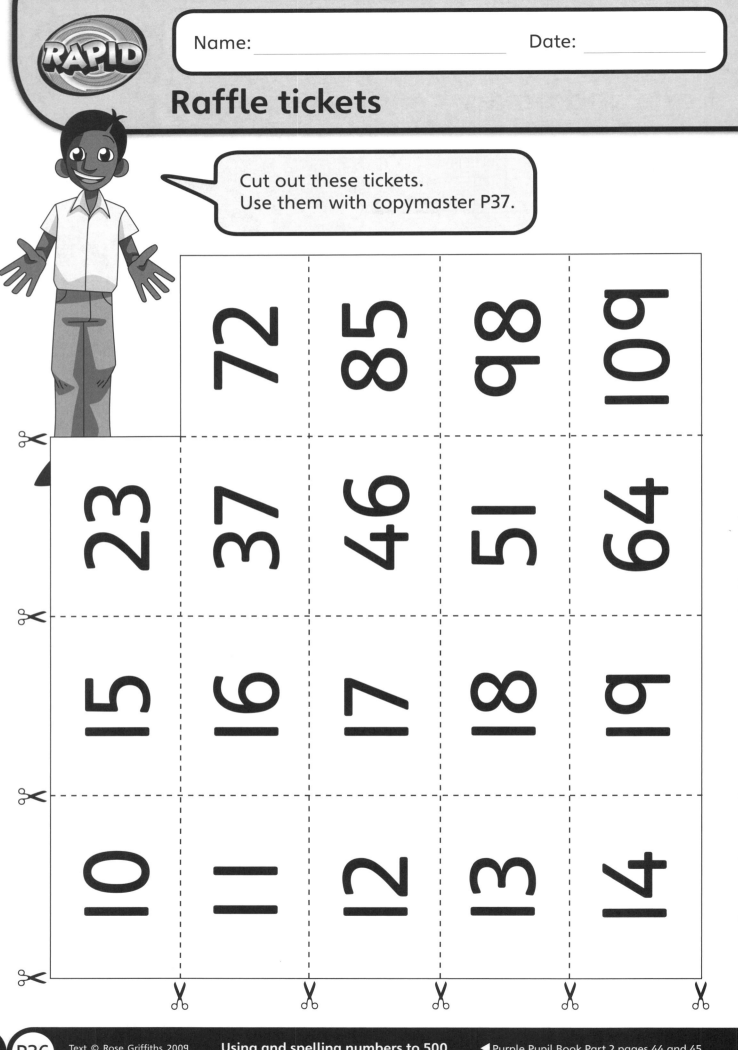

Raffle tickets

Work with a partner to practise your spelling.

Cut out the tickets on Copymaster P36.

Fold the tickets and put them in a tub or bag.

Take turns to pick a number to spell.

Check your spellings here.

1	one	11	eleven	30	thirty
2	two	12	twelve	40	forty
3	three	13	thirteen	50	fifty
4	four	14	fourteen	60	sixty
5	five	15	fifteen	70	seventy
6	six	16	sixteen	80	eighty
7	seven	17	seventeen	90	ninety
8	eight	18	eighteen	100	hundred
9	nine	19	nineteen		
10	ten	20	twenty		

Which numbers do <u>you</u> think are the hardest to spell?

_____   _____

_____   _____

Hundred squares

Fill in the missing numbers.

351	352	353	354	355		357	358	359	360
361			364	365	366	367			370
371	372	373		375	376			379	
381			384	385	386	387	388	389	
	392	393	394				398	399	400
	402	403		405		407	408		
411	412	413	414		416	417		419	420
	422			425	426		428		430
431		433		435		437		439	
	442	443	444		446				

Use the hundred square.

395 + 40 = ____   398 + 37 = ____

439 – 62 = ____   351 + 93 = ____

371 + 58 = ____   426 – 71 = ____

417 – 40 = ____   404 + 43 = ____

Hundred squares

One number is __wrong__ on this hundred square.

Find it and put it right.

401	402	403	404	405	406	407	408	409	410
411	412	413	414	415	416	417	418	419	420
421	422	423	424	425	426	427	428	429	430
431	432	433	434	435	436	437	438	439	440
441	442	443	444	445	446	447	448	449	450
451	452	453	454	455	456	457	458	459	460
461	462	463	464	465	466	467	468	469	470
471	472	473	474	475	476	477	478	478	480
481	482	483	484	485	486	487	488	489	490
491	492	493	494	495	496	497	498	499	500

Fill in the missing numbers.

443 + ☐ = 473

☐ + 60 = 487

480 − 19 = ☐

446 + ☐ = 500

462 − 45 = ☐

488 − ☐ = 428

405 + 27 = ☐

☐ + 20 = 444

493 − 51 = ☐

☐ + 34 = 459

◀ Purple Pupil Book Part 2 pages 46 and 47
Copymaster P40

Addition and subtraction within 500

Text © Rose Griffiths 2009
Pearson Education Ltd

P39

Name: _____ Date: _____

Speedy tables I   1 2 3 minute test

4 × 6 = _____	27 ÷ 3 = _____	8 × 9 = _____
5 × 3 = _____	9 ÷ 9 = _____	16 ÷ 4 = _____
2 × 7 = _____	40 ÷ 5 = _____	0 × 8 = _____
9 × 9 = _____	21 ÷ 7 = _____	42 ÷ 6 = _____
8 × 6 = _____	63 ÷ 9 = _____	10 × 4 = _____
5 × 5 = _____	48 ÷ 6 = _____	54 ÷ 6 = _____
7 × 4 = _____	70 ÷ 10 = _____	Score: _____

Text © Rose Griffiths 2009
Pearson Education Ltd

Mental recall of tables facts

◀ Purple Pupil Book Part 2
pages 48 and 49 onwards

Name: _____ Date: _____

Speedy tables J   1 2 3 minute test

4 × 9 = _____	24 ÷ 6 = _____	3 × 7 = _____
4 × 7 = _____	35 ÷ 5 = _____	18 ÷ 2 = _____
6 × 6 = _____	60 ÷ 10 = _____	7 × 6 = _____
9 × 8 = _____	32 ÷ 4 = _____	24 ÷ 3 = _____
3 × 0 = _____	5 ÷ 5 = _____	9 × 6 = _____
9 × 7 = _____	42 ÷ 6 = _____	81 ÷ 9 = _____
5 × 8 = _____	45 ÷ 9 = _____	Score: _____

 Text © Rose Griffiths 2009
Pearson Education Ltd

Mental recall of tables facts

◀ Purple Pupil Book Part 2
pages 48 and 49 onwards

Hoops

Fill in the missing numbers.

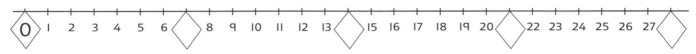

◇ 0 │ 1 2 3 4 5 6 ◇ 8 9 10 11 12 13 ◇ 15 16 17 18 19 20 ◇ 22 23 24 25 26 27 ◇

1	2	3	4	5	6	7
8	9	10	11	12	13	
15	16	17	18	19	20	
22	23	24	25	26	27	
29	30	31	32	33	34	
36	37	38	39	40	41	
43	44	45	46	47	48	

$$7 + 7 = \underline{\qquad}$$

$$14 + 7 = \underline{\qquad}$$

$$21 + 7 = \underline{\qquad}$$

$$28 + 7 = \underline{\qquad}$$

$$35 + 7 = \underline{\qquad}$$

$$42 + 7 = \underline{\qquad}$$

$$35 - 14 = \underline{\qquad}$$

$$49 - 14 = \underline{\qquad}$$

$$42 - 14 = \underline{\qquad}$$

$$49 - 21 = \underline{\qquad}$$

7, 14, 21, _____, _____.

7, 14, _____, 28, 35, _____.

7, 14, 21, _____, _____, 42, _____.

◀ Purple Pupil Book Part 2 pages 50 and 51
Copymaster P42

Multiples of 7 to 49

Text © Rose Griffiths 2009
Pearson Education Ltd

P41

 Score 7 points for each hoop.
Draw hoops to make these scores.

14 points

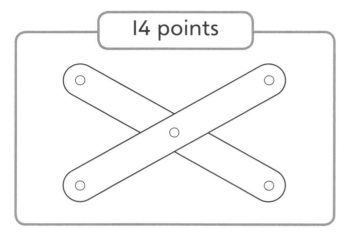

21 points

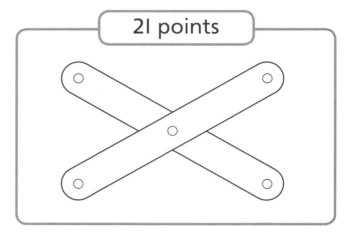

28 points

35 points

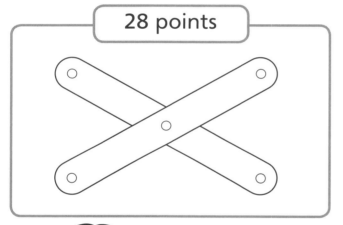

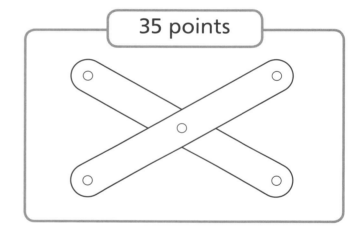

7 hoops.
How many points?

_____

5 × 7 = _____

7 × 5 = _____

35 ÷ 7 = _____

35 ÷ 5 = _____

6 × 7 = _____

7 × 6 = _____

42 ÷ 7 = _____

42 ÷ 6 = _____

Multiples of 7 to 49   ◄ Purple Pupil Book Part 2 pages 50 and 51

What's the difference?

What's the difference between the amounts in each bag?

Use coins and notes if you want to.

£1.95 £5.00

£4.50 £2.80

£5.00 £2.60

£3.75 £4.65

£70 £24

£1.40 £8.50

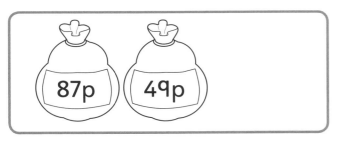

87p 49p

£267 £368

£146 £86

 ✔ or ✘

◀ Purple Pupil Book Part 2 pages 52 and 53
Copymaster P44

Subtraction within 500

Text © Rose Griffiths 2009
Pearson Education Ltd

P43

Name: ______________________ Date: ______________

What's the difference?

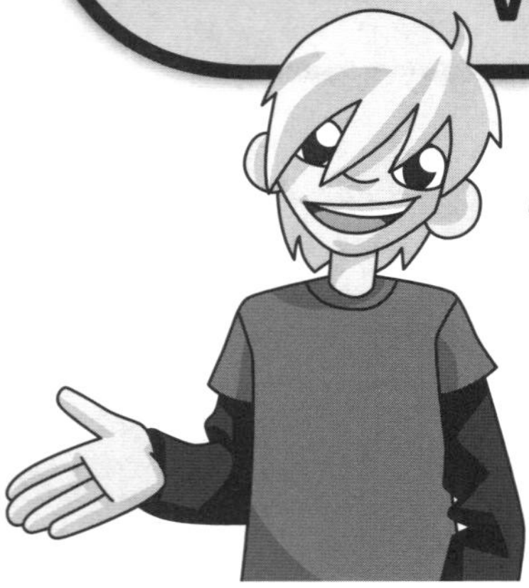

Work with a partner.
Talk about <u>how</u> you work these out.

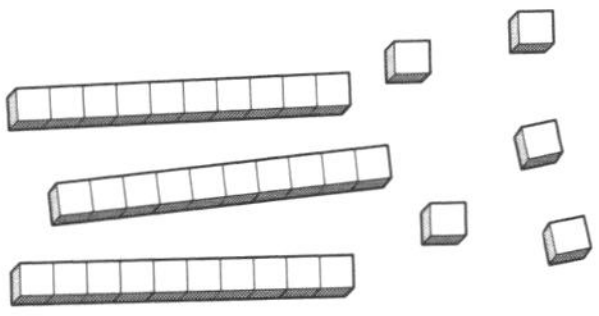

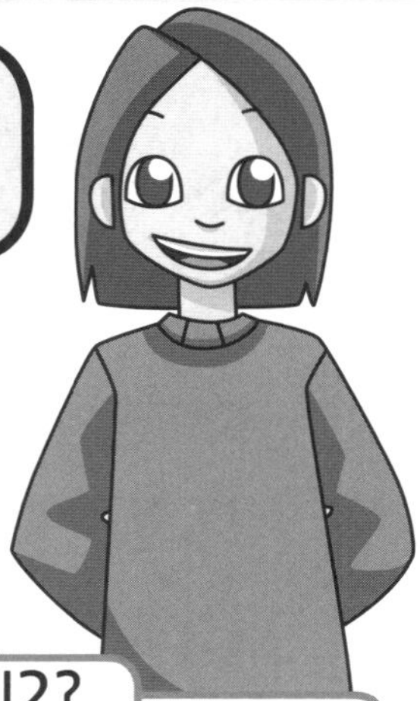

What's the difference between:

85 and 95?

99 and 412?

500 and 115?

136 and 123?

99 and 190?

341 and 450?

299 and 306?

400 and 175?

◀ Purple Pupil Book Part 2 pages 52 and 53

More raffle tickets

Practise adding!

147	147
230	+ 230
	_____

| 92 |
| 132 |

| 209 | |
| 164 | |

| 193 |
| 197 |

78	184
184	78
3	+ 3
	_____

| 63 |
| 145 |
| 207 |

142	159	97	114
+ 57	+ 213	+ 232	+ 185
_____	_____	_____	_____

126	243	59	248
+ 127	+ 136	+ 241	+ 249
_____	_____	_____	_____

More raffle tickets

Take away the smaller number from the bigger one.

121	238
238	− 121
	_____

202
43

112
187

225
107

144
139

58
221

$$
\begin{array}{r} 163 \\ -\ \ \ 4 \\ \hline \\ \hline \end{array}
\qquad
\begin{array}{r} 108 \\ -\ 99 \\ \hline \\ \hline \end{array}
\qquad
\begin{array}{r} 249 \\ -156 \\ \hline \\ \hline \end{array}
\qquad
\begin{array}{r} 211 \\ -\ 60 \\ \hline \\ \hline \end{array}
$$

$$
\begin{array}{r} 178 \\ -177 \\ \hline \\ \hline \end{array}
\qquad
\begin{array}{r} 162 \\ -\ 92 \\ \hline \\ \hline \end{array}
\qquad
\begin{array}{r} 222 \\ -111 \\ \hline \\ \hline \end{array}
\qquad
\begin{array}{r} 250 \\ -183 \\ \hline \\ \hline \end{array}
$$

Name: _____ **Date:** _____

Multiplying

Use hundreds, tens and ones. Draw them. Then multiply on paper.

121 times 2

121 times 3

121 times 4

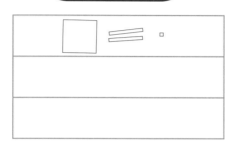

$$\begin{array}{r} 121 \\ \times\ \ 2 \\ \hline \\ \hline \end{array}$$

$$\begin{array}{r} 121 \\ \times\ \ 3 \\ \hline \\ \hline \end{array}$$

$$\begin{array}{r} 121 \\ \times\ \ 4 \\ \hline \\ \hline \end{array}$$

Use hundreds, tens and ones. <u>Then</u> multiply on paper.

$$\begin{array}{r} 161 \\ \times\ \ 3 \\ \hline \\ \hline \end{array}$$

$$\begin{array}{r} 85 \\ \times\ \ 3 \\ \hline \\ \hline \end{array}$$

$$\begin{array}{r} 227 \\ \times\ \ 2 \\ \hline \\ \hline \end{array}$$

$$\begin{array}{r} 108 \\ \times\ \ 2 \\ \hline \\ \hline \end{array}$$

$$\begin{array}{r} 113 \\ \times\ \ 4 \\ \hline \\ \hline \end{array}$$

$$\begin{array}{r} 65 \\ \times\ \ 4 \\ \hline \\ \hline \end{array}$$

$$\begin{array}{r} 100 \\ \times\ \ 5 \\ \hline \\ \hline \end{array}$$

 ✔ or ✘

◄ Purple Pupil Book Part 2 pages 56 and 57
Copymaster P48

Multiplication within 500

Text © Rose Griffiths 2009
Pearson Education Ltd

P47

Multiplying

Use hundreds, tens and ones. Draw them.
Then multiply on paper.

144 times 2   155 times 2   166 times 2

   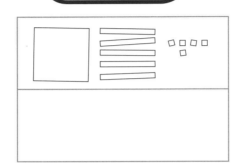   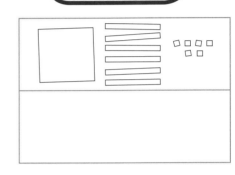

144	155	166
× 2	× 2	× 2
___	___	___

Multiply on paper. __Then__ use hundreds, tens and ones.

183	63	147	152
× 2	× 3	× 3	× 3
___	___	___	___

114	48	108	
× 4	× 5	× 4	✔ or ✗
___	___	___	

Seven times table

Cut out the eleven tables facts.
Fold along the dotted line and glue flat.

Ask how to practise with these.

5 × 7	35
0 × 7	0	6 × 7	42
1 × 7	7	7 × 7	49
2 × 7	14	8 × 7	56
3 × 7	21	9 × 7	63
4 × 7	28	10 × 7	70

Seven times tables

Fill in the missing numbers.

Check.

$7 \times 7 = \boxed{}$

$49 \div 7 = \boxed{}$

$9 \times 7 = \boxed{}$

$63 \div 9 = \boxed{}$

$6 \times 7 = \boxed{}$

$42 \div 7 = \boxed{}$

$7 \times 8 = \boxed{}$

$56 \div 7 = \boxed{}$

$10 \times 7 = \boxed{}$

$\boxed{} \times 7 = 63$

$8 \times 7 = \boxed{}$

$7 \times 7 = \boxed{}$

$\boxed{} \times 7 = 42$

$5 \times 7 = \boxed{}$

$\boxed{} \times 7 = 28$

$\boxed{} \times 7 = 21$

$2 \times 7 = \boxed{}$

$\boxed{} \times 7 = 7$

$0 \times 7 = \boxed{}$

What is 9 times 7?

What is 8 times 7?

_____ _____

Tenths

How much cake is on each plate?

Write the fractions.

two tenths

five tenths

nine tenths

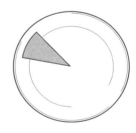

$\frac{2}{10}$

□

□

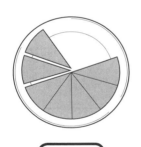

□   □   □

How much cake is on this tray?

$1\frac{4}{10}$

How much on this tray?

_____

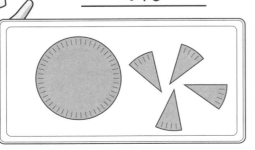

◀ Purple Pupil Book Part 2 pages 60 and 61
Copymaster P52

Using halves and tenths

Text © Rose Griffiths 2009
Pearson Education Ltd

P51

Tenths

Name: _____ **Date:** _____

Measure each pencil to the nearest half a centimetre.

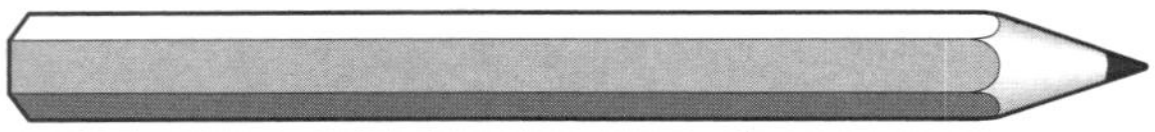

7.5 cm

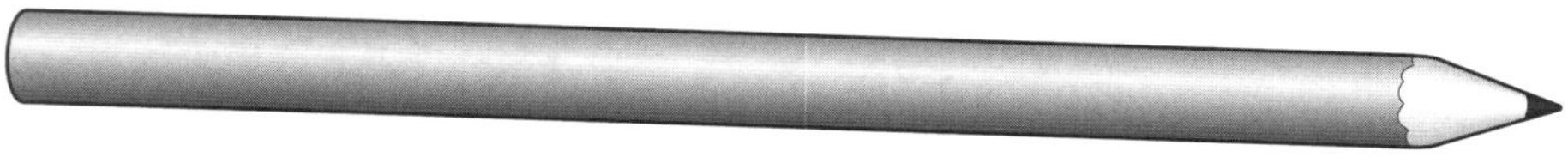

_____

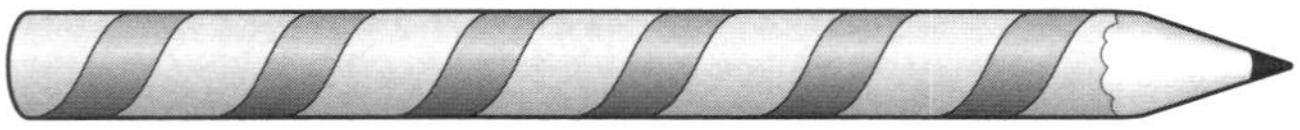

_____

_____

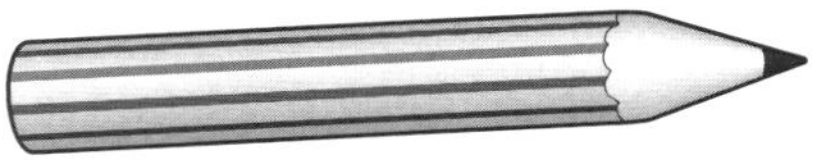

_____

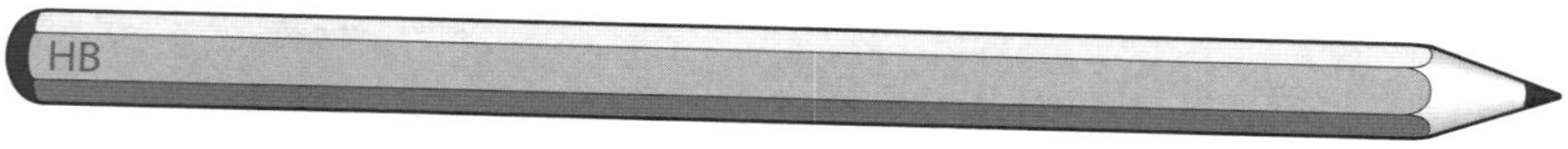

_____

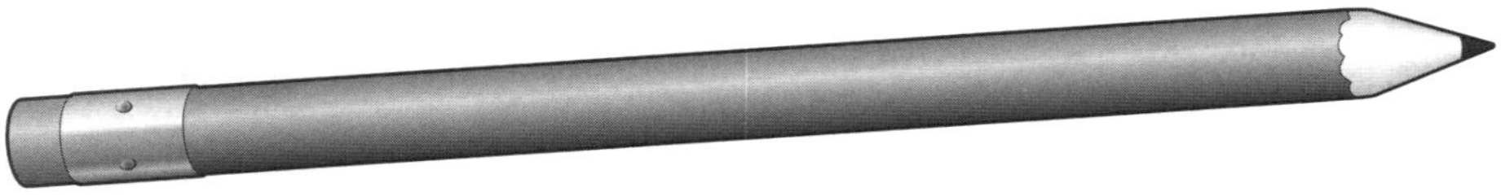

_____

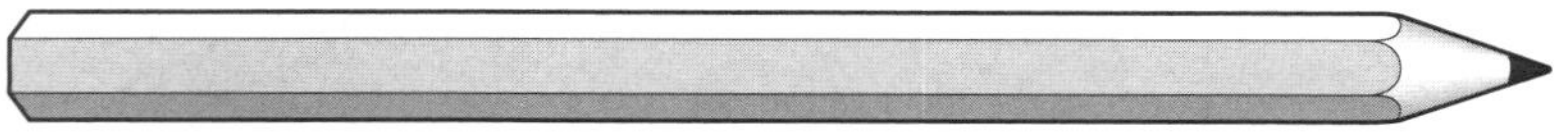

_____

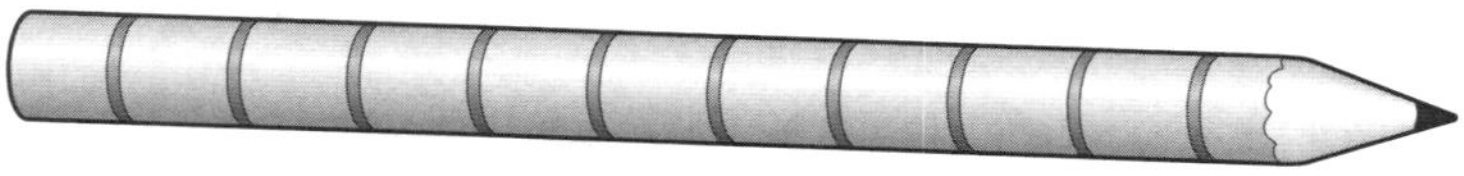

_____

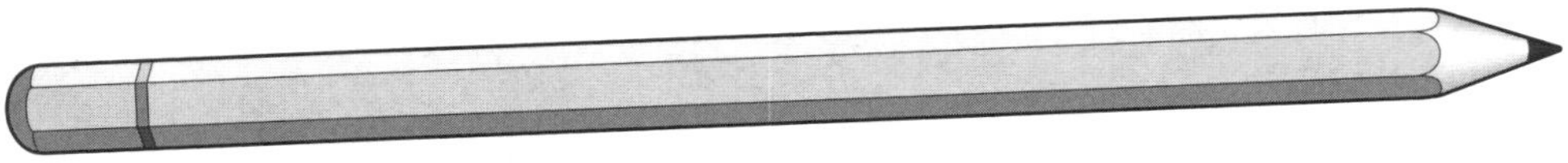

Name: _____ **Date:** _____

Car boot sale

How much money is this? _____

Divide it by three.   How much each? _____

How much left over? _____

Fill in the gaps in our chart.

Use coins and notes to help you.

Ready reckoner for sharing money between three people

How much altogether?	How much each?	How much altogether?	How much each?
£30	£10	£1	33p
£60	£20	£2	
£90		£3	£1
£120		£6	£2
	£50	£9	
£180		£12	
£210		£15	
£240		£18	
£270		£21	
£300		£24	
		£27	

Car boot sale

You can use your ready reckoner for any amount up to £300.

In July, we made £83 altogether.

That's £60 + £21 + £2

So we got £20 + £7 + 66p each. £27.66p each.

Use your ready reckoner for these.

Check with notes and coins.

Ready reckoner for sharing money between 3 people			
How much altogether?	How much each?	How much altogether?	How much each?
£30	£10	£1	33p
£60	£20	£2	66p
£90	£30	£3	£1
£120	£40	£6	£2
£150	£50	£9	£3
£180	£60	£12	£4
£210	£70	£15	£5
£240	£80	£18	£6
£270	£90	£21	£7
£300	£100	£24	£8
		£27	£9

August
£133 altogether.
How much each?

September
£151 altogether.
How much each?

October
£240 altogether.
How much each?

November
£284 altogether.
How much each?

December
£192 altogether.
How much each?

What's missing?

> Write the missing numbers.

| 2 | 3 | 6 | – | | | | = | 1 | 3 | 5 |

| 1 | | 8 | + | 1 | 1 | 5 | = | 2 | 4 | 3 |

| 1 | 0 | 0 | – | 7 | 2 | = | | 8 |

| 1 | 9 | 9 | + | | 9 | = | 2 | 8 | 8 |

Check

> Now try these.

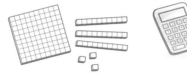

```
  1 4 8            1 3 5            2 3 2
+   5 □          + 1 2 □          –   1 1 □
-------          -------          -------
  2 0 2            2 6 3            1 1 7
```

```
  1 9 4            1 3 □            □ □
×     □          ×     2          ×     3
-------          -------          -------
  3 8 8            2 7 6            2 4 6
```

6		6	=	3	6

3	6		6	=	6

7		5	=	3	5

6		9	=	5	4

4	5		9	=	5

3	6		9	=	4

3	7	4		2	=	1	8	7

4	0	4		2	=	2	0	2

4	0	4		2	=	4	0	6

4	0	4		2	=	4	0	2

1	8		3	=	5	4

1	8	0		7	9	=	2	5	9

2	5	0	=	5	0		5

One hundred bingo

Print these on card. You can use them again.

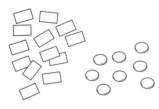

One hundred bingo

A game for 2, 3 or 4 people.

- **Before you start**
  You need a bingo card and eight counters each.
  Shuffle the 15 question cards.
  Put them in a pile, face down.

- **How to play**

Take a question card and read it to everyone.

If the answer is on their bingo card, they cover it with a counter.

Now it is your partner's go.

- **Keep going until someone says 'Bingo' because they have covered up all their numbers.**

Purple Pupil Book Part 2   **Addition and subtraction to 100**

One hundred bingo	One hundred bingo	One hundred bingo	One hundred bingo	One hundred bingo
100 – 3	100 – 12	100 – 17	100 – 25	100 – 36
One hundred bingo	One hundred bingo	One hundred bingo	One hundred bingo	One hundred bingo
100 – 42	100 – 48	100 – 50	100 – 61	100 – 64
One hundred bingo	One hundred bingo	One hundred bingo	One hundred bingo	One hundred bingo
100 – 79	100 – 81	100 – 83	100 – 90	100 – 99

One hundred bingo

sheet 2 of 2

Print these on card. You can use them again.

Cut out the instructions card, 4 bingo cards, and 15 question cards.
Store in a clear zip-top wallet or in an envelope. If possible, include 32 counters.

One hundred bingo

97	50		10
	36	64	19
1		88	

One hundred bingo

	64	58	17
36	10		75
	1		83

One hundred bingo

75	39	21	
10		1	
	58	97	

One hundred bingo

	19		1
75	10	83	
52		21	50

◄ Purple Pupil Book Part 2; use from
pages 40 and 41 onwards

Forty-nine game

Print these on card. You can use them again.
Cut out the instructions card and 16 star cards. Colour the stars if wished.
Store in a clear zip-top wallet or in an envelope.

Forty-nine

A game for 1, 2 or 3 people.

- **Before you start**
  Shuffle the cards.
  Spread them out on the table, face down.

- **How to play**

Turn over 3 cards.
Count the stars.

If you get exactly 49 stars,
keep the cards.
If not, turn the cards
back over.

Now it is your
partner's go.

- **Keep going until no one can make any more 49s.**

Purple Pupil Book Part 2   **Multiples of 7 to 49**   Text © Rose Griffiths 2009
Pearson Education Ltd

Forty-nine ☆ ☆ ☆ ☆ ☆ ☆ ☆

Forty-nine ☆ ☆ ☆ ☆ ☆ ☆ ☆

Forty-nine ☆ ☆ ☆ ☆ ☆ ☆ ☆ ☆ ☆ ☆ ☆ ☆ ☆ ☆

Forty-nine ☆ ☆ ☆ ☆ ☆ ☆ ☆ ☆ ☆ ☆ ☆ ☆ ☆ ☆

Forty-nine game

Print these on card. You can use them again.

Forty-nine

Forty-nine

Forty-nine

Forty-nine

Forty-nine

Forty-nine

Forty-nine

Forty-nine

Forty-nine

Forty-nine

Forty-nine

Forty-nine

One thousand

There are hundreds of people watching us!

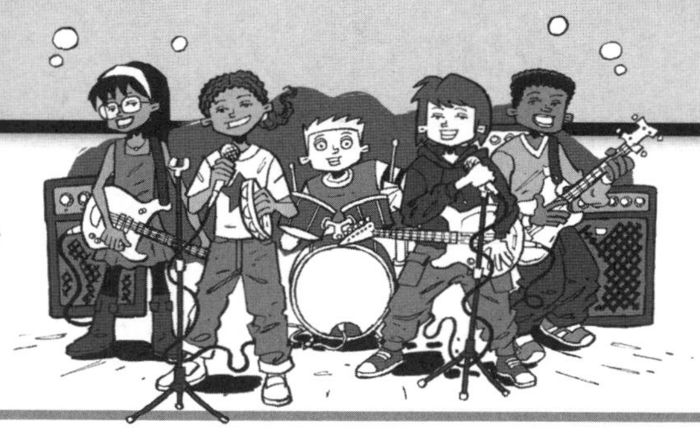

How many people in this row?

_____

How many people in this block?

_____

How many people in this block?

_____

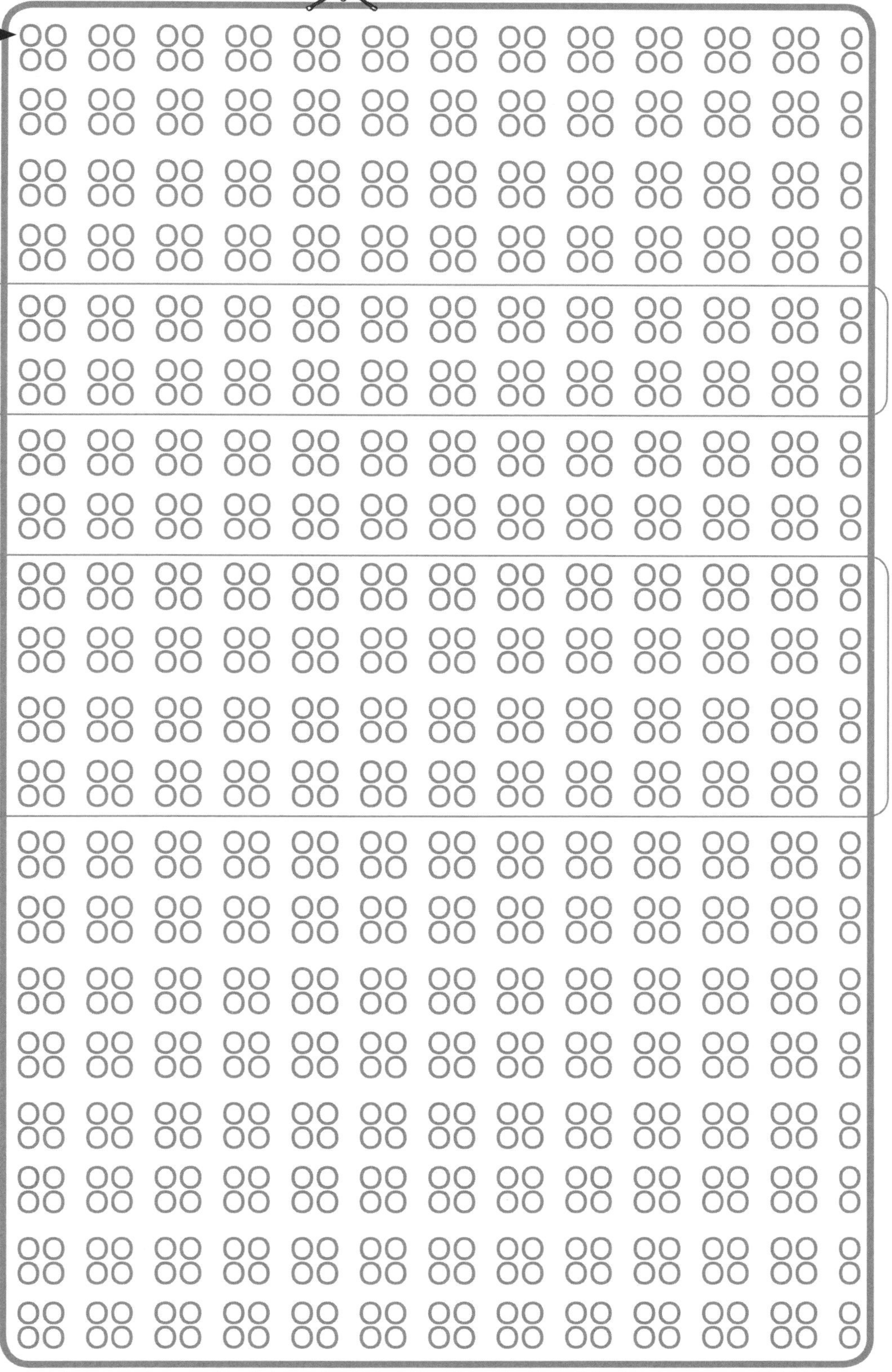

How many people watching altogether?

_____

Rounding

Name: _____ **Date:** _____

This
number line
belongs to
_____

GLUE

GLUE

GLUE

GLUE

0 10 20 30 40 50 60 70 80 90 100 110 120 130 140 150 160 170 180 190 200

210 220 230 240 250 260 270 280 290 300 310 320 330 340 350 360 370 380 390 400

410 420 430 440 450 460 470 480 490 500 510 520 530 540 550 560 570 580 590 600

610 620 630 640 650 660 670 680 690 700 710 720 730 740 750 760 770 780 790 800

810 820 830 840 850 860 870 880 890 900 910 920 930 940 950 960 970 980 990 1000

Rounding

Make each number with hundreds, tens and ones ... then fill in the chart.

Number	Where is it on the number line?	Rounded to the nearest ten
77	20 30 40 50 60 70 80 90 100	80
163	90 100 110 120 130 140 150 160 170	
251	240 250 260 270 280 290 300 310 320	
419	380 390 400 410 420 430 440 450 460	
582	510 520 530 540 550 560 570 580 590	
675	660 670 680 690 700 710 720 730 740	
896	830 840 850 860 870 880 890 900 910	
999	920 930 940 950 960 970 980 990 1000	

◀ Purple Pupil Book Part 3 pages 70-71
Copymaster P64

Rounding to the nearest 10 or 100

Text © Rose Griffiths 2009
Pearson Education Ltd

P63

Rounding

Make each number with hundreds, tens and ones ... then fill in the chart.

Number	Where is it on the number line?	Rounded to the nearest hundred
331	300 310 320 330 340 350 360 370 380 390 400 410	300
175	90 100 110 120 130 140 150 160 170 180 190 200 210	
392	290 300 310 320 330 340 350 360 370 380 390 400 410	
714	690 700 710 720 730 740 750 760 770 780 790 800 810	
246	190 200 210 220 230 240 250 260 270 280 290 300 310	
483	390 400 410 420 430 440 450 460 470 480 490 500 510	
550	490 500 510 520 530 540 550 560 570 580 590 600 610	
668	590 600 610 620 630 640 650 660 670 680 690 700 710	

Text © Rose Griffiths 2009
Pearson Education Ltd
Rounding to the nearest 10 or 100
◀ Purple Pupil Book Part 3 pages 70 and 71
Copymaster P65

Rough answers

Five sums are wrong! Can you find them?

Write a rough answer for each sum to help you find the mistakes.

52p
+ 39p
91p ✔

Rough answer:
50p + 40p = 90p

£1·95
+ £7·90
£8·85

Rough answer:

£1·35
+ £4·20
£5·55

Rough answer:

£18·10
+£ 3·15
£24·05

Rough answer:

£2·99
+£1·98
£4·97

Rough answer:

68p
+   71p
£1·59

Rough answer:

£16·40
+£21·95
£38·35

Rough answer:

27p
+ 27p
44p

Rough answer:

£39·50
+£69·95
£101·45

Rough answer:

Hundred squares

Use the hundred squares.

Fill in the missing numbers.

$64 + \boxed{} = 114$

$\boxed{} + 30 = 129$

$215 - 90 = \boxed{}$

$171 + 80 = \boxed{}$

$158 + \boxed{} = 218$

$86 + \boxed{} = 286$

$\boxed{} - 20 = 234$

$\boxed{} - 200 = 83$

$165 - 70 = \boxed{}$

$137 + 80 = \boxed{}$

$111 + \boxed{} = 221$

Check. ✔ or ✗

1	2	3	4	5	6	7	8	9	10
11	12	13	14	15	16	17	18	19	20
21	22	23	24	25	26	27	28	29	30
31	32	33	34	35	36	37	38	39	40
41	42	43	44	45	46	47	48	49	50
51	52	53	54	55	56	57	58	59	60
61	62	63	64	65	66	67	68	69	70
71	72	73	74	75	76	77	78	79	80
81	82	83	84	85	86	87	88	89	90
91	92	93	94	95	96	97	98	99	100

101	102	103	104	105	106	107	108	109	110
111	112	113	114	115	116	117	118	119	120
121	122	123	124	125	126	127	128	129	130
131	132	133	134	135	136	137	138	139	140
141	142	143	144	145	146	147	148	149	150
151	152	153	154	155	156	157	158	159	160
161	162	163	164	165	166	167	168	169	170
171	172	173	174	175	176	177	178	179	180
181	182	183	184	185	186	187	188	189	190
191	192	193	194	195	196	197	198	199	200

201	202	203	204	205	206	207	208	209	210
211	212	213	214	215	216	217	218	219	220
221	222	223	224	225	226	227	228	229	230
231	232	233	234	235	236	237	238	239	240
241	242	243	244	245	246	247	248	249	250
251	252	253	254	255	256	257	258	259	260
261	262	263	264	265	266	267	268	269	270
271	272	273	274	275	276	277	278	279	280
281	282	283	284	285	286	287	288	289	290
291	292	293	294	295	296	297	298	299	300

Hundred squares

Use the hundred squares.

267 − 32 = _____

298 − 32 = _____

313 − 32 = _____

324 + 43 = _____

357 + 43 = _____

415 + 43 = _____

229 + 101 = _____

323 + 101 = _____

399 + 101 = _____

295 − 50 = _____

425 − 50 = _____

376 − 50 = _____

328 + 33 = _____

249 + 33 = _____

156 + 33 = _____

[____] + 33 = 500

Check.   ✔ or ✘

201	202	203	204	205	206	207	208	209	210
211	212	213	214	215	216	217	218	219	220
221	222	223	224	225	226	227	228	229	230
231	232	233	234	235	236	237	238	239	240
241	242	243	244	245	246	247	248	249	250
251	252	253	254	255	256	257	258	259	260
261	262	263	264	265	266	267	268	269	270
271	272	273	274	275	276	277	278	279	280
281	282	283	284	285	286	287	288	289	290
291	292	293	294	295	296	297	298	299	300

301	302	303	304	305	306	307	308	309	310
311	312	313	314	315	316	317	318	319	320
321	322	323	324	325	326	327	328	329	330
331	332	333	334	335	336	337	338	339	340
341	342	343	344	345	346	347	348	349	350
351	352	353	354	355	356	357	358	359	360
361	362	363	364	365	366	367	368	369	370
371	372	373	374	375	376	377	378	379	380
381	382	383	384	385	386	387	388	389	390
391	392	393	394	395	396	397	398	399	400

401	402	403	404	405	406	407	408	409	410
411	412	413	414	415	416	417	418	419	420
421	422	423	424	425	426	427	428	429	430
431	432	433	434	435	436	437	438	439	440
441	442	443	444	445	446	447	448	449	450
451	452	453	454	455	456	457	458	459	460
461	462	463	464	465	466	467	468	469	470
471	472	473	474	475	476	477	478	479	480
481	482	483	484	485	486	487	488	489	490
491	492	493	494	495	496	497	498	499	500

Place value cards

Check your spelling with
place value cards (Copymaster P89).

| 4 | 2 | 3 |

Shuffle the cards. Use them to make 9 numbers.
Write each number ... and its spelling.

_____

_____

_____

_____

_____

_____

_____

_____

_____

Ask your teacher to check your spelling. Practise any you got wrong.

Place value cards

Use place value cards (Copymaster P89) to make up sums.

Don't use | 900 | 800 | 700 | 600 | or | 500 |

4 4 3
1 0 8

$$443 + 108$$

Do the sums yourself ...
or give them to your partner!

Check.    ✔ or ✘

Name: _____   Date: _____

Boxes and bones

30 ink cartridges in a box
How many in:

2 boxes? _____

4 boxes? _____

5 boxes? _____

8 boxes? _____

10 boxes? _____

Fill in the missing numbers:

| 0 | 30 | 60 | | 120 | | 180 | | 240 |

| 300 | 270 | | | 180 | 150 | 120 | | |

90 + 30 = ____

90 + 60 = ____

90 + 90 = ____

90 + 120 = ____

90 + 150 = ____

90 + 180 = ____

```
  30        30        30
×  3      ×  4      ×  6
____      ____      ____

____      ____      ____
```

```
  30        30        30
×  7      ×  8      ×  9
____      ____      ____

____      ____      ____
```

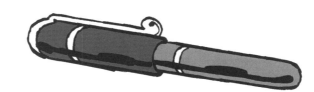

Boxes and bones

APPROX. is short for APPROXIMATE.

What does it mean?

_____

_____

How many drawing pins in:

2 boxes? _____   3 boxes? _____   4 boxes? _____

I need 4 drawing pins to put up a picture.

How many drawing pins for:

3 pictures? _____   7 pictures? _____   8 pictures? _____

10 pictures? _____   11 pictures? _____   12 pictures? _____

How many pictures could I put up with 60 drawing pins?   _____

$4 \overline{)80}$ $4 \overline{)100}$ $4 \overline{)700}$

Name: _____ Date: _____

Stamps

The machine sells books of 4 stamps.

How many stamps in:

6 books? _____   10 books? _____   16 books? _____

How many stamps in:

20 books? _____   3 books? _____   23 books? _____

How many stamps in:

11 books? _____   8 books? _____   19 books? _____

I need 16 stamps. How many books of 4?

_____

I need 10 stamps. How many books of 4?

_____

34	17	22	50	92
× 4	× 4	× 4	× 4	× 4

4) 60   4) 92   4) 68

Stamps

Put stamps on each parcel.
Don't stick them on until you've tried all four!

This needs £3.40

Mo Smith,
24 Forest Road,
Blaby.

This needs £1.60

Jenny Roberts,
39 Bagg Lane,
Wanstead.

This needs 92p

K. Parkar,
147 Leicester Road,
London
N12 8PQ

This needs £1.45

Mr & Mrs Price,
56 Meadow Street,
Leeds.

FRAGILE

Did you have any stamps left over? _____

Name: _____ **Date:** _____

More place value cards

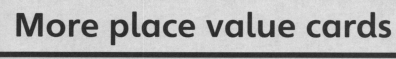

Add these.

2 9 7 6 1 2	6 9 7 2 1 2
4 3 5 8 0	5 4 3 8 0
1 0 2 4 0 9	1 0 9 4 0 2
3 4 5 2 8 9	3 8 9 2 4 5

Check. ✔ or ✗

Text © Rose Griffiths 2009
Pearson Education Ltd
Addition within 1000 ◀ Purple Pupil Book Part 3 pages 82 and 83
Copymaster P75

More place value cards

Use place value cards to make up sums.

<u>Don't</u> use | 9 0 0 | 8 0 0 | 7 0 0 | 6 0 0 | or | 5 0 0 |

Do the sums yourself ...
or give them to your partner.

400+100+40+2 =

Write each number.

Write what you do.

☐ ☐ ☐ + ☐ ☐ ☐

_____

☐ ☐ ☐ + ☐ ☐ ☐

_____

☐ ☐ ☐ + ☐ ☐ ☐

_____

☐ ☐ ☐ + ☐ ☐ ☐

_____

☐ ☐ ☐ + ☐ ☐ ☐

_____

☐ ☐ ☐ + ☐ ☐ ☐

_____

☐ ☐ ☐ + ☐ ☐ ☐

◀ Purple Pupil Book Part 3
pages 82 and 83

Addition within 1000

Text © Rose Griffiths 2009
Pearson Education Ltd

P75

Name: _____ Date: _____

Eight times table

Cut out the eleven tables facts.
Fold along the dotted line and glue flat.

Ask how to practise with these.

		5 × 8	40
0 × 8	0	6 × 8	48
1 × 8	8	7 × 8	56
2 × 8	16	8 × 8	64
3 × 8	24	9 × 8	72
4 × 8	32	10 × 8	80

Eight times table

Fill in the missing numbers.
Check with a calculator.

8 × 8 = ☐
64 ÷ 8 = ☐

7 × 8 = ☐
56 ÷ 8 = ☐

6 × 8 = ☐
48 ÷ 8 = ☐

9 × 8 = ☐
72 ÷ 8 = ☐

10 × 8 = ☐
☐ × 8 = 72
8 × 8 = ☐
☐ × 8 = 56
☐ × 8 = 48
5 × 8 = ☐
☐ × 8 = 32
3 × 8 = ☐
2 × 8 = ☐
☐ × 8 = 8
0 × 8 = ☐

What is
7 times 8?

_____

What is
8 times 8?

_____

Eight times table   Text © Rose Griffiths 2009
Pearson Education Ltd   P77

Add or take away

Find these adding and taking away words.

B	A	D	D	C	M	O	R	E
T	A	K	E	A	W	A	Y	Z
D	E	H	C	G	I	L	J	S
I	N	C	R	E	A	S	E	U
M	N	F	E	K	O	L	P	B
R	S	U	A	Q	T	E	V	T
P	L	U	S	T	O	S	X	R
Y	A	C	E	E	T	S	F	A
Z	D	W	B	H	A	I	J	C
M	I	N	U	S	L	G	K	T

+

add
plus
increase
more
total

−

take away
minus
decrease
less
subtract

Fill in [+] or [−].

128 [ ] 19 = 147   500 [ ] 136 = 364

128 [ ] 19 = 109   500 [ ] 136 = 636

```
   263              76             199             462
 + 148           + 451          + 299           + 485
 _____           _____          _____           _____

 _____           _____          _____           _____

   390             528             660             750
 − 154           − 250          − 142           − 209
 _____           _____          _____           _____

 _____           _____          _____           _____
```

Add or take away

Write each sum and work it out.

Seven hundred and fifty take away ninety-three

750
− 93
_____

_____

Twenty-eight add three hundred and forty-seven

Four hundred and sixty-five plus one hundred and thirty-nine

The difference between six hundred, and four hundred

Five hundred and seventy minus two hundred and one

Two hundred and fifty-eight add one hundred and forty-two

One hundred and twenty-four subtract eighty-three

Six hundred and seventy-two take away one hundred and thirteen

Name: _____ Date: _____

Speedy tables K 1 2 3 minute test

6 × 4 = _____   100 ÷ 10 = _____   9 × 9 = _____

8 × 0 = _____   56 ÷ 7 = _____   25 ÷ 5 = _____

7 × 6 = _____   48 ÷ 8 = _____   4 × 8 = _____

3 × 9 = _____   21 ÷ 3 = _____   64 ÷ 8 = _____

6 × 6 = _____   45 ÷ 9 = _____   5 × 6 = _____

9 × 8 = _____   70 ÷ 7 = _____   16 ÷ 4 = _____

2 × 8 = _____   28 ÷ 4 = _____   Score: _____

◀Purple Pupil Book Part 3 pages 88 and 89 onwards   **Mental recall of tables facts**   Text © Rose Griffiths 2009 Pearson Education Ltd

Name: _____ Date: _____

Speedy tables L 1 2 3 minute test

3 × 6 = _____   24 ÷ 4 = _____   8 × 8 = _____

6 × 7 = _____   80 ÷ 10 = _____   100 ÷ 10 = _____

5 × 8 = _____   49 ÷ 7 = _____   7 × 9 = _____

9 × 6 = _____   81 ÷ 9 = _____   2 ÷ 2 = _____

0 × 4 = _____   56 ÷ 8 = _____   4 × 9 = _____

8 × 9 = _____   21 ÷ 7 = _____   36 ÷ 6 = _____

6 × 8 = _____   24 ÷ 3 = _____   Score: _____

Text © Rose Griffiths 2009 Pearson Education Ltd   **Mental recall of tables facts**   ◀Purple Pupil Book Part 3 pages 88 and 89 onwards

Name: _____   Date: _____

More multiplying

Draw hundreds, tens and ones.
Then multiply on paper.

135 times 3	135 times 4	135 times 5

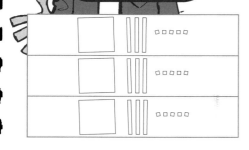
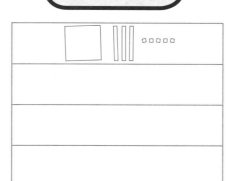
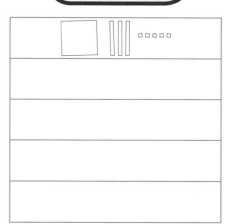

135		135		135
× 3		× 4		× 5

Use hundreds, tens and ones. <u>Then</u> multiply on paper.

170	150	199	156
× 4	× 5	× 3	× 4

184	207	98
× 4	× 3	× 5

 ✔ or ✘

More multiplying

1 0 3 × 6 = _____ 3 × 6 = _____ so 1 0 3 × 6 = _____	103 × 6 ————— —————
1 0 0 × 5 = _____ 4 0 × 5 = _____ 7 × 5 = _____ so 1 4 7 × 5 = _____	147 × 5 ————— —————
9 0 × 6 = _____ 4 × 6 = _____ so 9 4 × 6 = _____	94 × 6 ————— —————
1 0 0 × 4 = _____ 8 0 × 4 = _____ so 1 8 0 × 4 = _____	180 × 4 ————— —————
8 0 × 5 = _____ 9 × 5 = _____ so 8 9 × 5 = _____	89 × 5 ————— —————

Text © Rose Griffiths 2009
Pearson Education Ltd
Multiplication within 750   ◀ Purple Pupil Book Part 3 pages 90 and 91

Halves

I'll meet you half-way!

×

Measure the line: __11__ cm.

Halve the length: __5.5__ cm.

Measure the line and put a cross half-way along.

Measure the line: _____ cm.

Halve the length: _____ cm.

Measure the line and put a cross half-way along.

Measure the line: _____ cm.

Halve it: _____ cm.

Put a cross half-way.

Measure the line: _____ cm.

Halve it: _____ cm.

Put a cross half-way.

Measure the line: _____ cm.

Halve it: _____ cm.

Put a cross half-way.

Holidays

Use notes and coins to help you.

Check

Chalet in Scotland

£590

(maximum 5 people)

How much per person ...

- if 2 people go? _____
- if 3 people go? _____
- if 4 people go? _____
- if 5 people go? _____

Villa on the Costa del Sol

£720

(maximum 6 people)

How much per person ...

- if 2 people go? _____
- if 3 people go? _____
- if 4 people go? _____
- if 5 people go? _____

Caravan in Hunstanton

£380

(maximum 6 people)

How much per person ...

- if 2 people go? _____
- if 3 people go? _____
- if 4 people go? _____
- if 5 people go? _____

Holidays

Work with a partner.

Make up some holiday questions for each other.

Fantastic caravan in ....

£.......

(maximum 5 people)

How much per person ...
- if [ ] people go? _____
- if [ ] people go? _____

Chalet in ....

£.......

(maximum 6 people)

How much per person ...
- if [ ] people go? _____
- if [ ] people go? _____

Villa in ....

£.......

(maximum 5 people)

How much per person ...
- if [ ] people go? _____
- if [ ] people go? _____

Rough total game

Print these on card. You can use them again.
Cut out the instructions card and 24 playing cards.
Store in a clear zip-top wallet or in an envelope.

Rough total

A game for 2 or 3 people.

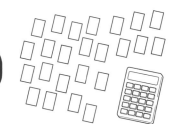

- **Before you start**
  Shuffle the cards.
  Spread them out on the table, face down.

- **How to play**

Turn over three cards.
Add up a rough total in your head ...

while your partner adds them exactly, on the calculator.

10p + 30p + 40p ...

rough total is 80p.

10p + 27p + 39p ...

exact total is 76p.

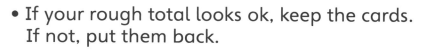

- If your rough total looks ok, keep the cards.
  If not, put them back.

- **Now it is your partner's go.**

Purple Pupil Book Part 3;   **Rounding, using money**   Text © Rose Griffiths 2009
Pearson Education Ltd

◄Purple Pupil Book Part 3; use from
pages 72 and 73 onwards

Rough total game

sheet 2 of 2
Print two copies of these on card. You can use them again.
Colour them in if you wish. Cut into 24 cards.

Rough total			Rough total		
Rough total	Lemon Lolly	34p	Rough total	Cat Stickers	66p
Rough total	CRISPS	27p	Rough total	*(pen)*	62p
Rough total	ERASER	23p	Rough total	CHOCO SHAKE	48p
Rough total	Cheese Biscuits	21p	Rough total	Pineapple Juice	45p
Rough total	ORANGE POP	19p	Rough total	Strawberry Juice	42p
Rough total	Ice Pop	10p	Rough total	WOW! COMIC	39p

999 game

Print these on card. You can use them again.
Cut out the instructions card and 27 place value cards.
Store in a clear zip-top wallet or in an envelope.

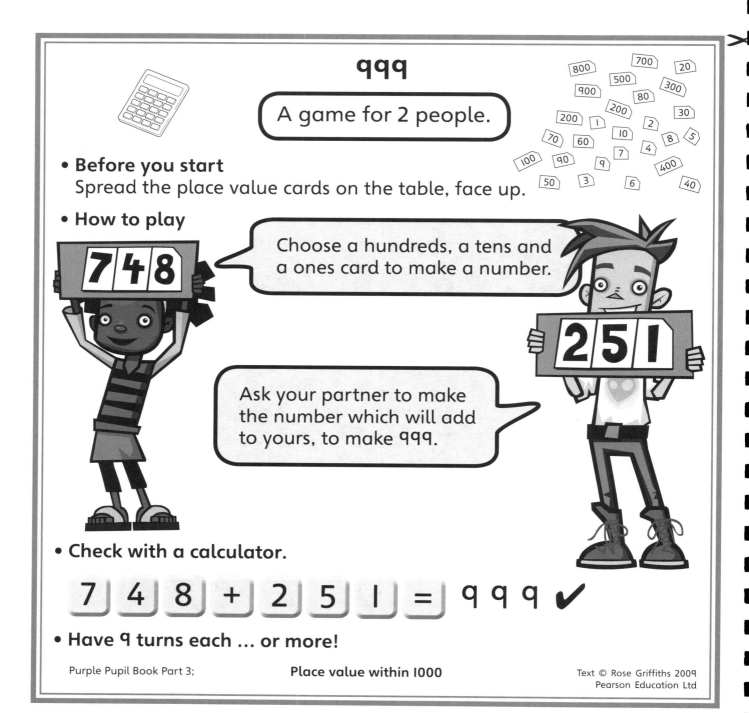

999

A game for 2 people.

- **Before you start**
  Spread the place value cards on the table, face up.

- **How to play**

Choose a hundreds, a tens and a ones card to make a number.

748

251

Ask your partner to make the number which will add to yours, to make 999.

- **Check with a calculator.**

7 4 8 + 2 5 1 = 9 9 9 ✔

- **Have 9 turns each ... or more!**

Purple Pupil Book Part 3; **Place value within 1000**

qqq game

Print these on card. You can use them again.
Cut into 27 corner cards, with one corner cut off each.

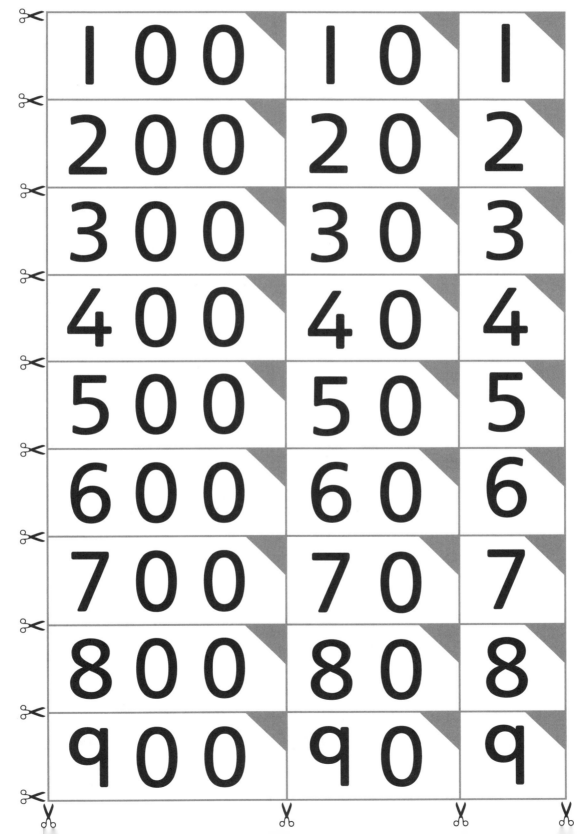

1 0 0	1 0	1
2 0 0	2 0	2
3 0 0	3 0	3
4 0 0	4 0	4
5 0 0	5 0	5
6 0 0	6 0	6
7 0 0	7 0	7
8 0 0	8 0	8
9 0 0	9 0	9

Eights game

Print these on card. You can use them again.
Cut out the instructions card and 9 stamp cards. Colour the stamps if you wish.
Store in a clear zip-top wallet or in an envelope.

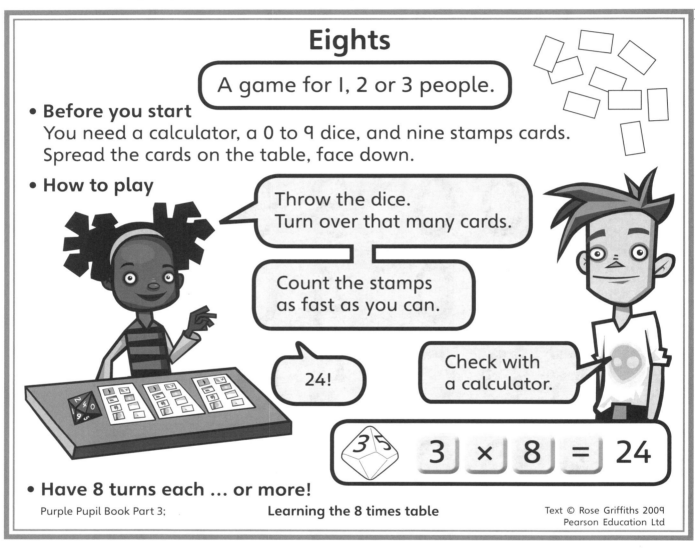

Eights

A game for 1, 2 or 3 people.

- **Before you start**
  You need a calculator, a 0 to 9 dice, and nine stamps cards.
  Spread the cards on the table, face down.

- **How to play**

  Throw the dice.
  Turn over that many cards.

  Count the stamps
  as fast as you can.

  24!

  Check with
  a calculator.

  3 × 8 = 24

- **Have 8 turns each ... or more!**

  Purple Pupil Book Part 3;   **Learning the 8 times table**   Text © Rose Griffiths 2009
  Pearson Education Ltd

If you wish,
make your own
stamps cards,
using real stamps.

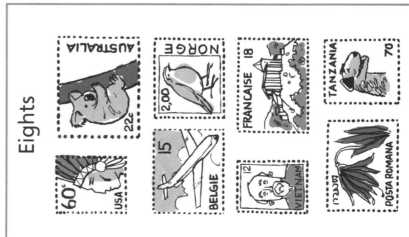

Eights game

Print these on card. You can use them again.

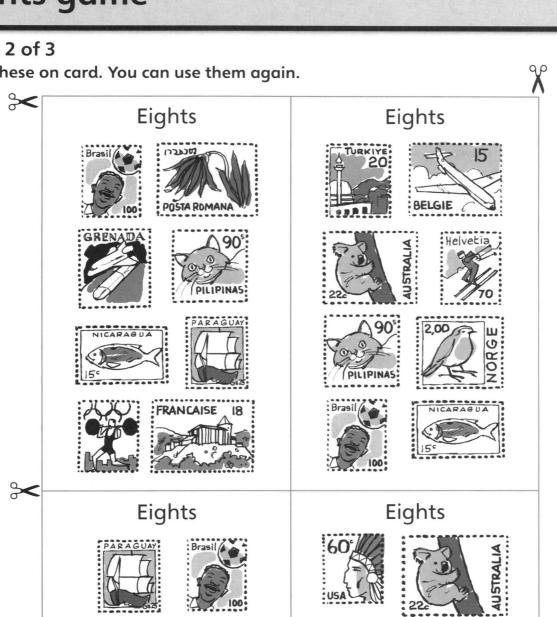

Eights game

sheet 3 of 3
Print these on card. You can use them again.

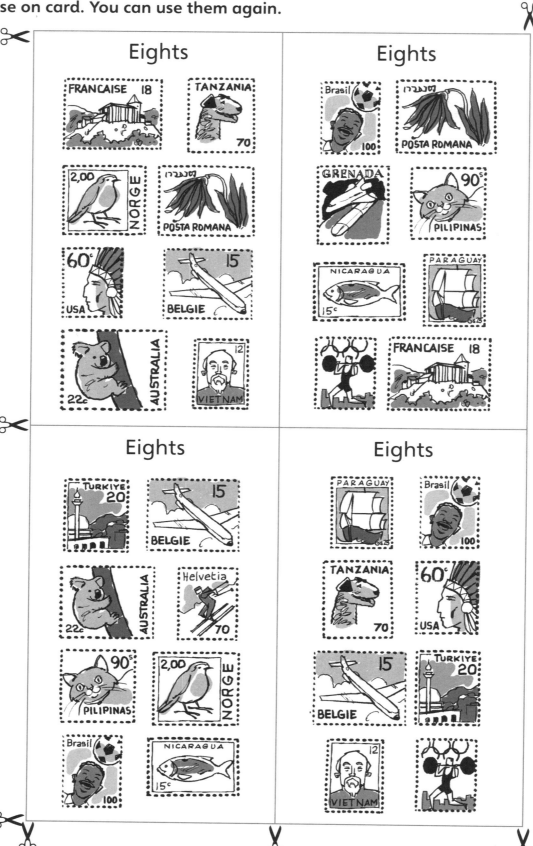